English Phonetics and Pro Practice

English Phonetics and Pronunciation Practice provides a unique introduction to basic articulatory phonetics for students of English. Built around an extensive collection of practice materials, this book teaches the pronunciation of modern standard non-regional British English to intermediate and advanced learners worldwide.

This book:

- provides an up-to-date description of the pronunciation of modern British English;
- demonstrates the use of each English phoneme with a selection of high-frequency words, both alone and in context in sentences, idiomatic phrases and dialogues;
- provides examples and practice material on commonly confused sounds;
- is supported by a companion website featuring phonetic transcriptions and over 30 hours of practice audio material to check your pronunciation against;
- can be used not only for studying pronunciation in the classroom but also for independent student practice.

English Phonetics and Pronunciation Practice is essential reading for any student studying this topic.

Paul Carley has held posts at the University of Applied Sciences, Utrecht, and the universities of Bedfordshire and Leicester. He is a regular lecturer on the University College London Summer Course in English Phonetics.

Inger M. Mees is Associate Professor in the Department of Management, Society and Communication at the Copenhagen Business School. She has formerly held lectureships at the universities of Leiden and Copenhagen. She is on the academic staff of the University College London Summer Course in English Phonetics.

Beverley Collins (1938–2014) held lectureships at the universities of Lancaster and Leiden and was Visiting Professor at Ghent University. He was also a lecturer on the University College London Summer Course in Phonetics.

English Phonetics and Pronunciation Practice

Paul Carley, Inger M. Mees
and Beverley Collins

LONDON AND NEW YORK

First published 2018
by Routledge
2 Park Square, Milton Park, Abingdon, Oxon OX14 4RN

and by Routledge
711 Third Avenue, New York, NY 10017

Routledge is an imprint of the Taylor & Francis Group, an informa business

British Library Cataloguing-in-Publication Data
A catalogue record for this book is available from the British Library

Library of Congress Cataloging-in-Publication Data
A catalog record for this title has been requested

ISBN: 978-1-138-88633-9 (hbk)
ISBN: 978-1-138-88634-6 (pbk)
ISBN: 978-1-315-16394-9 (ebk)

Typeset in Times New Roman
by Apex CoVantage, LLC

Visit the companion website: www.routledge.com/cw/carley

To our dear friend Beverley Collins (1938–2014)

Contents

7 Practice: Vowel contrasts   **197**

English phonemic transcription key

Consonants

Voiceless			Voiced		
Plosives					
p	pet, lap	pet, læp	b	bet, lab	bet, læb
t	town, mat	taʊn, mæt	d	down, mad	daʊn, mæd
k	cap, lock	kæp, lɒk	g	gap, log	kæb, lɒg
Affricates					
ʧ	chin, batch	ʧɪn, bæʧ	ʤ	gin, badge	ʤɪn, bæʤ
Fricatives					
f	fast, safe	fɑːst, seɪf	v	vast, save	vɑːst, seɪv
θ	thigh, loath	θaɪ, ləʊθ	ð	thy, loathe	ðaɪ, ləʊð
s	sink, face	sɪŋk, feɪs	z	zinc, phase	zɪŋk, feɪz
ʃ	shy, wish	ʃaɪ, wɪʃ	ʒ	measure	ˈmeʒə
h	hat	hæt –			
Nasals					
			m	meet, team	miːt, tiːm
			n	nice, fine	naɪs, faɪn
			ŋ	– long	lɒŋ
Approximants					
Lateral (approximant)			l	late, sail	leɪt, seɪl
(Median) **approximants**			j	yes –	jes
			w	wait –	weɪt
			r	race –	reɪs

Notes
1 This phonemic transcription system is the same as that to be found in the *Cambridge English Pronouncing Dictionary* (Jones et al. 2011) and in the *Longman Pronunciation Dictionary* (Wells 2008).
2 Examples show initial and final position. Note that /ŋ/ does not occur initially; /ʒ/ is virtually restricted to medial position; /h j w r/ do not occur finally.
3 The voiceless/voiced contrast is found only in the plosives, affricates and fricatives.

Vowels

The words shown in SMALL CAPITALS are the **keywords** used throughout this book to refer to the vowels. These were first introduced by Wells (1982) and are also found in Wells's (2008) *Longman Pronunciation Dictionary*.

Vowel	Keyword	Additional spellings
Checked		
ɪ	KIT /kɪt/	gym, manage, busy, England, guilt
e	DRESS /dres/	bread, friend, said
æ	TRAP /træp/	plaid
ʌ	STRUT /strʌt/	son, young, blood
ɒ	LOT /lɒt/	swan, because, knowledge
ʊ	FOOT /fʊt/	put, would, woman
Free monophthongs		
iː	FLEECE /fliːs/	neat, these, technique, belief
ɑː	PALM /pɑːm/	start, clerk, heart, memoir
ɜː	NURSE /nɜːs/	girl, term, heard, word, journey
ɔː	THOUGHT /θɔːt/	short, caught, war, saw, walk, broad
uː	GOOSE /guːs/	rude, soup, shoe, do, crew
eə	SQUARE /skweə/	fair, their, mayor, vary
Free diphthongs		
eɪ	FACE /feɪs/	laid, may, weigh, they, break
aɪ	PRICE /praɪs/	try, lie, buy, guide
ɔɪ	CHOICE /tʃɔɪs/	boy
əʊ	GOAT /gəʊt/	nose, blow, soul, toe
aʊ	MOUTH /maʊθ/	drown
ɪə	NEAR /nɪə/	beer, pierce, zero, weird
ʊə	CURE /kjʊə/	tour, Europe, moor
Weak vowels		
ə	Schwa	comma, ability, useless, under, forget, bonus, famous
i	Weak FLEECE	happy, money, hippie, mediate, pretend
u	Weak GOOSE	graduate, to (weak form), thank you
ɪ	Weak KIT	cottage, watches, expect
ʊ	Weak FOOT	accurate, regular

Instead of PALM we also sometimes find the keyword START used to refer to the set of words pronounced with /ɑː/ in GB. START comprises a set of items containing <r>, e.g. <ar, er, ear, aar> (*hard, sergeant, heart, bazaar*); in General American (GA) they would be pronounced /ɑːr/. PALM includes other words which in GB and GA are pronounced /ɑː/ (e.g. *calm, father*). Since there is no distinction between the pronunciation of PALM and START words in GB, both keywords can be used to denote this vowel. For convenience we refer to this vowel as PALM only.

Phonetic symbols and diacritics

This is a list of the phonetic symbols used in this book. We have not included here the symbols used for English phonemic transcription (see previous pages).

[ç]   voiceless palatal fricative, as a realisation of /hj/, e.g. *huge*
[ɦ]   voiced glottal fricative, e.g. *ahead*
[ɫ]   voiced velarised alveolar lateral approximant ('dark /l/'), e.g. *well*
[ɹ]   voiced post-alveolar approximant, e.g. *very*
[ʔ]   glottal plosive, e.g. as a realisation of /t/ before consonants, *at school* [ə ʔ 'skuːl], or glottal reinforcement of a voiceless plosive, e.g. *background* ['bæʔkgraʊnd]
[̥]   devoiced consonant, e.g. [b̥] (normally below the symbol, but above for descending symbols, e.g. [g̊])
[ʰ]   aspirated, e.g. [pʰ]
[̩]   (normally beneath the symbol, but above if it is a descending symbol) syllabic consonant, e.g. *Britain* ['brɪtn̩], *bacon* /'beɪkŋ̍/
[']   primary stress, e.g. *intend* [ɪn'tend]
[ˌ]   secondary stress, e.g. *entertain* /ˌentə'teɪn/
[ː]   long, used with vowels, e.g. /iː/
[']   ejective, e.g. *back* [bæk']
/ /   phonemic transcription
[ ]   phonetic transcription
< >   orthographic form
→   is realised as
*   incorrect or unattested form

THE INTERNATIONAL PHONETIC ALPHABET (revised to 2015)

CONSONANTS (PULMONIC)

© 2015 IPA

	Bilabial	Labiodental	Dental	Alveolar	Postalveolar	Retroflex	Palatal	Velar	Uvular	Pharyngeal	Glottal
Plosive	p b			t d		ʈ ɖ	c ɟ	k ɡ	q ɢ		ʔ
Nasal	m	ɱ		n		ɳ	ɲ	ŋ	N		
Trill	ʙ			r					ʀ		
Tap or Flap		ⱱ		ɾ		ɽ					
Fricative	ɸ β	f v	θ ð	s z	ʃ ʒ	ʂ ʐ	ç ʝ	x ɣ	χ ʁ	ħ ʕ	h ɦ
Lateral fricative				ɬ ɮ							
Approximant		ʋ		ɹ		ɻ	j	ɰ			
Lateral approximant				l		ɭ	ʎ	ʟ			

Symbols to the right in a cell are voiced, to the left are voiceless. Shaded areas denote articulations judged impossible.

CONSONANTS (NON-PULMONIC)

Clicks	Voiced implosives	Ejectives
ʘ Bilabial	ɓ Bilabial	ʼ Examples:
ǀ Dental	ɗ Dental/alveolar	pʼ Bilabial
ǃ (Post)alveolar	ʄ Palatal	tʼ Dental/alveolar
ǂ Palatoalveolar	ɠ Velar	kʼ Velar
ǁ Alveolar lateral	ʛ Uvular	sʼ Alveolar fricative

OTHER SYMBOLS

ʍ Voiceless labial-velar fricative

w Voiced labial-velar approximant

ɥ Voiced labial-palatal approximant

ʜ Voiceless epiglottal fricative

ʢ Voiced epiglottal fricative

ʡ Epiglottal plosive

ɕ ʑ Alveolo-palatal fricatives

ɺ Voiced alveolar lateral flap

ɧ Simultaneous ʃ and x

Affricates and double articulations can be represented by two symbols joined by a tie bar if necessary. t͡s k͡p

VOWELS

	Front	Central	Back
Close	i • y	ɨ • ʉ	ɯ • u
	ɪ ʏ		ʊ
Close-mid	e • ø	ɘ • ɵ	ɤ • o
		ə	
Open-mid	ɛ • œ	ɜ • ɞ	ʌ • ɔ
	æ	ɐ	
Open	a • ɶ		ɑ • ɒ

Where symbols appear in pairs, the one to the right represents a rounded vowel.

SUPRASEGMENTALS

ˈ	Primary stress
ˌ	Secondary stress
ː	Long
ˑ	Half-long
˘	Extra-short
ǀ	Minor (foot) group
ǁ	Major (intonation) group
.	Syllable break
‿	Linking (absence of a break)

ˌfoʊnəˈtɪʃən

eː eˑ ĕ

ɹi.ækt

DIACRITICS

Some diacritics may be placed above a symbol with a descender, e.g. ŋ̊

̥ Voiceless	n̥ d̥	̤ Breathy voiced	b̤ a̤	̪ Dental	t̪ d̪
̬ Voiced	s̬ t̬	̰ Creaky voiced	b̰ a̰	̺ Apical	t̺ d̺
ʰ Aspirated	tʰ dʰ	̼ Linguolabial	t̼ d̼	̻ Laminal	t̻ d̻
̹ More rounded	ɔ̹	ʷ Labialized	tʷ dʷ	̃ Nasalized	ẽ
̜ Less rounded	ɔ̜	ʲ Palatalized	tʲ dʲ	ⁿ Nasal release	dⁿ
̟ Advanced	u̟	ˠ Velarized	tˠ dˠ	ˡ Lateral release	dˡ
̠ Retracted	e̠	ˤ Pharyngealized	tˤ dˤ	̚ No audible release	d̚
̈ Centralized	ë	̴ Velarized or pharyngealized	ɫ		
̽ Mid-centralized	e̽	̝ Raised	e̝ (ɹ̝ = voiced alveolar fricative)		
̩ Syllabic	n̩	̞ Lowered	e̞ (β̞ = voiced bilabial approximant)		
̯ Non-syllabic	e̯	̘ Advanced Tongue Root	e̘		
˞ Rhoticity	ɚ a˞	̙ Retracted Tongue Root	e̙		

TONES AND WORD ACCENTS

LEVEL		CONTOUR	
e̋ or ˥	Extra high	ě or ˩˥	Rising
é ˦	High	ê ˥˩	Falling
ē ˧	Mid	e᷄ ˧˥	High rising
è ˨	Low	e᷅ ˩˧	Low rising
ȅ ˩	Extra low	e᷈ ˦˥˦	Rising-falling
↓	Downstep	↗	Global rise
↑	Upstep	↘	Global fall

Preface

English Phonetics and Pronunciation Practice (*EPPP*) is unique in combining an introduction to English phonetics with extensive material for practising English pronunciation. It presents a twenty-first-century model of educated British English, 'General British' (GB), and is supported by a website containing complete recordings and phonetic transcriptions of all exercises.

Modern corpus-based descriptions of colloquial English have been used to create materials that teach pronunciation while simultaneously practising useful idiomatic language. Each English phoneme is demonstrated in high-frequency words in different phonetic contexts, in common phrases, in sentences and in dialogues. Moreover, each phoneme is also extensively practised in contrast with similar, confusable sounds in minimal pairs, phrases and sentences.

Beyond the segmental level of vowels and consonants, considerable attention is given to the difference between strong and weak syllables – a very important component of English rhythm – and two complete chapters are dedicated to the difficult area of consonant clusters.

Learners who will benefit from *EPPP* include:

- Students of English language and linguistics
- Trainee English teachers
- Learners of English as a foreign language
- Professionals wishing to speak English with clarity and accuracy

Paul Carley and Inger M. Mees
Aberdare and Copenhagen, December 2016

Acknowledgements

The core concept of this work – to combine a description of English phonetics with copious pronunciation practice material – was originally conceived of by Beverley (Bev) Collins, and we gladly joined our dear friend and colleague as co-authors. Sadly, Bev died suddenly before the project got beyond the planning stage. Since then the book has grown and developed considerably in the writing, but we feel confident that we have remained true to his vision and produced a work which will, as he intended, help learners worldwide improve their pronunciation using solid phonetic principles.

Our thanks go to students and staff on the University College London Summer Course in English Phonetics, who have shared their experience and insights with us over a number of years. Among the staff, Jack Windsor Lewis, Jane Setter and Geoff Lindsey have been particularly supportive. We hope we have been successful in writing the textbook our students have been asking for.

The recordings accompanying the book are an absolutely essential component and therefore we heartily thank Toby Williams and Roselyn Opio for lending us their voices, and Peter Rawbone for lending us his skills as an audio engineer.

We are grateful to Petr Rösel for his perceptive comments.

Finally, we gratefully acknowledge the patience shown and help given by our editors at Routledge – Nadia Seemungal-Owen and Helen Tredget.

Chapter 1

Basic concepts

1.1 Pronunciation priorities

When learning to pronounce a new language it's essential to get your priorities right. The most important sounds are the ones that can change the meaning of words. These are called **phonemes** (see section 1.2). If you say *pin* and it sounds like *bin*, people will misunderstand you. And if you say *I hid them* and it sounds like *I hit them*, there will also be a breakdown in communication. Furthermore, you should be aware that sounds may be pronounced differently in different contexts, e.g. **pre-vocalically** (before vowels), **intervocalically** (between vowels) or **pre-consonantally** (before consonants). They may also be pronounced differently in different positions in the word – at the beginning (**initial**), in the middle (**medial**) and at the end (**final**). For instance, /p/ is more like a /b/ when it occurs after /s/, e.g. *port* vs. *sport*; /r/ sounds different in *red* and *tread*; the two /l/ sounds in *global* are said differently; and the quality of <oa> is different in *goat* and *goal*. Note that when we refer to the letters in a word – as opposed to the sounds – we show them in **angle brackets**, e.g. <f> or <ie>. Phonemes are shown in **slant brackets**, e.g. /r/ or /e/. The word *spread* would be shown phonemically as /spred/.

Even if people can understand what you are saying, an off-target pronunciation may still sound *comical, irritating* or *distracting* to listeners. For instance, if you say English /r/ with a back articulation (in your throat) instead of a front articulation (with your tongue-tip), it may sound funny to people who aren't used to it. If listeners are distracted because of a false pronunciation, they may stop concentrating on what you are trying to say. Or if they need to invest a lot of effort in deciphering what you are saying, they may lose track of your message. Furthermore, judgements of your overall ability in English are likely to be based on the impression your pronunciation makes: if you sound like a beginner, you may be treated like a beginner, even if your level is advanced in terms of grammar, vocabulary, reading and writing.

The best approach is to aim for a pronunciation that (1) can be understood without any difficulty and (2) doesn't irritate or distract your listeners. Note that there's more to learning the pronunciation of a language than mastering the **segments** (vowels and consonants). You have to pay attention to several other points. For instance, correct use of **weak forms** helps to get the speech **rhythm** right. **Contractions**, e.g. *don't, it's, we'll*, improve the fluency. To make your pronunciation more authentic, it's important to have a knowledge of **assimilation** (sounds that change under the influence of neighbouring sounds; e.g. *when* becomes /wem/ in *when my*), **elision** (disappearing sounds; e.g. /t/ is often lost in *strictly*) and **liaison** (linking of sounds across word boundaries, e.g. /r/ in *far away*).

1.2 Phonemes and allophones

Some sound differences matter a great deal, whereas others are of little significance. The ones that matter most are those that can change the meaning of otherwise identical words. In English, the words *bit*, *bet*, *boat* are distinguished only by the vowels; in *bit*, *sit*, *wit*, only the initial consonant is different. In *bit*, *bill*, *bin*, it's the final consonant that brings about the change in meaning. Sounds which can distinguish meaning are called **phonemes** (adjective: **phonemic**). A *pair* of words distinguished by a single phoneme is called a **minimal pair**, e.g. *bit – hit*. The variety of English taught in this book (see section 1.7) has 24 consonant phonemes and 20 vowel phonemes.

Not every sound difference can change the meaning of a word. Listen carefully to *feet* and *feed*. You can hear a distinct difference in the length of the two vowels. But the native English speaker interprets these vowels as two variants of the same phoneme /iː/; the different vowel lengths are the result of the influence of the following consonants /t/ and /d/. Similarly, the two /k/ sounds in *keen* and *corn* are different, the first being formed more forward and the second further back in the mouth, but English speakers hear both as variants of the phoneme /k/.

When you say the /d/ in *deal*, your lips are unrounded during the consonant, but when you say the /d/ in *door*, they are rounded. In *deal* the vowel is unrounded, and in *door* the vowel is rounded. When we say *deal* and *door*, our lips are getting ready for the vowel during the articulation of the consonant. So the lip shape of the consonant is affected by the lip shape of the following vowel. Each phoneme is composed of a number of such different variants. These are termed **allophones** (adjective: **allophonic**). Allophones may occur in **complementary distribution** or in **free variation**. Our *deal/door* example is an instance of allophones in complementary distribution. This means that the different allophones complement each other; where one occurs, the other cannot occur. In other words, we can write a rule for the occurrence of the two allophones: /d/ with rounded lips occurs before lip-rounded sounds while /d/ with unrounded lips occurs before all other sounds. Vowels are shortened before voiceless consonants like /s/ while they retain full length before voiced consonants like /z/; for example, the vowel in *price* /praɪs/ is clearly shorter than that in *prize* /praɪz/. Again, the allophones are in complementary distribution. If allophones are in free variation, their occurrence cannot be predicted from the phonetic context. An example of this would be the different possible pronunciations of /t/ in word-final position, as in *hat*. It's possible to pronounce the /t/ with or without glottal reinforcement (see section 2.7.3). Many speakers vary between these two possibilities, and we cannot predict which of the two they are going to use. The glottally reinforced and non-glottally reinforced variants are therefore said to be in free variation.

Unfortunately for the learner, different languages generally don't have the same phoneme system, and they certainly don't have the same range of allophones. So the learner has to work out the phonemic inventory of the new language and all the phonetic variants. Your first task is to make sure you never lose a phoneme contrast. This isn't easy to do in practice. Even though two phonemes may sound very similar, or identical, to the learner, to the native speaker they are completely different. This is something native speakers and learners are often not aware of. Native speakers are frequently surprised to hear that the vowels in the English words *seat* /siːt/ and *sit* /sɪt/ sound identical to speakers of most other languages, who hear them as the same vowel because they count as allophones of the same phoneme in their languages. Many learners find it difficult to separate the phonemes in *Luke* /luːk/ and *look*

/lɒk/. Others find it difficult to distinguish between *cat* /æ/, *cut* /ʌ/ and *cart* /ɑː/. Yet others can't hear and/or make the difference between the initial consonants in *three* /θ/ and *tree* /t/, or *three* /θ/ and *free* /f/, or *theme* /θ/ and *seem* /s/. In this book we have provided exercises for 29 consonant contrasts and 26 vowel contrasts. You'll find that some of these don't pose a problem for speakers of your language while others will take a long time to master. If making a particular contrast isn't difficult for you, you can still use the contrast section as extra material to help you get the two sounds just right. Note that a full command of the contrasts involves being able to say all the different allophones of a phoneme in their appropriate contexts.

Remember that allophones can never change the meaning of words. English /t/ can be said in many different ways (i.e. there are many different allophones or variants), but if we substitute one allophone for another, the meaning remains the same. It will merely sound a bit odd. However, if we replace /t/ in *tight* by /s/, /f/ or /k/, then it turns into *sight*, *fight* or *kite*, and the result is a new word with a different meaning; /t s k/ are therefore examples of phonemes in English. The English phoneme system is shown in the 'English Phonemic Transcription Key' at the start of this book.

1.3 Spelling and sound

English **orthography** (i.e. spelling) is notoriously unreliable. For instance, the vowel /iː/ can be spelt in numerous ways. All the letters underlined in the following words represent /iː/: m*e*, s*ee*, s*ea*, bel*ie*ve, rec*ei*ve, p*i*zza, p*eo*ple, k*ey*, q*uay*, q*ui*che, Portug*ue*se, f*oe*tus. Most other phonemes can also be spelt in many different ways, especially vowels. So instead of relying on the orthography, phoneticians use **transcription**. There are two types: (1) **Phonemic transcription** indicates phonemes only; this type, as we have seen, is normally placed inside slant brackets / /, e.g. *part* /pɑːt/. The sign – is used to show **phoneme contrasts**, e.g. *let* – *met* /let – met/. (2) **Phonetic transcription** shows more detailed allophonic distinctions, enclosed by **square brackets** [ ], e.g. *part* [pʰɑːt]. To indicate the allophonic distinctions, we often make use of **diacritics**, i.e. marks added to symbols to provide extra information, e.g. [pʰ] and [ʔt]. The rounded allophone of /t/ is shown as [tʷ]; as /t/ said with unrounded lips is the default, there's no special symbol to denote it.

Sometimes words with different meanings are spelt completely differently but are pronounced in the same way, as in *key* and *quay* above. Such words are called **homophones** (same pronunciation, different meaning). English has a great many of these. Other examples of homophones are *wait*/*weight*, *know*/*no*, *sea*/*see*, *cite*/*sight*/*site*. To confuse matters even more, the opposite also occurs. It's possible for words that are spelt identically to be pronounced differently. The written word *row* can be said with the vowel in GOAT (when it means a 'line') or the vowel in MOUTH (when it means a 'quarrel'), and it's therefore impossible to tell from the spelling alone which meaning and pronunciation are intended. Words of this type are called **homographs** (same spelling, different pronunciation).

1.4 Phoneme symbols

Unfortunately, different writers sometimes use different symbols to represent the vowel and consonant phonemes of English. This is partly because writers have different personal preferences and partly because the pronunciation of English has changed over the years. It has consequently become necessary to adapt the symbols to fit in better with present-day pronunciation. On the whole, the consonants tend to be shown in the same way, but several of the vowel symbols differ. In this book we have followed the notation used in the two leading pronunciation dictionaries, the *Longman Pronunciation Dictionary* (Wells 2008) and the *Cambridge English Pronouncing Dictionary* (Jones et al. 2011). The transcription system used in these dictionaries is standard for all mainstream English language teaching materials which use British English as their model. Three of the vowel sounds that have recently undergone change are the vowels found in the words DRESS, TRAP and SQUARE. In this book we have shown them in the traditional manner, i.e. /e/, /æ/ and /eə/ (as in the two dictionaries mentioned above), but a more accurate reflection of modern British English pronunciation would be to use /ɛ/, /a/ and /ɛː/ (all three are found in the *Oxford Dictionary of Pronunciation*,[1] and the last two are found in Cruttenden 2014); see Chapter 5. Note that it's convenient to use a **keyword** to refer to the vowels of English, as in the examples above, DRESS, TRAP and SQUARE (keywords are shown in SMALL CAPITALS). Examples of other keywords are FLEECE, KIT, FOOT and THOUGHT. When we talk about the FOOT vowel, we mean /ʊ/, the vowel in *foot* and words like *cook, full, could* and *woman*.

1.5 The syllable

A syllable is a group of sounds that are pronounced together. Words can consist of a single syllable (**monosyllabic**), e.g. *tight, time*, or of two or more syllables (**polysyllabic**), e.g. *waiting* (two syllables – **disyllabic**), *tomato* (three syllables), *participate* (four syllables), *university* (five syllables), etc. A syllable nearly always contains a vowel (e.g. *eye* /aɪ/, *or* / ɔː/); this is called the **syllable nucleus**. The nucleus may be preceded or followed by one or more consonants (e.g. *tea, tree, stream, at, cat, cats, stamps*). The consonant or consonants preceding the nucleus are known as the **syllable onset**, and the consonants following the nucleus are called the **coda**. The English syllable can consist of up to three consonants in the onset (e.g. *strengths* /streŋθs/), and as many as four in the coda (e.g. *texts* /teksts/). Note that we are here concerned with *pronunciation*, so even though the word *time* looks as if it consists of two syllables because it has two vowel letters in the orthography, the word consists of only one syllable as the second vowel letter in the spelling doesn't represent a vowel sound. A syllable which has a coda (i.e. one or more closing consonants) is called a **closed syllable** while a syllable which ends with a vowel phoneme is called an **open syllable**.

Occasionally, a syllable consists of a consonant only, most frequently /n/ or /l/, e.g. *Britain* /'brɪtn̩/, *hidden* /'hɪdn̩/, *mission* /'mɪʃn̩/, *middle* /'mɪdl̩/, *apple* /'æpl̩/, *battle* /'bætl̩/. A consonant that forms a syllable without the aid of a vowel is called a **syllabic consonant**. Note that we show a syllabic consonant by means of a small vertical mark beneath the symbol (with descending symbols a superscript mark is used, e.g. *bacon* /'beɪkŋ̍/). A word like *apple* /'æpl̩/ consists of two syllables, but only the first contains a vowel; the second contains a syllabic consonant; see section 8.2.

1.6 Stress

Words consist of more than a set of segments (vowels and consonants) arranged in a certain order. Words of more than one syllable also have a distinctive rhythmic pattern depending on which syllables are pronounced with **stress** and which are not. Stressed syllables are pronounced with greater energy and effort than unstressed syllables, which results in greater **prominence**; i.e. they stand out more. The first syllable in *carpet* is **stressed** and the second **unstressed**; the second syllable in *decide* is stressed and the first unstressed. Stress is indicated by means of a vertical mark placed *before* the stressed syllable, and unstressed syllables are left unmarked, e.g. /ˈkɑːpɪt/, /dɪˈsaɪd/. The position of stress in an English word is an important factor in word recognition, and there are even words which are distinguished by stress alone, e.g. *billow* /ˈbɪləʊ/ vs. *below* /bɪˈləʊ/, the noun *import* /ˈɪmpɔːt/ and the verb *import* /ɪmˈpɔːt/.

Some words have more than one stressed syllable. In *entertain* the first and third syllables are stressed, while in *impossibility* the second and fourth syllables are stressed. In these examples, as in all cases of multiple stresses, the last stress sounds more prominent than the earlier stress, and this is why the term **primary stress** has been used for the last, more prominent stress, and **secondary stress** for any earlier, less prominent stresses. Primary stress is indicated with the usual stress mark, and secondary stress with the same symbol at a lower level, e.g. /ˌentəˈteɪn/, /ɪmˌpɒsəˈbɪləti/. Although the terminology and transcription seem to suggest that there are three different levels of stress – primary stress, secondary stress and unstressed – this isn't actually the case. There are only stressed and unstressed syllables, and the difference in prominence between the stresses in words such as *entertain* and *impossibility* is due to **pitch accent**.

An accented syllable is one which is accompanied by a change in the **pitch** of the voice. Pitch is related to the speed at which the vocal folds vibrate: faster vibration results in higher pitch, and slower vibration in lower pitch. When a word is pronounced in isolation, the syllable that takes primary stress is accented, i.e. accompanied by a pitch movement, usually a fall in pitch. When there's a 'secondary stress' earlier in the word, this is accompanied by a step up to a relatively high pitch before the pitch movement of the 'primary stress'. In terms of the English sound system, the pitch movement associated with the 'primary stress' is more salient than the step up in pitch associated with the 'secondary stress'. Thus the distinction between primary and secondary stress is really a difference between different kinds of pitch accent rather than stress.

When individual monosyllabic words are transcribed as examples, it's common practice not to use a stress mark. Every word must have at least one stressed syllable when pronounced in isolation, and therefore it's self-evident that the one and only syllable of a word is stressed. When we transcribe an individual polysyllabic word, we include all necessary stress marks, both primary and secondary. Not to do so would mean leaving out essential information about the pronunciation of the word. When we transcribe utterances longer than a single word, we use the stress mark whenever a syllable is stressed, meaning that monosyllabic words can receive a stress mark, but also that some stresses which appear when a word is said in isolation may disappear when the word is spoken in a phrase. As there's no real difference between primary and secondary stress, only the primary stress symbol is used in transcriptions of connected speech, and no attempt is made to indicate differences in prominence among stressed syllables caused by different types of pitch accent.

1.7 Pronunciation model

Every language has a number of different **accents**, that is, a pronunciation variety characteristic of a group of people. Accents can be **regional** or **social**. In Britain we find many different regional accents; examples are London ('Cockney'), Birmingham, Bristol, Liverpool, Leeds, Glasgow and Cardiff, spoken by most of the people who live in these areas. But unless you have reasons for specifically wishing to adopt one of these regional accents, it's best for learners not to use these as a **model** for imitation. The accent of British English we recommend is one heard from educated speakers throughout Britain. Although it's more common in England than in Scotland and Wales, and in the south of England more than in the north, everybody in Britain has as least a passive familiarity with it. We shall term this social accent **General British** (abbreviated to **GB**). If you listen regularly to programmes on British radio and television, you're probably already familiar with this accent, since it's the variety used by the majority of British presenters. It's sometimes even called 'BBC English'. It either is completely non-localisable (i.e. it's impossible to tell where speakers come from) or has very few regional traces. When people alter their pronunciation (consciously or unconsciously) to sound less regional, they change in the direction of GB. When there's an accent spectrum within a location, those at the lower end of the social scale speak with the local accent while those towards the other end of the social scale speak with an accent progressively more like GB. Thus GB can be taken as the common denominator of the speech of educated British people.

Apart from 'BBC English', other popular names have been used for this variety of English. For instance, it has been referred to as the 'Queen's English' and 'Oxford English'. But these are very inaccurate. Phoneticians have also employed a variety of names. The following are a selection:

Label	Abbreviation
Received Pronunciation	RP
Modern Received Pronunciation	MRP
Public School Pronunciation	PSP
Reference Pronunciation	RP
Southern British Standard	SBS
Southern England Standard Pronunciation	SESP
Standard Southern British English	SSBE
Non-regional Pronunciation	NRP

Until recently 'Received Pronunciation' (abbreviated to RP) was frequently used to refer to the prestige accent, 'received' meaning 'socially acceptable' in the Victorian era. It was originally defined as the speech of a small minority who had gone to one of the 'public schools' in Britain (in actual fact very expensive private schools). But as time went by, more and more people, notably in London and the wealthy south-east of England, acquired a variety very similar to RP even though they had not gone to public school, and this tendency increased greatly through the use of RP for broadcasting purposes. This means that the term is no longer appropriate. To make the label more inclusive, we have decided to use the more neutral term 'General British' to refer to the prestige variety.[2] It's influenced by London and the south-east of England, which is why some authors have termed it 'Standard Southern British English', or equivalent names. For instance, the widespread use of glottal reinforcement of the plosives (see section 2.7.3) and the vocalisation of /l/ (see section 2.14.3) have come into GB through Cockney. The English we describe in this book is the speech of the average modern GB speaker. Old-fashioned usages have been excluded, as have any 'trendy' pronunciations that are too recent to have gained widespread acceptance.

Notes

1 Upton, Clive, Kretzschmar, William A. and Konopka, Rafal (2001) *Oxford Dictionary of Pronunciation for Current English*. Oxford: Oxford University Press.
2 The name was first suggested by Jack Windsor Lewis in his (1972) *A Concise Pronouncing Dictionary of British and American English*. London: Oxford University Press, and has recently been adopted in Cruttenden (2014).

Chapter 2

Consonants

2.1 The vocal tract and tongue

Before we discuss how the 24 English consonant phonemes are made, or **articulated**, let's familiarise ourselves with the anatomy of the **vocal tract** (Figure 2.1) and **tongue** (Figure 2.2).

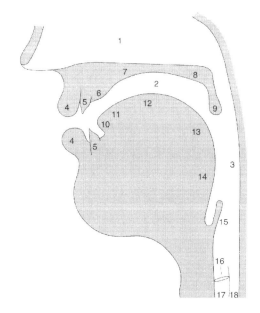

1. Nasal cavity	10. Tip of tongue
2. Oral cavity	11. Blade of tongue
3. Pharynx	12. Front of tongue
4. Lips	13. Back of tongue
5. Teeth	14. Root of tongue
6. Alveolar ridge	15. Epiglottis
7. Hard palate	16. Larynx, containing vocal folds
8. Soft palate (also termed 'velum')	17. Trachea
9. Uvula	18. Oesophagus

Figure 2.1 The anatomy of the vocal tract.

This diagram might appear strange to you at first. The tongue may be larger or smaller than you expected. It's small in the sense that the tip doesn't extend much further from the place at which it's attached to the lower jaw, and it's large in the sense that it extends deep into the mouth and throat, and almost completely fills the **oral cavity** (mouth).

If we start at the bottom of the diagram, we see that there are two passages. The **oesophagus** /ɪˈsɒfəɡəs/ (food pipe) leads to the stomach, and the **trachea** /trəˈkiːə/ (windpipe) leads to the lungs. It's the trachea which is of most interest for our purposes. During speech, air flows up from the lungs via the trachea, and the first point of interest that it meets is the **larynx** /ˈlærɪŋks/. The larynx joins the trachea to the pharynx (throat; see below) and is a box-like structure made of cartilage. It's larger in men than in women and is what makes the 'Adam's apple', the lump at the front of the throat. The larynx contains the **vocal folds**, a pair of lip-like structures which can be brought together to close off the trachea and lungs. If there's a need to expel something from the lungs or trachea, the vocal folds are brought tightly together, the muscles of the chest and abdomen squeeze the lungs strongly, and then the vocal folds are abruptly separated to let the trapped air below escape in an explosion which hopefully clears the blockage. This is a cough. The vocal folds also seal off the lungs to stabilise the chest during lifting or other types of physical exertion. You will notice that before you pick up something heavy, you take a breath and trap it in your lungs by bringing the vocal folds together, and then when you put the load down, you inevitably let out a gasp as you release the air you had trapped in your lungs.

The next feature is the **epiglottis** /ˌepɪˈɡlɒtɪs/, a flap of cartilage at the root of the tongue. It isn't involved in making speech sounds in English. Its biological function is to fold over the entrance to the larynx during swallowing in order to guide food and drink into the oesophagus.

The space above the larynx and behind the root of the tongue is called the **pharynx** /ˈfærɪŋks/. It's smaller when the tongue is pulled back in the mouth and larger when the tongue is pushed forward.

There is then a possible fork in the road for the **airstream**. In our diagram the **soft palate** /ˈpælət/ (also termed **velum** /ˈviːləm/) and the **uvula** /ˈjuːvjələ/ at its tip are shown in the lowered position, but it's also possible for the soft palate to form a seal against the back wall of the pharynx and close off the entrance to the **nasal cavity** (nose). This is known as a **velic closure**; see e.g. Fig. 2.3. Thus the airstream can potentially enter both the oral and nasal cavity (as in our diagram) or only the oral cavity (when the soft palate is raised and a velic closure is formed). There's little to be said about the nasal cavity itself because its dimensions are fixed; it's only the valve-like action of the soft palate opening and closing the entrance to it which is relevant for speech.

The oral cavity is bordered by the tongue at the bottom, the **palate** at the top, and the lips, cheeks and teeth at the front and sides. By opening and closing the jaw and pulling the tongue back and pushing it forward, the oral cavity can be made larger or smaller. The tongue, lower teeth and lip move with the lower jaw while the upper teeth and lip are in a fixed position.

Behind the upper front teeth is a lumpy area called the **alveolar ridge** /ˌælviˈəʊlə/, and to the rear of that is the palate. The palate is divided into the soft palate and the **hard palate**. If you explore your palate with the tip of your tongue, you'll find that it's indeed hard and bony at the front, and soft and fleshy at the back. At the very end of the soft palate is the uvula, which you can see hanging down when you look in the mirror.

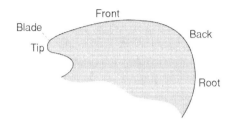

Figure 2.2 Divisions of the tongue.

The position shown in Figure 2.1 is actually a slightly unusual one, but it's useful for demonstration purposes. It shows the position assumed when breathing through the nose and mouth simultaneously. When not speaking, a healthy person would hold the jaws closer together with the lips and teeth touching, the tongue would fill the oral cavity, touching the roof of the mouth from the alveolar ridge to the soft palate, and the soft palate would be lowered (as in the diagram) to allow for normal breathing in and out via the nose.

The tongue has few obvious natural divisions in the way that the vocal tract does. However, phoneticians find it convenient to divide it into a number of parts for the sake of convenience when describing sounds and their articulations (see Figure 2.2).

The very point of the tongue is known as the **tip**; the part of the tongue which narrows to the tip and which lies under the alveolar ridge is the **blade** of the tongue. The part which lies under the hard palate and the part under the soft palate are called the **front** and **back** of the tongue respectively. This may seem strange at first, but front and back refer to the part of the tongue used in the articulation of vowels (see section 5.1.1) – the front is the part of the tongue used to form front vowels, and the back is the part used to form back vowels. The tip and blade remain low in the mouth and aren't involved in making vowels. Finally, the part of the tongue in the pharynx is the **root**.

2.2 Describing consonants

A consonant is a speech sound which involves an obstruction of the airstream as it passes through the vocal tract. Describing a consonant involves describing the nature of the obstruction, and there are three factors to be taken into consideration: **voicing, place of articulation** and **manner of articulation**.

2.2.1 Voicing

Voicing refers to the actions of the vocal folds during the articulation of a consonant. Different actions of the vocal folds produce **voiced** and **voiceless** sounds (Table 2.1).

It's easiest to appreciate the voicing in sounds like /v ð z ʒ m n ŋ l r/ because these can be prolonged. Put your hand on your throat as you say them and feel the vibration. Note how the vibration stops and starts as you stop and start the consonant.

A number of English consonants come in pairs, the only difference between them being that one is voiceless and one is voiced. These pairs are /f v/, /θ ð/, /s z/, /ʃ ʒ/, /p b/, /t d/, /k g/

Table 2.1 English voiced and voiceless consonants

Voicing	Description	Sounds
Voiced	The vocal folds are held gently together so that the airflow from the lungs causes them to vibrate.	/b d g dʒ v ð z ʒ m n ŋ l r j w/
Voiceless	The vocal folds are held apart as in the position for normal breathing.	/p t k tʃ f θ s ʃ h/

and /tʃ dʒ/. Take some of the pairs which can be easily lengthened, such as /f v/ and /s z/, and alternate between the voiceless and the voiced consonants and feel how the vibration in your larynx stops and starts.

Note that in our diagrams of consonant articulations we use a plus sign at the larynx to indicate that the consonant is voiced, and a minus sign if it's voiceless. If both signs are included (±), both voiced and voiceless articulations are possible.

2.2.2 Place of articulation

The second factor to take into account when describing a consonant is *where* in the vocal tract the obstruction is made. **Place of articulation** is described in terms of an **active articulator** which moves towards a **passive articulator** which is in a fixed position (Table 2.2).

The lip-rounding of labial-velar /w/ and the positioning of the vocal folds for glottal /h/ can't be analysed in terms of passive and active articulators because they involve two elements moving towards each other (the corners of the mouth for /w/ and the two vocal folds for /h/). The lips and vocal folds are therefore classified as both active and passive in our table.

Take some time to silently articulate the consonants listed in the table (or at least those you are confident you can correctly pronounce) in order to identify the different places of articulation.

Table 2.2 English consonants: place of articulation

Place	Active articulator	Passive articulator	Consonants
Bilabial	Lower lip	Upper lip	/p b m/
Labio-dental	Lower lip	Upper incisors	/f v/
Dental	Tongue-tip	Upper incisors	/θ ð/
Alveolar	Tongue-tip	Alveolar ridge	/t d n s z l/
Post-alveolar	Tongue-tip	Rear of alveolar ridge	/r/
Palato-alveolar	Tongue-tip, blade and front	Alveolar ridge and hard palate	/tʃ dʒ ʃ ʒ/
Palatal	Front of tongue	Hard palate	/j/
Velar	Back of tongue	Soft palate	/k g ŋ/
Glottal	Vocal folds	Vocal folds	/h/
Labial-velar	Back of tongue / Lips	Soft palate / Lips	/w/

Table 2.3 English consonants: manner of articulation

Manner	Description	Consonants
Plosive	A complete closure is formed in the vocal tract, blocking the airstream, and then released.	/p b t d k g/
Fricative	A narrowing is formed in the vocal tract, causing turbulence and fricative noise as the airstream is forced through.	/f v θ ð s z ʃ ʒ h/
Affricate	A complete closure is formed in the vocal tract and then released slowly, resulting in **homorganic friction**, i.e. fricative noise at the same place of articulation.	/ʧ ʤ/
Nasal	A complete closure is formed in the oral cavity, the soft palate is in the lowered position, and air exits via the nose.	/m n ŋ/
Approximant	A narrowing is formed in the vocal tract, but one not narrow enough to cause turbulence and noise as in the case of a fricative.	/r l j w/

2.2.3 Manner of articulation

Manner of articulation is the term used to describe the kind of obstruction involved in articulating a consonant. The five manners of articulation found in English are listed in Table 2.3.

Explore what these terms really mean by articulating some of the consonants you are confident of and feeling the different manners of articulation.

2.2.4 Double and secondary articulations

English /w/ is an example of a **double articulation**, meaning that two articulations of equal magnitude (i.e. two **primary articulations**) take place at the same time – an approximant articulation between the back of the tongue and the soft palate, and another approximant articulation consisting of the rounding of the lips. Other double articulations are possible but don't occur in English.

In the case of **secondary articulations**, the primary articulation is accompanied by an articulation of lesser magnitude. Examples of this in GB are the **labialisation** (i.e. lip-rounding) accompanying /ʃ ʒ ʧ ʤ r/ (see sections 2.12 and 2.14) and the approximation of the back of the tongue to the soft palate (**velarisation**) which accompanies /l/ in certain circumstances (see section 2.14.2).

2.2.5 Combining voicing, place and manner

When we bring together the key factors of voicing, place of articulation and manner of articulation, each English consonant phoneme has its own unique label which phoneticians use when referring to it (Table 2.4).

Strictly speaking, the IPA symbol for the English /r/ sound is [ɹ], but when making practical phonemic transcriptions for various languages, phoneticians often replace 'exotic' symbols with the nearest 'non-exotic' symbol for the sake of ease of printing and writing. In such cases there's no danger of confusion because the description of the sounds is included with the symbols, as we do here.

Table 2.4 English consonants: voicing, place and manner of articulation

Symbol	Consonant label	Symbol	Consonant label
/p/	voiceless bilabial plosive	/s/	voiceless alveolar fricative
/b/	voiced bilabial plosive	/z/	voiced alveolar fricative
/t/	voiceless alveolar plosive	/ʃ/	voiceless palato-alveolar fricative
/d/	voiced alveolar plosive	/ʒ/	voiced palato-alveolar fricative
/k/	voiceless velar plosive	/h/	voiceless glottal fricative
/g/	voiced velar plosive	/m/	voiced bilabial nasal
/ʧ/	voiceless palato-alveolar affricate	/n/	voiced alveolar nasal
/dʒ/	voiced palato-alveolar affricate	/ŋ/	voiced velar nasal
/f/	voiceless labio-dental fricative	/j/	voiced palatal approximant
/v/	voiced labio-dental fricative	/w/	voiced labial-velar approximant
/θ/	voiceless dental fricative	/l/	voiced alveolar lateral approximant
/ð/	voiced dental fricative	/r/	voiced post-alveolar approximant

Table 2.5 English consonant grid

	Bilabial	Labio-dental	Dental	Alveolar	Post-alveolar	Palato-alveolar	Palatal	Velar	Glottal	Labial-Velar
Plosives	p b			t d				k g		
Affricates						ʧ dʒ				
Fricatives		f v	θ ð	s z		ʃ ʒ			h	
Nasals	m			n				ŋ		
Approximants				l	r		j			w

Note that in the IPA chart (see p. xviii) the term *post-alveolar* is used for /ʧ dʒ ʃ ʒ/ and *alveolar* for /r/, but we prefer the terms traditionally used for English, *palato-alveolar* and *post-alveolar* respectively, because they better describe the English articulations.

2.3 The English consonants

Table 2.5 conveniently summarises the voicing, place of articulation and manner of articulation of the 24 English consonants. Within each cell, the sound on the left is voiceless, and the one on the right is voiced.

2.4 Obstruents and sonorants

Table 2.5 reveals that consonants fall into two groups: those that typically come in voiceless and voiced pairs, and those that don't. Plosives, affricates and fricatives are **obstruents** /'ɒbstruənts/, the most consonant-like of the consonants, involving the greatest degree of obstruction to the airstream. Nasals and approximants are **sonorants** /'sɒnərənts/ (as are vowels) and are the least consonant-like of the consonants, involving a lesser degree of obstruction.

2.4.1 Pre-fortis clipping

Voiceless (also known as *fortis*) obstruents shorten sonorants (including vowels, see section 5.3) which precede them in the same syllable. This phenomenon is termed **pre-fortis** clipping and results in /m/ being shortened before /p/ in *lump* and /f/ in *lymph*; /n/ before /t/ in *bent*, /s/ in *wince* and /ʧ/ in *bench*; /ŋ/ before /k/ in *bank*; and /l/ before /p/ in *help*, /t/ in *belt*, /k/ in *sulk*, /ʧ/ in *belch*, /f/ in *golf*, /θ/ in *health*, /s/ in *else* and /ʃ/ in *Welsh*.

2.4.2 Obstruent devoicing

Although we have so far referred to English consonants as either voiceless or voiced, English voiced obstruents are actually only *potentially* fully voiced. Depending on the phonetic context, they are often partially or even completely **devoiced** /ˌdiːˈvɔɪst/ (i.e. they partially or completely lose their voicing). For this reason the terms **fortis** and **lenis** are sometimes used for voiceless and voiced instead. Fortis means *strong* while lenis means *weak*, which reflects the fact that voiceless obstruents are articulated more forcefully than voiced obstruents. Force of articulation is a difficult feature to perceive, and many learners are confused by these terms because they feel that voiced sounds are louder and therefore strong, while voiceless sounds are quieter and therefore weak. It's preferable, therefore, to stick with the terms *voiceless* and *voiced*, with the understanding that when we refer to English /b d g dʒ v ð z ʒ/ as voiced obstruents, we actually mean 'potentially' fully voiced.

English voiced obstruents are typically fully voiced when they occur between voiced sounds, such as nasals, approximants and vowels (Table 2.6).

English voiced obstruents are typically partially or fully devoiced when they are preceded by a pause or a voiceless consonant, or when a pause or voiceless consonant follows (Table 2.7). A devoiced consonant is normally shown by means of a subscript circle under the consonant, e.g. [b̥], but with descending symbols a superscript circle is used, e.g. [g̊]. In the case of fricatives, the devoicing is greater before a voiceless consonant or pause than after a

Table 2.6 Examples of fully voiced obstruents

	Medial between vowels		Medial between sonorants and vowels		Word-initial between vowels		Word-final between vowels	
/b/	rabbit	[ˈræbɪt]	amber	[ˈæmbə]	a boat	[ə ˈbəʊt]	rub it	[ˈrʌb ɪt]
/d/	powder	[ˈpaʊdə]	balding	[ˈbɔːldɪŋ]	a dog	[ə ˈdɒg]	read it	[ˈriːd ɪt]
/g/	ago	[əˈgəʊ]	finger	[ˈfɪŋgə]	my gate	[maɪ ˈgeɪt]	big oak	[ˈbɪg ˈəʊk]
/dʒ/	badger	[ˈbædʒə]	banjo	[ˈbændʒəʊ]	a joke	[ə ˈdʒəʊk]	page eight	[ˈpeɪdʒ ˈeɪt]
/v/	saving	[ˈseɪvɪŋ]	envy	[ˈenvi]	a view	[ə ˈvjuː]	move it	[ˈmuːv ɪt]
/ð/	other	[ˈʌðə]	southern	[ˈsʌðn̩]	for this	[fə ˈðɪs]	with it	[ˈwɪð ɪt]
/z/	loser	[ˈluːzə]	frenzy	[ˈfrenzi]	the zoo	[ðə ˈzuː]	his own	[hɪz ˈəʊn]
/ʒ/	treasure	[ˈtreʒə]	vision	[ˈvɪʒn̩]	a genre	[ə ˈʒɒnrə]	beige is	[ˈbeɪʒ ɪz]

Table 2.7 Examples of devoiced obstruents

	Following a pause		Preceding a pause		Following a voiceless consonant		Preceding a voiceless consonant	
/b/	boy	[b̥ɔɪ]	tab	[tæb̥]	this book	[ˈðɪs ˈb̥ʊk]	grab some	[ˈgræb̥ ˈsʌm]
/d/	day	[d̥eɪ]	load	[ləʊd̥]	this dog	[ˈðɪs ˈd̥ɒg]	hid some	[ˈhɪd̥ ˈsʌm]
/g/	gate	[g̊eɪt]	pig	[pɪg̊]	this guy	[ˈðɪs ˈg̊aɪ]	big sign	[ˈbɪg̊ ˈsaɪn]
/dʒ/	joy	[d̥ʒɔɪ]	page	[peɪd̥ʒ]	this joke	[ˈðɪs ˈd̥ʒəʊk]	cage fight	[ˈkeɪd̥ʒ ˈfaɪt]
/v/	van	[v̥æn]	cave	[keɪv̥]	this verb	[ˈðɪs ˈv̥ɜːb]	give time	[ˈgɪv̥ ˈtaɪm]
/ð/	this	[ð̥ɪs]	bathe	[beɪð̥]	miss that	[ˈmɪs ˈð̥æt]	with Tom	[wɪð̥ ˈtɒm]
/z/	zip	[z̥ɪp]	buzz	[bʌz̥]	that zone	[ˈðæt ˈz̥əʊn]	his turn	[hɪz̥ ˈtɜːn]
/ʒ/	genre	[ˈʒ̊ɒnrə]	beige	[beɪʒ̊]	what genre	[ˈwɒt ˈʒ̊ɒnrə]	beige top	[ˈbeɪʒ̊ ˈtɒp]

voiceless consonant or pause. When devoicing occurs, the difference between pairs of voiced and voiceless obstruents is less marked, but the contrast still remains – /b d g dʒ v ð z ʒ/ don't become /p t k tʃ f θ s ʃ/.

2.5 Stops

Plosives and affricates make up the category of **stops**. They have in common a combination of a velic closure and a closure in the oral cavity which results in a complete obstruction to the airstream (hence the term *stop*).

English has three pairs of voiceless and voiced plosives at the bilabial, alveolar and velar places of articulation.

- For /p/ and /b/, the lips come together and form a complete closure, stopping the airstream (see Figure 2.3).
- For /t/ and /d/, a complete closure is formed by the tip of the tongue against the alveolar ridge and by the sides of the tongue against the upper side teeth (see Figure 2.4).
- For /k/ and /g/, the back of the tongue forms a closure against the soft palate, and the rear of the sides of the tongue forms a seal against the rear upper side teeth (see Figure 2.5).

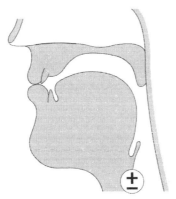

Figure 2.3 English plosives /p/ and /b/.

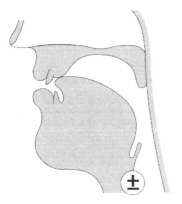

Figure 2.4 English plosives /t/ and /d/.

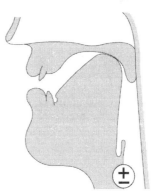

Figure 2.5 English plosives /k/ and /g/.

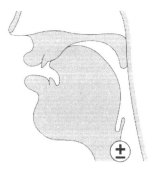
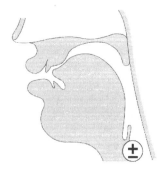

Figure 2.6 English affricates /ʧ/ and /ʤ/ showing palato-alveolar closure.

Figure 2.7 English affricates /ʧ/ and /ʤ/ showing palato-alveolar closure and release with homorganic friction.

English has a single pair of voiceless and voiced affricates at the palato-alveolar place of articulation.

- For /ʧ/ and /ʤ/, the tip and blade of the tongue form a closure against the rear part of the alveolar ridge, the front of the tongue is raised towards the hard palate, and the sides of the tongue form a seal against the upper side teeth (see Figure 2.6).
- The closure is released slowly, resulting in a brief moment of homorganic friction (Figure 2.7).

Although the phonemic symbols for the affricates consist of two elements, these phonemic affricates are single sounds, and although the first element of each symbol is the same as that used for the alveolar plosives, the place of articulation is different (as our diagrams demonstrate), the same symbols being used only for the sake of convenience.

2.5.1 The stages of stops

Stops have three stages (see Figure 2.8):

1   **approach**: the active articulator moves towards the passive articulator in order to form the closure;
2   **hold**: the closure is made, the airstream is blocked, and pressure builds up;
3   **release**: the active articulator moves away from the passive articulator, breaking the closure and releasing the compressed air.

The difference between plosives and affricates is that the release stage of affricates is slower and therefore accompanied by audible friction. Another key difference is that the fricative release stage of affricates is always present while the release stage of plosives is very variable.

2.6 Aspiration

When the voiceless plosives /p t k/ are at the beginning of a stressed syllable, they are released with **aspiration**. This means that there's a brief period of voicelessness

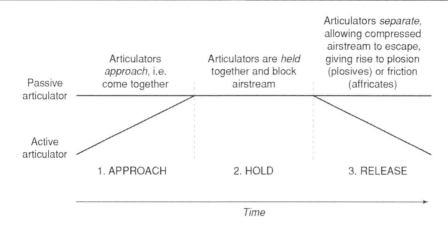

Figure 2.8 Articulation timing diagram showing the three stages of a stop.

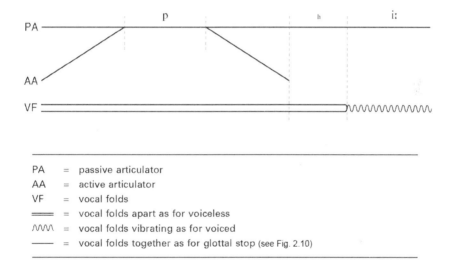

PA	=	passive articulator
AA	=	active articulator
VF	=	vocal folds
▬▬▬	=	vocal folds apart as for voiceless
∿∿∿	=	vocal folds vibrating as for voiced
——	=	vocal folds together as for glottal stop (see Fig. 2.10)

Figure 2.9 Aspiration in English /p/ as in *pea*. The diagram shows the brief period of voice-lessness after the release of the plosive and before the voicing for the vowel.

between the release of the plosive and the beginning of voicing for the next sounds (see Figure 2.9).

During this period the vocal folds remain open, and the air rushing through the vocal tract gives the impression of a short [h]; hence aspiration is shown with a raised [ʰ], e.g. [tʰ].

[pʰ]	*peas* [pʰiːz]	*palm* [pʰɑːm]	*pound* [pʰaʊnd]
[tʰ]	*toad* [tʰəʊd]	*tail* [tʰeɪl]	*torn* [tʰɔːn]
[kʰ]	*kind* [kʰaɪnd]	*care* [kʰeə]	*curb* [kʰɜːb]

When /p t k/ aren't at the beginning of a stressed syllable, they are weakly aspirated or unaspirated. This is the case at the beginning of unstressed syllables and at the end of syllables, but also, quite strikingly, when they are preceded by /s/ at the beginning of a syllable:

[p]	*perform* [pə'fɔːm]	*pacific* [pə'sɪfɪk]	*pyjamas* [pə'dʒɑːməz]
[t]	*today* [tə'deɪ]	*taboo* [tə'buː]	*together* [tə'geðə]
[k]	*concern* [kən'sɜːn]	*kebab* [kə'bæb]	*canal* [kə'næl]
[p]	*leap* [liːp]	*rope* [rəʊp]	*map* [mæp]
[t]	*fight* [faɪt]	*goat* [gəʊt]	*rate* [reɪt]
[k]	*like* [laɪk]	*sick* [sɪk]	*cheek* [tʃiːk]
[pʰ]	*pin* [pʰɪn]	*pot* [pʰɒt]	*pie* [pʰaɪ]
[p]	*spin* [spɪn]	*spot* [spɒt]	*spy* [spaɪ]
[tʰ]	*tone* [tʰəʊn]	*top* [tʰɒp]	*till* [tʰɪl]
[t]	*stone* [stəʊn]	*stop* [stɒp]	*still* [stɪl]
[kʰ]	*core* [kʰɔː]	*kill* [kʰɪl]	*cool* [kʰuːl]
[k]	*score* [skɔː]	*skill* [skɪl]	*school* [skuːl]

When aspirated /p t k/ are followed by approximants /l r w j/, the aspiration takes place during the articulation of the approximant, partially or fully devoicing the approximant [l̥ ɹ̥ j̊ w̥] and causing turbulence and fricative noise at the place of articulation of the approximant (Table 2.8).

When /s/ precedes these clusters, there's no aspiration, and therefore the approximants don't become devoiced or fricative: *splay* [spleɪ], *play* [pleɪ]; *spray* [spreɪ], *pray* [preɪ]; *spew* [spjuː], *pew* [pjuː]; *scream* [skriːm], *cream* [kriːm]; *skew* [skjuː], *queue* [kjuː]; *squad* [skwɒd], *quad* [kwɒd].

Because the voiced plosives are frequently partially or fully devoiced (see section 2.4.2), the presence of aspiration is an important cue for distinguishing /p t k/ from /b d g/.

Table 2.8 Examples of devoiced English approximants

	/l/	/r/	/j/	/w/
/p/	*plot* [pl̥ɒt]	*proud* [pr̥aʊd]	*pure* [pjɔː]	
/t/		*try* [tr̥aɪ]	*tune* [tj̊uːn]	*twin* [tw̥ɪn]
/k/	*clay* [kl̥eɪ]	*cry* [kr̥aɪ]	*cute* [kj̊uːt]	*quick* [kw̥ɪk]

2.7 Glottal plosive [ʔ]

In addition to the bilabial /p b/, alveolar /t d/ and velar /k g/ plosives, the glottal plosive [ʔ] (often referred to as the 'glottal stop') also occurs in English. The closure for a glottal plosive is made by bringing the vocal folds firmly together in an articulation similar to that of a very weak cough. The vocal folds are unable to vibrate during the production of a glottal plosive, and therefore the sound has no voiced equivalent. Although common, the glottal plosive isn't an independent phoneme in English (though it may be in other languages). The glottal plosive has a number of uses (see the sections below).

2.7.1 Hard attack

When a word starts with a vowel following a voiceless sound or a pause, the usual way to begin the vowel is to gently bring the vocal folds together into the position for voicing or, if the preceding sound is voiced, to continue the voicing as the articulators move into the position for the vowel. An alternative to this is to begin with a glottal plosive: irrespective of whether the vocal folds are apart for a preceding voiceless sound or pause, or vibrating for a preceding voiced sound, the vocal folds are brought tightly together and on release immediately take up the position for voicing, giving the impression of a very abrupt start to the vowel. This is known as **hard attack** and is used for emphasis in English, although in other languages this may be the most usual treatment of word-initial vowels.

> *Take this apple, not my orange.*
> With hard attack: ['teɪk ðɪs 'ʔæpl̩ 'nɒt maɪ 'ʔɒrɪndʒ]
> Without hard attack: ['teɪk ðɪs 'æpl̩ 'nɒt maɪ 'ɒrɪndʒ]

A similar use of the glottal plosive is to separate sequences of vowels within words. In words like *react* /ri'ækt/, *cooperate* /kəʊ'ɒpəreɪt/ and *deodorant* /di'əʊdərənt/, the transition from one vowel to the next usually consists of a rapid glide of the tongue from the first vowel position to the second. An alternative in emphatic speech is to insert a glottal plosive between the vowels as the tongue moves between the vowel positions. This is possible only when the second vowel is stressed, i.e. not in *serious* /'sɪəriəs/, *hire* /'haɪə/, *leotard* /'liːətɑːd/.

> **With glottal plosive:** *react* [ri'ʔækt], *cooperate* [kəʊ'ʔɒpəreɪt], *deodorant* [di'ʔəʊdərənt]
> **Without glottal plosive:** *react* [ri'ækt], *cooperate* [kəʊ'ɒpəreɪt], *deodorant* [di'əʊdərənt]

2.7.2 Glottal replacement

The most important occurrence of the glottal plosive in English is as an allophone of the /t/ phoneme. This is known as **glottal replacement**. Glottal replacement occurs in only a specific set of phonetic contexts: when /t/ is in a syllable coda, preceded by a sonorant (i.e. a vowel, nasal or approximant) and followed by another consonant:

> **Within words**: *butler* ['bʌʔlə], *lightning* ['laɪʔnɪŋ], *pitfall* ['pɪʔfɔːl], *cats* [kæʔs]
> **Between words**: *felt wrong* ['felʔ 'rɒŋ], *sent four* ['senʔ 'fɔː], *light rain* ['laɪʔ 'reɪn], *part time* ['pɑːʔ 'taɪm]

Although, in GB, [ʔ] doesn't occur between vowels in word-medial position, it can sometimes be heard in word-final position before a vowel in high-frequency words, for example *got a* ['gɒʔ ə], *let us* ['leʔ əs]. Some young speakers also use it before a pause, e.g. *wait* [weɪʔ].

The replacement of [t] by [ʔ] as a realisation of the /t/ phoneme in certain phonetic contexts is a very interesting and striking characteristic of modern English. Like the other uses of the glottal plosive, however, it's not obligatory, and using [t] in this context is never incorrect.

2.7.3 Glottal reinforcement

In addition to [ʔ] acting as an allophone of /t/, it can also occur together with /t/ and the other voiceless stops, /p k ʧ/, in a process known as **glottal reinforcement**. A glottal closure overlaps with the oral closure (see Figure 2.10): first the glottal closure is made, then the bilabial, alveolar, palato-alveolar or velar closure is made, then the glottal closure is released inaudibly behind the oral closure before finally the oral closure is released; this phenomenon is sometimes also referred to as 'pre-glottalisation'. Glottal reinforcement occurs in the same phonetic contexts as for glottal replacement of [t] (except for /ʧ/, which doesn't have to be followed by a consonant), and like glottal replacement, although it's common, it isn't obligatory.

captive [ˈkæʔptɪv]	*keep calm* [ˈkiːʔp ˈkɑːm]	
curtsey [ˈkɜːʔtsi]	*hot sauce* [ˈhɒʔt ˈsɔːs]	
action [ˈæʔkʃn̩]	*take five* [ˈteɪʔk ˈfaɪv]	
hatchet [ˈhæʔʧɪt]	*catch me* [ˈkæʔʧ mi]	*catch it* [ˈkæʔʧ ɪt]

2.7.4 Ejective /p t k/

A further way in which syllable-coda English voiceless plosives are associated with glottalic action is when they appear as **ejectives** in word-final position, particularly before a pause. Ejectives are sounds which use the larynx as a mechanism for creating an airstream. So far we have dealt only with the **pulmonic** airstream, consisting of air directly exiting the lungs, because this is the norm in English and in all other languages. It's also possible, however, to create an airstream by bringing the vocal folds together and raising the larynx to move the air above it. The ejectives [p' t' k'] are produced by forming the same velic and oral closures as for pulmonic [p t k], then closing the vocal folds, raising the larynx to compress the air behind the oral closure, and then releasing the closure. While ejective [k'] is noticeably more common than [t'] or [p'], none are obligatory in English.

quick [kwɪk']	*right* [raɪt']	*stop* [stɒp']

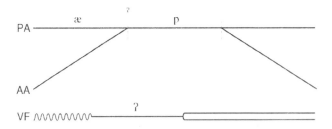

Figure 2.10 Glottal reinforcement in English /p/, as in *captive*. The reinforcing glottal plosive is formed before the hold stage of /p/ and released before the release of the bilabial plosive. (See Figure 2.9 for key to symbols.)

2.8 Nasal release

The bilabial /p b/ and alveolar /t d/ plosives have the same place of articulation as the bilabial /m/ and alveolar /n/ nasals respectively. They differ only in the soft palate being in the raised position (forming a velic closure) for the plosives and in the lowered position for the nasals. Consequently, it's possible to move from /p/ or /b/ to /m/, and from /t/ or /d/ to /n/, by lowering the soft palate only and leaving the oral closure in place. This is called **nasal release** and is usual in English when plosives are followed by their nasal equivalents. It's not usual for velar plosives /k g/ because the velar nasal /ŋ/ doesn't occur at the beginning of syllables.

/pm/	chipmunk /'ʧɪpmʌŋk/	ripe melon /'raɪp 'melən/	
/bm/	submit /səb'mɪt/	drab mood /'dræb 'muːd/	
/tn/	witness /'wɪtnəs/	got none /'gɒt 'nʌn/	
/dn/	kidney /'kɪdni/	good news /'gʊd 'njuːz/	

Nasal release often results in syllabic /n/. In recent decades this variant has become less universal than it was formerly (see section 8.2.2). Syllabic /m/ and /ŋ/ occur only in such contexts as the result of assimilation (see section 12.3.1).

[tn̩]	button ['bʌtn̩]	cotton ['kɒtn̩]	pattern ['pætn̩]
[dn̩]	burden ['bɜːdn̩]	sudden ['sʌdn̩]	modern ['mɒdn̩]

2.9 Lateral release

A similar process to nasal release occurs when /l/ follows /t/ or /d/. It's possible to go from the /t d/ position to the /l/ position simply by lowering one or both sides of the tongue, this being the only difference in the articulation of the sounds. This is called **lateral release**.

/tl/	atlas /'ætləs/	at least /ət 'liːst/
/dl/	badly /'bædli/	hard luck /'hɑːd 'lʌk/

Lateral release often results in syllabic /l/ (see sections 2.14.4 and 8.2.1).

[tl̩]	bottle ['bɒtl̩]	total ['təʊtl̩]	crystal ['krɪstl̩]
[dl̩]	idol ['aɪdl̩]	model ['mɒdl̩]	cradle ['kreɪdl̩]

When the non-alveolar plosives, bilabial /p b/ and velar /k g/, are followed by /l/, **lateral escape** occurs. This means that the tongue-tip contact for /l/ is in place during the hold stage of the bilabial and velar plosives, and when released, the pent-up air in the vocal tract travels around the side(s) of this obstruction.

/pl/	stripling /'strɪplɪŋ/	stop lying /'stɒp 'laɪɪŋ/	
/bl/	public /'pʌblɪk/	grab lunch /'græb 'lʌnʧ/	
/kl/	backlash /'bæklæʃ/	thick legs /'θɪk 'legz/	
/gl/	burglar /'bɜːglə/	big lights /'bɪg 'laɪts/	

Lateral escape also often results in syllabic /l/ (see sections 2.14.4 and 8.2.1).

[pḷ]	*apple* ['æpḷ]	*pupil* ['pjuːpḷ]	*opal* ['əʊpḷ]
[bḷ]	*double* ['dʌbḷ]	*label* ['leɪbḷ]	*global* ['gləʊbḷ]
[kḷ]	*tackle* ['tækḷ]	*local* ['ləʊkḷ]	*snorkel* ['snɔːkḷ]
[gḷ]	*eagle* ['iːgḷ]	*legal* ['liːgḷ]	*single* ['sɪŋgḷ]

2.10 Stop sequences

When two identical plosives occur in sequence, the first usually isn't released. Instead, the sequence is realised as a single long plosive. This means that there's an approach stage followed by a long hold stage and a release stage:

/pp/ *ripe pear* /'raɪp 'peə/   /tt/ *get two* /'get 'tuː/   /kk/ *black car* /'blæk 'kɑː/
/bb/ *grab both* /'græb 'bəʊθ/   /dd/ *red door* /'red 'dɔː/   /gg/ *big guy* /'bɪg 'gaɪ/

When two identical affricates occur in sequence, the first must be released; i.e. the fricative release stage must be present in the case of both consonants:

/ʧʧ/ *rich cheese* /'rɪʧ 'ʧiːz/   /ʤʤ/ *large jaw* /'lɑːʤ 'ʤɔː/

The first plosive is also usually unreleased when the plosives have the same place of articulation but differ in voicing:

/pb/ *stop by* /'stɒp 'baɪ/   /bp/ *rob people* /'rɒb 'piːpḷ/
/td/ *hot dinner* /'hɒt 'dɪnə/   /dt/ *red tie* /'red 'taɪ/
/kg/ *black gown* /'blæk 'gaʊn/   /gk/ *big cat* /'bɪg 'kæt/

Again, the first affricate must be released when the following affricate differs in voicing:

/ʧʤ/ *which job* /'wɪʧ 'ʤɒb/   /ʤʧ/ *large child* /'lɑːʤ 'ʧaɪld/

When plosives occur in sequence at different places of articulation, the closure for the second plosive is made before the closure for the first plosive is released. Consequently, the release of the first plosive is **inaudible** because a closure has already been made further forward in the mouth, or because a closure further back in the mouth holds back the compressed air.

Second plosive further forward than first plosive:

/tp/ *that part* /'ðæt 'pɑːt/   /tb/ *what beach* /'wɒt 'biːʧ/
/dp/ *bad place* /'bæd 'pleɪs/   /db/ *good boy* /'gʊd 'bɔɪ/
/kp/ *black pony* /'blæk 'pəʊni/   /kb/ *thick book* /'θɪk 'bʊk/
/gp/ *big picture* /'bɪg 'pɪkʧə/   /gb/ *big bang* /'bɪg 'bæŋ/
/kt/ *lack time* /'læk 'taɪm/   /kd/ *back door* /'bæk 'dɔː/
/gt/ *big town* /'bɪg 'taʊn/   /gd/ *big dog* /'bɪg 'dɒg/

Second plosive further back than first plosive:

/pt/ *top team* /'tɒp 'tiːm/	/pd/ *strap down* /'stræp 'daʊn/
/bt/ *grab two* /'græb 'tuː/	/bd/ *job done* /'dʒɒb 'dʌn/
/pk/ *deep trouble* /'diːp 'trʌbl̩/	/pg/ *cheap gift* /'ʧiːp 'gɪft/
/bk/ *drab colours* /'dræb 'kʌləz/	/bg/ *superb garden* /su'pɜːb 'gɑːdn̩/
/tk/ *what car* /'wɒt 'kɑː/	/tg/ *that guy* /'ðæt 'gaɪ/
/dk/ *sad case* /'sæd 'keɪs/	/dg/ *hard game* /'hɑːd 'geɪm/

(Alternatively, the first /t d/ in the sequence could assimilate in these positions (see section 12.3.1), or /t/ could undergo glottal replacement (see section 2.7.2), but the release would still typically be inaudible.)

The same isn't true of affricates. If a plosive follows, the affricate is released before the closure for the plosive is made.

/ʧp/ *HP* /'eɪʧ 'piː/	/ʧb/ *catch both* /'kæʧ 'bəʊθ/
/ʧt/ *each time* /'iːʧ 'taɪm/	/ʧd/ *each day* /'iːʧ 'deɪ/
/ʧk/ *reach Cardiff* /'riːʧ 'kɑːdɪf/	/ʧg/ *teach grammar* /'tiːʧ 'græmə/
/dʒp/ *barge past* /'bɑːdʒ 'pɑːst/	/dʒb/ *edge back* /'edʒ 'bæk/
/dʒt/ *large team* /'lɑːdʒ 'tiːm/	/dʒd/ *charge down* /'ʧɑːdʒ 'daʊn/
/dʒk/ *large cuts* /'lɑːdʒ 'kʌts/	/dʒg/ *huge grin* /'hjuːdʒ 'grɪn/

2.11 Affricates

So far, as is usual in phonetics textbooks, we have been using the term *affricate* a little imprecisely. There's a distinction between **phonetic affricates** and **phonemic affricates** which we should bear in mind. Phonetically, an affricate is a sound which consists of a complete closure followed by homorganic friction. Accordingly, English /ʧ/ and /dʒ/ are phonetic affricates because both the stop element and the fricative element are palato-alveolar. But by our definition, the alveolar sequences /ts dz/ are also phonetic affricates. The reason we consider /ʧ/ and /dʒ/ to be phonemic as well as phonetic affricates is that they behave as single indivisible units in the English sound system and are felt to be single sounds by native speakers. /ts dz/, on the other hand, behave like sequences and are felt to be sequences by natives.

Another pair of non-phonemic phonetic affricates is formed when /r/ follows /t/ or /d/. The closure for the /t/ or /d/ is post-alveolar in anticipation of the following /r/ (see Figure 2.11), and the release into the position for /r/ results in homorganic friction. The acoustic effect of /tr/ and /dr/ is similar to that of /ʧ/ and /dʒ/, but the two sets of sounds remain distinct: *chain* /ʧeɪn/ vs. *train* /treɪn/, *Jane* /dʒeɪn/ vs. *drain* /dreɪn/.

2.12 Fricatives

English has four pairs of voiceless and voiced fricatives at the labio-dental, dental, alveolar and palato-alveolar places of articulation, and a single voiceless glottal fricative.

- For /f/ and /v/, the lower lip lightly touches the upper incisors, and the airstream is forced through the gap (see Figure 2.12).

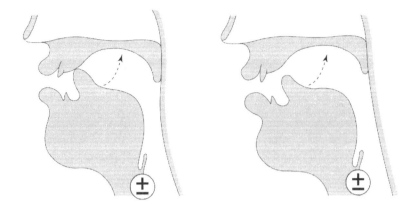

Figure 2.11 The hold and release stages of the English post-alveolar (phonetic) affricates /tr/ and /dr/ [tʃ, dʒ] as in *train*, *drain*. The arrow indicates the raising of the sides of the tongue towards the back teeth.

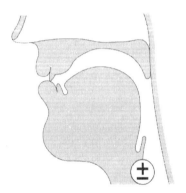

Figure 2.12 English fricatives /f/ and /v/.

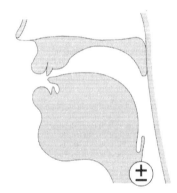

Figure 2.13 English fricatives /θ/ and /ð/.

- For /θ/ and /ð/, the sides of the tongue form a seal against the side teeth, and the airstream is forced through a gap between the tongue-tip and the rear of the upper incisors (see Figure 2.13).
- For /s/ and /z/, the airstream is forced through a gap between the tongue-tip/blade and the alveolar ridge, while the sides of the tongue form a seal against the upper side teeth (see Figure 2.14).
- For /ʃ/ and /ʒ/, the sides of the tongue form a seal against the upper side teeth, forcing the airstream through a narrow gap between the tongue-tip/blade and the alveolar ridge, and between the front of the tongue and the hard palate (see Figure 2.15). The primary articulation is accompanied by a simultaneous secondary articulation – rounding and protrusion of the lips.
- For /h/, the airstream is forced through the vocal tract with stronger than usual pressure, resulting in friction throughout the vocal tract and particularly at the narrowest point – the **glottis**, the space between the open vocal folds.

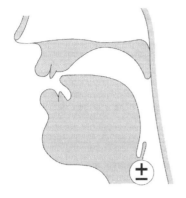

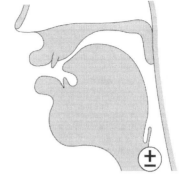

Figure 2.14 English fricatives /s/ and /z/.   *Figure 2.15* English fricatives /ʃ/ and /ʒ/.

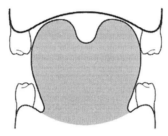

Figure 2.16 Mouth viewed from the front showing grooved tongue shape for /s z/.

Each fricative is accompanied by the raising of the soft palate, forming a velic closure blocking the entrance to the nasal cavity.

2.12.1 Sibilants

Fricatives can be divided into the sub-classes of **sibilant** fricatives /s z ʃ ʒ/ and **non-sibilant** fricatives /f v θ ð h/. The tongue assumes a longitudinal **grooved** shape for sibilants (see Figure 2.16) and a flatter shape for non-sibilants. The grooving of the tongue channels the airstream into a jet which becomes turbulent and noisy when it strikes an obstruction further forward in the mouth – the teeth. In the case of non-sibilant fricatives, the turbulence and noise are generated at the stricture itself. The jet-of-air method of producing noisy turbulence is more effective than simple narrowing of the articulators, and hence sibilants are noticeably louder than non-sibilant fricatives. In the case of the English voiced non-sibilants, /v/ and /ð/, there's often very little fricative noise, and the difference between them and their approximant equivalents can be very slight.

2.12.2 /h/

During the articulation of /h/, the vocal tract assumes the position for the following sound, usually a vowel, which gives /h/ the quality of a voiceless or fricative version of the following sound. Thus, when isolated, the /h/ in *heart* is noticeably different from the /h/ in *hit*, the first having the quality of [ɑ̥] and the second of [ɪ̥]. In the case of a following /j/, as in *huge*, the /h/ is usually [ç], a voiceless palatal fricative. Fricative realisations of /h/ are also sometimes heard before back vowels – pharyngeal before /ɒ/, uvular before /ɔː/ or velar before /uː/.

Between vowels, as in *ahead* or *a house*, a voiced glottal fricative [ɦ] is a common, but not obligatory, realisation. The [ɦ] articulation involves a brief period of **breathy voice**, where the vibrating vocal folds don't fully come together as they vibrate, allowing air to escape between them and resulting in a 'breathy' quality.

2.12.3 Distribution of fricatives

Some of the fricatives are restricted in their distribution. /h/ appears only in syllable onsets before vowels (e.g. *hot, who, home*) or /j/ (e.g. *human, hue*), but not in syllable codas. /ʒ/ mainly occurs medially (e.g. *treasure, pleasure, vision*), being found initially and finally only in relatively recent loanwords (e.g. *genre, camouflage*), which often have alternative variants with /dʒ/.

2.13 Nasals

English has three nasals, all voiced, at the bilabial, alveolar and velar places of articulation:

- For /m/, the lips come together and form a complete closure while the soft palate lowers to allow air to exit via the nose (Figure 2.17).
- For /n/, a complete closure is formed in the oral cavity by the tip of the tongue against the alveolar ridge and by the sides of the tongue against the upper side teeth. Simultaneously, the soft palate is lowered, allowing air to escape via the nose (Figure 2.18).
- For /ŋ/, the back of the tongue forms a closure against the soft palate, and the rear of the sides of the tongue forms a seal against the rear upper side teeth. The soft palate is in the lowered position, allowing air to exit via the nose (Figure 2.19).

Note that these three articulations are the same as those for the bilabial /p b/, alveolar /t d/ and velar /k g/ plosives, differing only in the position of the soft palate – raised for plosives, lowered for nasals.

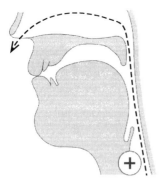

Figure 2.17 English nasal /m/. The arrow indicates the escape of the airstream through the nose.

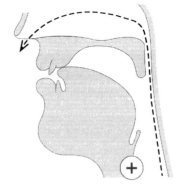

Figure 2.18 English nasal /n/. The arrow indicates the escape of the airstream through the nose.

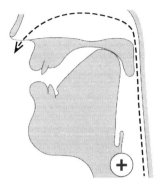

Figure 2.19 English nasal /ŋ/. The arrow indicates the escape of the airstream through the nose.

2.13.1 Distribution of nasals

Historically, the voiced plosives /b/ and /g/ have been lost from the word-final clusters /mb/ and /ŋg/.

This leaves /d/ as the only voiced plosive which can occur morpheme-finally after a nasal.

Table 2.9 demonstrates that *within* a morpheme, nasal + plosive clusters must be homorganic, i.e. have the same place of articulation – bilabial /m/ + bilabial /p/, alveolar /n/ + alveolar /t d/, velar /ŋ/ + velar /k/. Across a morpheme boundary, however, a nasal and a following plosive don't have to be homorganic. Within a syllable, /m/ and /ŋ/ can be followed by /d/ realising the <-ed> inflection (see section 2.15), and between syllables all sequences are possible (Table 2.10).

The velar nasal /ŋ/ is restricted to syllable-coda position (e.g. *sing* /sɪŋ/, *sink* /sɪŋk/). When a suffix is added to a word ending in /ŋ/, the pronunciation remains /g/-less even though it's

Table 2.9 Distribution of English nasals

	Voiceless plosive	Voiced plosive
/m/	*stamp* /stæmp/	*comb* /kəʊm/ (not */kəʊmb/)
/n/	*hint* /hɪnt/	*land* /lænd/
/ŋ/	*bank* /bæŋk/	*ring* /rɪŋ/ (not */rɪŋg/)

Note that erroneous or unattested forms are shown with an asterisk * before the incorrect transcription.

Table 2.10 Non-homorganic nasal + plosive clusters across morpheme boundaries

	<-ed>	/p/	/b/	/t/	/d/	/k/	/g/
/m/	*rammed* /ræmd/	*homepage* /ˈhəʊmpeɪdʒ/	*steamboat* /ˈstiːmbəʊt/	*timetable* /ˈtaɪmteɪbl̩/	*someday* /ˈsʌmdeɪ/	*tomcat* /ˈtɒmkæt/	*filmgoer* /ˈfɪlmgəʊə/
/n/		*pinpoint* /ˈpɪnpɔɪnt/	*sunbed* /ˈsʌnbed/	*suntan* /ˈsʌntæn/	*fandom* /ˈfændəm/	*pancake* /ˈpænkeɪk/	*wineglass* /ˈwaɪnglɑːs/
/ŋ/	*banged* /bæŋd/	*ringpull* /ˈrɪŋpʊl/	*songbird* /ˈsɒŋbɜːd/	*Paddington* /ˈpædɪŋtən/	*kingdom* /ˈkɪŋdəm/	*spring-clean* /ˈsprɪŋkliːn/	*dressing-gown* /ˈdresɪŋgaʊn/

Note that /n/ is likely to assimilate when followed by /p b/ or /k g/; see section 12.3.1.

now in word-medial position: *ring* /rɪŋ/, *ringing* /ˈrɪŋɪŋ/; *hang* /hæŋ/, *hanger* /ˈhæŋə/, etc. This leads to the generalisation that word-medially, /ŋ/ is found at the end of morphemes (e.g. *singer*, *hanging*) and /ŋg/ within morphemes (e.g. *finger*, *angry*, *angle*, *bongo*) because in the latter words /ŋg/ was never word-final and therefore /g/ was never lost. Exceptions to this rule are the words *long*, *young* and *strong* in their comparative and superlative forms, which retain the historical /g/ lost elsewhere:

long /lɒŋ/	*longer* /ˈlɒŋgə/	*longest* /ˈlɒŋgɪst/
young /jʌŋ/	*younger* /ˈjʌŋgə/	*youngest* /ˈjʌŋgɪst/
strong /strɒŋ/	*stronger* /ˈstrɒŋgə/	*strongest* /ˈstrɒŋgɪst/

2.13.2 Syllabic nasals

The syllables /əm/, /ən/ and /əŋ/ can in certain circumstances (see section 8.2) be realised as the syllabic consonants [m̩], [n̩] and [ŋ̩], meaning that the schwa /ə/ isn't articulated and the nasal becomes the nucleus of the syllable. Of the three nasals, however, syllabic /n/ is much more common than the other two (see section 8.2.2), and syllabic /ŋ/ occurs only as a result of assimilation. Syllabic consonants are very common in GB, but not completely obligatory.

[m̩]	*chasm* /ˈkæzm̩/	*a dozen miles* /ə ˈdʌzm̩ ˈmaɪlz/
[n̩]	*raisin* /ˈreɪzn̩/	*a dozen nights* /əˈdʌzn̩ ˈnaɪts/
[ŋ̩]	*taken* /ˈteɪkŋ̩/	*a dozen cats* /ə ˈdʌzŋ̩ ˈkæts/

2.14 Approximants

English has four approximants, all voiced, at the alveolar, post-alveolar, palatal and labial-velar places of articulation:

- For /l/, the tongue-tip touches the alveolar ridge while one or both of the sides of the tongue remain lowered, not making a seal with the side teeth and allowing air to flow around the tongue-tip contact (see Figure 2.20).
- For /r/, the tongue blade and front hollow while the tongue-tip curls slightly upwards towards the rear part of the alveolar ridge (see Figure 2.21). The lips are often weakly rounded.
- For /j/, the front of the tongue moves towards the hard palate (see Figure 2.22).
- For /w/, the back of the tongue moves towards the soft palate, and the lips round (see Figure 2.23).

Each approximant is accompanied by the raising of the soft palate, forming a velic closure blocking the entrance to the nasal cavity.

The double place name **labial-velar** reflects the fact that /w/ is a **double articulation**, i.e. one which involves two simultaneous articulations of equal degree – labial and velar approximants.

The approximants, like the nasals (and vowels), are sonorants and do not undergo the kind of devoicing which obstruents are subject to when adjacent to voiceless segments or pauses. However, when they are preceded by an aspirated voiceless plosive, the aspiration takes place during the articulation of the approximant and partially or completely devoices it, while the increased airflow through the approximant stricture causes friction (see section 2.6).

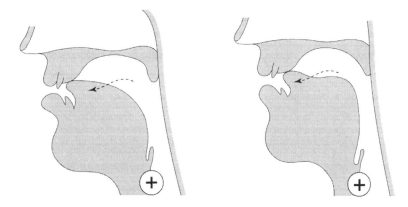

Figure 2.20 English lateral /l/. Left: clear /l/. Right: dark /l/ showing velarised tongue shape. The arrows indicate the passage of the airstream along the lowered sides of the tongue.

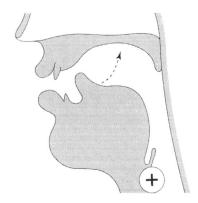

Figure 2.21 English approximant /r/. The arrow indicates the raising of the sides of the tongue towards the back teeth.

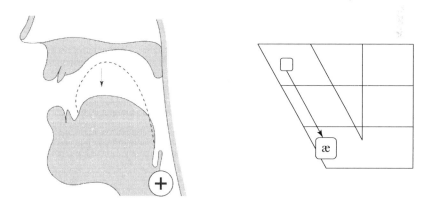

Figure 2.22 English /j/: sequence /jæ/ as in *yak*. The diagram shows the approximate change in tongue shape. Since /j/ is a semi-vowel, it can be indicated on a vowel diagram.

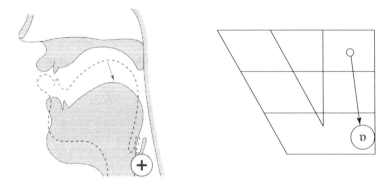

Figure 2.23 English /w/: sequence /wɒ/ as in *wash*. The diagram shows the approximate change in tongue shape. Since /w/ is a semi-vowel, it can be indicated on a vowel diagram.

2.14.1 Median and lateral approximants

The approximants can be divided into **lateral** (/l/) and **median** approximants (/r j w/). As the names suggest, the airstream flows to the side of an obstruction for lateral approximants, and along the midline of the oral cavity for the median approximants. You can test this by putting your tongue in the position for /l/ and breathing in deeply. You'll notice that one or both sides of your tongue feel cold because of the lateral airflow. Since /l/ is the only lateral approximant, it's often simply called a 'lateral', and since all other approximants are median, the label 'median' isn't usually included for them.

2.14.2 Clear and dark /l/

Since only tongue-tip contact with the alveolar ridge is necessary for the articulation of /l/, the rest of the tongue, a very flexible articulator, is able to take up a range of different shapes. When a vowel (including the semi-vowel /j/) follows, the tongue takes a relatively neutral position and anticipates the position of the following vowel. This is described as a **clear** variety of /l/ (see Figure 2.20). Before a consonant (except /j/) or in word-final position before a pause, the back of the tongue is raised towards the soft palate (see Figure 2.20), forming a secondary articulation. This is known as a **dark /l/** or **velarised /l/**. The symbol for dark /l/ is [ɫ].

> Clear /l/: *lead* [liːd], *let* [let], *lap* [læp], *luck* [lʌk], *law* [lɔː], *loose* [luːs]
> Dark /l/: *well* [weɫ], *dull* [dʌɫ], *fall* [fɔːɫ], *tool* [tuːɫ], *milk* [mɪɫk], *help* [heɫp], *salt* [sɔːɫt], *model* ['mɒdɫ], *pedal* ['pedɫ]

2.14.3 /l/-vocalisation

There's a tendency in the accents of southern England for the tongue-tip contact with the alveolar ridge to be lost when dark /l/ is pronounced. When this happens, only the raised back of the tongue remains, which results in a close back [ʊ]-like vowel. This process is known as **/l/-vocalisation**. When /l/-vocalisation happens with syllabic /l/, the result is a vowel in the [ʊ] ~ [u] area:

people ['piːpɫ] vs. ['piːpʊ]   *middle* ['mɪdɫ] vs. ['mɪdʊ]   *castle* ['kɑːsɫ] vs. ['kɑːsʊ]

With non-syllabic /l/, /l/-vocalisation results in a diphthong with a glide towards the close back position:

self [seɫf] vs. [seʊf]   *milk* [mɪɫk] vs. [mɪʊk]   *canal* [kə'næɫ] vs. [kə'næʊ]

/l/-vocalisation can sometimes be heard from GB speakers, especially those influenced by local southern English accents.

2.14.4 Syllabic /l/

The syllable /əl/ is very often realised as syllabic /l/, i.e. [l̩] (see section 8.2.1). The articulators move directly from the preceding consonant to /l/, the schwa /ə/ isn't articulated, and the /l/ becomes the nucleus of the syllable. Syllabic /l/ is the most common syllabic consonant in GB, occurring in a greater range of contexts than syllabic /n/.

> Syllabic /l/: *people* ['piːpl̩], *devil* ['devl̩], *satchel* ['sæʧl̩], *camel* ['kæml̩], *giggle* ['gɪgl̩]

2.14.5 Semi-vowels

Another way of grouping the approximants is according to the part of the tongue involved in their articulation, giving the terms **semi-vowel**, /j/ and /w/, and **non-semivowel**, /l/ and /r/. The semi-vowels are articulated with the parts of the tongue which are used to articulate vowels – the front and the back. The positions for /j/ and /w/ are the same as for the [i] and [u] vowels respectively. [j] and [i] both consist of an approximation of the front of the tongue to the hard palate, and [w] and [u] both consist of an approximation of the back of the tongue to the soft palate accompanied by simultaneous lip-rounding. Thus [j] and [w] are glides from these vowel positions to a vowel of longer duration. The non-semivowels involve the tip and blade of the tongue, which aren't used in the articulation of vowels.

2.14.6 Distribution of semi-vowels

The semi-vowels /j/ and /w/ occur only in syllable onsets in English (e.g. *young* /jʌŋ/, *unit* /'juːnɪt/, *few* /fjuː/, *one* /wʌn/, *wax* /wæks/, *twin* /twɪn/). Learners from other language backgrounds may feel that /j/ and /w/ can also occur in syllable codas, but in English such non-onset glides towards the [i] and [u] positions are best analysed as part of the syllable nucleus, forming diphthongs (see section 5.2.3):

FACE:	*cake* /keɪk/	*sail* /seɪl/	*day* /deɪ/
PRICE:	*like* /laɪk/	*ride* /raɪd/	*try* /traɪ/
CHOICE:	*voice* /vɔɪs/	*coin* /kɔɪn/	*boy* /bɔɪ/
GOAT:	*oak* /əʊk/	*rose* /rəʊz/	*no* /nəʊ/
MOUTH:	*shout* /ʃaʊt/	*clown* /klaʊn/	*plough* /plaʊ/

2.14.7 Distribution of /r/: rhoticity

GB is an example of a **non-rhotic** accent, meaning that /r/ occurs only in syllable onsets, or, to put it another way, only before vowels (e.g. *red* /red/) and not before consonants (e.g. *card* /kɑːd/), nor before a pause (e.g. *car* /kɑː/). Although /r/ has been lost in non-rhotic accents in syllable codas, historical /r/ in these positions continues to be represented in the orthography (because this was standardised before /r/ was lost) and is heard in the pronunciation of speakers of **rhotic** accents, such as most American, Scottish and Irish speakers. When /r/ was lost from syllable codas in the ancestor of modern GB, it resulted in the development of new vowel phonemes (NEAR, CURE, SQUARE, NURSE) and contributed to the stock of words representing already existing vowels (THOUGHT, PALM, schwa):

NEAR:	*deer* /dɪə/	*here* /hɪə/	*fear* /fɪə/
CURE:	*tour* /tʊə/ (/tɔː/)	*poor* /pʊə/ (/pɔː/)	*sure* /ʃʊə/ (/ʃɔː/)
SQUARE:	*bare* /beə/	*pair* /peə/	*wear* /weə/
NURSE:	*hurt* /hɜːt/	*bird* /bɜːd/	*verb* /vɜːb/
THOUGHT:	*north* /nɔːθ/	*force* /fɔːs/	*door* /dɔː/
PALM:	*start* /stɑːt/	*farm* /fɑːm/	*heart* /hɑːt/
schwa	*surprise* /sə'praɪz/	*offer* /'ɒfə/	*donor* /'dəʊnə/

Note that although /r/ has been lost in non-rhotic accents word-finally before a pause, it remains when there's no pause and the next word begins with a vowel (e.g. *far away* /'fɑːr ə'weɪ/), leading to the phenomenon of **/r/-liaison** (see sections 5.4 and 12.4).

2.14.8 Yod-dropping

We've seen that /j/ occurs only in syllable onsets, but even in onsets /j/ tends to be lost in certain positions, a phenomenon known as **yod-dropping**. Historically, /j/ has been lost after palato-alveolars (*chute* /ʃuːt/, *chew* /ʧuː/, *juice* /ʤuːs/), /r/ (*rude* /ruːd/) and /l/ preceded by a consonant (*blue* /bluː/, *flew* /fluː/). This tendency continues to spread, and it's now usual to drop /j/ after single /l/ (*lute* /luːt/, *allude* /ə'luːd/) and after word-initial /s/ (*suit* /suːt/), and common to drop /j/ after word-internal /s/ (*assume* /ə'suːm/), /z/ (*presume* /prɪ'zuːm/) and /θ/ (*enthusiasm* /ɪn'θuːziæzm̩/). In short, /j/ is dropped after certain tongue-tip consonants (dentals and alveolars) but always retained after labials and velars.

2.14.9 Yod-coalescence

When /j/ is preceded by /t/ or /d/ in words such as *tuna, mature, Tuesday* and *duty, reduce, duke*, the /tj/ and /dj/ clusters are increasingly replaced by /ʧ/ and /ʤ/ respectively. This process of **yod-coalescence**, /j/ combining with /t/ and /d/ to form /ʧ/ and /ʤ/, has already happened historically in unstressed syllables (e.g. in *nature* and *question*, *soldier* and *procedure*) and thus appears to be spreading to stressed syllables. It's also common across word boundaries with *you* and *your*, e.g. *don't you*, *did you*, in what is called coalescent assimilation (see section 12.3.2).

As a consequence of yod-dropping and yod-coalescence, /j/ is only reliably found in clusters after labials (*few*, *view*, *pure*, *beauty*) and velars (*cute*, *argue*).

2.15 Inflections

The pronunciation of the **-s** suffix (ending), occurring in plurals (e.g. *cats*), third person present tense endings (e.g. *thinks*) and possessives (e.g. *John's*), is determined by the preceding sound. It's pronounced /ɪz/ following sibilants, /s/ following all other voiceless consonants and /z/ following all other voiced sounds. See Table 2.11.

The same rule applies in contractions involving auxiliary *has* and *is* (see sections 8.7.2 and 8.6.2), such as *what's (happened)*, *that's (good)*, *Mike's (left)*, *it's (difficult)*, *where's (Pete)*, *who's (seen him)*, *Emma's (arrived)* /wɒts, ðæts, maɪks, ɪts, weəz, huːz, 'eməz/. Note, though, that if the preceding word ends in a sibilant, *has* is /əz/, and not /ɪz/, e.g. *George's (disappeared)*, *the ice's melted* /dʒɔːdʒ əz, aɪs əz/.

The pronunciation of the ending <-ed> (e.g. *talked*) is also governed by the preceding sound. It's pronounced /ɪd/ following /t/ or /d/, /t/ following all other voiceless consonants and /d/ following all other voiced sounds. See Table 2.12.

Table 2.11 Rules for pronunciation of the inflectional suffix <-s>

Suffix (-s)	Examples
/ɪz/	buses, Alice's, seizes, Rose's, wishes, churches, catches, judges, George's, camouflages
/s/	stops, lips, hats, Pete's, thinks, Mike's, laughs, Jeff's, months, Beth's
/z/	Bob's, needs, bags, leaves, breathes, seems, Jean's, things, Jill's, bees, Sue's, cars, shores, stirs, ways, Joe's, lies, cows, toys, fears, cures, cares, Hilda's

Table 2.12 Rules for pronunciation of the inflectional suffix <-ed>

Suffix (-ed)	Examples
/ɪd/	waited, needed
/t/	stopped, thanked, laughed, unearthed, kissed, wished, watched
/d/	robbed, begged, saved, breathed, judged, seemed, frowned, banged, sailed, starred, stirred, ignored, played, sighed, allowed, employed, showed, feared, toured, cared

Note that certain adjectives, e.g. *crooked, dogged, naked, -legged, wicked*, take the /ɪd/ ending.

Chapter 3

Practice

Individual consonants

This chapter provides practice in pronouncing the English consonants and their various allophones. The exercise material includes the target sounds in different positions in the word or syllable, in words and phrases where they occur multiple times, in sentences and in dialogues.

3.1 Stops: summary of key features

The stops consist of the plosives /p b t d k g/ and affricates /ʧ dʒ/. Their key features are:

1   With the soft palate raised, a closure is formed in the oral cavity, and the airstream is blocked completely.
2   In the case of affricates, the release stage is obligatory and is slower than that of plosives, resulting in homorganic friction.
3   The release stage for plosives is variable. It may be absent when a homorganic stop follows, inaudible when a non-homorganic stop follows, nasal when a nasal follows or lateral when /l/ follows.
4   Together with fricatives, the stops are obstruents and behave similarly in the following ways:

   a)   they come in voiceless and voiced pairs;
   b)   voiced stops are typically devoiced when adjacent to voiceless sounds or a pause, and only usually fully voiced between voiced sounds;
   c)   voiceless stops shorten preceding sonorants (nasals, approximants and vowels) in the same syllable.

5   Aspiration accompanies voiceless plosives /p t k/ at the beginning of stressed syllables. In other contexts they are weakly aspirated or unaspirated.
6   Approximants following aspirated /p t k/ become devoiced and fricative.
7   The voiceless stops /p t k ʧ/ can optionally undergo glottal reinforcement.
8   /t/ can optionally undergo glottal replacement.
10   Word-final voiceless plosives /p t k/ may occasionally be replaced by the equivalent ejectives [p' t' k'].
11   The sequences /tr/ and /dr/ form phonetic affricates at the post-alveolar place of articulation.
12   In stressed syllables /tj/ and /dj/ are increasingly replaced by /ʧ/ and /dʒ/ (yod-coalescence).

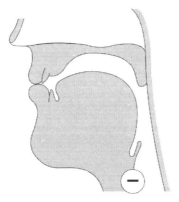

Figure 3.1 English /p/ (hold stage).

Plosives

3.2 Voiceless bilabial plosive /p/

3.2.1 Description

Voiceless bilabial plosive. With the soft palate raised, the lips come together to form a complete closure, blocking the airflow through the vocal tract. The tongue is free to anticipate the position of a following consonant or vowel.

3.2.2 Spelling

    <p> pay, apart, space, stop
    <pp> happy, puppy, stopped

Note that <p> is silent in certain words, e.g. *coup, corps, cupboard, raspberry, receipt, pneumonia, pneumatic, psychology, psychological, psychiatrist, psychotic, pterodactyl, psalm, pseudo.*

Unusual spellings

    hiccou**gh**

3.2.3 Aspirated

a)   *Stressed syllable-initial*
      pack, page, pain, paint, pair/pear, palace, pale, palm, pan, panda, panic, parcel, pardon, parent, park, part, partner, party, pass, passenger, past, pasta, pastry, pat, path, patient, paw, pay, pea, peace, peach, peak, peg, pen, pencil, pension, perfect (adj.), personal, petrol, pick, picture, pie, piece, pig, pile, pill, pillow, pilot, pin, pinch, pine, pink, pint, pirate, pit, pity, pocket, point, poison, pole, pond, pony, pool, port, positive, post, pot, pound, pour, powder, power, public, puddle, pull, punch, purse,

push, put, apart, apology, appear, department, disappoint, opinion, oppose, repeat, report, superb, superior, suppose

b) ***Before /r/***

precious, present (n.), press, pretty, price, pride, print, prison, prize, problem, profit, promise, proof, proper, practice, pray

c) ***Before /l/***

place, plain/plane, plan, planet, plank, plant, plaster, plastic, plate, play, player, pleasant, please, pleasure, plenty, plot, plough, plug, plum, plumber, plump, plural, plus

d) ***Before /j/***

pew, pewter, puberty, puce, puerile, puny, pupil, pure, putrid

3.2.4 Unaspirated or weakly aspirated

a) ***Syllable-final***

cap, cheap, chip, chop, clap, clip, cope, cup, deep, dip, drip, drop, escape, gap, gossip, grape, grip, group, heap, hip, hoop, hop, hope, keep, lap, leap, lip, loop, map, mop, ripe, rope, scrape, shape, sharp, sheep, ship, shop, sip, skip, slap, sleep, slip, slope, snap, soap, soup, steep, step, stop, strap, strip, stripe, swap, tap, tip, top, trap, trip, troop, tulip, type, up, weep, whip, wipe, wrap, zip, capital, carpenter, carpet, happy, leopard, open, rapid, stupid, super, supper, topic, typical, copper, copy

b) **/sp/**

space, spade, span, spaniel, spare, spark, sparrow, sparse, speak, spear, specialist, specify, specimen, spectacles, speech, speed, spell, spend, spice, spill, spin, spinach, spine, spirit, spit, spite, spoil, spoken, sponge, spoon, sport, spot, spy

c) **/spr/**

sprain, sprawl, spray, spread, spring, sprinkle, sprint, sprog, sprout, spruce

d) **/spl/**

splash, splay, spleen, splendid, splice, splinter, split, splutter

e) **/spj/**

spew, spume, spurious, sputum

f) ***Unstressed syllable-initial***

particular, peculiar, potato, police, pathetic, patrol, percent, perform, persist, polite, position, precise, predict, prefer, protect, provide

3.2.5 Multiple

paper, puppy, popular, pipe, proper, pamper, parsnip, pauper, peep, people, pepper, pickpocket, pimple, pineapple, plump, pompous, poppy, prepare, pupil, purple, purpose, pump, perhaps

3.2.6 Phrases

put pen to paper, a profound apology, keeping up appearances, apple pie, bumper to bumper, perfectly capable, an Olympic champion, comparatively cheap, a pork chop, a paper clip, a copper pipe, a spare copy, a happy couple, a packet of crisps, pay a deposit, a piece of gossip, purple grapes, an appeal for help, a hip replacement operation, a paper napkin, spray paint, pots and pans, wrapping paper, post a parcel, spare parts, a surprise party, pea soup, peer pressure, a sharp pencil, a petrol pump, sleeping pills, a pickpocket, a police patrol, an opinion poll, a paddling pool, proof of purchase, a skipping rope, a slippery slope, a picnic spot, step by step, a shopping trip, paint stripper, scrap paper

3.2.7 Sentences

1 Pass me the pepper please, Paul.
2 She wrapped his present in purple paper.
3 Pauline's performance is just past its peak.
4 Patricia put a piece of apple pie on the plate.
5 The patient proved to be susceptible to hypnosis.
6 They weren't prepared to compromise their principles.
7 Percy's completely dependent on his parents for support.
8 He played an important part in shaping European policies.
9 This particular shop specialises in maps, posters and prints.
10 Patrick adopted a pragmatic approach to this complex topic.
11 She couldn't appreciate the deeper implications of the poem.
12 They took precautionary steps to prevent the spread of polio.
13 Pete stopped punching to avoid crippling his sparring partner.
14 The most important passage in the pamphlet is the opening paragraph.
15 After he'd dropped off the Polish passengers, he picked up the Portuguese.
16 Particular groups are disproportionately represented among the poor population.
17 She was disappointed that her patient experienced post-operative complications.
18 The press put a positive spin on the pessimistic report that appeared in September.
19 Philip gave an inspiring PowerPoint presentation on how to prepare a paper for publication.
20 He's keeping his options open hoping that unexpected opportunities might present themselves.

3.2.8 Dialogue

A: Perhaps Peter could propose a plan.
B: But all Peter's previous plans have been completely preposterous.
A: Stop picking on poor Peter. He can't help pitching peculiar proposals.
B: I suppose so. But please oppose any project involving leopards, pumas, pandas or puppies.
A: Yes, Peter needed police protection after the last episode!

3.3 Voiced bilabial plosive /b/

3.3.1 Description

Voiced bilabial plosive /b/. With the soft palate raised, the lips come together to form a complete closure, blocking the airflow through the vocal tract. The tongue is free to anticipate the position of a following consonant or vowel.

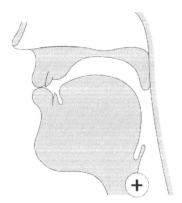

Figure 3.2 English /b/ (hold stage).

3.3.2 Spelling

<b> back, sober, verb
<bb> rabbit, robber

<b> is silent in certain words, e.g. *debt, doubt, subtle.* Also inflected forms, e.g. *debtor, doubtful.* Note in particular silent <b> in final <mb>, e.g. *aplomb, bomb, climb, comb, crumb, dumb, lamb, limb, numb, plumb, succumb, thumb, tomb, womb.* Also derived forms, e.g. *bomber, climber, dumbest, plumbing.* Otherwise, medial <mb> is pronounced, e.g. *amber, limbo, lumber, timber.*

3.3.3 Word-initial

back, bad, badge, bag, bake, balance, balcony, bald, ball, balloon, banana, band, bandage, bang, bank, bar, bare/bear, bargain, barn, barrel, barrier, basic, basket, bat, bath, battle, bay, beach, bead, beak, beam, bean, beard, beat, become, bed, bee, beef, beer, before, beg, begin, behaviour, behind, believe, bell, belong, below, belt, bench, bend, benefit, bent, berry, beside, best, bet, better, between, big, bike, bin, bird, birthday, bit, bite, bitter, board, boast, boat, body, boil, bone, bonus, book, boot, border, boss, both, bottle, bottom, bounce, box, boy, bucket, budget, bull, bullet, bully, bump, bun, bunch, burglar, burst, bury, burn, bush, business, busy, butcher, button, buy

3.3.4 Word-medial

ability, above, abroad, acrobat, alphabet, cabbage, cabin, cucumber, cupboard, debate, exhibition, habit, harbour, hobby, labour, mobile, neighbour, orbit, rabbit, ribbon, robber, robot, rubber, sober, tobacco, tribute

3.3.5 Word-final

club, crab, cube, describe, dub, globe, grab, herb, jab, job, kerb, knob, mob, probe, proverb, pub, robe, rub, scrub, shrub, slab, snob, sob, stab, superb, tab, throb, tribe, tub, tube, verb, wardrobe, web

3.3.6 Multiple

hubbub, suburb, baby, barbecue, rhubarb, absorb, bamboo, barber, backbone, bribe, bubble, bumblebee, cobweb, probably

3.3.7 Phrases

a burning ambition, a baby boy, a rubbish bag, bank balance, a bunch of bananas, a brass band, the big bang, a bank robber, a breakfast bar, a beer barrel, back to basics, a baseball bat, bubble bath, a bitter battle, a beautiful beach, amber beads, a bushy beard, bed and breakfast, a beer belly, bits and bobs, as blind as a bat, a rubber band, break every bone in your body, rubber boots, brown bread, bad breath, blood brothers, blow bubbles, a book club, a boring job, a paperback book, a double bed, bread and butter

3.3.8 Sentences

1   Toby has both brains and brawn.
2   Their baby boy was born in Bedford.
3   Barbara banged her elbow on the table.
4   Her book was published as a paperback.
5   It's not beyond the bounds of possibility.
6   I believe he broke every bone in his body.
7   His laboured breathing was barely audible.
8   My brother's a member of a basketball club.
9   Bill's bald but has bushy eyebrows and a beard.
10   Is it possible to borrow albums from the library?
11   Phoebe's husband's job is their bread and butter.
12   Abigail was deliberately ambiguous about her birthdate.
13   The rebels were based along the border with Bangladesh.
14   The bilingual brochures are now available for distribution.
15   Bob and Betty bought a bungalow in a respectable suburb.
16   The building was beset with problems from the beginning.
17   Rechargeable batteries are better than disposable batteries.
18   He brought the business back from the brink of bankruptcy.
19   Isobel had an unshakeable belief in the importance of personal liberty.
20   The bluebells burst into bloom, and there were bumblebees in the bushes.

3.3.9 Dialogue

A: How's your brother Bob doing in Blackburn?
B: He's got a job breaking biscuits, and his bank balance is getting bigger and bigger.
A: A job breaking biscuits? That sounds a bit bonkers!
B: You've bought broken biscuits before. Who do you think breaks them into bits?

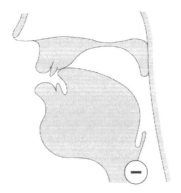

Figure 3.3 English /t/ (hold stage).

3.4 Voiceless alveolar plosive /t/

3.4.1 Description

Voiceless alveolar plosive. With the soft palate raised, the tip of the tongue forms a closure at the alveolar ridge while the sides of the tongue form a closure against the upper side teeth, blocking the airflow through the vocal tract. The lips are free to take the position for a following vowel or consonant.

3.4.2 Spelling

<t> tea, waiter, stop, bet
<tt> pretty, letter, bottle
<th> Anthony, Esther, Thames, Thomas, Thai, thyme
<z, tz, zz> = /ts/ schizophrenia, blitz, chutzpah, spritzer, Ritz, pizza
<ed> in inflections (see section 2.15) hoped, wished

Note that <t> is silent in <tle>, e.g. *apostle, bristle, bustle, castle, hustle, nestle, rustle, thistle, whistle, wrestle,* and in <sten>, e.g. *fasten, glisten, listen, moisten, soften.* <t> is also silent in *Christmas* and *mortgage,* and in recent French loans, e.g. *bouquet, ballet, buffet, cachet, chalet, crochet, depot, sachet, ragout.* The word *often* is said both with and without /t/ (even by the same speaker).

3.4.3 Aspirated

a) *Stressed syllable-initial*
table, take, tale, tall, tank, tap, tape, task, tax, tea, teacher, team, tear (from the eye), teeth, tell, ten, tennis, terror, tidy, time, tin, tiny, tip, tired, toe, tongue, tool, tooth, top, topic, torch, touch, tough, tour, towel, toy, turn, type, antique, attach, attack, competition, contain, maintain, material, return

b) *Before /r/*
track, trade, traffic, train, trap, tray, treasure, treat, tree, trick, trip, trouble, trousers, truck, true, trumpet, trunk, trust, truth, try, control

c) *Before* /j/ *(/tj/ or /ʧ/)*
   tube, Tuesday, tuition, tulip, tumultuous, tumour, tuna, tune, tunic, tutor
d) *Before* /w/
   twaddle, twang, tweak, tweed, tweet, tweezers, twelve, twice, twiddle, twig, twilight, twin, twinkle, twirl, twist, twitter, between

3.4.4 Unaspirated or weakly aspirated

a) *Syllable-final*
   beat, bet, bite, boat, bright, cat, chat, cheat, coat, complete, court, date, debt, defeat, delete, despite, dirt, doubt, eat, flat, flight, float, foot, forget, fright, fruit, gate, great, hate, heart, heat, height, hot, hurt, hut, invite, kite, knot, late, light, meat/meet, net, night, note, nut, pat, pet, plate, plot, polite, port, pot, quite, rat, regret, repeat, root, rot, seat, sheet, shirt, short, shout, shut, smart, sort, support, sweet, thought, threat, weight, wet, white, alphabet, basket, benefit, biscuit, budget, carpet, concert, credit, delicate, exit, expert, effort, habit, jacket, market, minute (n.), opposite, packet, pirate, pocket, profit, puppet, rabbit, riot, robot, quiet, secret, visit, atom, attic, beauty, better, bottom, butter, certain, city, computer, cottage, critic, data, ditto, duty, exotic, item, letter, lettuce, litter, motto, native, notice, party, pasta, pity, pretty, quarter, theatre, water, witty
b) /st/
   disturb, status, stab, staff, stage, stain, stamp, stand, star, stare, starve, station, steal/steel, steam, steep, steer, step, stick, stiff, still, stole, stone, stop, store, storm, story, stuff
c) /str/
   straight, strain, strand, strange, strangle, strap, straw, stream, street, strength, stress, stretch, strict, strike, string, stripe, strong, structure, struggle, destroy
d) /stj/
   stew, steward, student, studio, studious, stupefy, stupendous, stupid
e) *Unstressed syllable-initial*
   today, towards, taboo, tobacco, tomato, tomorrow

3.4.5 Multiple /t/

institute, teetotal, tent, test, text, ticket, title, tablet, talent, taste, temperature, total, activity, appetite, architect, contact, contract (n.), protect, contest (n.), straight, state, street, start, constant, contestant, instant, instinct, instrument, substitute, artist, assistant, attractive, automatic, centimetre, content (n.), dentist, distant, important, intelligent, interest, irritate, portrait, potato, quantity, status, target, tight, toast, toilet, tourist, traitor, treat, trust, twenty, twist

3.4.6 Phrases

a table-tennis table, tell tales, a water tank, a tax collector, tea for two, burst into tears, rotten teeth, a tennis racket, neat and tidy, tell the time, a wet towel, a bite to eat, a stray cat, at a later date, admit defeat, a flight attendant, ten minutes late, a night out, fitted sheets, a photo shoot, not a pretty sight, sit still, as white as a sheet, the letters of the alphabet, an irritating habit, wait a minute, top secret, a return ticket, a letter to the editor, at short notice, what a pity, a matter of taste, marital status, an estate agent, nuts and bolts, a constant effort, tight-fisted, a gentle giant, a subtle hint, a coat of paint, test results, a shooting star, set in stone, off the beaten track, caught in a trap, twin sisters, a complete waste of time, write a letter

3.4.7 Sentences

1   Tom's parents taught him the tricks of the trade.
2   The most important titles are printed in italic type.
3   The meeting was a complete and utter waste of time.
4   Peter was determined to get to the root of the matter.
5   We had a light breakfast of tea and hot buttered toast.
6   Is it true that bottled water tastes better than tap water?
7   Most of the students completed the assignment on time.
8   It turns out he was a secret agent for British Intelligence.
9   Ted was in no fit state to take part in the tennis tournament.
10   Victoria told us that she was still waiting for the test results.
11   I felt just a twinge of guilt as I left her standing on the platform.
12   Apparently Betty dropped out of university when she was twenty.
13   I was truly grateful to Patrick for taking the trouble to write to me.
14   It's difficult to alter the habits of a lifetime without continued support.
15   Visitors can expect to be treated with respect and courtesy by our staff.
16   Efforts are being made to appoint part-time teachers in different subjects.
17   Natasha bought two packets of tea and a tin of chocolate digestive biscuits.
18   Robert wanted to get a flat that was within commuting distance of the city centre.
19   Yesterday we took our first tentative steps towards establishing contact with potential clients.
20   We rented a beautiful little cottage in the Cotswolds and invited my twin sister to stay with us.

3.4.8 Dialogue

A: There are twenty-two letters on the table waiting for your attention.
B: Twenty-two Valentine's cards from twenty-two secret admirers, you meant to say. Tell me how many you got, Tony.
A: I'm not interested in trite platitudes and tacky greetings cards.
B: I'll take that to mean you got exactly twenty-two fewer than I got.

3.5 Voiced alveolar plosive /d/

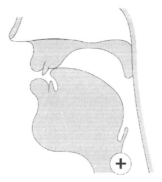

Figure 3.4 English /d/ (hold stage).

3.5.1 Description

Voiced alveolar plosive. With the soft palate raised, the tip of the tongue forms a closure at the alveolar ridge while the sides of the tongue form a closure against the upper side teeth, blocking the airflow through the vocal tract. The lips are free to take the position for a following vowel or consonant.

3.5.2 Spelling

<d> day, shadow, mad
<dd> sudden, wedding, address, add

3.5.3 Word-initial

damage, damp, dance, dare, dark, data, date, daughter, day, deaf, deal, debt, deep, deliver, dentist, describe, design, desire, desk, detail, develop, die, different, difficult, dinner, dirt, dish, dive, divorce, dizzy, dock, doctor, dog, doll, dollar, donkey, door, dot, double, doubt, down, duck, dull, dump, dust

3.5.4 Word-medial

adopt, audition, body, comedy, corridor, credit, edit, freedom, hideous, idea, idiom, idiot, ladder, lady, meadow, melody, murder, powder, predict, product, pudding, ready, ridiculous, shadow, shudder, spider, studio, study, tradition, widow

3.5.5 Before /r/

address, drab, draft, drag, dragon, drain, drama, drink, draw, dread, dream, dreary, drench, dress, dribble, drift, drill, drip, drive, drone, drop, drown, drug, drum, dry

3.5.6 Word-final

abroad, add, afford, afraid, aid, award, bad, bead, beard, bed, bird, blade, bleed, blood, board, bread, bride, broad, bud, card, cloud, code, coward, fade, feed, flood, food, glad, good, grade, greed, guard, guide, hard, head, heard, hide, hood, include, instead, lid, load, lord, loud, method, mood, mud, need, nod, odd, proud, rapid, read, red, ride, road, sad, salad, seed, shade, shed, side, speed, spread, sword, thread, timid, trade, ward, weed, weird, wide, wood, word

3.5.7 Multiple

dead, decide, daffodil, decade, dedicate, deed, defend, demand, depend, divide

3.5.8 Phrases

a dreadful accident, an added advantage, an adventure playground, sound advice, a reddish beard, a dead body, an ideal candidate, widespread damage, today's date, dead and buried, a good deed, a deep desire, draw a diagram, the dish of the day, without a shadow of doubt, a bad dream, a drunk driver, from dawn to dusk, food and drink, holding hands, a stupid idiot, needle and thread, respond accordingly, middle of the road, shoulder blades, the speed of sound, double standards, weird and wonderful, words of wisdom, an ideal world, the good old days

3.5.9 Sentences

1　Did it happen by accident or by design?
2　By Friday the scandal had spread worldwide.
3　The farmhands toiled in the fields from dawn to dusk.
4　My friend's understanding made a world of difference.
5　The ducks are paddling like mad round the garden pond.
6　The gold pendant is studded with diamonds and emeralds.
7　They drove on down the dead-end road and then turned around.
8　Linda needed a friendly word of advice to provide some direction.
9　Richard decided to stand as a candidate for the Board of Directors.
10　Outdated words and idioms should be excluded from the dictionary.
11　Suddenly a deafening sound of thunder could be heard in the distance.
12　These Scandinavian designers deserve credit for daring to be different.
13　The document concluded that the incident had been handled adequately.
14　I can recommend this comedy if you don't mind suspending your disbelief.
15　Appendix D describes the data and the methodology adopted for this study.
16　My husband ordered the dish of the day and I had a delicious seafood salad.
17　They endeavoured to remedy the fundamental design defects in the building.
18　The doctors admitted that the medical records had been accidentally destroyed.
19　Danny's daughter dreams of spending her birthday in Disney World in Orlando, Florida.
20　The head of department decided to include on the agenda a discussion of academic freedom.

3.5.10 Dialogue

A:　Did Dean do the dishes yesterday?
B:　He said he would, but in the end Fred had to do them.
A:　I told you so, didn't I? I said you should definitely doubt Dean's word.
B:　I decided to find out for myself, and he indeed proved to be a devious devil and avoided washing the dirty dishes after dinner.

3.6 Voiceless velar plosive /k/

3.6.1 Description

Voiceless velar plosive. The back of the tongue forms a closure against the soft palate, which is raised, and the rear sides of the tongue form a closure against the rear upper side teeth, blocking the airflow through the vocal tract. The lips and the tongue-tip, blade and front are free to take the position for a following vowel or consonant.

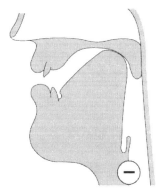

Figure 3.5 English /k/ (hold stage).

3.6.2 Spelling

<c> cost, country

<ch> chaos, character, scheme, school, echo, ache. Also in derived forms aching, chaotic, characteristic, etc.

<cc (+a/o/u)> occasion, account, occur

<ck> tricky, back, stick

<k> keep, awake, speaker, work

<kk> trekking

<qu, cqu> = /kw/ quick, acquaintance

<x> = /ks/ box, fix, suffix, exit

Note that initial <k> is silent in words like *knack, knapsack, knave, knead, knee, kneel, knell, knew, knickers, knife, knight, knit, knob, knock, knot, know, knowledge, knuckle.*

3.6.3 Aspirated

a) **Stressed syllable-initial**

cab, café, cake, call, calm, camp, cancel, capital, car, card, care, carpet, carrot, carry, case, castle, catch, cause, coach, coast, code, coffee, cold, collar, college, colour, comb, come, comedy, comfort, comma, comment, common, concert, confidence, cook, cool, copy, cord, core, cork, corner, cost, cottage, count, country, couple, course, cousin, cover, cow, cuddle, cup, curl, curry, curse, curtain, custom, cut, keen, keep, key, kid, kill, kind, king, kiss, kit, kitchen, kitten, accommodation, accomplish, accountant, application, become, education

b) **Before /r/**

crab, crack, craft, crash, cream, crease, credit, creep, crew, crime, crisis, critic, cross, crowd, crude, crumb, cry, crystal

c) **Before /l/**

claim, clap, class, claw, clay, clean, clear, clever, click, client, cliff, climate, climax, clinic, clip, cloak, clock, cloth, clothes, cloud, clover, clown, club, clue, clutter

d) **Before /j/**

cube, cucumber, cue/queue, cumulative, cumin, cure, curious, cute

e) **Before /w/**

quack, quaint, qualification, qualify, quality, quantity, quarrel, quarry, queen, queer, query, quest, question, questionnaire, quick, quiet, quilt, quit, quite, quiver, quiz, quota, quote, choir

3.6.4 Unaspirated or weakly aspirated

a) **Syllable-final**

attack, awake, back, basic, bike, black, block, book, brake/break, brick, chalk, check, dark, duck, garlic, hike, hook, joke, knock, lack, lake, leak, like, lock, look, luck, magic, make, mark, neck, oak, pack, panic, park, peak, pick, public, remark, rock, sack, sake, seek, shake, shock, sick, smoke, snake, sneak, soak, sock, speak, stick, strike, take, talk, thick, tick, topic, track, trick, wake, walk, weak/week, work, baker, bracket, broken, bucket, chicken, circus, echo, focus, hockey, jacket, market, packet, parking, second, token, turkey, vacant

b) **/sk/**

discussion, escape, scale, scarce, scatter, scheme, scholar, school, scone, score, skate, sketch, skill, skim, skin, skirt, sky

c) **/skj/**

skew, skewer

d) **/skw/**

squabble, squad, squalid, squalor, squander, square, squash, squat, squeak, squeal, squeeze, squelch, squid, squiggle, squint, squirm, squirrel, squirt

e) **/skr/**

scrap, scrape, scratch, scrawl, scream, screen, screw, scribble, script, scroll, scrounge, scrub, scruffy, scruple, scrutiny

f) **Unstressed syllable-initial**

career, command, complete, condition, canal, canoe, casino, cathedral, collect, comedian, compare, complete, complain, computer, concern, consider, contain

3.6.5 Multiple

academic, acoustic, architect, backpack, bookcase, bookmark, cactus, cake, calculate, caretaker, character, chemical, classic, click, clinic, cloak, clock, coconut, collect, communicate, conclusion, conquer, cook, cork, correct, crack, creak, critic, croak, cuckoo, expect, kick, kiosk, mechanic, picnic, practical, quack, quick, skunk, squeak, tactic, technique, toxic

3.6.6 Phrases

a close acquaintance, a broken ankle, back ache, background music, a bank account, a picnic basket, a packet of chocolate biscuits, the black market, an electric blanket, take a break, a plastic bucket, carrot cake, a wake-up call, a company car, a pack of cards, a magic carpet, a cause for concern, crystal clear, a cuckoo clock, black coffee, communication skills, keep in contact, cool, calm and collected, a topic for discussion, a quick drink, cause and effect, a close encounter, a quick fix, a clove of garlic, a sick joke, next of kin, a panic attack, a parking ticket, keep quiet, a rescue worker, a fraction of a second, keep a secret, an electric shock, a think tank

3.6.7 Sentences

1   Michael speaks with a thick Cockney accent.
2   Frank comes from a working-class background.
3   We kept the school equipment under lock and key.
4   Catherine can't shake off her cold and hacking cough.
5   Keith was scared he'd go completely blank with panic.
6   We had black coffee and chocolate cake at the corner café.
7   The couple couldn't accept the consequences of their actions.
8   The crying kid came to me for a comforting kiss and a cuddle.
9   Christine looked frantically for the ticket in her jacket pocket.
10 Rebecca shook back her dark curls and looked into the camera.
11 The seconds ticked by on the clock at the back of the classroom.
12 The secret of his success is dedication and his incredible work ethic.
13 The experiments were conducted under strictly controlled conditions.
14 We had cocoa and scones with thick clotted cream after our brisk walk.
15 There's no justification for the scathing remarks directed at his colleagues.
16 Is there a connection between academic skills and workplace productivity?
17 They discussed the security considerations that had to be taken into account.
18 Mark completed his college education without encouragement from any quarter.
19 The catalogue contains colour reproductions of the pictures with accompanying text.
20 There was a complete breakdown in communication between the company and the client.

3.6.8 Dialogues

A: Colin was caught copying chemical equations from a concealed crib sheet during the chemistry exam.
B: Can they kick him off the course for academic misconduct?
A: He's making excuses, and it looks like he could escape with a basic caution.
B: He's quite a character, our Colin. He's as cunning as a fox when copying in class and as cool as a cucumber when caught and questioned.

3.7 Voiced velar plosive /g/

3.7.1 Description

Voiced velar plosive. The back of the tongue forms a closure against the soft palate, which is raised, and the rear sides of the tongue form a closure against the rear upper side teeth, blocking the airflow through the vocal tract. The lips and the tongue-tip, blade and front are free to take the position for a following vowel or consonant.

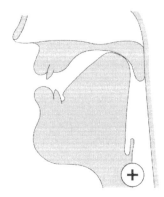

Figure 3.6 English /g/ (hold stage).

3.7.2 Spelling

<g> game, eager, again, dog
<gg> luggage, trigger
<gh> aghast, ghastly, ghost, spaghetti, gherkin, ghetto
<gu, gue> guest, guide, figure, vague, league
<x> = /gz/ exact, exam, exaggerate, exist
<xh> = /gz/ exhaust, exhaustion, exhilarate, exhilaration, exhort
<g> + <e/i/y> may be either /g/ or /dʒ/, e.g. *get* vs. *gel, gift* vs. *gin, gynaecologist* vs. *gypsy*

Note that <g> is silent in words like *paradigm, phlegm, diaphragm, gnarled, gnaw, gnome, align, assign, benign, campaign, champagne, cologne, design, foreign, reign, resign, sign.*

    <gh> is silent in the following words: *although, bough, bought, borough, breakthrough, brought, bright, caught, daughter, dough, doughnut, drought, eight, fight, fought, fraught, fright, haughty, height, high, light, might, mighty, naughty, neighbour, night, nought, ought, plough, right, sigh, sight, slaughter, sleigh, sought, straight, taught, thigh, thorough, though, thought, through, weigh, weight.*

3.7.3 Word-initial

gain, gallery, gamble, game, gap, garden, garlic, gas, gash, gasp, gate, gather, gauge, gaunt, gaze, gear, ghost, gift, girl, give, go, goal, goat, gold, golf, good, goose, gorgeous, gorilla, gossip, guarantee, guard, guess, guest, guide, guilty, guitar, gulp, gum, gun

3.7.4 Word-medial

again, aghast, agony, arrogant, asparagus, August, baggage, baggy, bargain, beggar, begin, burger, cigar, dagger, dragon, eager, elegant, figure, forget, forgive, haggard, investigation, legacy, logo, luggage, magazine, meagre, navigate, negative, organ, regard, rigour, slogan, sluggish, soggy, spaghetti, sugar, target, tiger, together, trigger, vinegar, wagon, yoga, yogurt

3.7.5 Word-final

bag, beg, big, dig, dog, drag, drug, egg, fatigue, flag, fog, frog, hug, jog, jug, leg, log, mug, peg, pig, plague, plug, rag, rug, shrug, smug, snag, snug, tug, twig, vague, wig

3.7.6 Multiple

gag, gargle, giggle

3.7.7 Phrases

a doggie bag, a guide dog, an illegal drug, give an example, a good figure, forgive and forget, give the game away, gold nuggets, a golf buggy, green grass, dig a grave, get a grip, a good guess, a regular guest, a big hug, an illegal immigrant, a glossy magazine, a legal obligation, a group photograph, give him my regards

3.7.8 Sentences

 1   Give Douglas my kind regards.
 2   Get your grubby fingers off my glass jug!
 3   Regrettably I forgot to give them their gifts.
 4   Megan's got a degree in English linguistics.
 5   She wasn't eager to give up her ill-gotten gains.
 6   My grandparents are going to Portugal in August.
 7   The guest extinguished his cigarette on the ground.
 8   The grass is growing and gradually getting greener.
 9   Are you going to go to the rugby game in Glasgow?
10   He guarantees that the grapes are organically grown.
11   The gangster had his finger on the trigger of the gun.
12   Gordon said goodbye to Margaret giving her a big hug.
13   They negotiated an agreement with the Greek government.
14   I'm good at forgiving and forgetting – I don't hold grudges.
15   My grandmother was engrossed in her gardening magazine.
16   Graham's gaze lingered on the photograph of his girlfriend.
17   There's a significant degree of ambiguity in your argument.
18   This was a flagrant disregard of the examination regulations.
19   Give Angus and Morag our congratulations on their engagement.
20   A great big dog was growling at the girls who were gathered in our garden.

3.7.9 Dialogue

A: What an elegant gown, Gwen! What a gorgeous figure you've got!
B: Gary's going to be staggered when he gets a glimpse of what he gave up.
A: Agreed. You're too good for that guy.
B: I'll never forgive the rogue for going off with that grotesque magnate's granddaughter and forgetting me, his gorgeous girlfriend.

Affricates

3.8 Voiceless palato-alveolar affricate /ʧ/

3.8.1 Description

Voiceless palato-alveolar affricate. With the soft palate raised, the tip, blade and front of the tongue form a closure with the alveolar ridge and the front of the hard palate, and the sides of the tongue form a closure with the upper side teeth, completely blocking the airflow. Air is compressed behind the closure and released relatively slowly, resulting in homorganic friction. The lips are rounded and protruded.

3.8.2 Spelling

<ch> child, achieve, teacher, touch
<tch> catch, watch, kitchen
<ti> congestion, exhaustion, question, suggestion
<tu> following a stressed syllable, e.g. century, future, mutual, statue. Nowadays, also stressed syllable-initially, e.g. tube, tutor, Tuesday.

Unusual spellings

cello, concerto, Czech

Note that <ch> is pronounced /k/ in scholarly words of Greek origin, e.g. *chaos, chasm, charismatic, archaeology, hierarchy, psychology*; <ch> is silent in *yacht* /jɒt/.

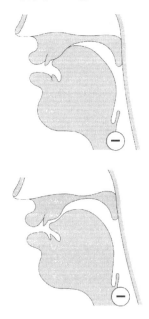

Figure 3.7 English /ʧ/ showing palato-alveolar closure (left) and release with homorganic friction (right). Note trumpet-shaped lip-rounding.

3.8.3 Word-initial

chain, chair, chalk, challenge, chamber, champion, chance, change, chant, chap, charge, charm, chart, chase, chat, cheap, cheat, check, cheek, cheer, cheese, cherish, cherry, chess, chest, chew, chicken, chief, child, chill, chimney, chimp, chip, chocolate, choice, choke, choose, chop, chore, chunk

3.8.4 Word-medial

achieve, adventurous, bachelor, butcher, feature, fortune, future, kitchen, literature, mutual, nature, orchard, ritual, situation, statue, teacher, virtual, virtue, wretched

3.8.5 Word-final

aitch, approach, arch, attach, batch, beach, bench, bleach, blotch, branch, breach, brooch, bunch, catch, coach, crouch, crutch, detach, each, fetch, itch, march, match, much, patch, peach, pitch, reach, rich, scorch, scratch, screech, sketch, snatch, speech, stitch, stretch, such, switch, teach, torch, touch, watch, witch

3.8.6 Multiple

church

3.8.7 Phrases

a challenging question, matching chairs, an intellectual challenge, a torture chamber, check your change, a chunk of cheese, a bunch of cherries, a chess champion, chicken and chips, a mischievous child, catch a chill, chocolate chips, eye-catching features, a change of fortune, scratch an itch, a church porch, a catch-22 situation, a charcoal sketch, Cheddar cheese, a spiritual teacher, chiselled features

3.8.8 Sentences

1   I had chicken and chips for lunch.
2   Rachel reached out to touch his cheek.
3   Add the chocolate chips to the mixture.
4   The child was chased from the church porch.
5   The chimp let out a high-pitched screech.
6   She teaches Chinese literature and culture.
7   These mid-century kitchen chairs are charming.
8   You have a choice of Cheddar or Dutch cheese.
9   I munched a peach and a whole bunch of cherries.
10   I watched the chess championship with my chums.
11   How much did the butcher charge for those chops?
12   If the temperature changes, you might catch a chill.
13   The adventurers eventually reached Chile in March.
14   He saw the chance of a change in their future fortune.

15   We approached the eye-catching statues on the beach.
16   This charcoal sketch of Charlie Chaplin is worth a fortune.
17   The coach congratulated them on the victory over Chelsea.
18   That chap with the chiselled features is our French lecturer.
19   He preaches the virtues of a contextual approach to research.
20   We tried to catch snatches of the exchange between Richard and Chad.

3.8.9 Dialogue

A: Mitch chose cheap Cheddar cheese for lunch.
B: So it's cheese and chips again from the Chinese chip shop. I'm itching for a change. Cheese and chips daily is a challenge.
A: If in future you reach into your own pocket, you can choose your own lunch – chicken, pork chops, fresh cherries, peaches . . .
B: Maybe melted cheese on chips from the Chinese isn't such a bad choice after all. Mitch is such a charitable chap.

3.9 Voiced palato-alveolar affricate /ʤ/

3.9.1 Description

Voiced palato-alveolar affricate. With the soft palate raised, the tip, blade and front of the tongue form a closure with the alveolar ridge and the front of the hard palate, and the sides of the tongue form a closure with the upper side teeth, completely blocking the airflow. Air is compressed behind the closure and released relatively slowly, resulting in homorganic friction. The lips are rounded and protruded.

3.9.2 Spelling

<j> jam, joke
<g> + <e/i/y> gentle, ginger, gym, suggest, danger, logic, apology, rage. This spelling can
   also represent /g/; see section 3.7.2.

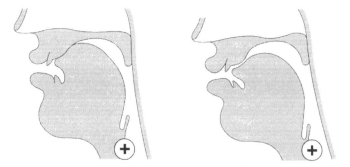

Figure 3.8 English /ʤ/ showing palato-alveolar closure (left) and release with homorganic
   friction (right). Note trumpet-shaped lip-rounding.

<dg> budget, edge
<di, dj> soldier, adjourn, adjust
<du> gradual, procedure; also produce, duke (see yod-coalescence, section 2.14.9)
<gg> suggest(ion), exaggerate, exaggeration

Unusual spellings

sandwich, Harwich (both also pronounced with /ʧ/), margarine

3.9.3 Word-initial

jail, general, gentle, genuine, geography, giant, gin, ginger, gym, jab, jacket, jade, jam, jar, jaw, jazz, jealous, jelly, jet, job, jockey, join, joke, jolly, journal, joy, judge, juice, jumble, jump, junk, jury, just

3.9.4 Word-medial

agenda, agent, agile, allergy, allergic, analogy, angel, apology, badger, budget, contagious, danger, energy, fidget, fragile, gadget, imagine, intelligent, legend, logic, magic, majestic, major, margin, origin, outrageous, pigeon, procedure, project (n.), pyjamas, region, reject (v.), rigid, suggest, surgeon, teenager, urgent

3.9.5 Word-final

allege, badge, baggage, barge, beverage, bridge, cabbage, cage, charge, college, cottage, courage, damage, dodge, edge, emerge, fridge, hedge, huge, image, knowledge, language, large, lodge, luggage, manage, marriage, merge, message, nudge, package, page, passage, porridge, rage, rampage, ridge, sausage, siege, sledge, smudge, stage, storage, urge, verge, village, voyage, wage, wedge, grudge

3.9.6 Multiple

George, ginger, judge

3.9.7 Phrases

an age range, an intelligence agent, pledge allegiance, an avenging angel, an abject apology, a large budget, a huge challenge, a gradual change, psychological damage, a jagged edge, an energy shortage, a jet engine, a gentle giant, a digital image, average intelligence, a storage jar, a twinge of jealousy, a jumbo jet, a challenging job, jump for joy, a junior manager, an arranged marriage, an urgent message, a gentle nudge, a surgical procedure, a jealous rage, a siege engine, change the subject, the average wage, a bungee jump

3.9.8 Sentences

 1 This region's ecologically fragile.
 2 The orange juice is in the fridge, Judy.
 3 Joan engaged Jeff as her project manager.
 4 The images were arranged chronologically.
 5 Angela hugely enjoyed her voyage to Egypt.
 6 Eugene gradually got the gist of the message.
 7 Benjamin's allergic to oranges and tangerines.
 8 We produce a large range of engines for generators.
 9 It's a major technological challenge for our engineers.
10 Jean jumped for joy when the surgeon discharged her.
11 Gerald and Jane tried to salvage their fragile marriage.
12 How dangerous is bungee jumping in terms of injuries?
13 D'you know the average age range for college students?
14 We have a generous budget for our journey to Argentina.
15 Jenny urged him to reject the outrageous suggestions for change.
16 The teenagers were rigid with rage when their luggage was damaged.
17 Marjorie's vegetarian sausages and ginger-fried vegetables were gorgeous.
18 I can just imagine how jealous Gemma must have been of his job in Geneva.
19 Joseph has a huge knowledge of languages, including German and Japanese.
20 Jessica encouraged me to lodge with her in her cottage at the edge of the village.

3.9.9 Dialogue

A: Would you suggest to Jim that he jives to his jazz music more gently?

B: I've urged him to jump about less energetically, but he just doesn't get the message.

A: If Reg flies into a rage and charges at him, not even Jim's agile jaw will dodge his giant fists.

B: Apart from his jazz jiving jam sessions, Jim's a jolly good lodger; but his outrageous gymnastics are no joke.

3.10 Fricatives: summary of key features

There are nine fricatives: /f v θ ð s z ʃ ʒ h/. Their key features are:

1   With the soft palate raised, the articulators move close together to form a narrow gap. Forced through this stricture, the airstream becomes turbulent, resulting in audible friction.

2   Together with stops, fricatives make up the obstruent class of consonants and therefore behave similarly in the following ways:

    a)   they come in voiceless and voiced pairs (except /h/);

    b)   voiced fricatives are typically devoiced when adjacent to voiceless sounds and silence – more so when followed by voiceless sounds or silence than when preceded by them – and are only reliably fully voiced between voiced sounds;

    c)   voiceless fricatives shorten sonorants (nasals, approximants and vowels) preceding them in a syllable.

3   [ɦ], a voiced allophone of /h/, is possible between voiced sounds.
4   The fricatives can be divided into sibilants /s z ʃ ʒ/ and non-sibilants /f v θ ð h/:

   a)   sibilants involve a longitudinal groove in the tongue channelling the airstream into a
        jet which produces turbulence and fricative noise when it hits an obstruction further
        along in the vocal tract (the teeth);
   b)   non-sibilant fricatives involve no grooving of the tongue, and consequently their
        fricative noise is due to turbulence at the stricture itself;
   c)   the fricative noise produced by the sibilants is strong while the non-sibilants pro-
        duce rather weak fricative noise, especially the voiced ones, which sometimes verge
        on being approximants.

5   During the glottal fricative /h/, friction is produced not only at the glottis but also
    throughout the whole vocal tract, and since the articulators take the position for the fol-
    lowing vowel during the articulation of /h/, there are as many allophones of /h/ as there
    are vowels.
6   The glottal fricative /h/ occurs only in syllable onsets.

3.11 Voiceless labio-dental fricative /f/

3.11.1 Description

Voiceless labio-dental fricative. The lower lip makes a light contact with the upper incisors.
The soft palate is in the raised position. The air escapes with labio-dental friction. The tongue
is free to anticipate the position of a following sound.

3.11.2 Spelling

   <f> fail, force, benefit, brief
   <ff> coffee, staff
   <ph> photo, philosophy, graph
   <gh> laugh, enough, rough

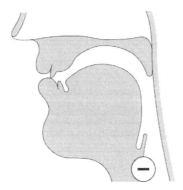

Figure 3.9 English /f/.

Unusual spellings

have to /'hæftə/

3.11.3 Word-initial

fabric, fabulous, face, fact, factory, fade, fail, faint, fair, fake, fall, false, fame, family, famous, fan, fancy, fantastic, fantasy, far, farm, fashion, fast, fat, fate, father, fault, favour, favourite, fear, feast, feather, feature, fee, feed, feel, fence, fetch, fever, fiction, fight, figure, file, fill, film, final, find, fine, finger, finish, fire, firm, first, fish, fist, fit, five, fix, foam, fog, foil, fold, follow, food, fool, foot, force, foreign, forest, forever, forget, forgive, fork, form, four, fox, full, fun, fund, fur, phone, photo

3.11.4 Word-medial

afford, before, benefit, buffalo, coffee, coffin, defeat, defend, define, differ, difficult, effort, muffin, nephew, offer, office, orphan, perfect (adj.), perform, prefer, professor, profit, qualify, refer, referee, suffer, terrific, trophy, uniform

3.11.5 Word-final

beef, belief, brief, chief, cliff, cough, deaf, enough, grief, half, if, knife, laugh, loaf, off, proof, relief, roof, rough, safe, scarf, sniff, staff, stiff, stuff, thief, tough, wife

3.11.6 Multiple

faithful, falafel, falsify, fanfare, fearful, fifteen, fifty, firefly, fluff, forefinger, fulfil, funfair, philosophy, photograph

3.11.7 Phrases

a familiar face, facts and figures, fear of failure, fame and fortune, family and friends, famine relief, a lifelong fan, a fruit farm, an awful fate, follow in your father's footsteps, a film festival, fact or fiction, a fair fight, official figures, freshwater fish, as fit as a fiddle, the first floor, difficult to follow, frozen food, forgive and forget, a knife and fork, fill in a form, a faithful friend, a coughing fit, half and half, a flat roof, the phonetic alphabet, fringe benefits, fresh coffee, a futile effort, a free gift, a fall in profits, for future reference, the facts of life, a father figure, a fish knife

3.11.8 Sentences

1   A fond farewell to our faithful friends!
2   This colourful floral fabric's fabulous.
3   Humphrey had a fierce frown on his face.
4   Jennifer stuffed herself with comfort food.
5   I infinitely prefer fresh fruit to frozen fruit.
6   Daphne was profoundly deaf in her left ear.

7   Don't forget that a first draft isn't a final draft.
8   There were four or five familiar faces on the staff.
9   We found the perfect gift for our unforgettable friend.
10   Fiona and her fiancé had terrific fun at the folk festival.
11   Fortunately there was a friendly atmosphere in the office.
12   Philip feared that they would laugh in his girlfriend's face.
13   Frank's former wife finds it difficult to forgive and forget.
14   Ralph's photos of the butterflies and flowers are beautiful.
15   Phoebe had suffered from whooping cough in her childhood.
16   Christopher was grateful when we offered him a lift to Oxford.
17   To Fred's relief there was a brief bibliography in the pamphlet.
18   The conference facilities were first class, and the food was fantastic.
19   My father intensified his efforts to find sufficient funds to finance the deficit.
20   We had hoped to find fresh footprints the following afternoon but failed to do so.

3.11.9 Dialogue

A: Enough is enough. I'm finished with fatty foods forever.
B: Muffins? French fries? Fudge? Fried fish fingers? Fast food?
A: I'm off fat forever. From now on, it's coffee and fags for me. I'll be as fit as a fiddle.
B: That's daft. You're having a laugh.
A: It's the famous coughing diet.
B: The infamous coffin diet, more like.

3.12 Voiced labio-dental fricative /v/

3.12.1 Description

Voiced labio-dental fricative. The lower lip makes a light contact with the upper incisors. The soft palate is in the raised position. The air escapes with labio-dental friction. The tongue is free to anticipate the position of a following sound.

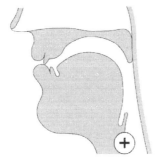

Figure 3.10 English /v/.

3.12.2 Spelling

<v> van, avoid, ever, give

Unusual spellings

of (though note that *of course* is occasionally said with /f/), nephew (traditionally pronounced with /v/, but more and more frequently with /f/ under the influence of the spelling)

3.12.3 Word-initial

vague, vain, valiant, valid, value, vampire, van, vandal, vanilla, vanish, varnish, vary, vase, vast, vault, vegetable, vegetarian, veil, vein, vengeance, venom, vent, venture, venue, veranda, verbal, verge, verify, vermin, verse, versus, vertical, vest, vet, vibrate, vice, vicious, victim, victory, vigour, vile, village, villain, vine, vinegar, vineyard, vintage, violence, violin, virgin, virtue, virus, visible, vision, visit, vital, vocabulary, vocal, voice, volcano, volume, volunteer, vomit, vote, voucher, vowel, voyage, vulgar, vulture

3.12.4 Word-medial

activate, aggravate, alleviate, ambivalent, anchovy, anniversary, approval, arrival, availability, available, avenue, average, avid, avoid, beaver, believer, brevity, clever, clover, cover, deliver, develop, device, devote, discover, divide, divorce, driver, event, ever, fever, flavour, forever, gravy, harvest, heavy, hover, ivy, lava, livid, navy, nervous, over, poverty, prevent, private, provide, quiver, reveal, revenge, reverse, river, savage, service, severe, shiver, survey, universe

3.12.5 Word-final

above, achieve, active, alive, approve, arrive, attractive, behave, believe, brave, carve, cave, curve, deserve, detective, dive, dove, drive, expensive, five, forgive, give, glove, grave, improve, leave, live (v.), love, massive, move, nerve, observe, olive, prove, receive, remove, reserve, save, serve, shave, shove, starve, wave

3.12.6 Multiple

involve, inventive, overactive, overview, pervasive, revive, revolve, survive, valve, velvet, verve, vindictive, vivacious, vivid

3.12.7 Phrases

vice versa, an impressive achievement, provide an attractive alternative, above average, aggressive behaviour, a private conversation, a duvet cover, a delivery van, an undercover detective, a voyage of discovery, divide evenly, a lovely evening, prohibitively expensive, develop a fever, a distinctive flavour, oven gloves, a harvest festival, a private individual, give an interview, massive investment, silver knives, a clever manoeuvre, a brave move, on the verge of a nervous breakdown, achieve an objective, a rave review, a devoted servant, a slave driver, a time-saving device, a wave of violence, a viable alternative, a detective novel

3.12.8 Sentences

1 The removal van'll arrive at twelve.
2 Vernon's like a vulture hovering overhead.
3 Sylvia's novel received very favourable reviews.
4 Voting behaviour varies from province to province.
5 We have a variety of sleeveless pullovers and vests.
6 This gives them a positive advantage over their rivals.
7 Microwave ovens are marvellous time-saving devices.
8 Steven lives in a villa in an attractive village in Devon.
9 Olivia's survey involved interviews with seventy-seven individuals.
10 Oliver vowed he'd never leave his beloved Venice.
11 Our services are reserved exclusively for private individuals.
12 You leave me with no alternative but to reveal your motives.
13 Remove the vegetables from the oven and serve with the veal.
14 Clive swerved violently to avoid driving into the delivery van.
15 These progressive views were virtually universal in the 1770s.
16 Kelvin discovered that we have several living relatives in Liverpool.
17 Vanilla's prohibitively expensive as harvesting it is so labour-intensive.
18 Vicki makes every endeavour to provide them with advice on visiting Vietnam.
19 While Val lived in Bratislava, she developed an extensive vocabulary in Slovak.
20 The television viewers were given live coverage of Slovenia's victory over Bolivia.

3.12.9 Dialogue

A: I'm very versatile. I've done a variety of volunteer jobs.
B: Have you ever handled doves?
A: I love doves. They're very attractive birds.
B: You'll be serving the doves to the vipers. Have you developed a resistance to venom? If not, our vet can provide vials of anti-venom. Our lovely vipers are very mischievous little savages.

3.13 Voiceless dental fricative /θ/

3.13.1 Description

Voiceless dental fricative. The tip of the tongue is raised towards the rear of the upper incisors, forming a narrow gap. The sides of the tongue form a seal against the upper side teeth. Unlike /s z/ there's no groove along the centre of the tongue so that the air escapes diffusely over the whole surface of the tongue.

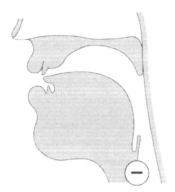

Figure 3.11 English /θ/.

3.13.2 Spelling

<th> think, author, month

Note that <th> is often pronounced /ð/; see section 3.14.2 below. It is silent in *asthma* and *isthmus.*

3.13.3 Word-initial

thank, thaw, theatre, theft, theme, theory, therapy, thesis, thick, thief, thigh, thimble, thin, thing, think, third, thirsty, thirty, thistle, thorn, thorough, thought, thousand, three, thread, threat, thriller, throat, throng, throw, through, thug, thumb, thump, thunder

3.13.4 Word-medial

anything, apathy, authentic, author, authority, cathedral, empathy, ethics, ethos, every-thing, Gothic, hypothesis, method, nothing, orthodox, orthography, pathetic, sympathetic, sympathy

3.13.5 Word-final

bath, beneath, birth, both, breath, broth, cloth, death, earth, eightieth, faith, fortieth, fourth, froth, growth, heath, hearth, henceforth, mirth, moth, mouth, myth, ninetieth, north, oath, path, seventieth, sixteenth, sixtieth, smith, south, teeth, tooth, truth, twentieth, worth, wreath, youth

3.13.6 Multiple

forthwith, thirteenth, thirtieth

3.13.7 Phrases

the length and breadth, death threats, diphthongs and monophthongs, a Gothic cathedral, healthy growth, a mathematical theory, mouth-to-mouth, north and south, an orthodox theory, from strength to strength, through thick and thin, something to think about, think things through, a threat to your health, death throes, a length of cloth

3.13.8 Sentences

1   Theo was in the throes of death.
2   It's Thelma's thirty-third birthday.
3   Are there any panthers in Ethiopia?
4   Elizabeth brings warmth and empathy.
5   Margaret Thatcher was born in Grantham.
6   This strengthened the author's hypothesis.
7   What's the length and breadth of the cloth?
8   He threw himself into mathematical theories.
9   She thinks Agatha Christie's thrillers are enthralling.
10   What is the width of the path through the south of Bath?
11   Kenneth needed therapy and time to think things through.
12   Matthew and Meredith are both enthusiastic about the theatre.
13   This author doesn't think much of the orthodox theory of growth.
14   Arthur was healthy and wealthy and had the enthusiasm of youth.
15   Dorothy wants to be a goldsmith and Gareth is an enthusiastic athlete.
16   Keith was faithful to Judith and stayed with her through thick and thin.
17   How many monophthongs and diphthongs are there in Northumbrian?
18   Ethnographic methods are sometimes used in anthropological research.
19   Ruth visited the cathedrals in Northampton, Plymouth and Portsmouth.
20   Her health was threatened from the fourth to the sixth month of her pregnancy.

3.13.9 Dialogue

A: There's been a theft from the theatre.
B: I thought I heard something about some threatening thugs.
A: They climbed through a window on the fourth floor.
B: Did the thieves take anything worth much?
A: They stole my thunder!

3.14 Voiced dental fricative /ð/

3.14.1 Description

Voiced dental fricative. The tip of the tongue is raised towards the rear of the upper incisors, forming a narrow gap. The sides of the tongue form a seal against the side teeth. Unlike /s z/ there's no groove along the centre of the tongue so that the air escapes diffusely over the whole surface of the tongue.

3.14.2 Spelling

<th> Word-initially in grammatical words such as *this*, *them*, *those*; medially in native words like *brother*, *father*, *mother*, *either*, *other*, *northern*, *southern*; and

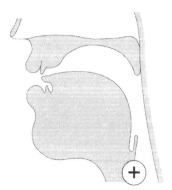

Figure 3.12 English /ð/.

in a small number of words in final position, e.g. *smooth*, *with*. Otherwise, <th> tends to be /θ/.

<the> clothe, breathe, soothe

3.14.3 Word-initial

the, this, that, these, those, they, them, then, thus, there/their, theirs, though, than

3.14.4 Word-medial

another, bother, brother, clothing, dither, either, farther/father, feather, further, gather, together, heather, lather, leather, mother, neither, nevertheless, northerly, northerner, worthy, other, scathing, slither, smoothie, soothing, withhold, wither

3.14.5 Word-final

bathe, breathe, mouth (v.), scythe, sheathe, smooth, soothe, swathe, clothe, loathe, with

3.14.6 Phrases

with or without, mother and father, gather together, hither and thither, the Netherlands, without any bother

3.14.7 Sentences

1 I can't fathom this weather.
2 His forefathers were heathens.
3 My brother sheathed the scythe.
4 It's a rather monotonous rhythm.
5 My grandfather worked in a smithy.
6 She's loud-mouthed and featherbrained.
7 Wuthering Heights is worthy literature.

8 My godmother lives in the Netherlands.
9 My stepfather was at the end of his tether.
10 No denim or leather clothing may be worn.
11 I'm putting together a menu for a get-together.
12 Neither my mother nor my father will be there.
13 We went to Carmarthenshire to gather heather.
14 He was a northerner born in the town of Blyth.
15 We found the smoothie bar without any bother.
16 Heather has a soothing influence on my brother.
17 He didn't smother her or breathe down her neck.
18 Her grandmother bequeathed her clothes to my mother.
19 I loathe his scathing remarks and holier-than-thou attitude.
20 It was inlaid with mother-of-pearl and wreathed with feathers.

3.14.8 Dialogue

A: My brother's mother's rather bothersome.
B: Your brother's mother? That's *your* mother.
A: No. My brother's mother and my father got together after my mother ran off with my father's brother.
B: Ah, so your father's your brother's father, but your mother isn't your brother's mother.
A: Yes, he's my brother from another mother.

3.15 Voiceless alveolar fricative /s/

3.15.1 Description

Voiceless alveolar fricative. The tip and blade of the tongue are raised in the direction of the alveolar ridge, forming a narrow gap. The sides of the tongue are held against the upper side teeth. There's a clear groove along the centre of the tongue.

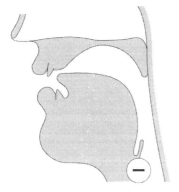

Figure 3.13 English /s/.

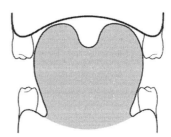

Figure 3.14 Mouth viewed from the front showing grooved tongue shape for /s/.

3.15.2 Spelling

<s> six, basic, yes
<se> sense, case, grease
<sce, sci> coalesce, scissors, condescend, scene, scent, fascinating, science
<ss> classic, assist, loss
<c (+e/i/y)> cell, circle, bicycle, race, receive, source, excellent, except
<x> = /ks/ box, expand

Note that <s> is silent in *aisle, isle, island, viscount, chassis, debris, précis, corps* /kɔ:/, *rendezvous, chamois.*

3.15.3 Word-initial

ceiling, cellar, centre, certain, cigar, circle, cycle, sack, sad, safe, sail/sale, salad, salmon, salt, same, sample, sand, saw, say, sea, search, second, secret, section, see, seem, self, sell, send, sick, side, sign, sight, silk, silver, simple, sing, sink, sip, sit, size, soak, soap, sob, sober, sock, soft, soil, solid, son, song, sore, sorry, sort, sound, soup, sour, south, subject (n.), subtle, such, suffer, suit, summer, sun, super, supply, support, surround

3.15.4 Word-medial

basic, bicycle, bossy, classic, conversation, decide, essay, gossip, impressive, jealousy, massive, possible, receive, reception, recipe

3.15.5 Word-final

across, address, advice, atlas, base, bliss, bonus, bus, case, chase, chess, choice, class, course, cross, decrease, delicious, dress, face, famous, fierce, force, genius, glass, grease, guess, hiss, horse, house, kiss, less, lettuce, loose, loss, mess, nice, notice, office, pass, peace/piece, place, plus, press, price, promise, purse, race, trace, twice, verse, voice, worse, yes

3.15.6 Multiple

access, ancestor, assassin, assess, assistant, basis, cease, circus, consist, crisis, discuss, distance, sentence, serious, source/sauce, suggest, suppress, surface, insist, licence, precise, process, science, sense, service, silence, since, sister, six, slice, space, spice, sponsor, status, stress, success, system, useless

3.15.7 Phrases

accept responsibility, restricted access, a serious accident, sensible advice, a precise answer, a personal assistant, a false assumption, a gasp of astonishment, a sense of balance, a savage beast, a Christmas bonus, a confidence boost, breakfast cereal, a bus pass, a case study, a star-studded cast, a centre of excellence, miss a chance, smoke a cigar, express concern, customer service, a sense of decency, a unanimous decision, a stroke of genius, a ghost story, a safe guess, the rest is history, a spelling mistake, false modesty, bits and pieces, a press release, a recipe for success, a dress rehearsal, a sign of respect, a risk assessment, safe and sound, better safe than sorry, a sliding scale, stars of stage and screen, bursting at the seams, a split second, a false sense of security, a stainless steel sink, a slippery slope, burst into song, the speed of sound, suffer in silence

3.15.8 Sentences

1 Scott's face creased into a smile.
2 Sally tossed and dressed the salad.
3 Steven sat sipping a glass of whisky.
4 My sister missed the last bus yesterday.
5 The task was beyond the grasp of our son.
6 Selena sewed the seam with small stitches.
7 Sport's a constant source of fascination for us.
8 The selection process takes place next Saturday.
9 Spelling mistakes can be embarrassing and costly.
10 Samuel sprinkled the steak with a teaspoon of salt.
11 It's sometimes impossible to escape one's destiny.
12 Simon protested his innocence throughout the case.
13 Tess spoke without the slightest sign of nervousness.
14 Several scientists were conspicuous by their absence.
15 Laurence couldn't suppress the excitement in his voice.
16 The police arrested suspects during the house-to-house search.
17 Her relentless pursuit of artistic excellence is an inspiration to us.
18 The industrious students succeeded in grasping the basics of the science.
19 The house faces south-west and overlooks the surrounding countryside.
20 The security forces collapsed in the face of recent assaults by the militants.

3.15.9 Dialogue

A: I missed the bus yesterday. It didn't stop for us at the bus stop.
B: When it's stuffed full, they say you must wait for the next one.
A: So the season tickets I buy are for standing at the bus stop getting soaked, and not for sitting on a seat inside going to my destination?
B: Face facts. The bus service stinks. Save your sanity and take a taxi.

3.16 Voiced alveolar fricative /z/

3.16.1 Description

Voiced alveolar fricative. The tip and blade of the tongue are raised in the direction of the alveolar ridge, forming a stricture of close approximation. The sides of the tongue are held against the upper side teeth. There's a clear groove along the centre of the tongue.

3.16.2 Spelling

<z> zoo, bizarre, lazy, quiz
<ze> blaze, freeze, prize

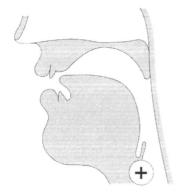

Figure 3.15 English /z/.

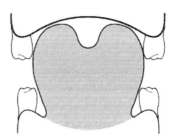

Figure 3.16 Mouth viewed from the front showing grooved tongue shape for /z/.

<zz> dizzy, jazz, buzz
<s, se> pleasant, always, museum, rise, wise, houses
<x> xenophobia, xylophone, anxiety
<x, xh> = /gz/ exam, exact, exist, exhilarate, exhausted
Also in -s endings, e.g. dogs, sees, John's; see section 2.15
After <pre-, de-, re->, e.g. preserve, desert, resist

Unusual spellings

<ss> possess, dissolve, scissors, dessert

3.16.3 Word-initial

zealous, zed, zest, zinc, zip, zone, zoo, zoom

3.16.4 Word-medial

adviser, amazing, bizarre, blazer, bulldozer, busy, closet, composer, cosy, crazy, cuisine, daisy, deposit, desert (n.), deserve, design, desire, dessert, disaster, dissolve, dizzy, drowsy, easy, fizzy, hazy, hesitate, laser, lazy, loser, miser, museum, music, physics, resist, scissors, user, visit

3.16.5 Word-final

accuse, advise, always, amaze, amuse, apologise, blouse, breeze, browse, bruise, buzz, cause, cheese, choose, cruise, daze, erase, freeze, fuse, gaze, hose, jazz, maze, news, noise, nose, pause, phrase, please, prize, quiz, realise, recognise, refuse (v.), revise, rose, seize, size, sneeze, squeeze, suppose, surprise, tease, vase, wise

3.16.6 Multiple

disease, measles, mesmerise, trousers, advisers, disasters, lasers, users, blouses, breezes, bruises, noises, noses, prizes, roses, sizes, houses

3.16.7 Phrases

easily absorbed, a careers adviser, a pleasant breeze, business studies, Parmesan cheese, a reasonable compromise, lose a deposit, transmit a disease, surprisingly easy, revise for an exam, jazz music, visit a museum, a buzzing noise, a seasoned observer, the laws of physics, easy to please, it stands to reason, rose petals, a surprise visit, visit the zoo, compose music, a pleasant surprise

3.16.8 Sentences

1   Please excuse my clumsy words.
2   These tools are surprisingly easy to use.
3   She grows herbs like basil, rosemary and chives.
4   Elizabeth's cheesecake with hazelnuts is tantalising.
5   Brussels sprouts with Parmesan cheese sounds bizarre.
6   He has master's degrees in tourism and business studies.
7   My cousin holds a position as a careers adviser in Leeds.
8   Alexandra adores flowers like azaleas, zinnias and roses.
9   She sounds exhausted and miserable although she denies it.
10 Why does she refuse what seems a reasonable compromise?
11 I'm amazed that anxiety can cause these physical symptoms.
12 Liz knows loads of words and phrases in Brazilian Portuguese.
13 They apologised to the passengers for the delays and cancellations.
14 I was surprised that they chose me to represent their values and ideas.
15 His findings aren't implausible and deserve to be examined exhaustively.
16 When James opens the browser, he hears a buzzing noise in his headphones.
17 He loves visiting the zoo and observing animals like zebras and chimpanzees.
18 My husband appears to be losing his enthusiasm for his jazz music magazines.
19 In the mornings and evenings there was always a pleasant breeze from the mountains.
20 Our offices are closed on Tuesday and Wednesday but will resume business on Thursday.

3.16.9 Dialogue

A: The zoo's closed on Tuesdays, Wednesdays and Thursdays.
B: How surprising! Is it wise to stay closed during the holidays?
A: The owner's very lazy and prefers an easy life to a busy one.
B: How bizarre! Surely he feeds and cares for the animals when the zoo's closed to visitors anyway.

3.17 Voiceless palato-alveolar fricative /ʃ/

3.17.1 Description

Voiceless palato-alveolar fricative. The tip, blade and front of the tongue are raised in the direction of the alveolar ridge and the front of the hard palate, forming a narrow gap. The sides of the tongue are held against the upper side teeth, thus forming a groove along the

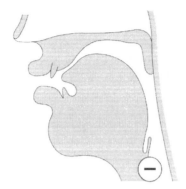

Figure 3.17 English /ʃ/. Note trumpet-shaped lip-rounding.

centre of the tongue. The groove is shallower than for /s z/ and also further back. The lips are rounded and protruded.

3.17.2 Spelling

<sh> ship, sushi, cash
<ti> station, portion, education
<ch> machine, brochure, chef, champagne
<su> sure, insure
<ssu> assure, pressure
<ci> special, precious
<si> following a consonant letter, e.g. controversial, compulsion, passion, expansion
<sci> conscious, conscience
<x> = /kʃ/ anxious, obnoxious, luxury

Unusual spellings

ocean, schedule (nowadays also with /sk/)

3.17.3 Word-initial

chauffeur, chef, shade, shadow, shake, shallow, shame, shampoo, shandy, shape, share, shark, sharp, shawl, shave, sheep, sheet, shelf, shell, shelter, shepherd, shield, shift, ship, shirt, shin, shiver, shock, shoe, shoot, shop, short, shot, should, shout, shove, show, shower, shuffle, shun, shut, shy, sugar, sure

3.17.4 Word-medial

assure, audacious, auspicious, bishop, delicious, issue, ambition, ancient, anxious, ashtray, auction, audition, banshee, beneficial, caption, cashmere, mushroom, action, caution, session, connection, edition, emotion, fashion, fiction, lotion, magician, mission, motion, ocean, passion, portion, ration, station

3.17.5 Word-final

gash, gush, hush, leash, niche, quiche, rash, stash, establish, clash, bash, blemish, banish, ambush, abolish, anguish, astonish, blush, brush, bush, cash, crash, crush, dash, English, finish, fish, flash, flesh, flush, fresh, push, rush, smash, splash, squash, varnish, wash, wish

3.17.6 Multiple

appreciation, initiation, negotiation, sheepish, shellfish, shush

3.17.7 Phrases

cherish an ambition, a shaving brush, a cash machine, short of cash, a champagne reception, fresh fish, a controversial issue, shampoo and conditioner, sheep shearing, fresh sheets, a makeshift shelter, a fresh shirt, the initial shock, shoe polish, a fashion shoot, a shoe shop, wishy-washy, a fashion show

3.17.8 Sentences

1   Joshua polished his shoes till they shone.
2   He shrank back into the shadow of a shrub.
3   Are there any sugar plantations in Bangladesh?
4   Sharon and Sean went shark fishing in the ocean.
5   The fashion show was shot on location in Chicago.
6   They wished to publish a special issue on education.
7   He rode roughshod over the wishes of the shareholders.
8   Our destination was a sheep-shearing station in the bush.
9   An ancient ship was washed up on the shores of Croatia.
10   We specialise in pashmina ponchos and crocheted shawls.
11   If you're short of cash, there's a cash machine at the station.
12   The optician refurbished his old-fashioned shop in Sheffield.
13   Ashley's dish was garnished with mushrooms and fresh radishes.
14   I'm partial to sherry, but I find traditional British shandy atrocious.
15   Sheila shrugged her shoulders impatiently and shivered with repulsion.
16   Shirley was anxious that her shorts would shrink in the washing machine.
17   Natasha has an astonishing collection of Chopin, Schubert and Schumann.
18   We took exception to his wishy-washy positions on this contentious issue.
19   We have a sensational selection of shampoos and conditioners on our shelves.
20   We had fish and shrimps washed down with Danish schnapps and champagne.

3.17.9 Dialogue

A: I wish you'd shut up about fashion.
B: I wish you'd shut up about fishing.
A: Your collection of shiny shoes should be sent to the rubbish dump.
B: Your fishing contraptions should be shoved into the ocean.

3.18 Voiced palato-alveolar fricative /ʒ/

3.18.1 Description

Voiced palato-alveolar fricative. The tip, blade and front of the tongue are raised in the direction of the alveolar ridge and the front of the hard palate, forming a narrow gap. The sides of the tongue are held against the upper side teeth, thus forming a groove along the centre of the tongue. The groove is shallower than for /s z/ and also further back. The lips are rounded and protruded.

/ʒ/ virtually only occurs in intervocalic position, e.g. *treasure*, though it's sometimes found initially and finally in recent French loanwords, e.g. *genre*, *beige*, *prestige*. In many cases, there are alternative pronunciations with /dʒ/.

3.18.2 Spelling

<si> following a vowel, e.g. confusion, decision, collision, occasion
<su> pleasure, casual, usual
<g(+e/i)> genre, courgette, regime, prestige
<zu> seizure

3.18.3 Word-initial

genre

3.18.4 Word-medial

illusion, intrusion, invasion, occasion, persuasion, precision, delusion, diffusion, elision, enclosure, envision, erosion, exclusion, excursion, explosion, exposure, corrosion, confusion, conclusion, allusion, aubergine, closure, collision, composure, courgette, decision, leisure, measure, pleasure, regime, seizure, treasure, profusion, provision, revision, supervision, television, vision

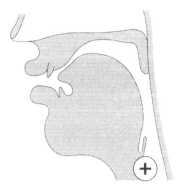

Figure 3.18 English /ʒ/ Note trumpet-shaped lip-rounding.

3.18.5 Word-final

barrage, beige, camouflage, collage, entourage, espionage, massage, prestige, rouge, sabotage

3.18.6 Phrases

television exposure

3.18.7 Sentences

1   The road closure led to confusion.
2   The explosion caused few casualties.
3   This added to the prestige of the genre.
4   Is it some sort of mirage or visual delusion?
5   The results led to a revision of the conclusion.
6   The measures of the regime were sabotaged.
7   Standard deviation's a measure of precision.
8   We can make a corsage that fits any occasion.
9   The star was surrounded by his usual entourage.
10 His new Peugeot was involved in a collision.
11 The soldiers were dressed in beige camouflage.
12 There's a profusion of courgettes and aubergines.
13 People with visual impairment experience exclusion.
14 Work's an unwelcome intrusion on my leisure time.
15 The damages may be caused by corrosion or erosion.
16 Beaujolais was the preferred wine of the bourgeoisie.
17 He accepted the treasurer's decision with composure.
18 It was such a pleasure to read Jane Austen's *Persuasion*.
19 He was met by a barrage of questions on the failed invasion.
20 It's debateable whether too much exposure to television is harmful.

3.18.8 Dialogue

A: I spend my leisure time searching for lost treasure.
B: I grow courgettes and aubergines.
A: There's no pleasure in watching television.
B: I agree. Television sabotages the mind.

3.19 Voiceless glottal fricative /h/

3.19.1 Description

Voiceless glottal fricative. The vocal folds are slightly narrowed, producing friction at the glottis. In addition, there is friction throughout the vocal tract. /h/ can be considered a strong voiceless beginning to the following sound (/j/ or a vowel) and therefore has the quality of a voiceless version of the following sound.

3.19.2 Spelling

<h> hand, home, perhaps
<wh> who, whose, whole, whore, wholesale, wholehearted, wholesome

Note that <h> is silent in words like *hour, honest(y), honour(able), heir(ess), annihilate, exhibit, exhaust, exhilarate, rhapsody, rhinoceros, rhotic, rhyme, rhythm, shepherd, silhouette, vehicle, vehement, vehemence.*

For words containing silent <gh>, as in *thought, through,* see section 3.7.2.

3.19.3 Word-initial

habit, hail, hair, half, hall, ham, hammer, hamster, hand, handle, happen, happy, harbour, hard, harm, harvest, hat, hate, head, heal, heap, hear, heart, heat, heavy, hedge, heel, hell, helmet, help, herb, hero, hesitate, hide, high, hike, hill, hip, hire, hiss, history, hit, hoax, hobby, hold, hole, holiday, home, honey, hook, hope, horn, horrible, horror, horse, hose, hospital, host, hot, house, hover, hug, hundred, hungry, hunt, hurry, hurt, husband, whole

3.19.4 Word-medial

abhor, abhorrent, alcohol, alcoholic, apprehend, apprehensive, apprehension, beehive, behalf, behave, behaviour, behind, coherent, cohort, comprehend, comprehension, comprehensive, enhance, inherit, perhaps, rehearse

3.19.5 Multiple

half-hearted, hand-holding, haphazard, headhunter, heavy-handed, heart-to-heart, hellhole, hitchhike, hobbyhorse, hot-headed, household, wholehearted

3.19.6 Phrases

a happy childhood, a horrible habit, half and half, a huge hall, holding hands, hard to handle, a hard hat, a health hazard, with head held high, the head of the household, a heavy heart, a head for heights, help is at hand, a childhood hero, a huge hit, a holiday home, have high hopes, not a hope in hell, honk a horn, a house husband, hands on hips, a home from home

3.19.7 Sentences

1 Heidi's hairstyle's hideous.
2 Hilary has no head for heights.
3 Herbert hasn't got a hope in hell.
4 A heat haze hung over the harbour.
5 Harry hung his head in humiliation.
6 Helen held her handbag over her head.
7 Humphrey was headhunted by Harvard.

8 We heard that the hurricane had hit Ohio.
9 Is Henry Higgins a hero or an anti-hero?
10 He had a happy and wholesome childhood.
11 His workaholic behaviour harms his health.
12 Here the husband was head of the household.
13 He hiked up a high hill in Haiti during his holidays.
14 Hugo held out his hand to his childhood sweetheart.
15 They were held hostage by the hot-headed hooligans.
16 The hound was howling its head off outside the house.
17 We helped ourselves to the heavenly hake and haddock.
18 Hugh is handsome with his hazel hair and high forehead.
19 The helicopter hovered above the house where he was hiding.
20 Harriet was so heavily dehydrated that we had to hurry her to hospital.

3.19.8 Dialogues

A: I can hardly hear Hugh's history lecture.
B: He's half asleep and hung over.
A: His alcohol habit is harming his career.
B: It's harming his home life too. A heavy drinker makes a horrible husband.

A: I half hoped to have the whole holiday here.
B: Henry, my husband, is happy here at the harbour too.
A: Perhaps hiking in the hills would be too hard.
B: In this heat it'd be horrible, hellish!

3.20 Nasals: summary of key features

There are three nasals: /m n ŋ/. Their key features are:

1 A complete closure is formed in the oral cavity while the soft palate is in the lowered position, allowing the airstream to exit via the nose.
2 The complete closures formed for /m n ŋ/ are identical to those for the bilabial /p b/, alveolar /t d/ and velar plosives /k g/. The difference is in the position of the soft palate: raised for the plosives, lowered for the nasals.
3 Together with approximants (and vowels), nasals are sonorants and act similarly in the following ways:

   a) they don't come in voiceless and voiced phonemic pairs;
   b) they aren't devoiced when adjacent to voiceless sounds or a pause;
   c) they are shortened by following voiceless consonants in the same syllable.

4 In word-final position, the alveolar nasal can be followed by both voiceless and voiced homorganic plosives – /nt/ and /nd/. Bilabial and velar nasals can only be followed by voiceless homorganic plosives in these positions – /mp/ and /ŋk/. See section 2.13.1.
5 Within a morpheme, nasals can only be followed by plosives that are homorganic.

6   In certain circumstances, nasals, particularly /n/, can become syllabic and form the nucleus of a syllable.

7   The velar nasal /ŋ/ doesn't occur in syllable onsets.

8   Apart from a small number of exceptions, /ŋg/ occurs within morphemes and /ŋ/ at the end of morphemes.

3.21 Voiced bilabial nasal /m/

3.21.1 Description

Voiced bilabial nasal. The lips form a closure, and the soft palate is lowered, thus preventing the airstream from exiting via the mouth and allowing it to escape through the nose. The vocal folds vibrate throughout the articulation.

3.21.2 Spelling

<m> map, amazing, human, aim
<mm> command, hammer
<mb> climb, lamb, comb, plumber
<mn> autumn, hymn, solemn, condemn
<gm> paradigm, phlegm, diaphragm

Note that in the word *mnemonic* <m> is silent.

3.21.3 Word-initial

machine, magnet, magic, mail/male, main, major, make, man, manage, manner, many, map, marble, march, margin, mark, market, marry, marsh, mask, master, mat, match, mate, material, maths, mattress, mature, may, maze, meadow, meal, mean, measure, meat/meet, medal, melt, mend, menu, mercy, merge, merit, merry, mess, metal, method, middle, mild, mile, milk, mind, mine, miss, mist, mistake, mix, moan, modern, money, monkey, month, mood, moon, morning, mother, mountain, mouth, move, much, music, mud, mug, murder, muscle, mustard

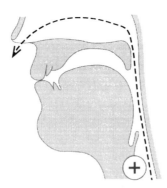

Figure 3.19 English /m/. The arrow indicates the escape of the airstream through the nose.

3.21.4 Word-medial

amateur, amazing, among, amount, blemish, charming, chemist, cinema, climate, comedy, comma, command, comment, common, customer, damage, demand, document (n.), domestic, drama, element, enemy, familiar, gimmick, glamour, grammar, hammer, human, humour, image, lemon, limit, permission, promise, puma, rumour, stomach, summer, woman

3.21.5 Word-final

aim, alarm, assume, atom, autumn, beam, bloom, blossom, bomb, bottom, calm, claim, climb, comb, cream, crime, crumb, dim, doom, dream, drum, dumb, exam, extreme, farm, firm, flame, foam, form, frame, game, gem, gloom, grim, gum, ham, harm, home, item, jam, lamb, name, numb, palm, plum, poem, pram, problem, programme, resume, room, same, scheme, scream, seem, shame, slim, steam, storm, sum, swim, team, theme, thumb, time, victim, volume, warm, welcome, womb, zoom

a)   *Clipped*

amp, blimp, bump, champ, chimp, chomp, chump, clump, crimp, imp, jump, lump, pump, scamp, stamp, stump, swamp, trump, wimp, bumf, lymph, nymph, triumph

b)   *Full length vs. clipped*

cam/camp, clam/clamp, cram/cramp, dam/damp, dumb/dump, hem/hemp, hum/hump, lamb/lamp, limb/limp, plum/plump, ram/ramp, skim/skimp, slum/slump, thumb/thump

3.21.6 Multiple

accomplishment, amusement, commitment, compartment, compliment (n.), compromise, embarrassment, mainstream, mammoth, meantime, measurement, medium, member, memo, memory, mermaid, mime, minimum, moment, movement, mumble, murmur, museum, premium, remember, sometimes, maximum

3.21.7 Phrases

an impressive achievement, a smoke alarm, a stamp album, a modest ambition, the maximum amount, a limited amount, the animal kingdom, a common assumption, a clumsy attempt, a time bomb, a claim for damages, in complete command, demand compensation, a famous composer, commit a crime, permanent damage, a simple diagram, a moment of drama, a family member, a team game, doom and gloom, welcome home, a meagre income, a musical instrument, plum jam, a time limit, a family man, man-made material, a simple meal, minced meat, a meeting of minds, a permanent memorial, a frame of mind, an elementary mistake, a memorable moment, tomorrow morning, climb a mountain, a smooth movement, a complete mystery, make a promise, a malicious rumour, a lump sum, this time tomorrow, an umbrella term, a farm animal, a computer game

3.21.8 Sentences

1   The moment's come to make a move.
2   That makes it something of a minor miracle!

3　Mary embraced the system with enthusiasm.
4　The maritime museum's marked on the map.
5　Mandy admitted she'd made a major mistake.
6　My family gave the newcomers a warm welcome.
7　Marilyn was completely immune to Tom's charms.
8　This matter was uppermost in my mind at the time.
9　Malcolm made himself comfortable in an armchair.
10　The computer comes with a comprehensive manual.
11　The mass media are an important means of communication.
12　A monument's been commissioned in his memory.
13　Emily supplemented her income with part-time journalism.
14　By this time tomorrow the temperature will have plummeted.
15　Cameras were employed to monitor the movement of animals.
16　Max aimed to cause the maximum amount of embarrassment.
17　Moira's a member of the management team for my company.
18　The musician demonstrated complete mastery of his instrument.
19　The government embarked on an ambitious programme of economic reforms.
20　Michael had no problem with his long-term memory, but his short-term memory was damaged.

3.21.9 Dialogue

A:　My mate's merely a mediocre musician who hammers away on his instrument for money.
B:　You might make him mad with your grim assessment of his competence.
A:　It's Mike's own assessment, not mine. He moans and moans about his drums.
B:　Then maybe he should make music with the tambourine.

3.22 Voiced alveolar nasal /n/

3.22.1 Description

Voiced alveolar nasal. The tip of the tongue forms a closure with the alveolar ridge, and the sides of the tongue with the side teeth. The soft palate is lowered, allowing air to escape through the nose. The vocal folds vibrate throughout the articulation.

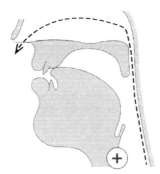

Figure 3.20 English /n/. The arrow indicates the escape of the airstream through the nose.

3.22.2 Spelling

<n> name, unite, money, burn
<nn> funny, tennis
<kn> knack, knee, kneel, know, knight, knife, knock, knob, knowledge, knit
<gn> gnaw, reign, sign, align, campaign, champagne, design, foreign (also derived forms,
    e.g. assignment, foreigner, designer)
<pn> pneumonia

Note that <n> is silent in final <mn>, e.g. *autumn, column, condemn, damn, hymn, solemn*.
/n/ returns in derived forms: e.g. *autumnal, condemnation, columnist*.

3.22.3 Word-initial

knee, knife, knob, knock, knot, know, naked, name, nap, narrow, nasty, nature, near, neck, needle, neighbour, nerve, next, nice, niece, night, no, nose, normal, note, nothing, now, numb, number, nurse, nor/gnaw

3.22.4 Word-medial

animal, corner, dinner, funny, honey, honour, manner, many, minor, minute (n.), money, owner, panic, piano, planet, pony, spinach, tennis, unite

3.22.5 Word-final

again, balloon, bargain, bean, begin, bin, born, brain, brown, burn, can, chain, chin, clean, clown, coin, common, crown, dawn, design, down, drown, earn, fan, fine, foreign, fortune, fountain, gain, green, grin, groan, gun, human, iron, keen, lawn, learn, lemon, line, lion, loan, machine, main, man, men, mine, moan, moon, open, pain, pan, pen, phone, pin, plan, plane, queen, sane, scan, shine, sin, skin, spin, stain, stolen, strain, sun, then, thin, token, tone, town, train, tune, turn, twin, vain, van, warn, weapon, when, whine/wine, win, woman, zone

a) Clipped
amount, aren't/aunt, blunt, can't, cent/sent, client, count, defiant, dent, don't, flaunt, flint, fluent, fount, front, gaunt, giant, glint, grant, grunt, hint, hunt, mint, point, print, quaint, rant, runt, saint, slant, splint, sprint, squint, stint, taint, taunt, want, weren't, won't, month, advance, announce, bounce, chance, convince, dance, defence, France, glance, lance, mince, once, ounce, pounce, prince, rinse, science, sense, trance, bench, branch, brunch, bunch, clench, crunch, drench, flinch, French, hunch, inch, launch, lunch, munch, pinch, punch, trench, wench, winch, wrench

b) Full length vs. clipped
burned/burnt, complained/complaint, dawned/daunt, feigned/faint, horned/haunt, joined/joint, lend/lent, mend/meant, mound/mount, pained/paint, panned/pant, pined/pint, punned/punt, rend/rent, scanned/scant, send/sent, shunned/shunt, skinned/skint, spend/spent, stunned/stunt, tend/tent, tinned/tint, vend/vent, wend/went, nine/ninth, ten/tenth, dens/dense, hens/hence, pens/pence, tens/tense, wins/wince, singe/cinch, lunge/lunch

3.22.6 Multiple

abandon, accountant, announce, banana, cannon, canteen, confident, consonant, contain, engine, entrance (n.), genuine, ignorant, innocent, London, napkin, nine, nineteen, nonsense, noon, noun, onion, opinion, suntan

3.22.7 Phrases

a pronounced foreign accent, a sunny afternoon, a wounded animal, won't take no for an answer, the beginning of the end, fringe benefits, brains and brawn, none of your business, the town centre, the turn of the century, a change of scene, not an ounce of common sense, danger money, a sense of destiny, squander a fortune, present a united front, genuinely funny, a gin and tonic, moan and groan, bound to happen, a gentle hint, a figment of your imagination, turn down an invitation, a blunt knife, behind enemy lines, a no-nonsense manner, friends and neighbours, a bundle of nerves, a handwritten note, a point of interest, a punch on the nose, answer a question, a brain scan, the monsoon season, maintain a stony silence, a banana skin, a tennis tournament, a train of events, vintage wine

3.22.8 Sentences

1   Only one question remains unanswered.
2   Nicholas grinned and nodded in confirmation.
3   Don't let the discussion end on a negative note.
4   Nancy doesn't have an ounce of common sense.
5   One of the men had a pronounced northern accent.
6   The students insisted that no offence was intended.
7   Cynthia's no-nonsense manner inspires confidence.
8   They'd confessed their sins and done their penance.
9   The parents confirmed that their son was born blind.
10   The town centre has changed beyond all recognition.
11   The next of kin have been informed about the accident.
12   The panel of scientists was drawn from the universities.
13   A nationwide hunt was launched for the dangerous gunman.
14   Simon and Jenny invested their money in government bonds.
15   Kenneth went from a no-win situation to a win-win situation.
16   Norman evidently wanted to be in control of his own destiny.
17   You'll need to be patient as change doesn't happen overnight.
18   His friend's experiences remained at the forefront of his mind.
19   None of the participants understood the meaning of the sentence.
20   Dominic eventually managed to convince them of his innocence.

3.22.9 Dialogue

A: No more nouns and pronouns!
B: We want to know about consonants – approximants, nasals, obstruents and sonorants.
A: Enough of determiners, tenses, inflections and inversion!
B: We demand to learn about the sounds of spoken English – phonetics!

3.23 Voiced velar nasal /ŋ/

3.23.1 Description

Voiced velar nasal. The back of the tongue forms a closure with the soft palate, and the rear of the sides of the tongue with the rear side teeth. The soft palate is lowered, allowing air to escape through the nose. Note that this means that there's a velar closure but no velic closure. The vocal folds vibrate throughout the articulation.

3.23.2 Spelling

<ng> singer, king, young
<nk> = /ŋk/ ankle, sink
<nc> = /ŋk/ uncle, zinc
<ng> = /ŋg/ anger, longer
<nx> = /ŋks/ lynx, larynx
<nq> = /ŋk/ banquet, tranquil

3.23.3 Word-final

a) *Full length*

along, among, bang, beginning, belong, boomerang, boxing, bring, building, ceiling, clearing, cling, clothing, cooking, craving, cunning, daring, darling, dumpling, dung, during, dwelling, evening, fling, gang, gong, hang, herring, king, lightning, long, lung, meringue, morning, nothing, oblong, pang, parking, pudding, railing, ring, rung, sing, slang, song, spring, sterling, sting, string, strong, swing, thing, throng, tongue, twang, wedding, wing, wring, wrong, young

b) *Full length vs. clipped*

bang/bank, bring/brink, bung/bunk, clang/clank, cling/clink, clung/clunk, dung/dunk, hung/hunk, ping/pink, rang/rank, ring/rink, sang/sank, sing/sink, sting/stink, stung/stunk, tang/tank, thing/think, wing/wink

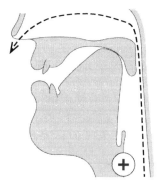

Figure 3.21 English /ŋ/. The arrow indicates the escape of the airstream through the nose.

3.23.4 Word-medial

a)   *Word-medial before /k/ (clipped)*

anchor, ankle, bank, banquet, blank, blanket, blink, brink, bunker, conquer, crinkle, donkey, drink, drunk, duckling, frank, hanker, ink, jinx, junk, link, mink, monk, monkey, pink, plank, prank, punk, rank, relinquish, rink, shrink, sink, sphinx, sprinkle, stink, tank, thank, think, tinker, tinkle, tranquil, trinket, trunk, twinkle, uncle, wink, wrinkle, zinc

b)   *Word-medial before /g/*

anger, angle, angora, angry, anguish, bingo, bungalow, distinguish, English, finger, flamingo, hunger, hungry, jingle, jungle, kangaroo, linger, mangle, mango, mingle, mongrel, nightingale, penguin, rectangle, single, strangle, tangle, tango, tingle, triangle, longer, stronger, younger, longest, youngest, strongest

3.23.5 Multiple

angling, long-running, long-standing, long-suffering, ping-pong, singsong, belongings, inkling, singing, stinking, banging, belongings, bringing, clinging, hanging, longing, ringing, singing, stinging, swinging, banking, blinking, conquering, drinking, hankering, linking, ranking, relinquishing, shrinking, sinking, thanking, thinking, tinkering, twinkling, winking, distinguishing, jingling, lingering, mingling, strangling, tingling

3.23.6 Phrases

growing anger, a wedding banquet, a boxing ring, on the brink of extinction, an imposing building, the wrong conclusion, a refreshing drink, strongly encourage, a spring evening, a sinking feeling, a surprising finding, my ring finger, hunger pangs, the fighting instinct, language learning, the missing link, a punctured lung, an angry meeting, shocking pink, a wedding ring, a younger sibling, rhyming slang, a drinking song, spring cleaning, a length of string, a long think, swimming trunks, a knowing wink

3.23.7 Sentences

1   It's a tranquil setting for a relaxing evening.
2   I've been feeling strong hunger pangs all morning.
3   We encourage you to be punctual for the meetings.
4   Angus was worrying about getting the timing wrong.
5   My siblings are playing ping-pong in the dining room.
6   My uncle was looking forward to his posting in Beijing.
7   We were dying to sing along with the best-selling songs.
8   Congratulations to Duncan and Bianca on getting engaged!
9   The youngsters are cycling from Nottingham to Birmingham.
10   We're travelling from Kings Cross St Pancras to Paddington.
11   I'm thinking of wearing long dangling earrings to the banquet.
12   Surprisingly she wasn't wearing a wedding ring on her finger.
13   Her findings were fascinating, but her conclusion was misleading.
14   It was so disappointing that they weren't willing to sing an encore.
15   We're moving from a crumbling building to a charming bungalow.
16   We were getting the hang of understanding the gang's rhyming slang.

17   He's trying to bring pink flamingos back from the brink of extinction.
18   I'll be studying English language and linguistics in Hong Kong next spring.
19   He was hoping he could relinquish the nagging anxiety that was weighing him down.
20   Learning to distinguish the diphthongs of Hungarian was proving to be a challenging undertaking.

3.23.8 Dialogue

A: Gangs of youngsters have been ringing my doorbell and running away.
B: I'd like to strangle those pranksters.
A: It's ruining my tranquil evenings.
B: I think I'll bring round my dog – an angry mongrel with long fangs.

3.24 Approximants: summary of key features

There are four approximants: /l r j w/. Their key features are:

1   With the soft palate raised, the articulators move towards each other to form a gap wider than that for fricatives and not narrow enough to cause turbulence and fricative noise.
2   Together with nasals (and vowels), approximants are sonorants and act similarly in the following ways:

a)   they don't come in voiceless and voiced phonemic pairs;
b)   they aren't devoiced when adjacent to voiceless sounds or a pause;
c)   they are shortened by a following voiceless consonant in the same syllable (/l/ only).

3   /j/ and /w/ are semi-vowels. They are articulated with parts of the tongue used to articulate vowels and are in essence glides from the [i] and [u] positions respectively.
4   While all other English phonemes involve the airstream travelling down the midline of the vocal tract, the lateral approximant /l/ forms a closure in the centre of the mouth and causes the airstream to flow on one or both sides of it.
5   When approximants follow aspirated voiceless plosives /p t k/, the aspiration takes place during the articulation of the approximants, causing them to become devoiced and fricative.
6   Three of the four approximants, /r j w/, occur only in syllable onsets.
7   /l/ has a velarised allophone, dark /l/, which occurs before consonants (except /j/) or a pause.
8   /j/ is lost after certain consonants.
9   The sequences /tj/ and /dj/ are increasingly replaced by /tʃ/ and /dʒ/ in stressed syllables.

Semi-vowels

3.25 Voiced palatal approximant /j/

3.25.1 Description

Voiced palatal median approximant. With the soft palate raised, the front of the tongue approaches the hard palate, but not close enough to result in friction. This is the same articulation as for a close front unrounded vowel; therefore, [j] can alternatively be described as

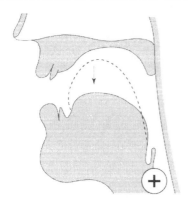
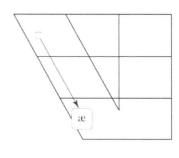

Figure 3.22 English /j/: sequence /jæ/ as in *yak*. The diagram shows the approximate change in tongue shape. Since /j/ is a semi-vowel, it can be indicated on a vowel diagram.

a glide from the [i] vowel position. If the following vowel is open, the approximation to the hard palate is less close, equating to a glide from an opener vowel position, for example [ɪ].

3.25.2 Spelling

    \<y\> year, yellow, youth
    \<u\> = /juː/ unit, useful, assume, music
    \<ue\> = /juː/ argue, value, venue, queue
    \<ew\> = /juː/ few, news, knew, view
    \<eu\> = /juː/ feud, neutral, Eugene
    \<i\> behaviour, dominion, saviour, William

Unusual spellings

    beautiful, Houston

3.25.3 Word-initial

ewe, UK, ukulele, Ukraine, unanimous, unicorn, uniform, union, unique, unit, unite, uni-verse, university, USA, useful, usual, utensil, utility, yacht, yard, yawn, year, yearn, yeast, yell, yellow, yes, yesterday, yet, yoga, yogurt, yolk, you, your, young, youth

3.25.4 Clusters

beauty, bugle, bureaucrat, steward, student, studio, stupid, feud, few, fuel, fume, funeral, fuse, futile, future, view, mule, museum, music, mute, mutiny, neutral, new, nuclear, nucleus, nude, huge, human, humid, humour, computer, accurate, ambulance, argument, behaviour, calculate, canyon, circulate, companion, curriculum, deputy, document (n.), emulate, execu-tive, fabulous, failure, formula, immaculate, jocular, manipulate, manuscript, monument, muscular, occupy, opinion, particular, popular, population, refuge, regular, singular, spec-tacular, speculate, stimulate, volume

3.25.5 Devoiced/fricative

pew, pewter, puberty, puce, puerile, puny, pupil, pure, putrid, cube, cucumber, cue/queue, cumulative, cumin, cure, curious, cute

3.25.6 /tj/ or /tʃ/

tube, Tuesday, tuition, tulip, tumour, tuna, tune, tunic, tutor

3.25.7 /dj/ or /dʒ/

dew/due, dual/duel, dubious, duke, dune, during, duty

3.25.8 Multiple

accumulate, tubular, uvula, yoyo

3.25.9 Phrases

a popular venue, yell abuse, argue furiously, a useful attribute, human behaviour, the undisputed champion, regular communication, a useful contribution, a miraculous cure, genuinely curious, youthful enthusiasm, the usual excuse, a humiliating failure, a newspaper interview, a user manual, beautiful music, popular opinion, an executive producer, the annual review, a university student, particularly stupid, make yourself useful, a neutral venue, a huge yawn, New Year's Eve

3.25.10 Sentences

1   His music's particularly popular in Europe.
2   Eugene refuses to speculate about the future.
3   Sonia looked beautiful in her new yellow tunic.
4   We saw pumas and jaguars in Uruguay in January.
5   Hugo made himself useful as a tutor for youngsters.
6   He contributed regularly to their communist newspaper.
7   This doesn't excuse his unusual behaviour yesterday.
8   William's a first-year student at the University of Houston.
9   The pupils found opportunities to use their new vocabulary.
10 Hubert calculated it meticulously and executed it scrupulously.
11 The monument was obscured from our view by a huge museum.
12 The computer manual's usually more useful than your intuition!
13 The document on nutrition was distributed to the youthful population.
14 There was a spectacular view from her luxurious studio in Euston.
15 This beautiful volume was produced as a tribute to his music tutor.
16 Ursula made a valuable contribution to the future of our community.
17 Matthew attributes his miraculous cure of pneumonia to acupuncture.
18 After her year-long recuperation, Muriel resumed her duties as a stewardess.
19 Stuart's enthusiastic to pursue a beautiful future with his new young wife.

20   My nephew had a manual occupation for years before becoming a communications
     executive.

3.25.11 Dialogue

A: The yoga instructor you recommended is useless.
B: Not true. I queued all day to see that beautiful new yoga teacher.
A: 'New' is true, and she's cute too, but she's a young student and knew very few
       moves.
B: *You* can do yoga with any old guru. *I* prefer to spend a few hours with a beautiful young
       tutor.

3.26 Voiced labial-velar approximant /w/

3.26.1 Description

Voiced labial-velar median approximant. With the soft palate raised, the back of the tongue
approaches the soft palate, but not close enough to cause friction, and, simultaneously, the
lips round. This is the same articulation as for a close back rounded vowel; therefore, [w] can
alternatively be described as a glide from the [u] position. If the following vowel is open, the
approximation to the soft palate is less close, equating to a glide from an opener position, for
example [ʊ]. /w/ is a double articulation consisting as it does of two strictures of equal rank:
velar and labial approximants.

3.26.2 Spelling

    <w> wait, world, awake
    <wh> whale, white, whether, what, where, when, which, why
    <qu> = /kw/ quite, query, acquire
    <ngu> = /ŋgw/ anguish, language, linguistics
    <su> = /sw/ assuage, persuade, suede, suite

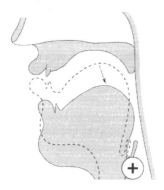
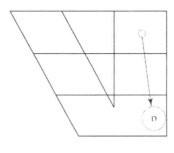

Figure 3.23 English /w/: sequence /wɒ/ as in *wash*. The diagram shows the approximate
    change in tongue shape. Since /w/ is a semi-vowel, it can be indicated on a vowel
    diagram.

Note that <w> is silent in *who, whose, whole, whore, answer, sword, two, Greenwich, Berwick*, and the second <w> in *Warwick*. <w> in initial <wr> is also silent, e.g. *wrack, wrangle, wrap, wrath, wreak, wreath, wreck, wreckage, wren, wrench, wrest, wrestle, wretch, wretched, wriggle, wring, wrinkle, wrist, write, writer, writhe, wrong, wrote, wrought, wrung, wry*.

3.26.3 Word-initial

one, wafer, wage, wagon, waist/waste, wait, wake, walk, wall, wallet, wander, want, war, wardrobe, warm, wash, wasp, watch, water, wave, wax, way, weak/week, wealthy, weapon, wear/where, weather, web, wedding, wedge, weed, weight, well, went, west, wet, wheel, while, whip, whistle, white, why, wide, wife, wig, wild, will, win, windy, window, wine, wing, wink, winter, wipe, wire, wish, witch, wolf, woman, wonder, wood, wool, word, work, world, worm, worry, worse, wound (n.), wound (past tense of *wind*), squad, square, squash, squeeze, squid, suede, suite/sweet, swallow, swim, swan, swap, swear, sweat, sweep, swing

3.26.4 Word-medial

awake, award, aware, away, awoke, backward, beware, farewell, firewood, foreword, forward, haywire, highway, keyword, kiwi, leeway, microwave, motorway, otherwise, paperweight, paperwork, reward, seaweed, towards, awkward, banquet, colloquial, conquest, equal, frequent (adj.), liquid, sequence, distinguish, extinguish, language, penguin

3.26.5 Devoiced/fricative

twaddle, twang, tweak, tweed, tweet, tweezers, twelve, twice, twenty, twiddle, twig, twilight, twin, twinkle, twirl, twist, twitter, between, quack, quaint, qualification, qualify, quality, quantity, quarrel, quarry, queen, queer, query, quest, question, questionnaire, quick, quiet, quilt, quit, quite, quiver, quiz, quota, quote, choir, acquaintance, acquire, enquire, equipment, request, require

3.26.6 Multiple

westward, one-to-one, one-way, quick-witted, swimwear, twenty-one, walkway, wall-to-wall, watchword, waterway, waterworks, waxwork, wayward, weather-worn, well-wisher, well-worn, werewolf, whirlwind, whitewash, wickerwork, wigwam, wishy-washy, woodwind, woodwork, woodworm, word-for-word, world-weary, worthwhile

3.26.7 Phrases

words of wisdom, wide awake, win an award, well aware, a farewell banquet, without equal, well equipped, watch your language, liquid waste, a qualified midwife, the motorway network, an awkward question, win a quiz, a railway worker, a white swan, work up a sweat, a quick swim, swing backwards and forwards, well worth the wait, a walk-in wardrobe, wonderfully warm weather, lukewarm water, the way forward, whatever the weather, a white wedding, watch one's weight, weird and wonderful, a welfare worker, a wishing well, a wealthy widow, wear a wig, white wine, wit and wisdom, wither away, wise words, walk to work, wakey wakey

3.26.8 Sentences

1   When it's wet, wear waterproof wellies.
2   Why worry about the weather, Edward?
3   William was wounded twice in World War I.
4   Wayne would do well to watch his language.
5   Gwen wore a white wig at the awards banquet.
6   I frequently quoted my wife's words of wisdom.
7   We watched the whales with wide-eyed wonder.
8   Wendy's unquestionably a woman of the world.
9   The women wept and wailed when he went away.
10 We were wondering why she quarrelled with the midwife.
11 Woollen sweaters should be washed with lukewarm water.
12 Gwyneth was woken up by the squeak of the wagon wheels.
13 The quality of his work's without equal in the Western world.
14 We watched the swimmers weave their way through the water.
15 Swansea City acquired an away-win over Watford this weekend.
16 The walkers watched the white-crested waves sweep towards them.
17 Wearing a turquoise swimsuit, she waded waist-deep into the water.
18 The watermelons were sweet, mouth-watering and thirst-quenching.
19 Walter switched between wanting to be a waiter and a welfare worker.
20 Watching wildlife in the wonderful tranquillity of the woods was rewarding.

3.26.9 Dialogue

A: Why won't you wear the woolly sweater I made you?
B: Itchy wool is the worst thing in the world.
A: It's wonderfully warm on windy days.
B: Well, if you want, I'll wait until winter and wear it then.

Non-semivowels

3.27 Voiced alveolar lateral approximant /l/

3.27.1 Description

Voiced alveolar lateral approximant. With the soft palate raised, the tip of the tongue forms a central closure with the alveolar ridge. One or both sides of the tongue are lowered, allowing the airstream to pass around the central obstruction. In non-prevocalic position, a velarised allophone is used (except before /j/).

3.27.2 Spelling

    <l> look, alone, elephant, build, bold
    <le> little, saddle, tackle, vile
    <ll> vanilla, bullet, wall

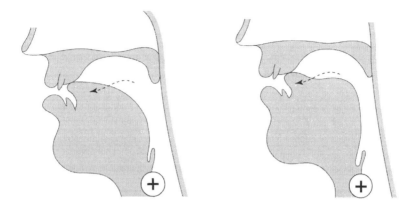

Figure 3.24 Left: English clear /l/. Right: dark /l/ showing velarised tongue shape. The arrow indicates that the airstream escapes over the lowered sides of the tongue.

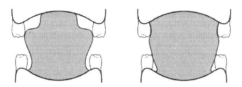

Figure 3.25 Mouth viewed from the front. Left: tongue sides lowered for lateral /l/. Right: tongue sides raised for non-lateral consonants.

Note that <l> is silent in *calm, palm, colonel, half, salmon, baulk, chalk, folk, Norfolk, Suffolk, talk, walk* and *yolk* and sometimes in *almond*. <l> is also silent in *could, should, would*. Otherwise, <l> is pronounced, e.g. *cold, field, told, milk, silk*.

3.27.3 Pre-vocalic

alarm, alert, alien, allergy, allow, alone, along, aloud, analyse, apology, balance, belief, belly, belong, bellow, bullet, bully, careless, ceiling, celery, cellar, collar, collect, college, colour, darling, delay, delicate, delight, deliver, early, elephant, follow, gallery, garlic, hollow, jelly, lady, lake, lamb, lamp, land, lane, large, last, late, laugh, law, leaf, leak, leap, learn, leave, left, lend, lesson, letter, lick, lid, life, lift, light, like, limit, line, lip, list, load, loaf, lock, log, long, look, lose, loss, loud, love, luck, melon, pillow, pilot, relax, relief, salad, shallow, silence, solid, trolley, vanilla, wallet, yellow

3.27.4 Pre-consonantal

album, balcony, bald, belt, bold, build, bulb, bulk, child, cold, culture, elbow, field, film, fold, gold, guilty, healthy, help, melt, mild, old, result, shelf, shelter, silk, silver, solve, vulgar, wild, wolf, world

3.27.5 Pre-pausal

aisle, all, appeal, ball, bell, bill, boil, bull, call, canal, cereal, chill, cool, crawl, curl, detail, doll, drill, dull, fall, feel, file, fool, girl, hall, heal/heel, hill, howl, ill, kneel, meal, mile, nail, oil, owl, pale, pearl, pill, pull, roll, rule, school, seal, sell, shell, skill, small, smell, smile, soil, spell, spill, steal/steel, still, style, tail, tall, tell, thrill, tool, trail, wall, well, wheel, while

3.27.6 Clipped

alp, gulp, help, kelp, pulp, scalp, whelp, yelp, asphalt, assault, belt, Celt, cobalt, colt, dealt, default, exalt, exult, fault, insult (v.), jilt, jolt, lilt, melt, pelt, quilt, result, revolt, salt, silt, stilt, tilt, vault, volt, bulk, elk, hulk, ilk, milk, silk, skulk, sulk, talc, whelk, belch, filch, mulch, zilch, elf, golf, gulf, self, wolf, filth, health, stealth, wealth, pulse, impulse, Welsh

3.27.7 Full length vs. clipped

bold/bolt, billed/built, culled/cult, doled/dolt, dwelled/dwelt, felled/felt, guild/guilt, hilled/hilt, killed/kilt, knelled/knelt, mauled/malt, mould/moult, smelled/smelt, spelled/spelt, spilled/spilt, willed/wilt, spoiled/spoilt, shelve/shelf, Ls/else, falls/false

3.27.8 Devoiced/fricative

place, plain/plane, plan, planet, plank, plant, plaster, plastic, plate, play, player, pleasant, please, pleasure, plenty, plot, plough, plug, plum, plumber, plump, plural, plus, claim, clap, class, claw, clay, clean, clear, clever, click, client, cliff, climate, climax, clinic, clip, cloak, clock, cloth, clothes, cloud, clover, clown, club, clue, clutter

3.27.9 Multiple

absolutely, alcohol, calculate, fulfil, legal, leaflet, level, lilac, lily, little, local, lonely, multiply, lovely, lolly, landlord, likely, lively

3.27.10 Phrases

install an alarm, low alcohol, mentally alert, call an ambulance, a letter of apology, polite applause, fall asleep, well balanced, a golf ball, a commonly held belief, demolish a building, a light bulb, a burglar alarm, lovely and clean, loud and clear, look for clues, live in exile, full of flavour, follow blindly, feel like a fool, wild garlic, a village hall, a call for help, manual labour, learn a language, built to last, a silent letter, lift the lid, flashing lights, drill for oil, swallow a pill, a helicopter pilot, learn to relax, fill shelves, build a shelter, a wall of silence, solid silver, a lack of skill, tall and slim, a cold spell, a dwindling supply, a bulging wallet, a lone wolf

3.27.11 Sentences

1 Oliver's planted fields full of sunflowers.
2 The local police were placed on full alert.

3 It's a sleepy little village in the Welsh hills.
4 Luke told me he'd fill me in on the details later.
5 The tail of Allan's plane was filled with bullet holes.
6 Malcolm was too lazy to consult the assembly manual.
7 The level of alcohol in his blood was below the legal limit.
8 These animals will curl up or roll into a ball when it's cold.
9 Carol volunteered to help children with learning difficulties.
10 Nicola chuckled softly to herself and then lapsed into silence.
11 Please familiarise yourselves with all the rules and regulations.
12 Michael has the ability to tackle problems from unusual angles.
13 Lesley published a collection of scholarly articles on linguistics.
14 The walls of the local library were lined with black steel shelves.
15 It was a cold-blooded killing of a defenceless eleven-year-old girl.
16 The old building was badly damaged and subsequently demolished.
17 Lucy felt overwhelmed with guilt for leaving her family in the lurch.
18 In this lesson the pupils will learn about the life cycle of the butterfly.
19 The council apologised for the delay in replying to Linda's complaint.
20 Dylan's accumulated wealth allowed him to live a life of luxury and leisure.

3.27.12 Dialogue

A: I'd like a little less salt and garlic in my meal next time, please.
B: Certainly. You clearly have a delicate palate.
A: I've lived for eleven years on salad and mineral water.
B: Well, that's healthy but slightly bland. Help yourself to trifle. It's delicious. It'll blow your mind!

3.28 Voiced post-alveolar approximant /r/

3.28.1 Description

Voiced post-alveolar approximant [ɹ]. With the soft palate in the raised position, the tip of the tongue approaches the rear of the alveolar ridge, but doesn't get close enough to cause turbulence. The centre of the tongue is lowered, giving rise to the distinct hollowing of the tongue characteristic of /r/, and the sides are held in contact with the upper back teeth. Weak lip-rounding is also frequently present.

3.28.2 Spelling

<r> rich, horizon, very
<rr> terrific, carrot, worry, error
<wr> wrap, write, wrong, playwright
<rh> rhyme, rhubarb, rhotic, rhythm, rhapsody, rhinoceros

Note that <r> is silent in *iron, aren't, weren't.*

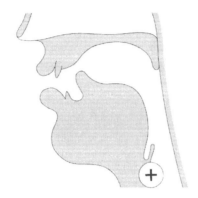

Figure 3.26 English /r/.

3.28.3 Word-initial

rabbit, radio, rain, raise, random, rare, rate, rather, reach, read, ready, reason, receive, recent, recover, red, reduce, refer, reflection, region, regret, regular, relative, relax, release, relief, rely, remember, remind, remove, rent, repeat, report, resign, respect, rest, result, retire, return, revenge, reverse, reward, rice, rich, ride, right, ring, river, road, rob, roll/role, roof, room, rope, rose, rough, round, rule, run, race, rack, recipe, reckon, rhyme, ribbon, rigid, ripe, root, rub, rude, rug, rush

3.28.4 Word-medial

appearance, area, arid, arrange, arrest, arrive, arrogant, arrow, barrier, berry/bury, boring, borrow, career, carrot, carry, cereal, charity, cherry, correct, curry, diary, encourage, error, ferry, flourish, foreign, forest, forever, guarantee, hero, horizon, horror, hurry, jury, marry, merry, mirror, narrow, orange, parent, parrot, safari, scary, series, sorry, story, terrific, terror, worry, afraid, agree, corridor, corrupt, giraffe, hungry, kangaroo, lorry, miracle, parade, parallel, perish, weary

3.28.5 Devoiced/fricative

precious, present (n.), press, pretty, price, pride, print, prison, prize, problem, profit, promise, proof, proper, practice, pray, crab, crack, craft, crash, cream, crease, credit, creep, crew, crime, crisis, critic, cross, crowd, crude, crumb, cry, crystal

3.28.6 Phonetic affricates /tr dr/

trace, track, trade, traffic, tragic, trail, train, traitor, tram, tramp, trance, trap, trauma, travel, trawl, tray, tread, treason, treasure, treat, tree, trek, trench, trend, tribe, trick, trim, trip, trolley, trophy, trouble, trousers, true, trunk, trust, truth, try, attract, betray, nutrition, patrol
draft, drag, dragon, drain, draw, dread, dream, dress, dribble, drill, drink, drip, drive, drone, drop, drown, drug, drum, dry, address

3.28.7 Multiple

abracadabra, appropriate, aristocrat, bridegroom, characteristic, dreary, fragrant, frustration, grapefruit, paragraph, primary, program, progress (n.), raindrop, rarity, rearrange, recruit, referee, regret, represent, strawberry

3.28.8 Phrases

reach an agreement, a practical approach, an area of interest, an arrest warrant, a broken arrow, break through a barrier, fresh bread, a breath of fresh air, a railway bridge, a promising career, red cherries, bribery and corruption, provoke criticism, correct an error, remain friends, ripe fruit, room for improvement, raw materials, proud parents, the root of the problem, a progress report, private property, a roof rack, torrential rain, on the road to recovery, fear of rejection, friends and relations, rest and relaxation, a rude remark, repeated requests, pioneering research, in every respect, recently restored, a rough ride, run a risk, red roses, rural surroundings, a reign of terror

3.28.9 Sentences

1   What was the real reason for the break-up of their marriage?
2   We reserve the right to refuse unreasonable requests.
3   Margaret bore a striking resemblance to her mother and brother.
4   Gerry refused to sacrifice his principles to improve his prospects.
5   Their receptionist was unprofessional, arrogant and downright rude.
6   Brian's on the road to recovery after suffering a serious brain injury.
7   Fear of rejection can result in very destructive behavioural problems.
8   The Central Library's recently been restored to its original appearance.
9   Throughout her career Harriet was troubled by moral and religious scruples.
10   The respondents had to rank their favourite beverages in order of preference.
11   Terry drew up a strategy for the recovery and growth of the region's industry.
12   Controlled experiments should preferably be carried out by trained researchers.
13   Reading improves children's comprehension, vocabulary, grammar and writing.
14   We browsed through the free travel brochures for countries in Central America.
15   There was a dramatic decrease in the number of residents with a graduate degree.
16   I'm intrigued by the story of Andrew's heroic struggle to provide for his offspring.
17   My parents are from Russia, and we can trace our roots through several generations.
18   Contrary to the predictions, the interest rates have risen during the period under review.
19   Lawrence hurried out of the room amid a chorus of protest from the angry unruly crowd.
20   The results of Roger's research and his recommendations are summarised in a brief report.

3.28.10 Dialogue

A: Is it right or wrong to use intrusive /r/ in English?
B: Is it really a matter of right or wrong? You very frequently hear it in the media and on radio.
A: Should foreign learners practise such pronunciations?
B: It's probably not very important to try to either avoid or imitate intrusive /r/. Foreign learners generally have more pressing pronunciation problems to worry about.

3.28.11 Distribution of /r/

GB is a non-rhotic accent, which means /r/ isn't pronounced before a consonant or a pause, e.g. *card*, *car* (sections 2.14.7 and 5.4). However, /r/ is sounded before a vowel, both within the word (e.g. *very*, *red*) and across a word boundary (termed /r/-liaison), as in *four apples* (see section 12.4). In the sections below, the occurrences of <r> that are not pronounced have been crossed out.

3.28.12 <r> in different contexts

the te~~r~~ms of an agreement, an area of conce~~r~~n, the fi~~r~~st to arrive, bedroom fu~~r~~nitu~~r~~e, junipe~~r~~ berries, squa~~r~~e brackets, bread and butte~~r~~, break down in tea~~r~~s, sho~~r~~t of breath, bricks and mo~~r~~ta~~r~~, da~~r~~k brown, a charity wo~~r~~ke~~r~~, ca~~r~~eful consideration, a contradiction in te~~r~~ms, gove~~r~~n a country, a~~r~~ts and crafts, sta~~r~~t a craze, sou~~r~~ cream, a sou~~r~~ce of disagreement, a jou~~r~~ney of discovery, a ma~~r~~gin of erro~~r~~, free of cha~~r~~ge, an a~~r~~t gallery, pu~~r~~ple grapes, ha~~r~~d of hearing, pee~~r~~ pressure, wo~~r~~k in progress, wa~~r~~m rega~~r~~ds, ma~~r~~ket resea~~r~~ch, a ma~~r~~k of respect, a rose ga~~r~~den, a pie~~r~~cing scream, tea~~r~~s of sorrow

3.28.13 Sentences

In the following sentences the letter <r> is pronounced in some cases and not in others.

1 Robe~~r~~t's red hai~~r~~ was smea~~r~~ed with grease.
2 The newspape~~r~~s a~~r~~e distributed free of cha~~r~~ge.
3 This mo~~r~~ning we reaped the fi~~r~~st fruits of ou~~r~~ labou~~r~~.
4 We hea~~r~~d a crack of thunde~~r~~ before it sta~~r~~ted pouring.
5 Afte~~r~~ the wa~~r~~, the chu~~r~~ch was resto~~r~~ed to its fo~~r~~me~~r~~ glory.
6 Unfo~~r~~tunately, Carol's ca~~r~~ brakes a~~r~~en't wo~~r~~king prope~~r~~ly.
7 Teenage~~r~~s a~~r~~e frequently vulnerable to pee~~r~~ group pressu~~r~~e.
8 Gregory igno~~r~~ed Pete~~r~~'s ha~~r~~sh rema~~r~~ks and wo~~r~~ds of reproach.
9 Carol was the fi~~r~~st to arrive and sta~~r~~t wa~~r~~ming up fo~~r~~ he~~r~~ wo~~r~~kout.
10 Cha~~r~~lotte's a fiery redhead, and Eleano~~r~~ has naturally da~~r~~k brown hai~~r~~.
11 This repo~~r~~t provides fu~~r~~ther info~~r~~mation on current resea~~r~~ch in literacy.
12 The wo~~r~~kshop was a true jou~~r~~ney of discovery for everyone conce~~r~~ned.
13 Pe~~r~~cy agreed to be Mary's bridge pa~~r~~tner at the tou~~r~~nament on Thu~~r~~sday.
14 Erica cried tea~~r~~s of relief when she lea~~r~~ned that he~~r~~ daughte~~r~~ was unha~~r~~med.
15 This playe~~r~~ has an incredible ene~~r~~gy and eno~~r~~mous powe~~r~~s of concentration.
16 The~~r~~e was a tremendous variety of mushrooms unde~~r~~ the gna~~r~~led roots of the tree.
17 The~~r~~e's no guarantee that the eme~~r~~gency measu~~r~~es will produce the desi~~r~~ed result.
18 Catherine ado~~r~~es ga~~r~~dening and is pa~~r~~ticularly proud of he~~r~~ wonde~~r~~ful rose ga~~r~~den.
19 We've experienced unfo~~r~~eseen problems and don't have the resou~~r~~ces to ove~~r~~come them.
20 We stress that ou~~r~~ primary conce~~r~~n is fo~~r~~ the welfa~~r~~e of the children who are entrusted to ou~~r~~ ca~~r~~e.

3.29 Silent letters

In the sections above you have practised making the 24 consonants found in GB. For each consonant we have shown the typical spellings. However, as you will have seen, English has quite a lot of silent letters. Below we have provided a range of examples of phrases and sentences containing silent letters. Consult the website for phonemic transcriptions.

3.29.1 Phrases containing silent letters (shown in bold-faced type)

an **exh**austing climb, like lam**b**s to the slaug**h**ter, foreign de**b**t, a slig**h**t doubt, ascending clim**b**ers, listen in fascination, cal**f** muscles, roug**h**ly aligned, a toug**h** assignment, the rig**h**tful **h**eir, a dou**b**tful **h**onour, eig**h**t **h**ours, **wh**eeled vehicles, **k**nead doug**h**, brig**h**t lig**h**ts, throug**h**-out the nig**h**t, rig**h**t and **w**rong, human rig**h**ts campaigners, a resigned sig**h**, a g**h**astly sig**h**t, **wh**olesale slaug**h**ter, lig**h**t weig**h**t, half an **h**our, a de**b**t to other **w**riters, spag**h**etti Bolognese, broug**h**t up in a g**h**etto, a **g**nawing doubt, a half r**h**yme, thig**h** muscles, **wh**isk egg **wh**ites, designed by an arc**h**itect, a **wh**ite C**h**ristmas, the reig**n**ing monarch, **wh**et a **k**nife, answer a **k**nock at the door, a tig**h**t **k**not, a chal**k** drawing, **w**rite a colum**n**, fasten tig**h**tly

3.29.2 Sentences containing silent letters (shown in bold-faced type)

1   Fasten your belt tig**h**tly.
2   R**h**ys was only half conscious.
3   Two **w**rongs don't make a rig**h**t.
4   She answered a **k**nock at the door.
5   I owe a great de**b**t to other **w**riters.
6   Leah's always so hig**h** and mig**h**ty.
7   **Wh**o cooked this delig**h**tful ragout?
8   You **k**now **wh**at I'm talking about!
9   The sea was strewn with **w**reckage.
10   They boug**h**t doug**h**nuts in Brig**h**ton.
11   Hug**h** is a human rig**h**ts campaigner.
12   Hanna**h** gave me the thum**b**s-up sign.
13   She does all the talking – I just listen.
14   My rig**h**t leg was num**b** from **k**neeling.
15   When are you off to the Isle of **W**ight?
16   She taug**h**t my eig**h**t-year-old daug**h**ter.
17   The weig**h**t of slaug**h**tered lam**b**s varies.
18   Priscilla **k**new she had rig**h**t on her side.
19   I could hear him coug**h**ing and **wh**eezing.
20   Honestly, it's too subtle to be worth**wh**ile.
21   Shepherd's pie should be made with lam**b**.
22   We have a buffet breakfast in half an **h**our.
23   She has really **w**rinkly palms and **k**nuckles.
24   We caug**h**t sig**h**t of a **wh**ite **wh**ale in the sea.
25   R**h**inos are being slaug**h**tered for their horns.
26   The g**h**ost is said to haunt the castle at nig**h**t.
27   Noa**h** had lost multiple lim**b**s in bom**b** blasts.
28   He couldn't cut throug**h** the **g**narled tree trunk.
29   She couldn't stand the sig**h**t of garden **g**nomes.
30   The **p**sychologist **w**restled with his conscience.

31   He couldn't answer two of the eight questions.
32   She was brought up in a ghetto in Birmingham.
33   He was asthmatic and often coughed up phlegm.
34   The scent of a calm autumn's night filled the air.
35   He sang a solemn hymn and then knelt in prayer.
36   Whisk the egg whites and add them to the dough.
37   Sarah usually wrote down her thoughts in rhyme.
38   Rhonda's teeth were white and perfectly straight.
39   I have a grade two injury in my right calf muscle.
40   I baulked at the thought of walking alone at night.
41   I'm writing an assignment on the history of ballet.
42   He acknowledged receipt of the written comments.
43   The frame of a vehicle's also known as the chassis.
44   The kids had a straightforward spaghetti Bolognese.
45   He finished without the slightest sign of exhaustion.
46   D'you know if the raspberry jam's in the cupboard?
47   Swords made of iron appear from the Early Iron Age.
48   She was frightened of being stalked by unknown men.
49   Louis wore the khaki beret he bought in Rhode Island.
50   Dwight is a lightweight boxer who comes from Berwick.
51   My thighs and knees still ached so I couldn't go climbing.
52   The bride walked down the aisle carrying a white bouquet.
53   Mr Walker didn't have the slightest doubt that he was right.
54   Hugh caught pneumonia during his trip to the Faroe Islands.
55   Mr Hughes wrote it as a ghostwriter on behalf of a celebrity.
56   The bread was made from white and wholemeal wheat flour.
57   Wrap the bouquet tightly in newspaper and leave it overnight.
58   Noah walked from Norwich in Norfolk to Dunwich in Suffolk.
59   He did the graphic design of the catalogues for the two exhibitions.
60   His eyes glistened in anger but softened at the sight of his daughter.
61   He wholeheartedly condemns foreign interference in Ghana's affairs.
62   These four-wheeled vehicles are designed for trekking through rough terrain.

Chapter 4

Practice

Consonant contrasts

This chapter provides practice in distinguishing between pairs of consonants which learners tend to confuse. The exercise material includes minimal pairs demonstrating the contrast in word-initial, word-medial and word-final positions, and words, phrases and sentences containing both sounds. The numbers in the table indicate the sections containing the contrasts.

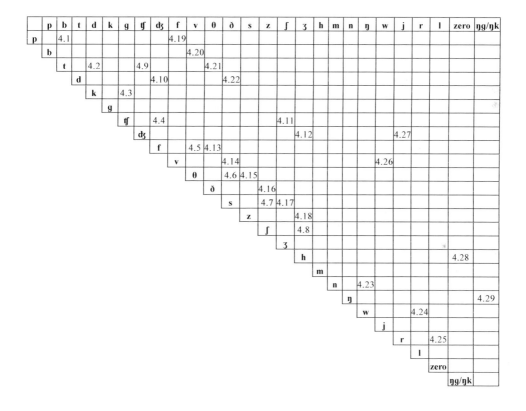

	p	b	t	d	k	g	ʧ	ʤ	f	v	θ	ð	s	z	ʃ	ʒ	h	m	n	ŋ	w	j	r	l	zero	ŋg/ŋk
p	p	4.1							4.19																	
b		b								4.20																
t			t	4.2			4.9				4.21															
d				d				4.10				4.22														
k					k	4.3																				
g						g																				
ʧ							ʧ	4.4							4.11											
ʤ								ʤ								4.12						4.27				
f									f	4.5	4.13															
v										v		4.14									4.26					
θ											θ	4.6	4.15													
ð												ð		4.16												
s													s	4.7	4.17											
z														z		4.18										
ʃ															ʃ	4.8										
ʒ																ʒ										
h																	h						4.28			
m																		m								
n																			n	4.23						
ŋ																				ŋ						4.29
w																					w	4.24				
j																						j				
r																							r	4.25		
l																								l		
zero																									zero	
ŋg/ŋk																										ŋg/ŋk

4.1 Voiceless bilabial plosive /p/ vs. voiced bilabial plosive /b/

4.1.1 Minimal pairs

a) *Word-initial*

pack/back, pad/bad, pair/bare, palm/balm, pan/ban, park/bark, pat/bat, patch/batch, path/bath, paw/bore, pawn/born, pay/bay, pea/bee, peach/beach, peak/beak, peg/beg, pest/best, pet/bet, pie/buy, pig/big, pill/bill, pin/bin, pit/bit, pole/bowl, port/bought, post/boast, pride/bride, pull/bull, pump/bump, punch/bunch, push/bush

b) *Word-final*

cap/cab, cup/cub, hop/hob, lap/lab, mop/mob, nip/nib, rip/rib, pup/pub, rope/robe, slap/slab, swap/swab, tap/tab, tripe/tribe

c) *Word-medial*

ample/amble, crumple/crumble, dapple/dabble, nipple/nibble, rapid/rabid, simple/symbol, staple/stable, repel/rebel (v.)

4.1.2 Words with /p/ and /b/

acceptable, capable, clipboard, culpable, disposable, hipbone, incapable, paintbrush, paperback, pebble, placebo, playboy, portable, possible, postbox, powerboat, probe, problem, prohibit, proverb, pub, public, publish, punchbag, scrapbook, superb, abrupt, bishop, backpack, backup, battleship, beep, blueprint, bookshop, bump, burp, subgroup, webpage

4.1.3 Phrases

a humble apology, a baseball cap, a broken cup, a bunch of grapes, a park bench, a birthday party, a bus pass, a bald patch, bits and pieces, break a promise, the push of a button, sleep like a baby, a bus stop, back pain, a paper bag, a picnic basket, a bird of prey, pitch black, deep blue, a paperback book, a proper job, pipe tobacco, a copper tube

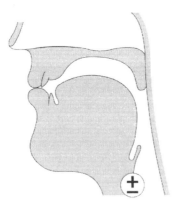

Figure 4.1 English /p/ and /b/ (hold stage).

4.1.4 Sentences

1 Pete's behaviour's simply beneath contempt.
2 Belinda responded with a barely audible whisper.
3 Patrick bought bananas, pears and a bunch of grapes.
4 This report's based on people's subjective experiences.
5 My husband's mobility has improved by leaps and bounds.
6 Reasonable expenses will be reimbursed by your employer.
7 Belinda dabbed some perfume on her temples and collarbone.
8 The company embarked on a programme to help the disabled.
9 Would you prefer baked or boiled potatoes with your pork chops?
10 This appealing book bears the unmistakable stamp of personal observation.

4.2 Voiceless alveolar plosive /t/ vs. voiced alveolar plosive /d/

4.2.1 Minimal pairs

a) Word-initial

tail/dale, tame/dame, tangle/dangle, tank/dank, tart/dart, taunt/daunt, tear (rip)/dare, tear (from the eye)/dear, ten/den, tense/dense, tie/die, time/dime, tin/din, tip/dip, tire/dire, toe/dough, tomb/doom, ton/done, two/do, torn/dawn, town/down, train/drain, trawl/drawl, tread/dread, trench/drench, trip/drip, trout/drought, trudge/drudge, true/drew, trunk/drunk, try/dry, tuck/duck, tusk/dusk

b) Word-final

bat/bad, beat/bead, bent/bend, bet/bed, bit/bid, bolt/bold, bought/bored, bright/bride, brought/broad, built/build, cart/card, caught/cord, coat/code, cot/cod, debt/dead, eight/aid, fate/fade, feet/feed, fought/ford, fright/fried, great/grade, greet/greed, grit/grid, hat/had, heart/hard, height/hide, hit/hid, hurt/heard, knot/nod, lent/lend, light/lied, mate/made, mat/mad, ought/awed, pat/pad, plate/played, rate/raid, right/ride, root/rude, rot/rod, sat/sad, seat/seed, sent/send, set/said, sight/side, slight/slide, slit/slid, sort/sword, spent/spend, squat/squad, tent/tend, tight/tide, thought/thawed,

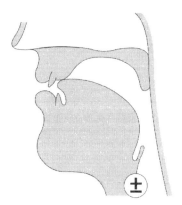

Figure 4.2 English /t/ and /d/ (hold stage).

threat/thread, wait/wade, want/wand, wheat/weed, white/wide, write/ride, wrote/road

c)   ***Word-medial***

centre/sender, title/tidal, traitor/trader, bitter/bidder, greater/grader, hurtle/hurdle, kitty/kiddy, latter/ladder, maternity/modernity, litre/leader, matter/madder, metal/medal, otter/odder, petal/pedal, shutter/shudder, utter/udder, water/warder, whiten/widen, writer/rider

4.2.2 Words with /t/ and /d/

attitude, antidote, astounding, attend, contend, contradict, devoted, gratitude, instead, intend, introduce, leotard, meltdown, standard, tap-dance, teardrop, teddy, tedious, tide, tidy, timid, tired, toad, today, trade, tradition, accident, adult, bandit, bloodshot, dart, data, date, daughter, debt, decent, decorate, defeat, delicate, delight, dent, dentist, department, detail, determined, devoted, dictator, diet, dirty, disaster, distant, donate, dot, doubt, dust, edit, idiot, modest

4.2.3 Phrases

a dinner table, a sad tale, a team leader, crocodile tears, tooth decay, dead tired, from head to toe, garden tools, a court order, today's date, as fit as a fiddle, a fruit salad, neat and tidy, a red carpet, bread and butter, drinking water, a dead-end street, a cloud of dust, a reading list, the dim and distant past, get out of bed, an identity card, a gifted child, a tap dancer, at a later date, day and night, sit at a desk, attention to detail, a dinner party, a bitter divorce, cast a shadow, wit and wisdom

4.2.4 Sentences

1   The two methods yielded identical results.
2   After dinner we headed to the historic city centre.
3   My elder sister's as blind as a bat and as deaf as a doorpost.
4   It happened in the dim and distant past and is best forgotten.
5   The leadership team decided to treat it as an isolated incident.
6   What's the difference between word stress and sentence stress?
7   Katie and her husband, Peter, are in the middle of a bitter divorce.
8   Hundreds of students have benefited from Derek's wit and wisdom.
9   Donald did a master's degree in statistics at the University of Sheffield.
10 For breakfast we were served a delicious fruit salad, home-made bread and hot tea.

4.3 Voiceless velar plosive /k/ vs. voiced velar plosive /g/

4.3.1 Minimal pairs

a)   ***Word-initial***

cage/gauge, calorie/gallery, came/game, cane/gain, cap/gap, card/guard, cause/gauze, cave/gave, class/glass, clue/glue, coal/goal, coast/ghost, coat/goat, cold/gold, come/gum, cot/got, could/good, crab/grab, craft/graft, crane/grain, crate/great, crave/

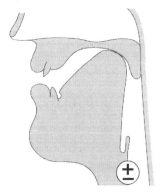

Figure 4.3 English /k/ and /g/ (hold stage).

grave, crease/grease, crew/grew, crime/grime, crow/grow, crumble/grumble, curl/ girl

b)   *Word-final*

back/bag, buck/bug, clock/clog, dock/dog, duck/dug, knack/nag, leak/league, lock/log, muck/mug, peck/peg, pick/pig, pluck/plug, rack/rag, sack/sag, snack/snag, stack/ stag, tack/tag, tuck/tug, wick/wig

c)   *Word-medial*

anchor/anger, ankle/angle, bicker/bigger, delicate/delegate (n.), mucky/muggy, nickel/ niggle, tinkle/tingle, vicar/vigour, decree/degree

4.3.2 Words with /k/ and /g/

backgammon, backlog, cardigan, cargo, catalogue, cog, colleague, congratulate, foxglove, kangaroo, keg, kilogram, recognise, agriculture, eggcup, exact, exotic, galaxy, garlic, geek, gherkin, graphic, magnetic, neglect, organic

4.3.3 Phrases

gain confidence, forget to ask, a dog basket, a card game, close together, a mug of coffee, regular contact, a golf course, hugs and kisses, beginner's luck, a gap in the market, a rock garden, a closely guarded secret, work in progress, a weak argument, a stomach bug, a duck egg, key figures, sticky fingers, computer games, a gas leak, a security guard, a lucky guess, kind regards, a catchy slogan, sugar cubes

4.3.4 Sentences

1   Agnes just scraped through her chemistry exam.
2   Gary caught a glimpse of the cat burglar in action.
3   The candidates must have a good command of English.
4   We recommend the guided walk through the botanical gardens.
5   She picked up a copy of a yoga magazine at the local supermarket.
6   Gwen was commissioned to think of a catchy slogan for the golf club.

7   Keith compiled a comprehensive bibliography in cognitive linguistics.
8   I've been asked to give a lecture at the School of Agriculture in August.
9   Chris comported himself with great dignity and integrity during the crisis.
10   Secret negotiations were conducted between the kidnappers and the government.

4.4 Voiceless palato-alveolar affricate /ʧ/ vs. voiced palato-alveolar affricate /ʤ/

4.4.1 Minimal pairs

a)   Word-initial
chain/Jane, char/jar, cheer/jeer, cheese/Gs, cherry/jerry, chess/Jess, chest/jest, Chester/
    jester, chew/Jew, chin/gin, chive/jive, choice/Joyce, choke/joke, chore/jaw, chunk/junk

b)   Word-final
batch/badge, cinch/singe, etch/edge, aitch/age, larch/large, lunch/lunge, march/Marge,
    match/Madge, perch/purge, retch/Reg, rich/ridge, search/surge

c)   Word-medial
lecher/ledger

4.4.2 Words with /ʧ/ and /ʤ/

challenge, charge, congestion, conjecture, digestion, gesture, stagecoach, suggestion

4.4.3 Phrases

a cheerful subject, a branch manager, a cabbage patch, a challenging question, a champion jockey, a change of strategy, a charming cottage, the chief surgeon, a coach journey,
a college lecturer, cultural heritage, a digital watch, a gentle touch, a huge challenge, a
huge statue, a job search, a juicy cherry, a large batch, a major change, a strange mixture,
cottage cheese, free-range chicken, Punch and Judy, broach a subject, capture the imagination, change the subject, check your luggage, choose a jury, join in the chase, launch
a project

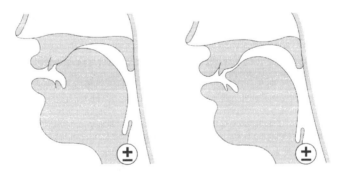

Figure 4.4 English /ʧ/ and /ʤ/. Left: hold stage. Right: release with homorganic friction. Note
    trumpet-shaped lip-rounding.

4.4.4 Sentences

1 Richard's major subject's cultural anthropology.
2 Jeff was a branch manager for a regional furniture chain.
3 Jim wouldn't budge an inch until Charlie had apologised.
4 They launched a research project on agricultural drainage.
5 The teenagers were charged with cheating in a geography project.
6 Gemma has a thatched cottage in a picturesque village in Cheshire.
7 We checked in our luggage and then trudged to the departure lounge.
8 Judith cringed when she approached the torture chambers and dungeons.
9 There was a large beech hedge around the vegetable patch and the charming orange orchard.
10 Joe indulged in a chicken and spinach sandwich while Gina munched on the juicy sumptuous cherries.

4.5 Voiceless labio-dental fricative /f/ vs. voiced labio-dental fricative /v/

4.5.1 Minimal pairs

a) **Word-initial**
fairy/vary, fail/veil, fan/van, fast/vast, fat/vat, fault/vault, fear/veer, fee/V, ferry/very, feud/viewed, few/view, fewer/viewer, figure/vigour, file/vile, fine/vine, fuse/views, final/vinyl

b) **Word-final**
belief/believe, calf/calve, grief/grieve, half/halve, leaf/leave, life/live (adj.), off/of, proof/prove, relief/relieve, safe/save, shelf/shelve, staff/starve, strife/strive, surf/serve, thief/thieve

c) **Word-medial**
deafen/Devon, infantry/inventory, reference/reverence, rifle/rival, safer/saver, shuffle/shovel, sniffle/snivel, surface/service, confection/convection, defied/divide, defies/devise, define/divine, infest/invest, refuse/reviews, wafer/waiver

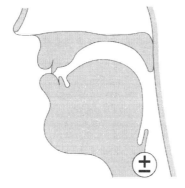

Figure 4.5 English /f/ and /v/.

4.5.2 Words with /f/ and /v/

aftershave, defective, defensive, definitive, effective, favour, festive, fever, five, flavour, forever, forgive, leftover, offensive, hovercraft, overdraft, overflow (v.), verify

4.5.3 Phrases

family values, a grave face, feel very faint, a devoted fan, live in fear, a moveable feast, viewing figures, wave a flag, reveal a flaw, invest in the future, a carving knife, living proof, a vast difference, a valiant effort, a gift voucher, an attractive offer, free advice, a safe alternative, a fascinating conversation, drive carefully, full of flavour, a love affair, a fast-flowing river, at face value, perfect vision

4.5.4 Sentences

1 Frank's funeral service was very moving.
2 It's November, and the leaves are falling fast.
3 My friend Valerie finally finished her first novel.
4 It's a fascinating film about love and forgiveness.
5 We deliver fresh fruit and vegetables in refrigerated vans.
6 My boyfriend and I visited the dolphins on Friday evening.
7 The university professors eventually resolved their conflict.
8 It definitely isn't difficult to find vegetarian food in Vietnam.
9 Phil vented his frustration at their failure to develop an effective vaccine.
10 It was painfully obvious to everyone that Phoebe had given false evidence.

4.6 Voiceless dental fricative /θ/ vs. voiced dental fricative /ð/

4.6.1 Minimal pairs

a) *Word-initial*
      thigh/thy
b) *Word-final*
      loath/loathe, mouth (n.)/mouth (v.), wreath/wreathe, sheath/sheathe, teeth/teethe

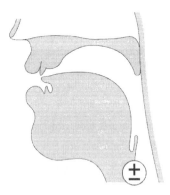

Figure 4.6 English /θ/ and /ð/.

4.6.2 Phrases

gather strength, breathe through your mouth, threaten to withdraw, without further thought, rather pathetic, further south, gather your thoughts

4.6.3 Sentences

1   Matthew and his grandfather withdrew from the throng.
2   Pleather's a type of synthetic leather made of polyethylene.
3   Without further thought Dorothy ruthlessly threw out all her clothes.
4   Catherine made a healthy smoothie to soothe Elspeth's throbbing throat.
5   Edith gathered the strength to tell Martha the truth about her father's death.
6   The three of us loathed his pathetic blather about the ethics of youth athletics.
7   Further north a path threads its way through a wealth of heather-covered heath.
8   It's healthiest to breathe in through the nose and to breathe out through the mouth.
9   It's her mother's seventieth and her brother's thirty-fifth birthday on the thirteenth.
10   That godfather of yours is economical with the truth; in fact, he lies through his teeth.

4.7 Voiceless alveolar fricative /s/ vs. voiced alveolar fricative /z/

4.7.1 Minimal pairs

a)   *Word-initial*
said/Z, sink/zinc, sip/zip, sown/zone, sue/zoo, sack/Zack

b)   *Word-final*
abuse (n.)/abuse (v.), advice/advise, bus/buzz, cease/seize, close (adj.)/close (v.), course/ cause, device/devise, diffuse (adj.)/diffuse (v.), dose/doze, excuse (n.)/excuse (v.), face/phase, fuss/fuzz, grace/graze, hearse/hers, hiss/his, house (n.)/house (v.), loose/ lose, price/prize, race/raise, rice/rise, use (n.)/use (v.)

c)   *Word-medial*
looser/loser, muscle/muzzle, precedent/president

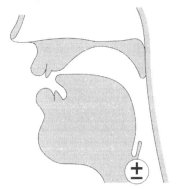 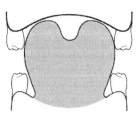

Figure 4.7 Left: English /s/ and /z/. Right: mouth viewed from the front showing grooved tongue shape.

4.7.2 Words with /s/ and /z/

Caesar, capsize, centralise, citizen, chastise, criticise, customise, despise, disclose, dispose, downstairs, emphasise, exercise, fantasise, missus, salesman, scales, scissors, season, seize, series, size, sneeze, snooze, sometimes, squeeze, summarise, supervise, surprise, business, cosmos, disaster, possess, residence, resist, zealous, zest

4.7.3 Phrases

easy access, a surprise announcement, cheese and biscuits, a blessing in disguise, a prison cell, deserve a chance, a wise choice, a cause for concern, hazard a guess, repossess a house, a recipe for disaster, a poisonous snake, ease of use, a serious accusation, a fierce blaze, a silk blouse, a sea breeze, Swiss cheese, cross a desert, a basic design, a strong desire, a contagious disease, pass an exam, a jealous husband, a jazz singer, a famous phrase, past and present, a jigsaw puzzle, the voice of reason, powerless to resist, a massive rise, different shapes and sizes, a crystal vase

4.7.4 Sentences

1   This mysterious disease spreads easily.
2   Steve raised his glass to propose a toast.
3   Zoe listens to classical music for relaxation.
4   This was my first tantalising glimpse of the islands.
5   James seized the chance to present his ideas to his boss.
6   The rise in taxes caused widespread resentment among investors.
7   Sebastian still hasn't paused to consider the reasons for these rules.
8   Zack suffered serious cuts and bruises after the accident last Thursday.
9   The owners were at pains to stress that there were no plans to close the restaurant.
10   The lecturers and students expressed surprise at the news of the dean's resignation.

4.8 Voiceless palato-alveolar fricative /ʃ/ vs. voiced palato-alveolar fricative /ʒ/

4.8.1 Minimal pairs

Aleutian/allusion, Confucian/confusion, dilution/delusion

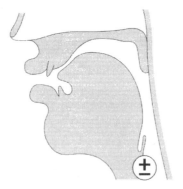

Figure 4.8 English /ʃ/ and /ʒ/. Note trumpet-shaped lip-rounding.

4.8.2 Phrases

a partial closure, a rash decision, a foolish delusion, social divisions, a population explosion, radiation exposure, an occasional flash, a special measure, malicious pleasure, a special regime, an unusual shape, national television, a national treasure, a special occasion

4.8.3 Sentences

1   This collection's a national treasure.
2   Elision's the deletion or omission of a sound.
3   The Caucasian patient was rushed to casualty.
4   Make a donation in celebration of a special occasion.
5   Overfishing led to the partial closure of the recreation area.
6   The conclusion is that education and working conditions are crucial.
7   The justification of this action was the prevention of sabotage and espionage.
8   There was substantial opposition to the introduction of commercial television.
9   The revision included the provision of information on legislation and regulations.
10 Schadenfreude is the satisfaction or malicious pleasure felt at somebody else's hardship.

4.9 Voiceless alveolar plosive /t/ vs. voiceless palato-alveolar affricate /ʧ/

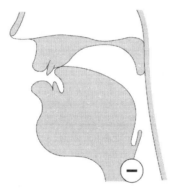

Figure 4.9 English /t/ (hold stage).

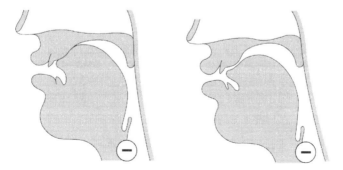

Figure 4.10 English /ʧ/. Left: hold stage. Right: release with homorganic friction. Note trumpet-shaped lip-rounding.

4.9.1 Minimal pairs

a)   *Word-initial*
   talk/chalk, tap/chap, tart/chart, tatty/chatty, tear (rip)/chair, tear (from the eye)/cheer, tease/cheese, test/chest, tick/chick, till/chill, tin/chin, tip/chip, toes/chose, two/ chew, top/chop, tore/chore

b)   *Word-final*
   art/arch, bat/batch, beat/beach, belt/belch, bent/bench, bit/bitch, cat/catch, coat/coach, eat/each, hat/hatch, hit/hitch, hut/hutch, it/itch, knot/notch, mat/match, pat/patch, pit/pitch, port/porch, rent/wrench, start/starch, taught/torch, what/watch, wit/which

c)   *Word-medial*
   artery/archery, jester/gesture

4.9.2 Words with /t/ and /tʃ/

artichoke, attach, teacher, touch, statue, stitch, stench, torch, torture, twitch, chant, chapter, chariot, charity, chart, chat, cheat, cheetah, chest, futuristic, merchant, ratchet

4.9.3 Phrases

kitchen table, a chilling tale, Chinese tea, a tennis coach, times have changed, watch your tongue, a beach towel, a change of heart, market research, a charming cottage, pitch a tent, a stretch of coast, a gift voucher, a witch hunt, a safety catch, a chain of events, cheese on toast, hot chocolate, an irritating itch, attend a lecture, a nasty scratch, a satirical sketch, get in touch

4.9.4 Sentences

   1   Ted can't stop scratching that irritating itch on his chest.
   2   We got tickets to watch a football match in Ipswich last March.
   3   If you've got any questions, don't hesitate to get in touch with Rachel.
   4   Archie got two bottles of water to quench his thirst in the scorching heat.
   5   Unfortunately the chief of staff didn't understand the gravity of the situation.
   6   The team coach stressed the importance of a culture based on mutual respect.
   7   Charles was appointed as a research assistant at the University of Manchester.
   8   The concepts and facts from each chapter were checked in a multiple choice test.
   9   Richard's lecture entitled 'Climate Challenges in the Twenty-first Century' was fascinating.
   10 That stupid teacher watched the children snatching my daughter's toys without interfering.

4.10 Voiced alveolar plosive /d/ vs. voiced palato-alveolar affricate /dʒ/

4.10.1 Minimal pairs

a)   *Word-initial*
   dab/jab, dam/jam, day/jay, dear/jeer, debt/jet, dental/gentle, din/gin, dog/jog, door/jaw, dust/just, dot/jot, dug/jug, dump/jump

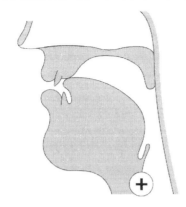

Figure 4.11 English /t/ (hold stage).

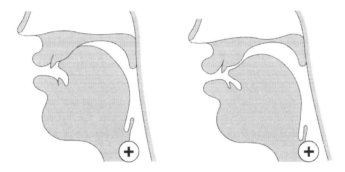

Figure 4.12 English /ʤ/. Left: hold stage. Right: release with homorganic friction. Note trumpet-shaped lip-rounding.

b) **Word-final**
    aid/age, bad/badge, chained/change, head/hedge, lard/large, lead (metal)/ledge, paid/
        page, posted/postage, raid/rage, rid/ridge, wade/wage
c) **Word-medial**
    murder/merger, buddy/budgie

4.10.2 Words with /d/ and /ʤ/

adage, advantage, appendage, bandage, bondage, damage, danger, dejected, deluge, deranged, detergent, didgeridoo, digest (v.), digit, dirge, diligent, discourage, diverge, dodge, dungeon, indulge, prodigy, agenda, frigid, gender, gingerbread, jackdaw, jade, jeopardy, judo, legend, rigid, tragedy

4.10.3 Phrases

a tragic accident, an adoption agency, a huge advantage, a prestigious award, a ginger beard, board and lodging, body language, this day and age, encourage debate, a voyage of discovery, flood damage, food shortage, a holiday cottage, a change of mood, a range of products, old age, a hidden agenda, a food allergy, build a bridge, change your mind, a vivid image, bread and jam, traditional jazz, a dirty job, a dead language, a sudden urge

4.10.4 Sentences

1   Jill's daughter's studying modern languages at Cambridge.
2   The older generation finds it hard to adapt to major changes.
3   The offender managed to avoid jail by pleading self-defence.
4   Jess denied all knowledge of what had happened to her lodger.
5   David's engineering project turned out to be a voyage of discovery.
6   We stayed in a delightful holiday cottage in the seaside village of Swanage.
7   Joe just couldn't understand the difference between adjectives and adverbs.
8   The original budget was exceeded by an average of a hundred pounds a day.
9   Dozens of passengers were stranded after floods damaged roads and bridges.
10 My friend Jenny was injured in a tragic road accident when she was a teenager.

4.11 Voiceless palato-alveolar affricate /ʧ/ vs. voiceless palato-alveolar fricative /ʃ/

4.11.1 Minimal pairs

a) *Word-initial*
   chair/share, chatter/shatter, cheer/sheer, cheat/sheet, cherry/sherry, chin/shin, chip/ship, chew/shoe, chop/shop, chore/shore

b) *Word-final*
   batch/bash, butch/bush, catch/cash, crutch/crush, ditch/dish, hutch/hush, latch/lash, leech/leash, march/marsh, match/mash, much/mush, watch/wash, witch/wish

4.11.2 Words with /ʧ/ and /ʃ/

archbishop, championship, cherish, childish, situation, pushchair, short-change

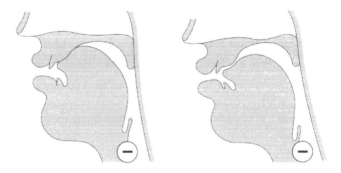

Figure 4.13 Left: hold stage of English /ʧ/. Right: the release of English /ʧ/ (with homorganic friction), identical to English /ʃ/. Note trumpet-shaped lip-rounding.

4.11.3 Phrases

boyish charm, a butcher's shop, a chain reaction, a chat show, a chip shop, a coach crash, a crucial match, culture shock, a delicious lunch, a distinguishing feature, a fresh approach, a short chat, a special feature, an English teacher, cheap champagne, fish and chips, such a shame, the finishing touch, catch a fish, launch a ship, watch a show, a charity shop, a refreshing change

4.11.4 Sentences

1   Sean's childhood shaped his future.
2   They wished to establish a branch in China.
3   The lunch special seemed suspiciously cheap.
4   The fisherman watched anxiously as the shark approached.
5   Charlie's donations to the charity shop were much appreciated.
6   The situation in Massachusetts had changed out of all recognition.
7   In March they established an association for the teaching of Dutch.
8   The British national squash championships were held in Manchester.
9   There was a short discussion on the relationship between nature and nurture.
10   Rachel put the finishing touches on her translation of the brochure into Czech.

4.12 Voiced palato-alveolar affricate /dʒ/ vs. voiced palato-alveolar fricative /ʒ/

4.12.1 Minimal pairs

lesion/legion, leisure/ledger

4.12.2 Phrases

an unusual arrangement, the logical conclusion, a majority decision, a dangerous delusion, a rigid division, a huge explosion, a gentle massage, a visual image, an emergency measure, a joyous occasion, precision engineering, a major revision

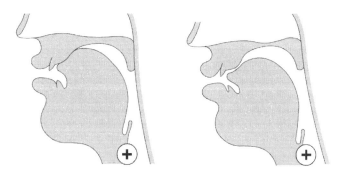

Figure 4.14 Left: hold stage of English /dʒ/. Right: the release of English /dʒ/ (with homorganic friction), identical to English /ʒ/. Note trumpet-shaped lip-rounding.

4.12.3 Sentences

1 John was injured in the explosion in June.
2 Jessica's graduation was a joyous occasion.
3 Add a generous measure of gin to the ginger ale.
4 The possessions were split with surgical precision.
5 Courgettes and aubergines are treasured vegetables.
6 I was overjoyed when a logical conclusion emerged.
7 Joe challenged the judge's decision to end supervision.
8 A strategy was needed for the diffusion of digital television.
9 Major changes generally have to start with gentle persuasion.
10 The archaeologists salvaged some of the religious treasures of Egypt.

4.13 Voiceless labio-dental fricative /f/ vs. voiceless dental fricative /θ/

4.13.1 Minimal pairs

a) *Word-initial*
      first/thirst, fin/thin, four/thaw, ford/thawed, fought/thought, Fred/thread, free/three,
          freeze/threes, frill/thrill
b) *Word-final*
      deaf/death, half/hearth, oaf/oath, roof/Ruth
c) *Word-medial*
      infuse/enthuse

4.13.2 Words with /f/ and /θ/

afterbirth, aftermath, afterthought, diphthong, facecloth, faith, filthy, footpath, fourth, free-
thinker, froth, life-and-death, monophthong, mouthful, thankful, theft, thief, thoughtful,
youthful

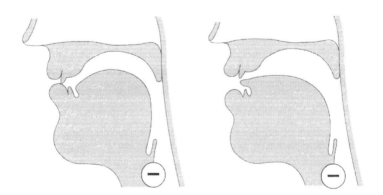

Figure 4.15 Left: English /f/. Right: English /θ/.

4.13.3 Phrases

thin fabric, a face like thunder, false enthusiasm, monthly fees, a fight to the death, fit and healthy, a thermos flask, thick fog, healthy food, lethal force, worth a fortune, a faithful friend, thick fur, going through a phase, three and a half, a thatched roof, nothing to be afraid of, a different author, twenty-first birthday, freeze to death, life on earth, farming methods, follow a path, a funny thing, thoughts and feelings, nothing to offer

4.13.4 Sentences

1   Cathy filled three thermos flasks with coffee.
2   Follow the path on the south side of the cliff.
3   This French Gothic cathedral's breathtakingly beautiful.
4   My friend Judith will perform at the theatre festival on Thursday.
5   There's a wealth of wildlife in the rainforest, from elephants to panthers.
6   His frame was thick-set and athletic, but his physical strength was failing.
7   My nephew's going through a health food phase and refuses to eat fast food.
8   Kenneth felt the author was thoroughly confused about the definition of faith.
9   Edith's stiff, arthritic fingers made it difficult for her to hold her knife and fork.
10   Keith threw the pamphlet on the floor and left the office with a face like thunder.

4.14 Voiced labio-dental fricative /v/ vs. voiced dental fricative /ð/

4.14.1 Minimal pairs

a)   *Word-initial*
     Vs/these, vale/they'll, van/than, vat/that
b)   *Word-final*
     loaves/loathes, clove/clothe
c)   *Word-medial*
     fervour/further, Ivor/either

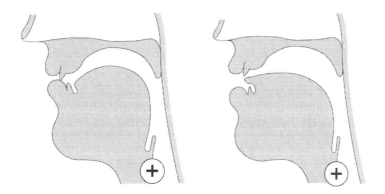

Figure 4.16 Left: English /v/. Right: English /ð/.

4.14.2 Words with /v/ and /ð/

nevertheless, themselves, weathervane

4.14.3 Phrases

breathe heavily, my beloved brother, expensive clothes, a loving father, develop a rhythm, relatively smooth, whatever the weather, with approval, rather clever, a smooth curve, leather gloves, further investment, absent without leave, soothe your nerves, a smooth shave, a worthy victory, protective clothing

4.14.4 Sentences

1   Heather has a very overbearing father.
2   My mother's mauve velvet clothes are lovely.
3   Vera advised us to invest in breathable clothes.
4   My brother ventures out whatever the weather.
5   Victoria's smooth voice was soothing and forgiving.
6   Oliver's intervention saved them the bother of having to leave Nevada.
7   They were envious of Steven's move to a southern province in the Netherlands.
8   My beloved half-brother voluntarily withdrew in favour of his loud-mouthed rival.
9   It was evident that the volunteers loathed the novice's holier-than-thou behaviour.
10 They were in seventh heaven when they discovered that their father had survived unscathed.

4.15 Voiceless alveolar fricative /s/ vs. voiceless dental fricative /θ/

4.15.1 Minimal pairs

a)   *Word-initial*
     symbol/thimble, sank/thank, saw/thaw, sawn/thorn, seam/theme, sick/thick, sigh/thigh, sin/thin, sink/think, song/thong, sort/thought, sum/thumb

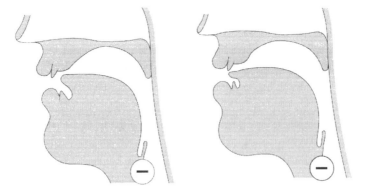

Figure 4.17 Left: English /s/. Right: English /θ/.

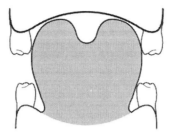

Figure 4.18 Mouth viewed from the front showing grooved tongue shape for /s/.

b) *Word-final*
   eights/eighth, face/faith, force/forth, frost/frothed, gross/growth, miss/myth, moss/
      moth, mouse/mouth, pass/path, tense/tenth, truce/truth, use (n.)/youth, worse/
      worth
c) *Medial*
   Essex/ethics, ensues/enthuse, unsinkable/unthinkable

4.15.2 Words with /s/ and /θ/

absinthe, anaesthetic, facecloth, henceforth, hyacinth, locksmith, psychopath, seventh,
south, stealth, stethoscope, strength, sympathy, amethyst, anthrax, arthritis, atheist, birth-
place, breathless, enthusiastic, faithless, hypothesis, mathematics, orthodox, pathos, thesau-
rus, thesis, thirsty, thrust, thanks

4.15.3 Phrases

an assessment method, thrown off balance, birthday celebrations, a death certificate, through
chance, the thrill of the chase, a thick crust, strengthen defences, a lengthy description, a thin
face, a thick mist, nothing to say, scared to death, a thin slice, a theme song, speech therapy,
a faithful servant, slow growth, a solemn oath, the tenth century, a central theme, thick-
skinned, stop a thief, a thorough search, a school of thought, a serious threat, a sore throat,
suck your thumb, speak the truth, lost youth, a thick sauce, sick to death

4.15.4 Sentences

1   Sue gave birth to a healthy son last Saturday.
2   Beth was threatened with the sack by the headmaster.
3   The cathedral's famous for its seventh-century ceiling.
4   The circus got an enthusiastic reception in Bath yesterday.
5   Psychologists now think there is such a thing as a sixth sense.
6   The discipline of mathematics develops at a breathtaking pace.
7   Matthew has produced an in-depth study of the symptoms of apathy.
8   I'm sick to death of listening to his hypotheses and unsound theories.
9   The authors stress that this is the least expensive method of assessment.
10 For the past six months I've been seeing a speech therapist who specialises in
      stammering.

4.16 Voiced alveolar fricative /z/ vs. voiced dental fricative /ð/

4.16.1 Minimal pairs

a)   *Word-initial*
Zen/then
b)   *Word-final*
bays/bathe, breeze/breathe, close (v.)/clothe, tease/teethe, whiz/with
c)   *Word-medial*
wizard/withered

4.16.2 Words with /z/ and /ð/

otherwise, theirs, these, those, bothers, breathes, brothers, dithers, feathers, loathes, mothers, northerners, others, newsworthy, praiseworthy

4.16.3 Phrases

a worthy cause, rather fuzzy, without realising, breathe easily, resemble your father, a further reason, rather bizarre

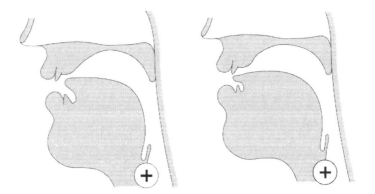

Figure 4.19 Left: English /z/. Right: English /ð/.

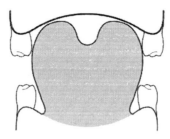

Figure 4.20 Mouth viewed from the front showing grooved tongue shape for /z/.

4.16.4 Sentences

1   My mother always wears designer clothes and shoes.
2   I loathe her jeans, turquoise blouse and leather blazer.
3   Although he pretends otherwise, he finds her irresistible.
4   He believes rhythmic breathing's a means of minimising anxiety.
5   Alexander raises funds from many sources to further worthy causes.
6   His stepfather's a rhythm and blues and jazz musician from Louisiana.
7   The weather has hitherto been pleasant for the season, but now it's freezing.
8   Heather resembles her mother physically with her hazel eyes and frizzy curls.
9   There was a reasonable breeze, but nevertheless the northern horizon was hazy.
10 Mr Kenworthy's transition from Kansas to southern Arizona caused a lot of misery.

4.17 Voiceless alveolar fricative /s/ vs. voiceless palato-alveolar fricative /ʃ/

4.17.1 Minimal pairs

a)   Word-initial

said/shed, sake/shake, sale/shale, same/shame, save/shave, sealed/shield, seat/sheet, self/shelf, sell/shell, sigh/shy, sign/shine, sin/shin, single/shingle, sip/ship, sofa/chauffeur, sock/shock, soccer/shocker, sort/short, sour/shower, sun/shun

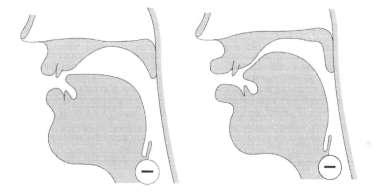

Figure 4.21 Left: English /s/. Right: English /ʃ/.

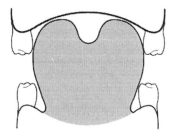

Figure 4.22 Mouth viewed from the front showing grooved tongue shape for /s/.

b)   Word-final
accomplice/accomplish, ass/ash, fist/fished, furnace/furnish, gas/gash, iris/Irish, lease/
leash, mass/mash, mess/mesh, Paris/parish, rust/rushed
c)   Word-medial
seesaw/seashore

4.17.2 Words with /s/ and /ʃ/

ambitious, anxious, assurance, atrocious, audacious, cautious, conscious, contentious, delicious, gracious, impatience, infectious, luscious, malicious, patience, precious, shameless,
shoelace, spacious, tenacious, vicious, social, astonish, celebration, censorship, circulation,
concession, conversation, deception, discretion, discussion, disruption, distinguish, special,
essential, establish, expression, horseradish, sachet, sash, seashore, section, session, slash,
slush, Spanish, special, splash, squash, superstition, sushi

4.17.3 Phrases

a modest ambition, rest assured, absolutely astonished, a stiff brush, spare cash, a glass
of champagne, a personality clash, a serious crash, from start to finish, fish soup, nice and
fresh, cast a shadow, a sense of shame, a distinctive shape, a silk sheet, sea shells, seek
shelter, a nasty shock, sensible shoes, an expensive shop, a shop assistant, show business,
a secret wish

4.17.4 Sentences

1   Tracy's voice sounded so shrill and sharp.
2   The ship sailed extremely close to the shore.
3   Susan was shivering in her short-sleeved shirt.
4   She pushed and shoved to get the best possible seat.
5   There wasn't a shred of evidence for this assumption.
6   There's a shuttle bus from the station to the city centre.
7   The ice fashion show was fabulous from start to finish.
8   Sharon's life's ambition was to be financially successful.
9   Sheila slipped between the sheets and was asleep in an instant.
10 The nurse must respect the patient's wish for confidentiality should this be
requested.

4.18 Voiced alveolar fricative /z/ vs. voiced palato-alveolar fricative /ʒ/

4.18.1 Minimal pairs

a)   Word-final
baize/beige, ruse/rouge
b)   Word-medial
Caesar/seizure, composer/composure, eraser/erasure

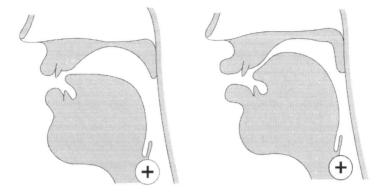

Figure 4.23 Left: English /z/. Right: English /ʒ/.

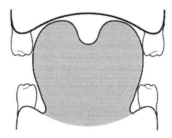

Figure 4.24 Mouth viewed from the front showing grooved tongue shape for /z/.

4.18.2 Phrases

a barrage of criticism, cause a collision, lose composure, cause confusion, a pleasure cruise, a wise decision, an organised excursion, minimise exposure, preserve an illusion, resist an invasion, easy to measure, a casual observer, rise to the occasion, use persuasion, lose prestige, business as usual

4.18.3 Sentences

1 Our treasurer has amazing powers of persuasion.
2 It's wise to minimise your children's exposure to television.
3 It was by no means unusual for James to lose his composure.
4 He was imprisoned for espionage activities against the regime.
5 The shows, films and television series are categorised by genre.
6 Elizabeth resented her husband's intrusion into her leisure activities.
7 The explosion was caused by soldiers disguised in desert camouflage.
8 The decision to close the business was met with a barrage of criticism.
9 Alexander hides his treasured beige Peugeot in the garage, refusing to let me use it.
10 The excursion to the museums of Rio de Janeiro was a pleasant conclusion to their cruise to Brazil.

4.19 Voiceless bilabial plosive /p/ vs. voiceless labio-dental fricative /f/

4.19.1 Minimal pairs

a)   *Word-initial*

pace/face, pad/fad, paid/fade, paint/faint, pair/fair, palm/farm, pan/fan, pass/farce, past/fast, pat/fat, paw/four, pea/fee, peel/feel, pier/fear, pierce/fierce, pig/fig, pile/file, pill/fill, pine/fine, pit/fit, poke/folk, pond/fond, pool/fool, pork/fork, port/fort, pound/found, prose/froze, pull/full, pun/fun, purr/fir, put/foot

b)   *Word-final*

carp/calf, cheap/chief, clip/cliff, cop/cough, cup/cuff, harp/half, leap/leaf, ripe/rife, sheep/sheaf, snip/sniff, whip/whiff, wipe/wife

c)   *Word-medial*

copy/coffee, puppy/puffy, reputation/refutation, supper/suffer, depend/defend

4.19.2 Words with /p/ and /f/

amplify, apostrophe, campfire, proof, grapefruit, helpful, perfect (adj.), leapfrog, perform, painful, pamphlet, paraffin, paragraph, penknife, platform, powerful, prefer, profession, professor, profile, profit, proof, puffin, shoplift, specify, uplift (v.), coffeepot, fingerprint, flap, flipper, half-price, off-peak, off-putting, self-pity

4.19.3 Phrases

a different approach, fitted carpet, a famous composer, fetch help, hopes and fears, a leap forward, the front page, pain relief, fresh paint, a fountain pen, a pillow fight, a fish pond, a gift shop, pull a face, pure fantasy, a pig farm, a deep fear, a feather pillow, an important feature, plain flour, pet food, a tropical forest, a picture frame, a special friend, a pension fund, a passport photo, a petty thief, a proper breakfast, a cup of coffee, a difference of opinion, for reference purposes

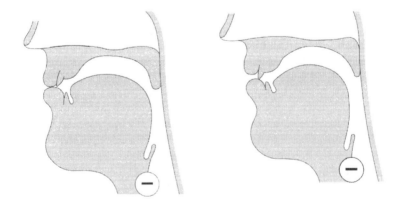

Figure 4.25 Left: English /p/ (hold stage). Right: English /f/.

4.19.4 Sentences

1 Please don't forget to pay the fifty pound membership fee.
2 For breakfast Fred typically has porridge and a piece of fruit.
3 An atmosphere of defeat and hopelessness pervaded the office.
4 It's difficult to compare and interpret the findings in these reports.
5 Pete's a super sportsman and in fact a former professional golf player.
6 My friends planned a surprise farewell party when I left the department.
7 After a bumpy flight over the Alps, we flew safely into one of the Paris airports.
8 He suffers from an inferiority complex, which explains his fear of public speaking.
9 We'd be happy to clarify any points of confusion before you make an appointment.
10 Providing positive feedback to your staff's a simple procedure but surprisingly effective.

4.20 Voiced bilabial plosive /b/ vs. voiced labio-dental fricative /v/

4.20.1 Minimal pairs

a) *Word-initial*
bee/V, bail/veil, banish/vanish, bat/vat, beard/veered, beer/veer, bent/vent, best/vest, bet/
vet, bigger/vigour, boat/vote, bolt/volt, bow/vow, bowel/vowel, bury/very

b) *Word-final*
curb/curve

c) *Word-medial*
cupboard/covered, dribble/drivel, fibre/fiver, marble/marvel, rebel (n.)/revel, sabre/savour

4.20.2 Words with /b/ and /v/

abbreviate, above, abusive, balaclava, beaver, beehive, behaviour, believe, beverage, brainwave, brave, observe, obvious, objective, subjective, available, divisible, everybody, invisible, lovable, lovebird, November, overbalance, overboard, proverb, riverbank, riverboat,
variable, verb, vibrant, vibrate

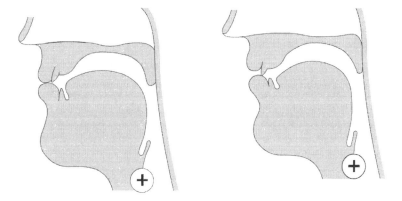

Figure 4.26 Left: English /b/ (hold stage). Right: English /v/.

4.20.3 Phrases

a big advantage, a bit of advice, public approval, above average, best behaviour, a book cover, a bitter divorce, a bus driver, rubber gloves, a brief interval, a job interview, a basic level, double vision, a booming voice, live bait, navy blue, a book review, a favourite hobby, reserve a table

4.20.4 Sentences

1   This bird has a distinctive curved beak.
2   The book covers the subject comprehensively.
3   Bill and Violet had breakfast at their favourite pub.
4   Toby has a reliable passive vocabulary in Bulgarian.
5   The boat'll leave the harbour at seven this evening.
6   These baked beans are suitable for vegetarians and vegans.
7   A number of villages were evacuated after the river burst its banks.
8   In November we celebrated the seventh anniversary of the rugby club.
9   He made an invaluable contribution to the development of the university.
10 Elizabeth's feedback provided a basis for improvements in our environment.

4.21 Voiceless alveolar plosive /t/ vs. voiceless dental fricative /θ/

4.21.1 Minimal pairs

a)   *Word-initial*
     tank/thank, taught/thought, team/theme, tie/thigh, tore/thaw, tick/thick, torn/thorn, trash/
         thrash, tread/thread, tree/three, true/threw, trust/thrust, tug/thug

b)   *Word-final*
     boat/both, debt/death, fate/faith, fought/fourth, heart/hearth, heat/heath, oat/oath, part/
         path, tent/tenth

4.21.2 Words with /t/ and /θ/

afterbirth, aftermath, afterthought, antipathy, antithesis, down-to-earth, eighth, eightieth, fortieth, tooth, truth, stealthy, stethoscope, telepathy, tenth, thirteenth, thirtieth, Timothy,

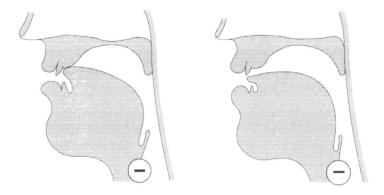

Figure 4.27 Left: English /t/ (hold stage). Right: English /θ/.

twentieth, amethyst, anaesthetic, apathetic, arithmetic, arthritis, atheist, athlete, authentic, authority, bathtub, birthrate, breathtaking, mathematics, pathetic, sympathetic, theatre, theft, thicket, thirsty, thirty, threat, throat, thrust

4.21.3 Phrases

a bath tap, a tax threshold, a sympathetic teacher, healthy teeth, the umpteenth time, a bath towel, thigh-length boots, a thin coat of paint, date of birth, eat healthily, a fate worse than death, fit and healthy, a thank-you note, a breathtaking sight, a death threat, a thick blanket, an enthusiastic amateur, a cathedral city, a thatched cottage, a mythical monster, worth the effort, a thing of the past, test a hypothesis, a test of strength, the tenth time, tell the truth

4.21.4 Sentences

1   I don't think it'll fit, but it's worth a try.
2   The city's Gothic cathedral's a breathtaking sight.
3   Ruth bought me a guitar as a thirtieth birthday present.
4   Arthur should do the decent thing and tell her the truth.
5   Edith gave birth to twins at two-thirty yesterday afternoon.
6   Thelma wrote a thorough report containing a wealth of detail.
7   Matthew sent a heartfelt thank-you letter to his maths teacher.
8   Agatha tried to determine the birth and death dates of her earliest ancestors.
9   Elizabeth spent the entire month of August in Gareth's beautiful thatched cottage.
10   They co-authored an article on the monophthongs and diphthongs of Estonian in 2013.

4.22 Voiced alveolar plosive /d/ vs. voiced dental fricative /ð/

4.22.1 Minimal pairs

breed/breathe, Ds/these, dale/they'll, Dan/than, dare/their, Dave/they've, day/they, den/then, dough/though, doze/those, header/heather, udder/other, wordy/worthy

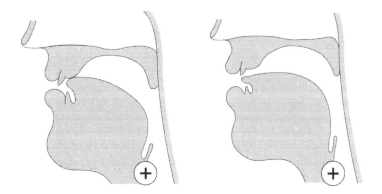

Figure 4.28 Left: English /d/ (hold stage). Right: English /ð/.

4.22.2 Words with /d/ and /ð/

creditworthy, dither, godfather, roadworthy, breathed, brotherhood, fatherhood, foul-mouthed, motherboard, motherhood, notwithstanding, otherworldly, unfathomed, unscathed, withdraw, withhold, withstand, bathed, blathered, bothered, clothed, fathered, fatherland, gathered, loathed, mothered, seethed, smothered, soothed, tethered, weathered, withered

4.22.3 Phrases

abandon altogether, withhold aid, a feather bed, a motherless child, gathering clouds, weather conditions, a rhythmic dance, gather data, these days, those were the days, a southern dialect, in a northerly direction, without further discussion, gathering dust, other ideas, a blithering idiot, pretend otherwise, a smooth ride, gather speed, breathe deeply, blood brothers, a devoted father, a doting mother, rather difficult

4.22.4 Sentences

1   Without further delay they headed in a northerly direction.
2   Judy's older brother's definitely worthy of our admiration.
3   Blend these dry ingredients together and then add the liquid.
4   Don's stupid loud-mouthed father needs his head examined.
5   They were blood brothers bound together by shared hardship.
6   David's a blithering idiot, and it's absurd to pretend otherwise.
7   The data for the second study was gathered in the Netherlands.
8   Heather's wonderful idea either failed or was abandoned altogether.
9   Within days his godfather had developed a delightful southern drawl.
10 Her grandfather was seated behind an old-fashioned leather-topped desk.

4.23 Voiced alveolar nasal /n/ vs. voiced velar nasal /ŋ/

4.23.1 Minimal pairs

a)   *Word-final*
     ban/bang, bun/bung, clan/clang, coffin/coughing, done/dung, fan/fang, gone/gong, kin/king, mountain/mounting, pan/pang, pin/ping, puffin/puffing, ran/rang, robin/robbing, Ron/wrong, run/rung, sin/sing, son/sung, tan/tang, thin/thing, ton/tongue, win/wing

b)   *Word-medial*
     banner/banger, hand/hanged, wind/winged

4.23.2 Phrases

pain and anguish, a broken ankle, a bank account, financial backing, an enormous bang, a new beginning, uneven breathing, winter clothing, a newspaper cutting, an unhappy ending, join a gang, hang on a minute, an emergency landing, thunder and lightning, earn a living, long enough, a sunny morning, an opening ceremony, extensive reading, singing lessons, strong enough, sense of timing, native tongue, a wedding present, the animal kingdom, a marching

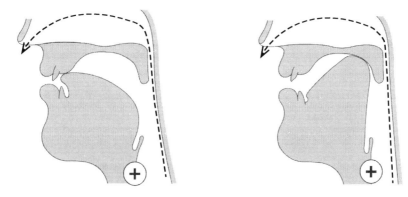

Figure 4.29 Left: English /n/. Right: English /ŋ/.The arrows indicate the escape of the air-stream through the nose.

band, a strong bond, a growing demand, distance learning, a young man, a fleeting moment, a throbbing pain, a frying pan, boiling point, hunting season, a long sentence, spring cleaning, train spotting, sparkling wine, slender fingers, the kitchen sink, many thanks, pineapple chunks, a pen and ink drawing

4.23.3 Sentences

1   My son Norman earns a living giving singing lessons.
2   Are your parents going to attend the meeting tonight?
3   It's been raining torrentially with distant thunder and lightning.
4   He's been working morning, noon and night on his writing assignment.
5   Joanna has a charming collection of pen and ink drawings of town scenes.
6   Wendy was waiting for her dancing partner at the main entrance of the building.
7   John and his girlfriend from Reading are making preparations for their wedding.
8   His children are in a stimulating environment where learning's fun and exciting.
9   I've been reading an intensely moving and thought-provoking novel about a lonely teenager.
10 I recommend this exhibition to anyone looking for an inspiring introduction to nineteenth-century painting.

4.24 Voiced post-alveolar approximant /r/ vs. voiced labial-velar approximant /w/

4.24.1 Minimal pairs

a)   Word-initial
rage/wage, raid/wade, rail/wail, raise/ways, rake/wake, rare/wear, rate/wait, ray/way, reel/wheel, rent/went, rest/west, rich/which, ride/wide, right/white, rinse/wince, rip/whip, ripe/wipe, roar/war, rod/wad, room/womb, run/one, wriggle/wiggle, write/white

b)   Word-medial
array/away

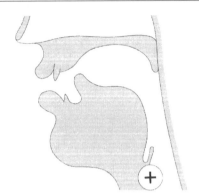

Figure 4.30 English /r/.

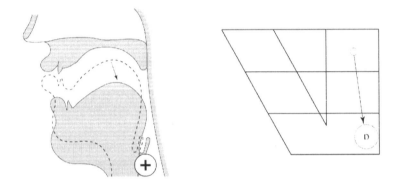

Figure 4.31 English /w/: sequence /wɒ/ in *wash*. The diagram shows the approximate change in tongue shape. Since /w/ is a semi-vowel, it can be indicated on a vowel diagram.

4.24.2 Words with both /r/ and /w/

brainwash, brainwave, breadwinner, breakaway, brickwork, crossword, driveway, everyone, faraway, framework, frequent (adj.), railway, require, request, reservoir, reward, roadworks, runway, straightaway, throwaway, aquamarine, aquarium, enquiry, equilibrium, mouth-watering, quarrel, quarry, query, squirrel, warrant, wary, watercress, weary, withdraw, worry

4.24.3 Phrases

choir practice, a farewell appearance, routine paperwork, the correct password, a rhetorical question, remain quiet, quiz programme, a generous reward, sworn to secrecy, a narrow waist, a war hero, a wrist watch, the wrong way, arrange a wedding, a rich widow, received wisdom, rotten wood, the right word

4.24.4 Sentences

1 Wendy broke down and wept uncontrollably.
2 The three workmen were stripped to the waist.

3   Walter received a serious wound during the war.
4   Wild waves crashed relentlessly against the rocks.
5   Rebecca always pronounces this word incorrectly.
6   Robert wants to go for a quick swim before breakfast.
7   The weather grew progressively worse and unpredictable.
8   The runners were dripping with sweat and screaming for water.
9   Edward broke off a dry twig from the tree and threw it into the well.
10 They carried out the fieldwork in whatever language was natural to the respondents.

4.25 Voiced alveolar lateral approximant /l/ vs. voiced post-alveolar approximant /r/

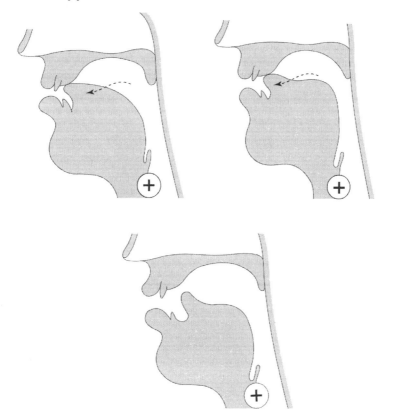

Figure 4.32 Left: English clear /l/. Right: dark /l/ showing velarised tongue shape. The arrow indicates that the airstream escapes over the lowered sides of the tongue. Bottom: English /r/.

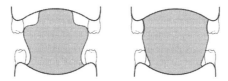

Figure 4.33 Mouth viewed from the front. Left: tongue sides lowered for lateral /l/. Right: tongue sides raised for /r/.

4.25.1 Minimal pairs

a)   Word-initial

lace/race, lack/rack, lake/rake, lamb/ram, lamp/ramp, lane/rain, late/rate, law/roar, lead/read, legion/region, light/right, list/wrist, liver/river, load/road, lock/rock, long/wrong, loot/root, lot/rot, bland/brand, blew/brew, blink/brink, bloom/broom, blouse/browse, blush/brush, clamp/cramp, clash/crash, clue/crew, climb/crime, cloud/crowd, clown/crown, flame/frame, flea/free, flesh/fresh, flight/fright, flute/fruit, fly/fry, glamour/grammar, glass/grass, glow/grow, pleasant/present

b)   Word-medial

belly/berry, palate/parrot, pilot/pirate, lolly/lorry, alive/arrive, belated/berated, believe/bereave, collect/correct, collection/correction

4.25.2 Words with both /l/ and /r/

accelerate, blackberry, bleary, burglary, calibrate, calorie, cavalry, celebrity, celery, chlorine, clarify, electric, florist, gallery, glamorous, glory, glossary, hilarious, larynx, laundry, lorry, lurid, luxury, lyric, military, plural, slurry, tolerate, aerial, aeroplane, agriculture, approval, arrival, barrel, brawl, brilliant, brutal, carol, central, cereal, control, coral, crawl, crocodile, cruel, crystal, drill, feral, frail, fragile, friendly, frill, gorilla, grill, growl, material, parallel, problem, profile, rail, realise, really, relative, relax, relic, relief, relish, rival, roll, rule

4.25.3 Phrases

a legal agreement, the seal of approval, the last to arrive, below average, wild berries, brain cells, garlic bread, buried alive, a railway carriage, black cherries, contrary to popular belief, a life of crime, split the difference, a look of disapproval, live in dread, a lifelong dream, old and frail, the national portrait gallery, a self-help group, hold a grudge, a look of horror, a loveless marriage, a press release, a price list, problem solving, lose a race, ready and willing, follow a recipe, a silly remark, a lack of respect, early retirement, the last straw, the least of your worries, crystal clear, fear of failure, green fields, a cry for help, pilot error, friends and relations, a regular supply

4.25.4 Sentences

1   Fresh barrels of ale were brought up from the cellar.
2   Brian's closing remarks were greeted with wild applause.
3   Carol's worries proved utterly and completely groundless.
4   The stress falls on the last syllable in *kangaroo* and *referee*.
5   Harry held up his trousers with braces and a cracked leather belt.
6   The fielders tried to retrieve the ball quickly and return it to the bowler.
7   Unfortunately, we ran up a very large hotel bill on a brief trip to London.
8   They had to drive slowly as the road was partially blocked by fallen logs.
9   The primary responsibility lies with the authorities of the individual countries.
10   The programme was broadcast live on national television on Friday the eleventh of April.

4.26 Voiced labio-dental fricative /v/ vs. voiced labial-velar approximant /w/

4.26.1 Minimal pairs

a) Word-initial

V/we, vale/wail, vary/wary, veal/wheel, veer/weir, veered/weird, vein/wane, vent/went, verse/worse, vest/west, vet/wet, vine/whine, viper/wiper, vow/wow

4.26.2 Words with /v/ and /w/

cavewoman, driveway, everyone, heavyweight, overqualified, overweight, overwork, reservoir, vanquish, wave, equivalent, weave, persuasive, quiver, swerve, twelve, whatever, wives

4.26.3 Phrases

an award for bravery, vaguely aware, a lavish banquet, a male-voice choir, solve a crossword, a private dwelling, vital equipment, wave farewell, at frequent intervals, a valid password, a

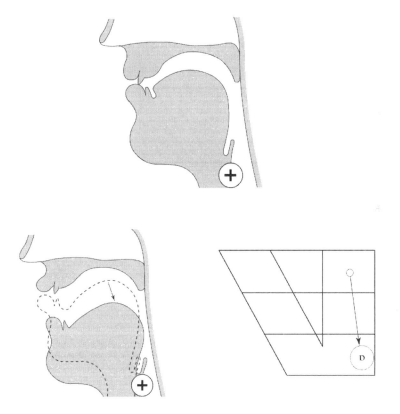

Figure 4.34 Top: English /v/. Bottom: English /w/. Note that English /w/ is a semi-vowel and can therefore be indicated on a vowel diagram. Here the sequence /wɒ/ in *wash* is shown.

violent quarrel, a railway service, available on request, covered in sweat, the average wage, an evening walk, a civil war, river water, heavy weapons, wedding vows, vintage wine, a word of advice, alive and well, revenge is sweet, a world view, well worth a visit, a live wire

4.26.4 Sentences

1 Victor wants to divorce his wife.
2 Oliver quickly recovered his wits.
3 Vera is wondering what the work will involve.
4 They served an expensive wine at the wedding.
5 We couldn't quite work out the value of the investment.
6 David invited Vanessa for a walk along the river on that warm evening.
7 Sweden won silver in women's volleyball in Venezuela on Wednesday.
8 My Welsh acquaintance was visibly moved by his visit to the war graves.
9 Walter and Gwen travelled to Cornwall on their seventeenth anniversary.
10 The women became involved in a quarrel with their supervisor at the workshop.

4.27 Voiced palato-alveolar affricate /ʤ/ vs. voiced palatal approximant /j/

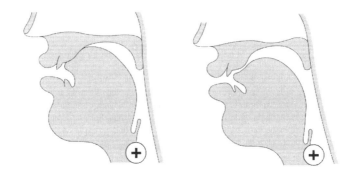

Figure 4.35 English /ʤ/. Left: hold stage. Right: release with homorganic friction. Note trumpet-shaped lip-rounding.

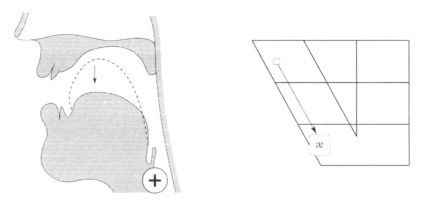

Figure 4.36 English /j/: sequence /jæ/ in *yak*. The diagram shows the approximate change in tongue shape. Since /j/ is a semi-vowel, it can be indicated on a vowel diagram.

4.27.1 Minimal pairs

Jew/you, Jews/use (v.), juice/use (n.), jot/yacht, jeer/year, gel/yell, jet/yet, job/yob, jaw/your

4.27.2 Words with /dʒ/ and /j/

genuine, ingenuity, jaguar, jocular, jugular, junkyard, centrifuge, fugitive, huge, musicology, refuge, usage

4.27.3 Phrases

the younger generation, jet fuel, gentle humour, a jazz musician, job security, an emergency unit, a surgical unit, a university graduate, in general usage, gentle yoga, youthful energy, an intelligence unit, at a young age, a storage unit

4.27.4 Sentences

1 Geoffrey's a popular jazz musician.
2 There's a huge Jewish community in New York.
3 Muriel used any excuse to indulge in orange juice.
4 Jack was on duty in the emergency unit yesterday.
5 Matthew's suggestions are outrageous and ridiculous.
6 Jenny graduated from the University of Munich in June.
7 The students had divergent views on gene manipulation.
8 Judith's an insecure, belligerent and rebellious teenager.
9 Eugene managed to enlarge his vocabulary at the engineering college in Houston.
10 We assumed that our ideologically neutral newspaper would have an objective opinion.

4.28 Voiceless glottal fricative /h/ vs. zero

4.28.1 Minimal pairs

Word-initial

had/add, hair/air, hake/ache, hall/all, harm/arm, heart/art, heal/eel, hear/ear, heat/eat, hedge/edge, high/eye, hill/ill, hit/it, hold/old, hotter/otter, hurl/earl

4.28.2 Phrases

an unhappy childhood, an annoying habit, auburn hair, an abrupt halt, easy to handle, irreparable harm, in absolute harmony, a head injury, intense heat, afraid of heights, expert help, ancient history, ice hockey, home address, an empty house

4.28.3 Sentences

1 Henry's eaten all the oranges as he was hungry.
2 Ellen heard an audible hiss through the headphones.
3 Here are eight helpful hints if you're afraid of heights.

4   The hedgehog emerged from hibernation in early April.
5   All hospitals have been equipped to handle emergencies.
6   I'm indebted to Hamish Hamilton for his invaluable assistance.
7   We hope we'll have an abundant harvest of apples in the autumn.
8   He helped in the areas that had been hit especially hard by the earthquake.
9   Hilary's husband happened to be in the house when the explosion occurred.
10   I was happy I'd insisted on an air-conditioned hotel as Hamburg was oppressively hot in
     August.

4.29 Voiced velar nasal + velar plosive /ŋk/ or /ŋg/ vs. voiced velar nasal /ŋ/

In many languages, the velar nasal [ŋ] occurs only before the velar plosives /k/ and /g/. In
English, however, /ŋ/ can occur with or without a following velar plosive. Word-medially, /ŋ/
contrasts with both /ŋk/ and /ŋg/, but word-finally only /ŋ/ and /ŋk/ are possible.

4.29.1 Minimal pairs

a)   *Word-final*
     think/thing, brink/bring, rink/ring, sink/sing, slink/sling, stink/sting, wink/wing, bank/
          bang, Hank/hang, rank/rang, sank/sang, bunk/bung, sunk/sung, clank/clang, clink/
          cling, clunk/clung, hunk/hung, pink/ping, stunk/stung, tank/tang
b)   *Word-medial*
     /ŋk/ vs. /ŋ/
     banker/banger, hanker/hanger, sinker/singer, stinker/stinger
     /ŋg/ vs. /ŋ/
     Bangor/banger, clangour/clanger

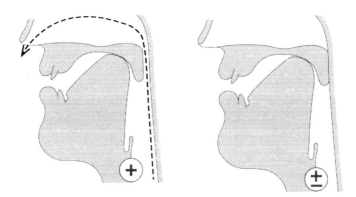

Figure 4.37 Left: English /ŋ/. The arrows indicate the escape of the airstream through the
          nose. Note that the soft palate is lowered. Right: If /ŋ/ is followed by a homor-
          ganic plosive (/k/ or /g/), the soft palate rises to form a velic closure.

4.29.2 Phrases

increasingly angry, along the bank, a wedding banquet, a strong drink, surprisingly frank, printing ink, the missing link, shocking pink, willing to relinquish, a long think, swimming trunks, a knowing wink, mounting anger, your ring finger, matching fingerprints, hunger pangs

4.29.3 Sentences

 1 We're buying a bungalow in Bangor.
 2 I'm growing increasingly angry with my uncle.
 3 Angus will be travelling to Helsinki in the spring.
 4 It was amusing to see the chattering monkeys in the jungle.
 5 Frank's developing a programming language for linguistics.
 6 Bianca's no longer wearing an engagement ring on her finger.
 7 Duncan and Ingrid are holding their wedding banquet in Hong Kong.
 8 Her handwriting's appalling, and her spelling and punctuation incorrect.
 9 Mr Jenkins is working on strengthening the link between planning and budgeting.
10 Why does Hank think pink flamingos and king penguins are on the brink of extinction?

Chapter 5

Vowels

5.1 Describing vowels

We saw in Chapter 2 that a consonant is a speech sound which involves an obstruction to the airstream on its way through the vocal tract. So what then is a vowel? A vowel is the opposite of a consonant: a sound made with *no* obstruction in the vocal tract to the air as it passes through it.

Say a long /ɑ:/, the sound doctors ask us to make when they want to look in our mouths, and feel how the air flows out through your mouth without any obstruction. Try the same for /i:/, the <ee> of *tree*, and /ɔ:/, the <aw> of *saw*. You will notice that the lips and tongue take different positions for these different vowels, but in each case there's no obstruction or blockage of the kind that we find in consonants.

If consonants are analysed in terms of the kind of obstruction involved and its location in the vocal tract, how can we analyse vowels, which have no such obstruction? Although the tongue and lips assume a wide range of complex shapes for the articulation of different vowels, a relatively simple system has been developed to describe them. Figure 5.1 shows the vowel diagram from the chart of the International Phonetic Association (IPA), which is based on this system of vowel description.

5.1.1 Tongue shape

In order to understand the system behind the diagram, the first step is to explore the limits of the range of tongue positions used to make vowels, known as the **vowel space**. There are two fixed articulatory reference points to the system. To find the first, you make a vowel with the front of the body of your tongue pushed as far forward and as far up towards the hard palate as possible. This is the position for the [i] vowel (see Figure 5.2). If you move your tongue any further forward or up, audible friction would result between the tongue and the hard palate, and the sound would no longer be a vowel. The second reference point is found by doing the opposite – opening your mouth and pulling your tongue as far down and back as possible without causing friction between the root of the tongue and the back wall of the pharynx (see Figure 5.3). This is the [ɑ] vowel. A further two positions can be identified by pushing the tongue as far up and back as possible (see Figure 5.4), which gives us the [u] vowel, and by pushing the tongue as far forward and down as possible (see Figure 5.5), which gives us the [a] vowel. Note that during the production of all these vowels, the tongue-tip and blade (see Figure 5.6) remain low in the mouth. They aren't involved in vowel production, and this is why the front of the tongue as a technical term isn't where non-phoneticians usually expect it to be. The front of the tongue is actually the front of the part used in vowel articulations, and is what lay people would think of as the centre or middle of the tongue.

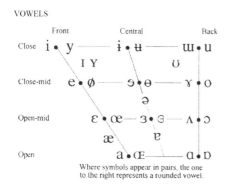

Figure 5.1 Vowel diagram from the IPA chart.

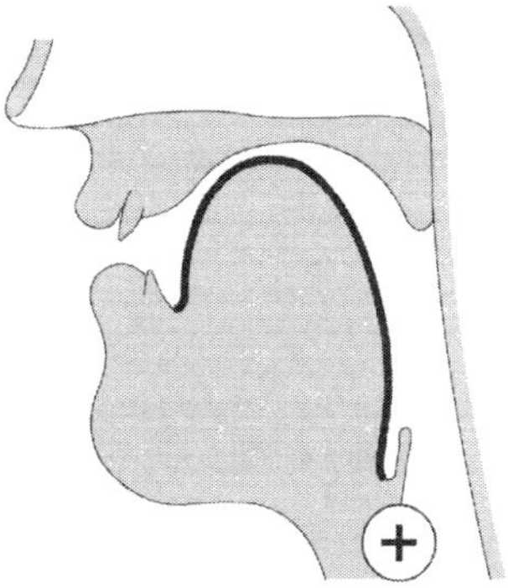

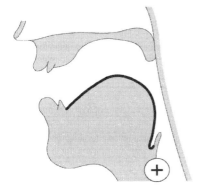

Figure 5.3 Tongue shape for [ɑ].

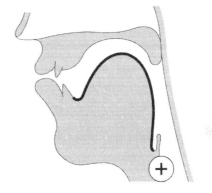

Figure 5.2 Tongue shape for [i].

Figure 5.4 Tongue shape for [u].

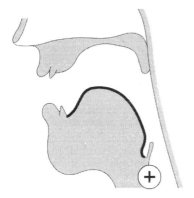

Figure 5.5 Tongue shape for [a].

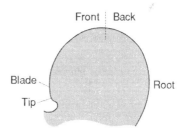

Figure 5.6 Tongue body raised and tip and blade lowered, as for vowel articulations.

Now spend some time exploring the limits of the vowel space. Paradoxical as it may seem, it's best to do this silently. If you voice the vowels as you articulate them, it makes you less able to appreciate the sensations of touch, movement and position you receive from your articulators. Start at the [i] position, then silently and slowly glide to the [u] position while keeping your tongue as close as possible to the palate without turning the sound into a

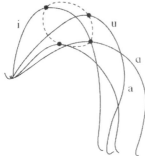

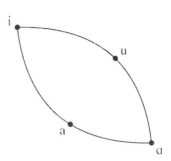

Figure 5.7 Tongue shapes for [i, u, a, ɑ] superimposed. Black dots indicate the highest point of the tongue for each of the vowels; the dashed line shows the limits of the vowel area.

Figure 5.8 The vowel area.

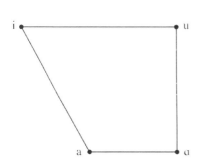

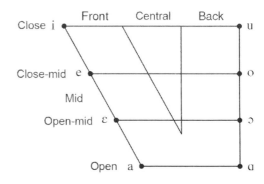

Figure 5.9 The vowel quadrilateral.

Figure 5.10 The eight basic reference vowels.

consonant. Next slowly glide to [ɑ], making sure to pull your tongue back to the lower back limit of the vowel space. Do the same from the [i] position to [a], and then to [ɑ], moving your tongue along the front limit of the vowel space. You will feel that your tongue is moving in an oval shape like that shown in Figures 5.7 and 5.8.

The oval is too awkward a shape for practical purposes, and so in a schematic representation its sides are straightened to give it the basic shape of the vowel quadrilateral (see Figure 5.9) that we are familiar with from the IPA chart.

The shape isn't a perfect square, which reflects the fact that there's greater distance between [i] and [u] than between [a] and [ɑ], and also more space between [i] and [a] than between [u] and [ɑ]. The vowel diagram is further elaborated on by providing symbols for four further positions equally spaced on the left [e ɛ] and right sides [o ɔ]. Finally, lines are added to divide the vowel space into manageable vertical and horizontal areas (see Figure 5.10)

Vertically, the positions are called **close**, **mid** and **open**, with mid being further divided into **close-mid** and **open-mid**. Horizontally, they are **front**, **central** and **back**.

5.1.2 Lip shape

So far we've only considered the position of the tongue, but the shape of the lips is also important. Since the tongue and lips can move independently of each other, every vowel position can be accompanied by either **unrounded** or **rounded** lips. This is why the symbols on the IPA vowel diagram mostly come in pairs, the left symbol having unrounded lips and the right symbol having rounded lips.

5.1.3 Vowel labels

Serendipitously, it turns out that as in the case of consonants, the basics of vowel description can be summarised in terms of three factors: vertical tongue position, horizontal tongue position and lip shape. The peripheral vowels, for example, are described as shown in Table 5.1; see also Figure 5.1.

Table 5.1 Labelling system for the peripheral vowels

Symbol	Label	Symbol	Label
[i]	close front unrounded	[ɯ]	close back unrounded
[y]	close front rounded	[u]	close back rounded
[e]	close-mid front unrounded	[ɤ]	close-mid back unrounded
[ø]	close-mid front rounded	[o]	close-mid back rounded
[ɛ]	open-mid front unrounded	[ʌ]	open-mid back unrounded
[œ]	open-mid front rounded	[ɔ]	open-mid back rounded
[a]	open front unrounded	[ɑ]	open back unrounded
[ɶ]	open front rounded	[ɒ]	open back rounded

5.2 English vowels

In the GB accent of English, there are 20 vowel phonemes.

In Table 5.2 we give the vowel symbols most widely used in dictionaries and teaching materials. Symbols are followed by the keyword (based on Wells 1982) which we will use when referring to the vowels. The schwa vowel /ə/ needs no keyword because the name 'schwa' is so well established.

The phonemic symbols used to represent English vowels aren't always a good indication of their exact phonetic quality. This is because (1) some vowels have changed since the phonemic symbols were chosen and (2) 'exotic' vowel symbols are sometimes avoided for the sake of ease of printing and writing. For example, the TRAP vowel has the phonemic symbol /æ/ because this is the quality it had about fifty years ago – a front unrounded vowel between open-mid and open. Nowadays it's a fully open vowel, and therefore /a/ would be a more appropriate phonemic symbol. The DRESS vowel has long been a front unrounded vowel closer to open-mid [ɛ] than to close-mid [e], but clearly the phonemic symbol /e/ is simpler for day-to-day teaching purposes than the more precise /ɛ/.

Table 5.3 shows the phonemic symbols some of the English vowels would have if the nearest IPA symbol (see Figure 5.1) to their vowel quality was used.

5.2.1 Strong and weak vowels

When describing English vowels, a distinction is made between the vowels which typically occur in stressed syllables and those which typically occur in unstressed syllables. The former are said to belong to the **strong vowel** system, and the latter to the **weak vowel** system.

Table 5.2 General British vowels

		Checked monophthongs	
/ɪ/	KIT	gym, busy, pretty, build, sieve, women
/ʊ/	FOOT	book, put, would, woman
/e/	DRESS	bread, friend, leisure, leopard, bury, said
/ɒ/	LOT	job, want, sausage, knowledge
/æ/	TRAP	cat, plait, meringue
/ʌ/	STRUT	mud, love, touch
		Free monophthongs	
/iː/	FLEECE	pea, bee, key, even, kilo, field
/uː/	GOOSE	food, blue, fruit, move, group, flew
/ɜː/	NURSE	fur, sir, word, earn, berth
/ɑː/	PALM	pass, park, heart, clerk
/ɔː/	THOUGHT	war, oar, door, sore, paw, fraud, fort
/eə/	SQUARE	rare, pair, wear, heir, aerial
		Free diphthongs – closing, fronting	
/eɪ/	FACE	pay, mail, take, break, vein, prey, gauge
/aɪ/	PRICE	pie, dry, dye, pi, high, aisle
/ɔɪ/	CHOICE	toy, foil, buoy
		Free diphthongs – closing, backing	
/aʊ/	MOUTH	now, loud
/əʊ/	GOAT	blow, hero, nose, hoax, soul
		Free diphthongs – centring	
/ɪə/	NEAR	fear, idea, era, cheer, weird, here, pier
/ʊə/	CURE	poor, tour, jury
		Weak vowels	
/ə/	schwa	fibre, water, forget, perform, future, about
/ɪ/	weak KIT	savage, naked, basic, invest
[i]	weak FLEECE	baby, honey, taxi, coffee, cookie, acne, react, serious
[u]	weak GOOSE	genuine, continuous, jaguar, virtual
/ʊ/	weak FOOT	accurate, deputy, regular

Table 5.3 Vowel phonemes shown with present symbol and closest IPA symbol

Keyword	Present symbol	Alternative symbol	Keyword	Present symbol	Alternative symbol
FOOT	/ʊ/	/o/	GOOSE	/uː/	/ʉː/
DRESS	/e/	/ɛ/	NURSE	/ɜː/	/əː/
LOT	/ɒ/	/ɔ/	THOUGHT	/ɔː/	/oː/
TRAP	/æ/	/a/	SQUARE	/eə/	/ɛː/
STRUT	/ʌ/	/ɐ/	CURE	/ʊə/	/oə/

There's a striking difference between the sets of vowels which are usually found in these two types of syllable, a distinction which isn't found in most other languages. All vowels except schwa are found in stressed syllables, but in unstressed syllables a much smaller set of vowels predominates – schwa, KIT, FLEECE, GOOSE and FOOT (see Chapter 9). This isn't to say that the other strong vowels can't occur in unstressed syllables, but rather that they are unusual in this context. Conversely, schwa is the only weak vowel which occurs exclusively in unstressed syllables, while the other four are also common in stressed syllables. You will notice from Table 5.2 that FLEECE and GOOSE have special symbols, [i] and [u], for when they appear as weak vowels. This is because, historically, they developed out of weak KIT and weak FOOT. Our transcription system therefore reflects a point in the late twentieth century when symbols were needed to cover two possibilities: [i], meaning 'FLEECE or KIT', and [u], meaning 'GOOSE or FOOT'. Nowadays, however, it would be distinctly old-fashioned to give these weak vowels the quality of KIT or FOOT, but we include the symbols in order for our transcription to be consistent with that most widely used in dictionaries and teaching materials.

5.2.2 Checked and free vowels

The strong vowels fall into two groups: **checked vowels** (Figure 5.11) and **free vowels** (Figures 5.12–5.15).

- Checked: KIT /ɪ/, FOOT /ʊ/, DRESS /e/, LOT /ɒ/, TRAP /æ/, STRUT /ʌ/.
- Free: FLEECE /iː/, GOOSE /uː/, THOUGHT /ɔː/, PALM /ɑː/, NURSE /ɜː/, SQUARE /eə/, FACE /eɪ/, PRICE /aɪ/, CHOICE /ɔɪ/, MOUTH /aʊ/, GOAT /əʊ/, NEAR /ɪə/, CURE /ʊə/.

Note that the shape of the lips is shown as follows on the vowel diagrams: a square ☐ for an unrounded vowel and a circle ○ for a rounded vowel. If the lip shape changes from unrounded to rounded, we show this by means of a square that becomes a circle, and if the lips change from rounded to unrounded, we show it as a circle that becomes a square.

The checked/free categorisation is based on the types of syllable the strong vowels occur in. Free vowels are 'free' to occur in both closed and open syllables. A **closed syllable** is one which has a coda, i.e. one or more consonants after the vowel, for example:

seed /siːd/, *lose* /luːz/, *sword* /sɔːd/, *hard* /hɑːd/, *bird* /bɜːd/, *pears* /peəz/, *haze* /heɪz/, *size* /saɪz/, *boys* /bɔɪz/, *town* /taʊn/, *load* /ləʊd/, *beard* /bɪəd/, *cures* /kjʊəz/

An open syllable is one which *doesn't* have a coda following the vowel, for example:

tea /tiː/, *do* /duː/, *law* /lɔː/, *star* /stɑː/, *sir* /sɜː/, *pair* /peə/, *pay* /peɪ/, *tie* /taɪ/, *boy* /bɔɪ/, *now* /naʊ/, *go* /gəʊ/, *fear* /fɪə/, *cure* /kjʊə/

Checked vowels are 'checked' in the sense that their distribution is restricted because they can only occur in closed syllables, for example:

sit /sɪt/, *put* /pʊt/, *head* /hed/, *boss* /bɒs/, *sad* /sæd/, *luck* /lʌk/

Can you think of any English words which have these vowels at the end, i.e. in an open syllable? Are there words like /nɪ/, /tʃʊ/, /de/, /plɒ/, /fæ/ or /lʌ/? No, there aren't any such words.

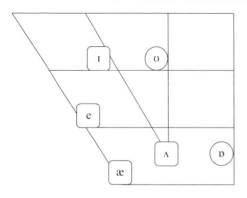

Figure 5.11 Checked vowels.

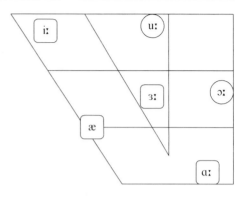

Figure 5.12 Free vowels: monophthongs.

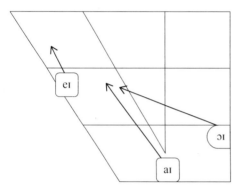

Figure 5.13 Free vowels: closing fronting diphthongs.

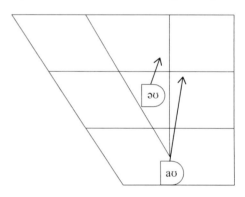

Figure 5.14 Free vowels: closing backing diphthongs.

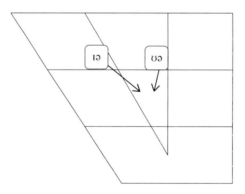

Figure 5.15 Free vowels: centring diphthongs.

The checked/free distinction has also been described as one of length. The checked vowels have been called the 'short' vowels, and the free vowels have been called the 'long' vowels. There's some truth in this generalisation because it's a fact that in the same phonetic context, the free vowels are consistently longer than the checked vowels, and this is why the phonemic symbols for the free monophthongs include the length symbol [ː]. However, there are many factors which affect vowel duration in English speech, meaning that the 'short'

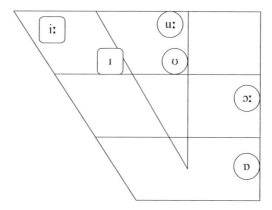

Figure 5.16 The different qualities of the pairs FLEECE/kit, goose/FOOT and THOUGHT/LOT.

checked vowels can sometimes be lengthened and, in particular, the 'long' free vowels are often shortened. It's better, therefore, to categorise the strong vowels according to the fixed, unchanging fact of their distribution in different types of syllables and not in terms of their variable duration.

The 'short/long' terminology has had implications for the choice of phonemic symbols. Formerly, KIT, FOOT and LOT were given the phonemic symbols /i/, /u/ and /ɔ/ respectively, while FLEECE, GOOSE and THOUGHT were written /iː/, /uː/ and /ɔː/, as they still are. This was done in order to simplify the transcription for printing purposes by avoiding 'exotic' symbols, and so the length mark [ː] was used to distinguish these pairs of vowels instead of giving the three checked vowels their own unique symbols. This had the unfortunate consequence, however, of leading learners to believe that the only difference between these pairs of vowels was their length. As Figure 5.16 demonstrates, this isn't true.

The pairs FLEECE/KIT, GOOSE/FOOT and THOUGHT/LOT differ in vowel quality (resulting from different tongue positions), and this is the most important feature which distinguishes them, their lengths being variable. It's simply not true, as some learners believe, that shortened FLEECE, GOOSE and THOUGHT become KIT, FOOT and LOT, or that lengthened KIT, FOOT and LOT become FLEECE, GOOSE and THOUGHT.

5.2.3 Monophthongs and diphthongs

Vowels can be further divided into **diphthongs**, which involve a glide from one vowel position towards another during their production, and **monophthongs**, during which there's no change of vowel position. The checked vowels are all monophthongs. The free vowel group contains both monophthongs and diphthongs (see Figures 5.12–5.15):

- **Free monophthongs**: FLEECE /iː/, GOOSE /uː/, THOUGHT /ɔː/, NURSE /ɜː/, PALM /ɑː/, SQUARE /eə/
- **Free diphthongs**: FACE /eɪ/, PRICE /aɪ/, CHOICE /ɔɪ/, MOUTH /aʊ/, GOAT /əʊ/, NEAR /ɪə/, CURE /ʊə/

Monophthongs are written with a single vowel symbol, while the diphthongs have two symbols. The first symbol represents the starting position of the diphthong, and the second gives the direction of the glide. The single exception to this method of representing monophthongs and diphthongs is the SQUARE /eə/ vowel, which has a double symbol despite nowadays being a monophthong. This is because this vowel was a diphthong when the phonemic symbol for it was chosen, but during the decades since, a monophthongal variant has taken over as the most usual realisation. We continue to use this slightly misleading symbol for the sake of consistency with the set of symbols used in English language teaching materials.

The diphthongs can be categorised according to the direction of the glide. The **centring** diphthongs (Figure 5.15) are those which glide towards the schwa position at the centre of the vowel space: NEAR /ɪə/ and CURE /ʊə/. As stated above, SQUARE /eə/ belonged to this category before it became a monophthong, as the phonemic symbol still indicates. The non-centring diphthongs are called **closing** diphthongs because the tongue moves towards the close position at the top of the vowel space as they are pronounced. The closing diphthongs can in turn be divided into the **fronting** diphthongs – FACE /eɪ/, PRICE /aɪ/ and CHOICE /ɔɪ/ – which glide towards the front of the vowel space (Figure 5.13), and the **backing** diphthongs – MOUTH /aʊ/ and GOAT /əʊ/ – which glide towards the back of the vowel space (Figure 5.14). The GB diphthongs are all **falling diphthongs**, which means that the first element is longer, and the second, gliding element is shorter and weaker. Consequently, the closing diphthongs only glide *towards* the close front and close back areas but rarely reach them. [ɪ] and [ʊ] are used in the phonemic symbols for the closing diphthongs to represent the general close front and close back areas; it's not meant that [ɪ] and [ʊ] are their actual targets. On our vowel diagrams we identify the starting point of a diphthong and represent the glide with an arrow.

An alternative way of categorising the diphthongs is according to the extent of the gliding element. Accordingly, PRICE /aɪ/, MOUTH /aʊ/ and CHOICE /ɔɪ/ are **wide diphthongs**, involving a relatively long glide, and FACE /eɪ/, GOAT /əʊ/, NEAR /ɪə/ and CURE /ʊə/ are **narrow diphthongs**, involving a rather short glide.

5.2.4 Triphthongs

Although the word 'triphthong' has been used in connection with English vowels in a number of works, there are no phonemic triphthongs in English. A diphthong is a vowel which glides from one position to another within a single syllable. A **triphthong**, therefore, is a vowel which glides from one position to another and then towards a third position, all *within* one syllable. The vowels which have been called triphthongs are in reality merely disyllabic sequences (= sequences of two syllables) of closing diphthongs followed by schwa /ə/. For example:

- PRICE /aɪ/ + schwa /ə/:   *fire* /ˈfaɪə/, *wire* /ˈwaɪə/, *choir* /ˈkwaɪə/, *iron* /ˈaɪən/
- MOUTH /aʊ/ + schwa /ə/:   *tower* /ˈtaʊə/, *sour* /ˈsaʊə/, *hour* /ˈaʊə/, *flour* /ˈflaʊə/
- FACE /eɪ/ + schwa /ə/:   *layer* /ˈleɪə/, *player* /ˈpleɪə/, *greyer* /ˈɡreɪə/, *slayer* /ˈsleɪə/
- GOAT /əʊ/ + schwa /ə/:   *lower* /ˈləʊə/, *mower* /ˈməʊə/, *rower* /ˈrəʊə/, *slower* /ˈsləʊə/
- CHOICE /ɔɪ/ + schwa /ə/:   *buoyant* /ˈbɔɪənt/, *employer* /ɪmˈplɔɪə/, *joyous* /ˈdʒɔɪəs/

Sequences with PRICE /aɪ/ and MOUTH /aʊ/ have been given the most attention because they occur in more words and are often found within a single morpheme. In sequences with FACE /eɪ/, GOAT /əʊ/ and CHOICE /ɔɪ/, on the other hand, the schwa is nearly always part of a suffix, as our examples demonstrate.

The situation is further complicated by a process known as **smoothing**, i.e. the partial or complete loss of an element in a vowel sequence. Since the gliding elements of the diphthongs are rather weak, they can be reduced to virtually nothing when schwa /ə/ follows, the tongue moving directly from the diphthong's starting position to the schwa position. The resulting vowel is monosyllabic (a single syllable) and a diphthong, e.g. *fire* [faə] and *sour* [saə]. This is more common in the case of PRICE /aɪ/ and MOUTH /aɪ/, for which the process may go a step further, the tongue not moving from the starting point of the diphthong. The result is a long monophthong, e.g. *fire* [faː] and *sour* [saː]. Smoothing is less usual for sequences of FACE /eɪ/, GOAT /əʊ/ and CHOICE /ɔɪ/ plus schwa because they are fewer in number and because speakers are conscious of the two elements which they normally consist of. Ultimately, however, although smoothing is an interesting phenomenon, it cannot be recommended for imitation by learners. Extensive use of smoothing is associated with socially conspicuous or 'posh' speech, and it's never obligatory to smooth sequences of diphthong and schwa. If the learner can correctly pronounce the individual diphthongs and schwa, then saying them in sequence should cause no more difficulty than any other sequence.

5.3 Pre-fortis clipping

Numerous factors affect vowel duration besides the inherent length of checked and free vowels, and many of these factors, such as speech rate, aren't unique to English. One universal tendency, however, which is notably exaggerated in English is the shortening of vowels (and other sonorants) when immediately followed by a voiceless consonant in the same syllable. This phenomenon is called **pre-fortis clipping**, 'fortis' being an alternative term for 'voiceless', and 'clipping' meaning 'shortening'. This shortening is most noticeable in the free vowels, since they are inherently rather long to begin with.

Compare: full length vs. shortened:

seed /siːd/ vs. *seat* /siːt/   *lose* /luːz/ vs. *loose* /luːs/
save /seɪv/ vs. *safe* /seɪf/   *side* /saɪd/ vs. *site* /saɪt/   *void* /vɔɪd/ vs. *voice* /vɔɪs/
code /kəʊd/ vs. *coat* /kəʊt/   *loud* /laʊd/ vs. *lout* /laʊt/

When diphthongs are clipped, it's the first part, not the glide, which is shortened, making them less obviously falling diphthongs.

The vowels in the above examples are either close monophthongs (FLEECE /iː/, GOOSE /uː/) or diphthongs which glide towards a close front (FACE /eɪ/, PRICE /aɪ/, CHOICE /ɔɪ/) or close back (GOAT /əʊ/, MOUTH /aʊ/) position. The degree of shortening is less striking in those free vowels which don't include a close element, i.e. the centring diphthongs and the open and mid monophthongs.

Compare: full length vs. slightly shortened:

peers /pɪəz/ vs. *pierce* /pɪəs/
heard /hɜːd/ vs. *hurt* /hɜːt/
cord /kɔːd/ vs. *court* /kɔːt/
card /kɑːd/ vs. *cart* /kɑːt/
scares /skeəz/ vs. *scarce* /skeəs/

Note the number of words which demonstrate the relevant context. There are none for CURE /ʊə/, very few for NEAR /ɪə/ and SQUARE /eə/, a moderate number for NURSE and CHOICE, and a good number for PALM /ɑː/ and THOUGHT /ɔː/.

The checked vowels are already inherently short, and therefore the extent of the shortening they undergo is also rather slight, but nevertheless still present.

Compare: full length vs. slightly clipped:

his /hɪz/ vs. *hiss* /hɪs/   *hood* /hʊd/ vs. *hook* /hʊk/
bed /bed/ vs. *bet* /bet/   *mug* /mʌg/ vs. *muck* /mʌk/
rag /ræg/ vs. *rack* /ræk/   *log* /lɒg/ vs. *lock* /lɒk/

Pre-fortis clipping affects all sonorants, not just vowels, which means that the lateral approximant /l/ and the nasals /m/, /n/ and /ŋ/ are shortened together with the vowel which precedes them (see section 2.4.1). It's typically checked vowels which can be followed by a sonorant and an obstruent, in which case the combined clipping of both the sonorant and the vowel is much more striking than when a checked vowel alone is clipped.

Compare: full length vs. shortened:

build /bɪld/ vs. *built* /bɪlt/   *bulb* /bʌlb/ vs. *pulp* /pʌlp/
hummed /hʌmd/ vs. *hump* /hʌmp/   *rammed* /ræmd/ vs. *ramp* /ræmp/
lend /lend/ vs. *lent* /lent/   *wand* /wɒnd/ vs. *want* /wɒnt/
wins /wɪnz/ vs. *wince* /wɪns/   *lunge* /lʌndʒ/ vs. *lunch* /lʌntʃ/
banged /bæŋd/ vs. *bank* /bæŋk/   *anger* /ˈæŋgə/ vs. *anchor* /ˈæŋkə/

Pre-fortis clipping is important not only for the correct pronunciation and recognition of vowels, but also as a cue to the identity of consonants. As we saw in section 2.4.2, English voiced obstruents (plosives, affricates and fricatives) are actually only potentially fully voiced – they are often only partially voiced or may even be fully devoiced. In such cases the length of the preceding sonorant (a vowel, nasal or approximant) can be an important indicator for distinguishing between voiced and voiceless obstruents.

5.4 Rhoticity

GB is a **non-rhotic** accent, which means that the phoneme /r/ occurs only before vowels and has been lost before consonants and at the end of words before a pause. In the rhotic accents of Scotland, Ireland and North America, /r/ was never lost in non-prevocalic positions and is still pronounced wherever there's an <r> in the spelling. As a consequence of the loss of /r/ in non-rhotic accents, a number of new vowels arose which are written with <r> but have no /r/ in their pronunciation:

- NEAR /ɪə/: *steer* /stɪə/, *here* /hɪə/, *fear* /fɪə/, *fierce* /fɪəs/, *beard* /bɪəd/
- SQUARE /eə/: *care* /keə/, *pair* /peə/, *bear* /beə/, *there* /ðeə/, *scarce* /skeəs/
- NURSE /ɜː/: *purse* /pɜːs/, *bird* /bɜːd/, *verb* /vɜːb/, *earth* /ɜːθ/, *word* /wɜːd/
- CURE /ʊə/: *moor* /mʊə/, *assure* /əˈʃʊə/

In another group of words the loss of /r/ in non-prevocalic position ultimately led to merger with another vowel and added to the stock of words representing that vowel:

- PALM /ɑː/: *start* /stɑːt/, *car* /kɑː/, *part* /pɑːt/, *card* /kɑːd/, *barn* /bɑːn/, *heart* /hɑːt/
- THOUGHT /ɔː/: *north* /nɔːθ/, *force* /fɔːs/, *warm* /wɔːm/, *more* /mɔː/, *roar* /rɔː/, *door* /dɔː/
- schwa /ə/: *litre* /ˈliːtə/, *surprise* /səˈpraɪz/, *grammar* /ˈgræmə/, *forgive* /fəˈgɪv/

Note that /r/ is always pronounced when another vowel follows (see also section 12.4):

- NEAR /ɪə/: *hero* /ˈhɪərəʊ/, *weary* /ˈwɪəri/, *hearing* /ˈhɪərɪŋ/, *clearer* /ˈklɪərə/
- SQUARE /eə/: *parent* /ˈpeərənt/, *vary* /ˈveəri/, *fairy* /ˈfeəri/, *wearing* /ˈweərɪŋ/
- NURSE /ɜː/: *furry* /ˈfɜːri/, *stirring* /ˈstɜːrɪŋ/, *blurry* /ˈblɜːri/, *purring* /ˈpɜːrɪŋ/
- CURE /ʊə/: *curious* /ˈkjʊəriəs/, *boorish* /ˈbʊərɪʃ/, *fury* /ˈfjʊəri/, *during* /ˈdʒʊərɪŋ/
- PALM /ɑː/: *starring* /ˈstɑːrɪŋ/, *guitarist* /ɡɪˈtɑːrɪst/, *Sahara* /səˈhɑːrə/
- THOUGHT /ɔː/: *warring* /ˈwɔːrɪŋ/, *Laura* /ˈlɔːrə/, *story* /ˈstɔːri/, *boring* /ˈbɔːrɪŋ/

It's important to take special care not to be misled by the spelling, and to be certain which words have /r/ and which words don't. With some practice, the habit of pronouncing /r/ only before vowels will come naturally.

Note that in non-rhotic accents such as GB, /r/ has been lost in word-final position when a pause or a word beginning with a consonant follows. When a word beginning with a vowel immediately follows, this counts as pre-vocalic position and /r/ is pronounced, leading to the phenomenon of **/r/-liaison** (see section 12.4):

- NEAR /ɪə/:   *here and there* /ˈhɪər ən ˈðeə/
- SQUARE /eə/:   *fair and square* /ˈfeər ən ˈskweə/
- NURSE /ɜː/:   *stir and strain* /ˈstɜːr ən ˈstreɪn/
- CURE /ʊə/:   *pure and simple* /ˈpjʊər ən ˈsɪmpl̩/
- PALM /ɑː/:   *far and wide* /ˈfɑːr ən ˈwaɪd/
- THOUGHT /ɔː/: *more and more* /ˈmɔːr ən ˈmɔː/

5.5 Influence of dark /l/

The raising of the back of the tongue (velarisation) for **dark /l/** (see section 2.14.2) has the effect of retracting a preceding vowel:

- **Checked vowels**: *sit* [sɪt] vs. *silt* [sɪɫt], *bet* [bet] vs. *belt* [beɫt], *pat* [pæt] vs. *pal* [pæɫ], *cut* [kʌt] vs. *cult* [kʌɫt], *dot* [dɒt] vs. *doll* [dɒɫ], *put* [pʊt] vs. *pull* [pʊɫ]
- **Free monophthongs**: *cur* [kɜː] vs. *curl* [kɜːɫ], *star* [stɑː] vs. *snarl* [snɑːɫ], *four* [fɔː] vs. *fall* [fɔːɫ], *food* [fuːd] vs. *fool* [fuːɫ]
- **Diphthongs**: *how* [haʊ] vs. *howl* [haʊɫ], *go* [ɡəʊ] vs. *goal* [ɡəʊɫ]

This is particularly striking in the case of GOAT, which has in recent decades developed an allophone with a backer, opener starting point [ɒʊ] in this position.

5.6 Pre-/l/ breaking

When dark /l/ follows the close front vowel FLEECE /iː/ or the closing fronting diphthongs (FACE /eɪ/, PRICE /aɪ/, CHOICE /ɔɪ/), which glide towards the close front position, a schwa /ə/ often develops between the vowel and the dark /l/. This is known as **pre-/l/ breaking**:

fee [fiː] vs. *feel* [ˈfiːəɫ]   *pay* [peɪ] vs. *pale* [ˈpeɪəɫ]
tie [taɪ] vs. *tile* [ˈtaɪəɫ]   *toy* [tɔɪ] vs. *toil* [ˈtɔɪəɫ]

When the word-final /l/ is followed by a suffix or word beginning with a vowel, the dark /l/ is replaced by a clear /l/, and the schwa element is lost:

feel ['fiːɬ] vs. *feeling* ['fiːlɪŋ] or *feel it* ['fiːl ɪt]
sail ['seɪɬ] vs. *sailing* ['seɪlɪŋ] or *sail along* ['seɪl ə'lɒŋ]
smile ['smaɪɬ] vs. *smiling* ['smaɪlɪŋ] or *smile at* ['smaɪl ət]
toil ['tɔɪɬ] vs. *toiling* ['tɔɪlɪŋ] or *toil away* ['tɔɪl ə'weɪ]

5.7 Recent developments

5.7.1 Fronting, lowering, raising

There has been a tendency since the middle of the last century for a number of GB monophthongs to move around the vowel space in an anti-clockwise direction. This is shown in Figure 5.17.

The most striking example of this is the fronting of GOOSE /uː/ (termed **GOOSE-fronting**) and FOOT /ʊ/ from back to central positions. At the same time DRESS /e/ and TRAP /æ/ have been **lowered** to open-mid and open positions, and LOT /ɒ/ and THOUGHT /ɔː/ have been **raised** to nearer the open-mid and close-mid positions. The only peripheral monophthongs (i.e. those at the edges of the vowel space) that have maintained their positions are those in the close front area – FLEECE /iː/ and KIT /ɪ/ – and PALM /ɑː/. During the second half of the twentieth century STRUT /ʌ/ was fronted, but it has since backed again, thus maintaining its distance from TRAP /æ/.

5.7.2 Monophthonging of centring diphthongs

It appears that the class of centring diphthongs is destined to be lost from the GB accent. Since at least the last quarter of the nineteenth century there has been alongside the diphthongal variant of SQUARE [ɛə] a monophthongal variant [ɛː], which lacks the glide to schwa [ə]. During the course of the twentieth century the monophthongal variant gradually became more common until it took over from the diphthongal variant as the most usual realisation. At the present time the monophthongal pronunciation is the norm while the minority diphthongal pronunciation has become rather old-fashioned. Despite this fact, we continue to use the phonemic symbol /ɛə/ for the sake of consistency with most other published materials and dictionaries.

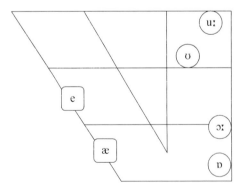 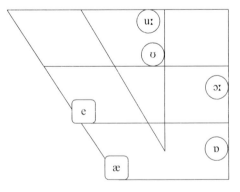

Figure 5.17 Left: English monophthongs in the twentieth century. Right: English monophthongs in the twenty-first century.

The NEAR vowel is undergoing the same monophthonging process, but it's a lot less advanced than that of SQUARE. Both [ɪː] and [ɪə] pronunciations are common, and neither is stereotyped as old-fashioned or excessively modern.

CURE is also undergoing monophthonging, especially after /j/, resulting in a long version of the modern fronted FOOT vowel: [ɵː]. More importantly, however, CURE has for a long time been merging with the THOUGHT vowel. Throughout the twentieth century the CURE vowel was increasingly replaced by THOUGHT, especially in high-frequency words such as *sure*, *your*, *poor*. This process is still incomplete, but it's far enough advanced to advise foreign learners that they can, for the sake of simplicity, pronounce all CURE words with the THOUGHT vowel without sounding un-English.

5.7.3 Happy tensing

Since about the middle of the twentieth century, the weak KIT vowel has in a certain set of phonetic environments developed into a new weak vowel – weak FLEECE. This has occurred in word-final position (*happy*, *coffee*, *movie*), in morpheme-final position (*anti-*, *multi-*, *semi-*), before vowels (*react*, *alien*, *piano*, *area*) and, more recently, in word-initial *be-* (*before*), *de-* (*delete*), *e-* (*elect*), *pre-* (*predict*) and *re-* (*repeat*). This phenomenon is known as **happy tensing**. Towards the end of the century, the symbol [i] and the keyword *happ*Y were introduced to indicate that at that time the older generations tended to pronounce such words with weak KIT and the younger generations with the new weak FLEECE vowel. At the present time, however, the weak FLEECE vowel is practically universal in these contexts, and weak KIT is now restricted to old-fashioned speech or certain regional accents. Now that the symbol [i] no longer means '*weak* KIT *or weak* FLEECE' but instead only '*now weak* FLEECE *but formerly weak* KIT', it isn't strictly necessary and only complicates our otherwise phonemic transcription. In many ways it would be better to show it as /iː/ and then to remember that it's shortened in unstressed syllables, just like all other vowels. We continue to use it, however, in order to be consistent with other published works.

A similar process occurred with weak FOOT, which in pre-vocalic position has been replaced by another new weak vowel, weak GOOSE (*tuition*, *annual*, *situation*). Weak FOOT occurred in many fewer words than weak KIT, and as a consequence it has almost completely been wiped out and replaced by weak GOOSE in pre-vocalic position and schwa in pre-consonantal position (*ridiculous*, *executive*, *singular*). Like weak FLEECE, weak GOOSE is represented by a superfluous symbol, [u], which we use here for the sake of consistency.

5.8 Vowel length and phonemic contrasts

It was noted in section 5.2.2 that an earlier, very popular style of transcription used the length mark to distinguish between the symbols for FLEECE /iː/ and KIT /i/, GOOSE /uː/ and FOOT /u/, and THOUGHT /ɔː/ and LOT /ɔ/, thereby giving the false impression that the only difference between these pairs of vowels was length, when in fact it's vowel quality (i.e. tongue and lip position) which distinguishes them. There are some vowels in English, however, which do form pairs distinguished by length alone. The NURSE /ɜː/ vowel, for example, was formerly represented by the schwa symbol accompanied by a length mark /əː/. In this case the symbol isn't misleading as NURSE is indeed merely a long schwa. The lowering of DRESS /e/ and monophthonging of SQUARE /eə/ mean that it's possible to use the same open-mid front unrounded vowel quality for both of them (*ferry* ['fɛri] vs. *fairy* ['fɛːri]). And if a speaker uses the monophthongal variant of NEAR /ɪə/, the result is a contrast between KIT /ɪ/ and NEAR /ɪə/ based on length alone (*bid* [bɪd] vs. *beard* [bɪːd]).

Chapter 6

Practice

Individual strong vowels

This chapter provides practice in pronouncing the English vowels and their various allophones. The exercise material includes the target sounds in different phonetic contexts, in words and phrases where they occur multiple times, in sentences and in dialogues.

6.1 Checked monophthongs: summary of key features

The six checked monophthongs are KIT /ɪ/, FOOT /ʊ/, DRESS /e/, TRAP /æ/, STRUT /ʌ/ and LOT /ɒ/. Their key features are:

1 As checked vowels, they must be followed by a syllable coda.
2 They are of relatively short duration when compared with the other strong vowels (and therefore are often referred to as *short* vowels). TRAP /æ/ is an exception. For many speakers it's rather long, especially before voiced consonants.
3 They are shortened when followed by a voiceless consonant in the same syllable (pre-fortis clipping).

   a) The shortening is slight because the checked vowels are already inherently rather short.
   b) The shortening is more noticeable when combined with the shortening of another sonorant (nasal or approximant).
   c) Shortening of vowels is an important cue for identifying whether a following obstruent is voiced or voiceless.

4 KIT /ɪ/, FOOT /ʊ/ and LOT /ɒ/ aren't merely short versions of FLEECE /iː/, GOOSE /uː/ and THOUGHT /ɔː/.
5 The vowel quality of DRESS /e/ can be used for SQUARE /eə/, and the two distinguished by means of length.
6 The modern TRAP /æ/ vowel is fully open.
7 The modern FOOT /ʊ/ vowel is no longer back, but central and only very slightly rounded.

6.2 KIT /ɪ/

6.2.1 Description

Just above close-mid, front-central, unrounded. KIT /ɪ/ is also a member of the weak vowel set.

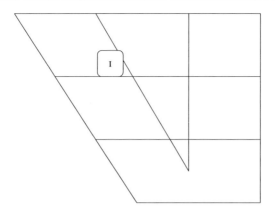

Figure 6.1 The KIT /ɪ/ vowel.

6.2.2 Spelling

    <i> big, lid, bill
    <y> typical, myth, symbol
    <e> English, establish, pretty, chicken
    <a> cottage, dotage

Unusual spellings

    sieve, busy, business, minute (n.), biscuit, build, guilt, women

6.2.3 Full length

big, bin, bridge, fin, fridge, give, grin, king, lid, pig, pin, ring, sing, skin, slim, quiz, spin, spring, sting, string, swim, swing, thin, thing, tin, twig, twin, wig, win, wind, wing

6.2.4 Clipped

bit, brick, brisk, chick, chip, click, cliff, clip, crisp, dip, dish, drip, fish, fist, fit, fix, gift, flip, hip, hiss, hit, kick, knit, lift, lip, list, miss, mist, mix, myth, pick, quick, quit, rich, rip, risk, shift, ship, sick, sit, six, slip, stick, stiff, switch, this, trick, trip, twist, which, whip, wish, wrist, zip

6.2.5 Full length vs. clipped

bid/bit, grid/grit, hid/hit, his/hiss, pig/pick, ridge/rich, wig/wick, kid/kit, lid/lit, slid/slit, nib/nip, rib/rip

6.2.6 Retracted before dark /l/

bill, chill, drill, fill, grill, hill, ill, kill, mill, pill, skill, spill, will, build, milk, silk, film, guilt, hilt, tilt, wilt

6.2.7 Multiple (including weak KIT)

biscuit, finish, image, limit, minute (n.), ticket, victim, visit, wicked, women, cricket, village, spinach, clinic, critic, lyric, mimic, picnic, building, spirit, vivid, timid, rigid, liquid, district, instinct, insist, diplomatic, disadvantage, disappointed, pyramid, vitamin, discourage, historic, hypnotic

6.2.8 Additional words

city, busy, begin, bitter, chicken, different, difficult, dinner, figure, guilty, idiot, injure, innocent, insect, interesting, kitchen, kitten, little, middle, mirror, opinion, picture, pillow, pity, pretty, river, scissors, silly, sister, sticky, tickle, tricky, typical, window, winter

6.2.9 Phrases

big business, binge drinking, a biscuit tin, a bitter wind, a brick building, silicon chips, a British citizen, the inner city, living conditions, a cricket pitch, a film critic, a difficult decision, an English dictionary, Christmas dinner, a fizzy drink, written English, cling film, a film script, fish fingers, a fitted kitchen, physically fit, a quick fix, flip a switch, a giggling fit, the village idiot, an innocent victim, a kiss on the lips, the kitchen sink, little children, skimmed milk, the missing link, a bitter pill, quick thinking, a sinking ship, thick-skinned, a kindred spirit, a stick insect, a stiff drink, finger prints, a business trip, a wicked witch, a tin whistle, a wish list, a big difference, build a bridge, fish and chips, English literature, as fit as a fiddle, lick your lips, sink or swim

6.2.10 Sentences

1   Phil's as fit as a fiddle.
2   Fill in the missing lyrics.
3   Isobel drinks skimmed milk.
4   Did Dylan win the competition?
5   Bridget lived in Italy for six years.
6   This put him in a difficult position.
7   Jim's kids are sick of chicken dinners.
8   Fish and chips is originally an English dish.
9   Christopher and Imogen are kindred spirits.
10   Jill didn't stick her fingers in the biscuit tin!
11   The living conditions in the inner city are abysmal.
12   Lydia lives in a little village in the middle of England.
13   Melissa's interested in the history of English literature.
14   Will Patricia give me her quick recipe for ginger biscuits?
15   My dictionary of English idioms went missing within fifteen minutes.
16   In my opinion Jim's quick thinking, but I think Sid's pretty dim-witted.
17   Who was commissioned to build the bridge across the Mississippi River?
18   My little sister's a bitter cynic, and my big sister's an interfering busybody.
19   It's fulfilled his ambition of becoming a minister in the Department of Business, Innovation and Skills.
20   We established a statistically significant difference between English and Finnish children.

6.2.11 Dialogues

A: He can mix six drinks in a minute.
B: Six is very quick.
A: He does it for a living.
B: For a living? Then six is a bit sluggish.

A: This is ridiculous!
B: It's silly!
A: Nearly fifty different symbols!
B: For nearly fifty different English sounds!

A: Give me a sip of your drink.
B: Only if you give me one of your fish fingers.
A: Is this a swindle?
B: Business is business . . .

6.3 FOOT /ʊ/

6.3.1 Description

Just above close-mid, central, weakly rounded.

6.3.2 Spelling

<ook> = /ʊk/ book, cook, look, took (exceptions: spooky, snooker)
Certain other words containing <oo> foot, good, hood, childhood, stood, gooseberry, wool
<ou, oul> could, should, would, courier
<o> woman, wolf, wolves, bosom
<ul, ull> = /ʊl/ full, pull, bullet, beautiful, useful, fulfil
<ush> = /ʊʃ/ bush, push
Certain other words with <u> sugar, put, pudding, butcher, cuckoo

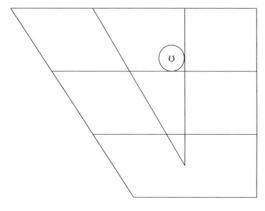

Figure 6.2 The FOOT /ʊ/ vowel.

Unusual spellings

Worcester, worsted

6.3.3 Full length

could, good, hood, should, stood, wood/would

6.3.4 Clipped

book, look, took, cook, hook, crook, rook, shook, brook, nook, foot, soot, put, bush, push, woof

6.3.5 Full length vs. clipped

could/cook, hood/hook, should/shook, wood/woof

6.3.6 Retracted before dark /l/

bull, full, pull, wool, wolf

6.3.7 Additional words

bushel, bullet, bulletin, crooked, rookie, wooden, bully, cuckoo, butcher, cushion, cushy, pudding, sugar, understood, woman, bosom, courier, gooseberry, ambush, fulfil, childhood

6.3.8 Phrases

a good look, by hook or by crook, a cook book, fully booked, a good footballer, here puss, puss, puss!, I would if I could, look at that rook!, pull the wool over his eyes, put your foot down, took a look, took the bull by the horns, woof, woof!, woollen goods, cook good food, push and pull, put your foot in it, good-looking

6.3.9 Sentences

1   He was hooked on books.
2   Kirundi's spoken in Burundi.
3   She stood barefoot in the brook.
4   The bully pushed him into the bush.
5   The crooks pulled down their hoods.
6   I would if I could, but it's just no good.
7   I bought woollen cushions in Pembroke.
8   The bulldogs chased him into the woods.
9   The cooking courses are all fully booked.
10   We picked bushels and bushels of mushrooms.
11   The bullfight was held at the Acapulco bullring.
12   He was a footballer before he became a butcher.
13   He fully understood why she'd put her foot down.
14   It would be good if you could put a full stop there.

15   He took a good look at her and then shook his head.
16   I didn't know whether to push him away or pull him closer.
17   My cuckoo clock stopped because the pendulum was crooked.
18   Could you cook a gooseberry pudding without putting sugar in?
19   The book looks at the bully's journey from childhood to manhood.
20   The football club's full name is the Wolverhampton Wanderers, but they're known as the Wolves.

6.3.10 Dialogues

A: You shouldn't cook that pudding anymore.
B: And *you* shouldn't bully the cook, should you.
A: I couldn't bully you, could I. You'd butcher me!
B: Good cooks have sharp knives!

A: Now look, how can I hook the heart of a good woman?
B: It took me a lot of looking to find a good woman.
A: How do I ambush the affections of a good woman?
B: Put your best foot forward, and by hook or by crook you'll find a good woman.
A: Is there a good book on how to look for a good woman?

A: For a good pudding you shouldn't add much sugar.
B: A good cook wouldn't add more than a spoonful.
A: A tablespoonful of sugar, or a teaspoonful of sugar?
B: I couldn't say. Let me have another look in the cookbook.
A: It wouldn't look good if we put too much sugar in the pudding, would it?
B: Goodness no! We'd look like a pair of woolly, wooden-headed cooks!

6.4 DRESS /e/

Description

Open-mid, front, unrounded.

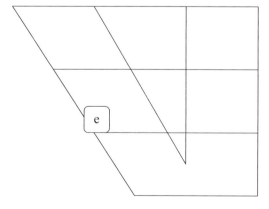

Figure 6.3 The DRESS /e/ vowel.

6.4.1 Spelling

<e> bed, beg, bell
<ea> bread, dead, breath, pleasure
<a> any, many

Unusual spellings

friend, ate, again, against, said, says, leopard, Geoff, jeopardy, bury, burial, Leicester

6.4.2 Full length

bed, bread, dead, edge, egg, end, fed, friend, head, hedge, leg, lend, pen, red, said, send, shed, spend, spread, ten, when

6.4.3 Clipped

best, bet, breath, check, chest, deaf, death, debt, desk, dress, fetch, fresh, get, guess, left, less, let, mess, neck, nest, net, next, pet, rest, step, stretch, sweat, test, wet, yes

6.4.4 Full length vs. clipped

bed/bet, led/let, dead/debt, edge/etch, wed/wet, said/set, peg/peck, rev/ref

6.4.5 Retracted before dark /l/

bell, sell/cell, fell, gel, hell, shell, smell, tell, well, weld, self, shelf, elk, elm, help, else, belt, felt, melt

6.4.6 Multiple

bedspread, bestseller, deathbed, egghead, eggshell, epilepsy, existential, extraterrestrial, headdress, headrest, headset, letterhead, nevertheless, recollect, recommend, redhead, referendum, represent, retrospect, self-centred, self-confessed, self-defence, self-help, self-possessed, self-respect, semiprecious, semi-professional, temperamental, trendsetter, well-bred, well-connected, well-fed, well-intentioned, well-read, whenever

6.4.7 Additional words

ahead, any, belly, bury, cellar, cherry, clever, credit, defend, desert (n.), develop, echo, elephant, energy, enemy, engine, error, feather, heavy, jealous, leather, lemon, many, measure, merry, pleasant, ready, weather, yellow, address, adventure, centre, collect, correct, dentist, event, healthy, letter, message, plenty, question, technique, index, context, access, alphabet, ancestor, comment

6.4.8 Phrases

a best friend, a dead end, a debt collector, a health centre, a special event, a buried treasure chest, a wedding ceremony, an electric fence, bed and breakfast, a breath of fresh air, correct an error, dead and buried, death threats, a defence mechanism, a desperate effort, dress sense, forensic tests, a French head chef, fresh eggs, gentle exercise, genuine leather, heavy metal, an intelligence test, a jet engine, lemon zest, a precious gem, a protective shell, red peppers, send a letter, a sense of adventure, a spelling error, stretch your legs, a wedding dress, wet cement, deadly enemies

6.4.9 Sentences

1   Beth has no sense of adventure.
2   The men were mending the nets.
3   The desert stretched out endlessly.
4   Ellen and Emma were best friends.
5   How can I tell if the eggs are fresh?
6   Ken has no dress sense whatsoever!
7   The breathalyser test proved negative.
8   Ted's bed and breakfast is exceptional.
9   Fred says he regularly gets death threats.
10 The hotel was excellent in every respect.
11 Derek wasn't ready to accept these tenets.
12 Dennis places a heavy emphasis on ethics.
13 Jenny made several perceptive suggestions.
14 Benjamin and Betty went everywhere together.
15 The empty desk suggested that Jeremy had left.
16 I'll never forget the expression on Edward's face.
17 Megan's always one step ahead of everyone else.
18 The elections are scheduled for December the seventh.
19 These sectors are heavily dependent on technology.
20 We had a very helpful attendant at the check-in desk.

6.4.10 Dialogues

A: Is this your best effort?
B: Yes, it's my very best attempt.
A: It's a terrible mess.
B: Well, I bet the rest aren't any better!

A: Fred, have you been sending death threats to Ted again?
B: I penned my ten best ever on Wednesday and sent them direct. A real treasure chest of devilish, hellish threats. A clever jest for my very best friend.
A: But you neglected to append your name and address, Fred! He read your letter and more or less wet the bed!
B: Wet the bed? What a terrible defence mechanism.
A: I meant he drenched it in sweat. Now get ready to tell him you sent the letter in error and you're terribly repentant.

A: Are you getting ready for your French test?
B: French is my best subject. The test'll be an effortless success.

A: Have you kept abreast of the expected content of the test – the irregular present tense and the imperative?

B: My friends said to expect questions about the feminine gender and inflections.

A: In the end, your friends aren't as friendly as you guessed!

6.5 TRAP /æ/

6.5.1 Description

Open, front, unrounded. This vowel has become increasingly open since the middle of the twentieth century and is now typically fully open. For many speakers, TRAP can be rather long before voiced consonants, almost as long as the free vowels.

6.5.2 Spelling

    <a> bang, cab, bank, mat, arrow, taxi

Unusual spellings

    plait, plaid, meringue, timbre

6.5.3 Full length

add, bad, badge, bag, band, bang, cab, can, drag, fan, gang, glad, grand, hand, hang, jam, have, land, man, pan, plan, rag, sad, sand, stand, van

6.5.4 Clipped

axe, back, bat, black, cash, cat, catch, chat, clap, crash, flash, flat, gap, gas, hat, lap, map, mat, match, pat, rat, scratch, snap, tap, tax, track, trap, wrap

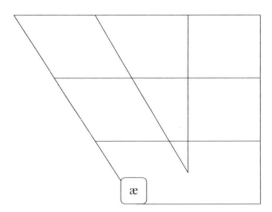

Figure 6.4 The TRAP /æ/ vowel.

6.5.5 Full length vs. clipped

add/at, bad/bat, badge/batch, bag/back, cab/cap, had/hat, rag/rack, lab/lap, plaid/plait, slab/slap, tab/tap, fad/fat, pad/pat, sad/sat, lag/lack, sag/sack, snag/snack, tag/tack

6.5.6 Retracted before dark /l/

canal, pal, talc, scalp, shall

6.5.7 Multiple

abnormality, abracadabra, abstract (n.), acrobat, anagram, Anglo-Saxon, anorak, anthrax, anti-climax, aristocrat, aromatic, backgammon, backhand, backlash, backpack, back-scratcher, backslash, backtrack, bandana, bandstand, bandwagon, battleaxe, blackjack, caravan, cataract, catnap, claptrap, crash-land, fantastic, flapjack, gangplank, gasman, granddad, handbag, handstand, haphazard, hatchback, jackass, magnanimous, malpractice, mantrap, manufacture, mathematics, no-man's-land, parallelogram, ransack, saddlebag, sandbag, satisfaction, slapdash

6.5.8 Additional words

action, actor, agony, amateur, anchor, anger, angry, animal, ankle, apple, arrow, attack, attractive, balcony, battle, blanket, cabbage, café, camera, cancel, candle, capital, carry, channel, chapter, character, damage, dragon, exam, fancy, fashion, gamble, grammar, habit, imagine, manage, manners, marry, massive, matter, narrow, natural, packet, panic, perhaps, plastic, practical, rabbit, shadow, tablet, talent, taxi, travel, understand, value, vanish, syntax, contact, climax

6.5.9 Phrases

a bad attitude, a balancing act, a bank manager, a black cab, a plastic carrier bag, a ham sandwich, a jazz band, a married man, a matter of fact, a narrow gap, natural talent, a panic attack, a bad back, a traffic jam, an asthma attack, an elastic band, as mad as a hatter, bank balance, black magic, a gambling man, hand in hand, happily married, natural gas, pack your bags, a plan of action, a rat catcher, a relaxed attitude, value added tax, a bad habit, a black cat

6.5.10 Sentences

1 Pack your bags.
2 Amanda was in absolute agony.
3 Andrew landed flat on his back.
4 Thanks for clarifying the matter.
5 Pat and Jack catch rabbits in traps.
6 Anna has a natural talent for languages.
7 Alan has a callous attitude towards cats.
8 My granddad had a massive heart attack.

9   Barry's a happily married family man.
10   Has Patrick got an accurate map of Japan?
11   Can you see the animal tracks in the sand?
12   The manager valiantly tackled the challenge.
13   Matthew was very practical and matter of fact.
14   Natasha understands how to handle the matter.
15   Annabel patted Janet on the back and dashed off.
16   Catherine wore a black jacket and a matching hat.
17   Sebastian still has panic attacks after his accident.
18   The sandwiches were packed in a plastic carrier bag.
19   Larry wrapped Alice in a blanket and carried her back.
20   Joanna had exams, so we had to cancel our plans to go camping.

6.5.11 Dialogues

A: I wish they'd scrap the tax on plastic carrier bags.
B: Hang on! They should scrap the bags, not the tax.
A: You're mad! A man can't carry masses of shopping back to the car without a bag.
B: If you had a stash of bags in the back of your car, you'd always have one to hand.

A: Is that a fat black rat you're carrying in your jacket?
B: Sally's a black rat, but she's not fat. Fancy embarrassing her like that! What bad manners!
A: Having a menagerie of angry animals jammed in your jacket pockets is bad manners and a very bad habit.
B: Don't exaggerate. A rabbit, a rat and a cat aren't a menagerie. Here, pat Sally on the back. She's saddened by your attack on her character.

A: Now that I'm a married man, I'm abandoning my bad habits.
B: Is Jan planning to abandon her bad habits?
A: What bad habits? Jan's a fantastic catch. She doesn't have any bad habits.
B: Marriage has a habit of bringing out bad manners in even the most fantastic catch.

6.6 STRUT /ʌ/

6.6.1 Description

Between open-mid and open, central, unrounded.

6.6.2 Spelling

    <u> sum, butter, curry
    <o> love, money, nothing, colour
    <ou> cousin, courage, trouble, enough, tough

Unusual spellings

    blood, flood, does

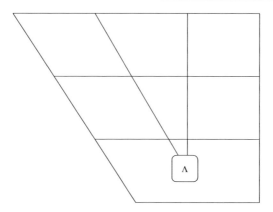

Figure 6.5 The STRUT /ʌ/ vowel.

6.6.3 Full length

blood, bud, bug, bun, buzz, club, come, crumb, cub, drug, drum, flood, fun, fund, gun, judge, jug, love, mud, plug, rub, rug, run, son/sun, sponge, stuff, suck, thumb, tongue, young

6.6.4 Clipped

blush, bust, crush, cup, cut, duck, dust, hut, luck, nut, rough, rush, shut, suck, touch, tough, trust

6.6.5 Full length vs. clipped

bud/but, bug/buck, buzz/bus, cub/cup, lug/luck, pub/pup, cud/cut, tug/tuck, mud/mutt, dug/duck, mug/muck, rug/ruck

6.6.6 Retracted before dark /l/

cull, dull, gull, hull, lull, skull, bulb, bulge, indulge, bulk, sulk, gulp, pulp, pulse, consult, cult, culture, result, vulture

6.6.7 Multiple

bloodsucker, bubblegum, buttercup, dumbstruck, fuddy-duddy, gunrunner, honeysuckle, humbug, humdrum, knuckle-duster, lovey-dovey, monkey-puzzle, multi-coloured, numbskull, punch-drunk, rough-and-tumble, runner-up, subculture, thumbs-up, unaccustomed, unbecoming, unbutton, uncomfortable, uncover, undercover, undercurrent, undercut (v.), underdone, undernourished, understudy, uninstructed, uninterrupted, upcoming, uppercut

6.6.8 Additional words

above, another, become, brother, bubble, bucket, buckle, budget, bundle, bungalow, butter, button, clumsy, colour, company, country, couple, cousin, cover, cuddle, culture, cupboard, curry, customer, discover, discovery, double, dozen, enough, funny, glove, honey, hundred, hungry, hurry, husband, lucky, money, monkey, mother, muscle, onion, oven, rubbish, stomach, sudden, suffer, summer, thorough, trouble, impulse, humbug, frustration, umbrella

6.6.9 Phrases

covered in blood, a younger brother, a dustpan and brush, a stomach bug, a currant bun, a London double-decker bus, at the touch of a button, lovely colours, a young couple, the front cover, lumpy custard, suddenly discover, a drug smuggler, a rubber duck, a rubbish dump, covered in dust, a sudden flood, just for fun, a trust fund, rubber gloves, runny honey, a loving husband, brotherly love, tough luck, a lump sum, Sunday lunch, run out of money, a couple of months, a young mother, stuck in mud, a tough nut, a rumbling stomach, a rust bucket, a wonder drug, oven gloves, the mother tongue

6.6.10 Sentences

1   Just my luck!
2   My husband loves currant buns.
3   Justin was unintentionally funny.
4   Don't be upset. It was just for fun.
5   Just dump the rubbish in the dustbin.
6   Douglas suffered the ultimate insult.
7   My son's truck got stuck in the mud.
8   The country was inundated by floods.
9   The young thug was covered in blood.
10   The gunfire rumbled like dull thunder.
11   Russell finds lumpy custard disgusting.
12   Russian and Dutch are my mother tongues.
13   Button mushrooms are cultivated in Hungary.
14   There are dozens of cups and mugs in the cupboard.
15   My cousin has become reluctant to trust other adults.
16   We indulged in a sumptuous Sunday lunch at the pub.
17   I subsequently discovered the company had gone bust.
18   The conductor grunted: 'Hurry up, love. Jump on the bus.'
19   For a month the government was unable to run the country.
20   You can indulge in another cup of coffee at the touch of a button.

6.6.11 Dialogues

A: Cover the muffins and buns!
B: Is your son suddenly coming back?
A: Let's stuff them back in the oven. Pass me another dozen of the big ones.
B: But your mother and brother said he was on a run with your cousin . . .

A: Coming duck hunting on Monday?
B: I love the countryside, but hunting ducks sounds too bloody for my weak stomach.

A: It's rubber ducks we hunt. My mother covers a couple in mud and hides them in the rubbish dump behind the pub near the country club.

B: Another one of your family's funny traditions? You really are a nutty bunch!

A: These currant buns are nothing like the ones that come out of my mother's oven.

B: I've had enough of your mother's currant buns. I love these ones and could munch dozens and dozens for lunch.

A: You'll suffer in the long run. A bulging stomach stuffed with buns, and your ugly mug covered in blood.

B: My ugly mug covered in blood?

A: When Mum hears you've had enough of her currant buns, she'll tug off her oven gloves and punch your ugly mug till it gushes with blood!

6.7 LOT /ɒ/

6.7.1 Description

Between open-mid and open, back, rounded.

6.7.2 Spelling

    <o> block, clock, frog
    <wa> = /wɒ/ swan, want, was, watch
    <qua> = /kwɒ/ equality, qualify, quality, quantity, quarrel
    <au> because, cauliflower, sausage, Austria, Australia

Unusual spellings

    cough, trough, knowledge, yacht

6.7.3 Full length

blob, bog, clog, cod, dog, fog, job, knob, lodge, log, mob, nod, odd, plod, pod, prod, rob, rod, snob, sob, solve

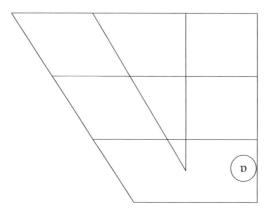

Figure 6.6 The LOT /ɒ/ vowel.

6.7.4 Clipped

block, boss, box, clock, cloth, cost, cot, cough, crop, cross, dock, dot, drop, fox, frost, hop, hot, knock, lock, loss, lost, lot, mock, mop, moss, moth, not, off, plot, pop, rock, rot, shock, shop, shot, sock, soft, spot, top, want, wash, wasp, watch, what, yacht

6.7.5 Full length vs. clipped

clog/clock, cod/cot, dog/dock, flog/flock, log/lock, mob/mop, nod/not, plod/plot, hob/hop, pod/pot, rod/rot, trod/trot, frog/frock

6.7.6 Retracted before dark /l/

alcohol, doll, dolphin, golf, absolve, dissolve, evolve, involve, resolve, solve

6.7.7 Multiple

chocoholic, choreography, coffeepot, compost, correspond, cosmos, dogsbody, foxtrot, gob-stopper, hogwash, horizontal, hotdog, hotpot, hotspot, lollipop, mollycoddle, monologue, monophthong, monstrosity, non-stop, not-for-profit, oblong, orange-blossom, poppycock, potshot, rock-bottom, shopaholic, stopcock, stopwatch, top-notch, watchdog

6.7.8 Additional words

accommodation, across, anonymous, apology, astonished, belong, body, bomb, borrow, bot-tle, bottom, chocolate, coffee, coffin, collar, comedy, common, copy, cottage, doctor, donkey, follow, forest, gossip, hobby, hollow, honest, honour, horrible, horror, hover, knowledge, modern, monster, office, pocket, popular, possible, profit, project (n.), promise, proper, quali-fied, quality, rocket, sausage, solid, sorry, swallow, topic, trolley, wallet, October, epoch, diphthong, tripod, apricot

6.7.9 Phrases

an atomic bomb, a body of knowledge, a bottle top, a box of chocolates, a coffee shop, com-mon knowledge, drop a bomb, a foreign body, the Foreign Office, a gossip column, a Gothic novel, a hot water bottle, job losses, the Loch Ness Monster, a long shot, a modest cost, a novel concept, orange squash, a rock concert, a pop song, a proper job, a qualified doctor, resolve a problem, a shopping trolley, solid rock, strong coffee, top quality, job prospects

6.7.10 Sentences

1 Joshua watched in horror.
2 It's a long shot, but why not?
3 They dropped an atomic bomb.
4 Dorothy has a soft spot for Oscar.
5 Tom's got a copy of the document.
6 Poverty's a complex phenomenon.
7 Molly got Bob a box of chocolates.

8   The box fell off the top of the lorry.
9   This shop sells top quality products.
10 John got a job in the Foreign Office.
11 Do you want coffee or hot chocolate?
12 Roger's job prospects are promising.
13 Dominic's a properly qualified doctor.
14 Horace Walpole was the first Gothic novelist.
15 Thomas had forgotten he'd lost his stopwatch.
16 Colin longed for a holiday on the Costa del Sol.
17 Oliver and Donna watched *Top of the Pops* online.
18 A majority of the respondents opted for the soft option.
19 How do we solve the problems of poverty and inequality?
20 Lots of Scots claim they've spotted the Loch Ness Monster.

6.7.11 Dialogues

A: Stop mocking John. It's wrong to sing such nasty songs.
B: It's wrong to wear odd socks.
A: It's a common problem if you're not conscientious.
B: A common problem if you're a rotten slob!

A: A pot of strong hot coffee will fix that cough.
B: The doctor said not to drink coffee until I've stopped coughing.
A: What a lot of nonsense! He's not a proper doctor. It's common knowledge that strong hot coffee's the top tonic for a cough.
B: Your top tonic makes me want to vomit.

A: It's so hot on this poxy yacht.
B: Get off if you want. I'm not stopping you.
A: You want me to drop to the bottom of the sea?
B: What an idiotic comment! We're in dock, you donkey. You can step off this poxy yacht if that's what you want.

6.8 Free monophthongs: summary of key features

The six free monophthongs are FLEECE /iː/, GOOSE /uː/, NURSE /ɜː/, PALM /ɑː/, THOUGHT /ɔː/ and SQUARE /eə/. Their key features are:

1   As free vowels, they can appear in syllables with or without a coda.
2   They are of relatively long duration when compared with the checked vowels (and therefore are often referred to as *long* vowels).
3   They are shortened when followed by a voiceless consonant in the same syllable (pre-fortis clipping).

   a)   The shortening of the close free monophthongs, FLEECE /iː/ and GOOSE /uː/, is greater than that of the non-close free monophthongs – NURSE /ɜː/, PALM /ɑː/, THOUGHT /ɔː/ and SQUARE /eə/.
   b)   Shortening of vowels is an important cue for identifying whether a following obstruent is voiced or voiceless.

4   FLEECE /iː/, GOOSE /uː/ and THOUGHT /ɔː/ aren't merely long versions of KIT /ɪ/, FOOT /ʊ/ and LOT /ɒ/.
5   GOOSE /uː/ is no longer a back vowel, but a central vowel with weak lip-rounding (GOOSE-fronting).
6   NURSE /ɜː/ is a long schwa.
7   A subgroup of PALM /ɑː/ words, called the BATH words, has TRAP /æ/, not PALM, in many of the accents of the north of England and North America (see section 6.12.1).
8   Both FLEECE /iː/ and GOOSE /uː/ have common slightly diphthongal variants – [ɪi] alongside [iː] for FLEECE and [ʊu] alongside [uː] for GOOSE.
9   SQUARE /eə/ was formerly a centring diphthong, and its phonemic symbol still reflects this.

6.9   FLEECE /iː/

6.9.1   Description

A little lower than close, a little backer than front, unrounded. Many speakers have a narrow diphthongal glide [ɪi] when the vowel has full length, notably in final positions, e.g. *free*. Before voiceless consonants, there's usually little or no glide, e.g. *feet*. Before dark /l/ a centring glide is heard, e.g. *reel*, *wheel* (pre-/l/ breaking; see section 5.6).

6.9.2   Spelling

    <ee> bee, see, glee
    <ea> sea, tea, season, reveal
    <ie> achieve, believe, grieve, niece
    <e> these, gene, scene
    <ei> seize, receive, ceiling
    <i> ski, niche, magazine

Unusual spellings

    people, Phoebe, foetus, Phoenix, key, quiche, suite, mosquito, Portuguese, quay

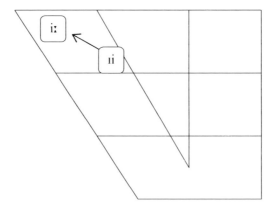

Figure 6.7 The FLEECE /iː/ vowel. The diagram shows both the monophthongal and diphthongal allophones.

6.9.3 Full length (open syllables)

bee, sea, key, ski, tea, tree, three, flea/flee, free, knee, pea, fee

6.9.4 Full length (closed syllables)

bead, bleed, breeze, cheese, feed, freeze, lead (v.), leave, need, please, read, seed, speed, squeeze, tease, weed, sleeve, bean, clean, cream, dream, gleam, green, jeans, keen, mean, queen, scene, scream, screen, steam, stream, team, seem

6.9.5 Pre-/l/ breaking

deal, feel, field, heal/heel, kneel, meal, peel, squeal, steel/steal, wheel, shield, reveal

6.9.6 Clipped

beach, beast, beat, beef, brief, cheap, cheat, cheek, deep, each, eat, feet, grease, heat, keep, leaf, leak/leek, meat/meet, neat, niece, peace/piece, peach, peak, reach, seat, sheep, sheet, sleep, sneak, speak, speech, steep, street, sweet, teach, teeth, thief, treat, weak/week, screech

6.9.7 Full length vs. clipped

bead/beat, seize/cease, seed/seat, weed/wheat, greed/greet, heed/heat, Swede/sweet, tweed/tweet, believe/belief, grieve/grief, leave/leaf, relieve/relief, thieve/thief, teethe/teeth, knees/niece, peas/peace

6.9.8 Multiple

beanfeast, beefeater, beekeeper, deep-sea, deep-seated, freewheel, heat-seeking, legalese, peacekeeper, piecemeal, seaweed, speed-read, squeaky-clean, tea-tree, 3-D, weak-kneed, BBC

6.9.9 Additional words

agree, asleep, cathedral, ceiling, colleague, complete, decent, defeat, delete, detail, disease, eager, easy, evening, extreme, feature, fever, freedom, indeed, litre, machine, magazine, medium, people, police, reason, release, repeat, secret, centipede, chlorine, colleague, hygiene, protein, vaccine

6.9.10 Phrases

green beans, a bleak scene, the queen bee, a deep-seated belief, a sea breeze, a brief meeting, a piece of cheese, a police chief, a street cleaner, the deep blue sea, a feeling of deep grief, delete an email, a devious scheme, complete disbelief, an easy read, an elite athlete, an evening meal, an evil creature, between two extremes, a key feature, keep a secret, legal fees, a reasonable fee, beneath your feet, a green field, free speech, green leaves, green tea, a clean handkerchief, a weak leader, lean meat, a weekly magazine, a secret meeting, keep your receipt, a key ingredient, a peace treaty, a sneak preview, sea creatures, a secret ingredient, clean sheets, a three-piece suite, VIP treatment, extreme heat, keep clean

6.9.11 Sentences

1 Please leave me in peace!
2 We believe in freedom of speech.
3 These wheels are extremely cheap.
4 An elite athlete needs a lean physique.
5 Eat a piece of cheese after every meal.
6 Anita and Peter sealed the deal at three p.m.
7 Phoebe completed a degree in Swedish.
8 Eve seems reasonably easy to deal with.
9 Denise received treatment for the disease.
10 The sea breeze decreased the feeling of heat.
11 Reading tea leaves can reveal people's secrets.
12 Steve's a beekeeper, and Amelia's a PE teacher.
13 We treated ourselves to a cream tea on the beach.
14 Keith has no redeeming features, but Sheila's sweet.
15 This is the first decent meal I've had in three weeks.
16 Pete speaks Greek, and Christina speaks Portuguese.
17 The thief succeeded in deceiving the chief of police.
18 I have a feeling of deep grief, but his death's a relief.
19 I'll leave the green beans and peas in the deep freeze.
20 The people of New Zealand are frequently called Kiwis.

6.9.12 Dialogues

A: You don't seem to be a keen reader.
B: Me? I read three magazines a week!
A: You need to read more signs. That one says 'Please keep feet off seats.'
B: Oh! I see what you mean.

A: Steve's a keen beekeeper.
B: He keeps bees? So if I need any honey . . .
A: He's a vegan. He doesn't agree with stealing from bees.
B: Why does he keep the creatures?
A: He breeds three endangered species of honeybee.

A: How sweet of you to meet me this evening!
B: I need to see you to feel complete. Believe me!
A: I'm speechless. I can't feel the ground beneath my feet.
B: I mean it. I dream of leading an extremely genial life with you. Please be my queen!

6.10 GOOSE /uː/

6.10.1 Description

Close, central, weakly rounded. Many speakers use a diphthongal glide [ʊu], especially in final position, e.g. *blue, true, do*. The lip-rounding is nowadays weak and may be entirely absent. The vowel has gradually become more front in the twenty-first century, especially following /j/, e.g. *use, beautiful*. The glide is lost before dark /l/, where a backer realisation is heard, e.g. *rule, cool*.

6.10.2 Spelling

<oo> boot, choose, food
<u> duty, amusing
<u-e> brute, cube, cute
<o> do, to (strong form), two, tomb, who
<o-e> move, lose, prove, whose
<ou> group, through, youth
<ui> bruise, fruit, juice, suit
<ue> blue, clue, true, venue
<eu> feud, manoeuvre, neutral, queue, pseudo-
<ew> blew, chew, crew, interview

Unusual spellings

beauty, beautiful, shoe

6.10.3 Full length (open syllables)

blue/blew, clue, chew, crew, dew/due, do, drew, few, glue, grew, new/knew, queue/cue, screw, shoe, through, true, two/too, view, who, you, zoo

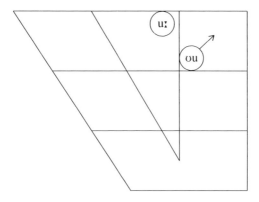

Figure 6.8 The GOOSE /uː/ vowel. The diagrams shows both the monophthongal and diphthongal allophones.

6.10.4 Full length (closed syllables)

bruise, choose, food, huge, mood, move, prove, smooth, moon, noon, room, soon, spoon, zoom

6.10.5 Clipped

boot, cute, flute, fruit, goose, hoot, juice, loop, loose, roof, root, shoot, suit, tooth

6.10.6 Full length vs. clipped

rude/root, sued/suit, prove/proof, booed/boot, brewed/brute, queued/cute, lose/loose, use (v.)/use (n.), abuse (v.)/abuse (n.)

6.10.7 Retracted before dark /l/

cool, fool, ghoul, mule, pool, rule, school, stool, tool

6.10.8 Multiple

cock-a-doodle-doo, foolproof, guru, supercomputer, supercool, superhuman, voodoo

6.10.9 Additional words

absolutely, afternoon, amusing, argue, balloon, beauty, computer, conclude, confusing, future, human, humour, improve, include, movie, music, remove, rumour, student, stupid, uniform, unit, bridegroom, costume, cuckoo, destitute, fortune, interview, issue, menu, module, nephew, persecute, substitute, volume

6.10.10 Phrases

a soup spoon, a room with a view, absolutely true, a beautiful view, choose from the menu, confuse the issue, fruit juice, doom and gloom, through the roof, human communication, improve your mood, junior school, lose enthusiasm, move smoothly, a music school, nuclear fusion, nutritious food, of dubious value, conclusive proof, remove your shoes, room for manoeuvre, a blue school uniform, use a computer, a useful clue, youthful enthusiasm, absolutely useless, lose a tooth, remove a tumour

6.10.11 Sentences

1   You stupid fool!
2   This view's too crude.
3   Fruit's a nutritious food.
4   Matthew was an astute pupil.
5   Luke was confusing the issue.
6   Ruth's suit's absolutely beautiful.
7   My tutor confused Judy with Lucy.

8 Drop your doom and gloom attitude.
9 Louis used it as an excuse to do it too.
10 The room was filled with huge suitcases.
11 Fruit juice can boost your immune system.
12 Music was played throughout the afternoon.
13 They unanimously approved the constitution.
14 The shoes and boots in that boutique are cute.
15 Do you usually listen to music at full volume?
16 Susan and Julie went to junior school together.
17 My computer guru will be back on Tuesday afternoon.
18 Hugh took the opportunity to interview some of the pupils.
19 Ruby knew that Andrew would soon lose his youthful enthusiasm.
20 A statue of Newton can be found at one of the Oxford University museums.

6.10.12 Dialogues

A: There are too few serious issues in the news.
B: Who wants doom and gloom in June?
A: I assume you disapprove of truth in the news, you fool.
B: I knew you'd choose a gloomy mood instead of good humour and amusement.

A: Sue says she's through with Bruce.
B: The rumours are absolutely true. I knew they were doomed when I saw Bruce with Judy outside the music school on Tuesday.
A: You zoom in on all the clues!
B: The brute had on a new puce suit and new blue shoes.
A: What a costume!

A: I don't know what to choose from the menu.
B: Do choose soon. I need food!
A: Don't be rude. I'll choose soon.
B: Just choose stew for you and goose for me.
A: No soup? No prune juice?
B: Choose soup and prune juice, but soon! I'm drooling!

6.11 NURSE /ɜː/

6.11.1 Description

Mid, central, unrounded.

6.11.2 Spelling

<er> herd, determined, fertile
<ur> fur, turn, occur, purpose
<ir> bird, girl, confirm, dirty
<ear> earth, rehearse, earnest

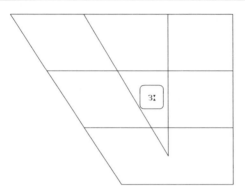

Figure 6.9 The NURSE /ɜ:/ vowel.

<our> adjourn, courteous, journey
<yr> myrtle, myrrh
<wor> = /wɜ:/ word, worthy, world, worth

Unusual spellings

colonel, attorney, milieu, entrepreneur (also sometimes *adieu*)

6.11.3 Full length (open syllables)

blur, fur, purr, stir, sir, spur, slur

6.11.4 Full length (closed syllables)

bird, burn, curb, curve, earn, fern, firm, germ, herb, learn, nerve, serve, stern, term, third, turn, word, worm

6.11.5 Clipped

birth, church, curse, dirt, earth, first, hurt, nurse, purse, search, shirt, skirt, surf, work, worse, worst, worth

6.11.6 Full length vs. clipped

heard/hurt, purrs/purse, serve/surf, curs/curse, surge/search, purge/perch, curd/curt, purred/pert

6.11.7 Retracted before dark /l/

curl, earl, girl, hurl, pearl, twirl, whirl, world

6.11.8 Multiple

earthworks, earthworm, hurly-burly, pervert (n.), word-for-word, word-perfect, Wordsworth

6.11.9 Additional words

alert, allergic, burden, burger, burglar, certain, circle, circuit, circus, commercial, concerned, confirm, curtain, deserve, dirty, early, emergency, eternal, expert, fertile, furniture, journal, merchant, murder, murmur, observe, perfect (adj.), permanent, person, prefer, purple, purpose, refer, reserve, return, reverse, servant, service, survey (n.), thirsty, turkey, version, advert, proverb, suburb

6.11.10 Phrases

a first-class service, a bird reserve, a church service, a circular journey, confirm the worst, a dirty word, an early bird, emergency first aid, the emergency services, an external observer, fertile earth, the First World War, in a perfect world, in no uncertain terms, permanent work, the person concerned, the return journey, first-degree burns, serve a purpose, slur your words, sterling work, virtually perfect, a turn for the worse, chirping birds, dirty work, early work, emergency surgery, the first anniversary

6.11.11 Sentences

1 Herbert did the dirty work.
2 The girls wore twirl skirts.
3 She worked as a nurse in Serbia.
4 Ernest needed emergency surgery.
5 Pearl's an expert on early furniture.
6 She worked like a whirling dervish.
7 I'm allergic to virtually all perfumes.
8 Earl deserved to come first, not third.
9 The first version was virtually perfect.
10 How do you determine a pearl's worth?
11 The return journey from Berlin was murder.
12 Thursdays are the worst for service workers.
13 The girls were determined to learn Burmese.
14 That advert in the *Observer* was certainly disturbing.
15 It's Bernard's thirty-third birthday on the thirty-first.
16 Curtis and Gertie journeyed from Germany to Turkey.
17 She seemed unperturbed by Vernon's curt, hurtful words.
18 Curse those chirping birds that disturb me so early!
19 Shirley's journey to Serbia turned out to be nerve-racking.
20 Ferdinand was told in no uncertain terms not to disturb Gertrude.

6.11.12 Dialogues

A: Vernon's certainly nervous about burglars.
B: His work as a pearl and fur merchant means his house is perfect for burglars.
A: And his furniture's worth a fortune.
B: You're certain he's out on Thursday for his birthday party?
A: Burglary's dirty work, but the economy's taken a turn for the worse and my girl's thirsty for pearls.

A: I'm concerned about Percy's thirst for sherbet.

B: It's worse than you know. The dental nurse told him to return to the dentist for more work on the surfaces of his teeth.

A: He's impervious to the threat of emergency surgery. His perverted thirst for sherbet has given him scurvy.

B: I'm certain he'll never learn. He says it's worth it for his precious sherbet.

A: The first person he murdered was a burglar.

B: Did the burglar deserve it?

A: The burglar wasn't at work. He only learnt later that burglary was that person's work.

B: Was the thirty-third murder victim also a burglar?

A: No, he murdered a colonel and then an earl.

B: This murderer went up in the world!

6.12 PALM /ɑː/

6.12.1 Description

Open, back-central, unrounded. Note that GB uses PALM /ɑː/ in a set of words known as the BATH words. These have TRAP /æ/ in General American. They typically occur when <a> is followed by a nasal + consonant, e.g. *plant*, *chance*, *command*, or a fricative, e.g. *class*, *past*, but there are many exceptions, e.g. *exam* with TRAP, *example* with PALM, *gas* with TRAP, *grass* with PALM.

6.12.2 Spelling

> <ar> bark, card, remark, target
> <a> dance, father, last

Unusual spellings

> clerk, Berkshire, Berkeley, Derby, sergeant, calf, calm, palm, half, heart, hearth, bourgeois, memoir, repertoire, reservoir

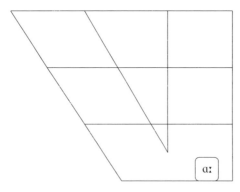

Figure 6.10 The PALM /ɑː/ vowel.

6.12.3 Full length

a) Open syllables

bar, bra, car, far, jar, scar, star, tar

b) Closed syllables

arm, barge, barn, calm, card, carve, charge, charm, farm, guard, hard, harm, large, palm, starve, vase

6.12.4 Clipped

art, aunt, bark, bath, blast, branch, brass, calf, carp, cart, cast, chance, chart, class, craft, daft, dance, dark, draft, fast, glance, glass, grasp, grass, half, heart, last, laugh, march, mark, marsh, park, part, pass, past, path, plant, scarf, shaft, shark, sharp, smart, spark, staff, start, task, vast

6.12.5 Full length vs. clipped

bras/brass, carve/calf, card/cart, hard/heart, halve/half, large/larch, starve/staff, starred/start

6.12.6 Retracted before dark /l/

banal, gnarl, morale, snarl

6.12.7 Multiple

aardvark, farmyard, half-hearted, half-mast, heart-to-heart, lah-di-dah, taskmaster

6.12.8 Additional words

advance, advantage, after, alarm, answer, argue, artist, bargain, basket, carpet, castle, demand, disaster, drama, example, farmer, father, garden, garlic, guardian, guitar, harbour, harvest, market, nasty, parcel, pardon, partner, rather, sample, sergeant, target, banana, giraffe, plaster, command, slander, memoir, placard, rhubarb

6.12.9 Phrases

an all-star cast, armed guards, arts and crafts, demand an answer, a barn dance, a hard bargain, far apart, a fast car, a garden path, a glass jar, half a chance, hard to grasp, the last laugh, a heart bypass, a jar of marmalade, a large part, a last chance, a marketing department, park a car, part-time staff, a safari park, start to laugh, a dancing class, a hearty laugh, a master class, a past master

6.12.10 Sentences

1   This is Arthur's last chance.
2   Barbara's father's charming.
3   Margaret's a hard taskmaster.
4   I've planted garlic in my garden.

5 Mark was granted a partial pardon.
6 The sergeant was charged with arson.
7 Martha can't master the art of dancing.
8 It's hard to forecast the demand for cars.
9 Alexandra has a master of arts in drama.
10 Charlotte's a marvellous sparring partner.
11 Let's have a barbecue party this afternoon.
12 We put the jars of marmalade in the basket.
13 I bought my aunt a cardigan and a glass vase.
14 My father spent the afternoon at Cardiff Castle.
15 Archie's a carpenter who's a real master of his craft.
16 You can get a large harvest of tomatoes from one plant.
17 Marsha answered that she'd kept to her part of the bargain.
18 Sandra performs arduous tasks in the marketing department.
19 We were charmed by the llamas and the aardvarks at the safari park.
20 Martin's remarks on the advantages of a large sample were unanswerable.

6.12.11 Dialogues

A: Marge! I can't start the blasted car again.
B: At last a chance to buy a faster car! This one's only good for parts.
A: Don't start demanding a large car we can't afford.
B: I'd rather starve than be laughed at in this nasty old car.

A: The drama Charles starred in was marred by a lack of harmony among the all-star cast.
B: Is there any chance he and his partner will attend the after-party?
A: They may have the last laugh and bypass the party.
B: It's all rather a farce. If Charles had half your charm, he would've demanded they all calm down and master their parts in advance.

A: This jar of marmalade has been started.
B: Carl was starving and took advantage of the unguarded jar.
A: A charming start to the afternoon. If I was still a sergeant in the army, I'd send him on a rather nasty march.
B: But you're not an army sergeant. So calm down, father, button up your cardigan, and eat your marmalade.

6.13 THOUGHT /ɔː/

6.13.1 Description

Below close-mid, back, rounded.

6.13.2 Spelling

 <or> north, sort, force, sword /sɔːd/
 <ore> before, more, score

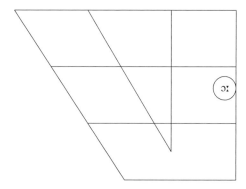

Figure 6.11 The THOUGHT /ɔː/ vowel.

<oar> board, soar
<oor> poor (formerly with CURE), door, floor
<quar> = /kwɔː/ quartet, quartz, quarter (also /ˈkɔːtə/)
<al> = /ɔːl/ also, always, false, salt (also /fɒls, sɒlt/)
<all> = /ɔːl/ all, fall, hall, tall
<au> author, launch, cause, fault (also /fɒlt/)
<ar> = /wɔː/ war, warm, reward
<aw> law, straw, dawn, awkward, awful
<our> your, you're (these used to be said with CURE), four, pour
<ur> sure, pure, cure (nowadays usually said with THOUGHT /ɔː/ but formerly with CURE /ʊə/)

Unusual spellings

daughter, caught, brought, ought, thought, broad, water

6.13.3 Full length

a) Open syllables
chore, claw, core, door, floor, four, jaw, law, more, pour, saw, score, shore, snore, store, straw, thaw, war

b) Closed syllables
board, broad, cause, clause, cord, fraud, lord, pause, sword, corn, form, horn, lawn, storm, thorn, warm, yawn

6.13.4 Clipped

brought, caught/court, chalk, course, force, fought, fork, horse, north, porch, pork, port, sauce/source, short, sort, sport, talk, taught, thought, walk

6.13.5 Full length vs. clipped

board/bought, broad/brought, cord/caught, cause/course, ford/fought, saws/sauce, sword/sort, thawed/thought, ward/wart, poured/port, toured/taught

6.13.6 Retracted before dark /l/

appal, ball/bawl, brawl, call, crawl, drawl, fall, hall/haul, install, maul, recall (v.), scrawl, shawl, small, sprawl, stall, tall, trawl, wall

6.13.7 Multiple

all-important, auditorium, broadsword, daughter-in-law, door-to-door, floorboard, hawthorn, short-haul, walkie-talkie, wall-to-wall, warlord, watercourse, waterfall

6.13.8 Additional words

abroad, afford, author, autumn, award, before, daughter, divorce, enormous, important, ignore, naughty, normal, orchard, reward, story, water, order, platform, acorn, audition, ordeal, jigsaw, tornado

6.13.9 Phrases

a short walk, water sports, all morning, an awkward pause, a chalk drawing, a court order, draw the short straw, law enforcement, fall to the floor, a formal report, former glory, an important resource, north of the border, pause for thought, pour water, restore order, a short course, a water shortage, a small fortune, small talk, a tall order, a war memorial, warm water, a divorce court, draw a portrait, a short story

6.13.10 Sentences

1   I bought it warts and all.
2   I always draw the short straw.
3   My daughter Gloria adores horses.
4   They sought to restore law and order.
5   Paul taught a course on the short story.
6   Audrey bought a gorgeous chalk drawing.
7   Paula's favourite water sport is snorkelling.
8   George went for a short walk around Newport.
9   Claudia caught the ball before it hit the floor.
10   He called upon them to withdraw their forces.
11   It's a Victorian fort restored to its former glory.
12   Small talk's very important in any organisation.
13   Unfortunately, my report was altogether ignored.
14   Laura was a staunch supporter of law enforcement.
15   Norman will formally launch the report this morning.
16   It's a memorial for the soldiers that fought in the war.
17   Claude gave a talk on George Orwell last autumn.
18   Explore the Norwegian fjords on board the *Queen Victoria*.
19   He was caught at the border of Portugal with a false passport.
20   There was an awkward pause before Walter walked out the door.

6.13.11 Dialogues (including CURE words)

A: You call that normal? You snore like a wild boar with a broken jaw!

B: There's nothing boring about my snoring. It's gorgeous.

A: I'll pour water on my naughty snoring boar before long.

B: Then a small brawl, some sort of law enforcement and a formal divorce court will follow.

A: I bought forty-four false passports this morning.

B: Touring northern Europe while avoiding the law courts is even more plausible than before.

A: When I was caught and brought before the law court in Norway last August, they poured scorn on me and I felt so forlorn.

B: Caution is the order of the day. There'll be no more forced walks across borders because of a shortage of resources.

A: Is Norman short or tall?

B: He's neither short nor tall, neither small nor enormous.

A: You're sure he's not at all poor?

B: His fortune isn't small, it's enormous.

A: You adore Norman because he's normal – neither short nor tall, neither small nor enormous.

B: Yes, his enormous fortune isn't important at all.

6.14 SQUARE /eə/

6.14.1 Description

Open-mid, front, unrounded. This vowel used to start from an open-mid front position and move towards open-mid central. However, nowadays the glide is usually absent, and some books and dictionaries now use the symbol /ɛː/ for SQUARE.

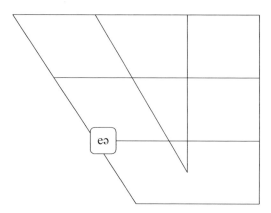

Figure 6.12 The SQUARE /eə/ vowel.

6.14.2 Spelling

<air> air, chair, flair, questionnaire
<are> bare, care, share, parent
<ar> scarce, scarcity, Sarah
<ary> = /eəri/ Mary, scary, canary
<aria> = /eəriə/ vegetarian, Hungarian, variable
<arious> = /eəriəs/ various, hilarious, gregarious
<ay> mayor, prayer
<ei> their, heir, heiress

Unusual spellings

they're, there, where

6.14.3 Full length

a)   Open syllables

air, bare/bear, blare, care, chair, dare, fair/fare, flair/flare, glare, hair, mare/mayor, pair/ pear, rare, share, spare, square, stair/stare, swear, tear (rip), there, wear/where, affair, aware, beware, billionaire, compare, declare, despair, millionaire, nightmare, prepare, questionnaire, repair, welfare

b)   Closed syllables

laird, cairn, airs, aired, bears, blares, blared, cares, cared, chairs, dares, dared, fares, fared, flares, flared, glares, glared, pairs/pears, paired, shares, shared, spares, spared, stairs/stares, stared, swears, tears (rips), wears

6.14.4 Clipped

scarce

6.14.5 Before /r/ (medial)

aerial, aeroplane, aquarium, area, barbarian, canary, dairy, fairy, hairy, hilarious, parent, prairie, scary, variable, various, vary, vegetarian, wary

6.14.6 Multiple

airfare, airy-fairy, fair-haired, shareware

6.14.7 Phrases

a fair share, a caring parent, fair hair, scarcely bear, vegetarian fare, wear and tear, wear your hair, prepare a questionnaire, fairly careful, prepared to swear

6.14.8 Sentences

1   He left his heirs all his shares.
2   Sarah was scarcely ever there.
3   The hardware was beyond repair.

4   Mary was aware of all his affairs.
5   He had a flair for writing fairy tales.
6   The chairman was a gregarious person.
7   I swear the pair of them looked hilarious.
8   Claire wouldn't share the airfare with him.
9   They made the mayor aware of their despair.
10   Care must be taken to wear suitable footwear.
11   We prepared the questionnaire with great care.
12   I can scarcely bear to see her in that wheelchair.
13   We tasted the carefully prepared vegetarian fare.
14   We had dairy-free éclairs with caramelised pears.
15   It's unfair to compare this area with the Canaries.
16   Her visual awareness was impaired after the scare.
17   It's rare for it to be colder upstairs than downstairs.
18   Enter if you dare, and prepare yourselves for a scare!
19   Her nightmares scared her, but her parents didn't care.
20   The Hungarian millionaire was wary of airy-fairy schemes.

6.14.9 Dialogues

A: Her parents don't care if she swears.
B: They're a pair! And look how she wears her hair.
A: I wasn't prepared for such a scare. She's a real nightmare.
B: And now she's in our care. Her parents just haven't done their fair share.

A: Will you share your spare pear with me?
B: I'm prepared to share my spare pear if you swear to share it fairly.
A: I swear. I'll be careful to share it fairly.
B: But where *is* my pear? It's not where I left it.
A: Don't despair. It's over there, on the chair.
B: What a scare!

A: Claire always wears her hair with flair.
B: You mean Claire's hair attracts stares.
A: To be fair, if you wear your hair with flair, you get stares.
B: I swear Clare's scary canary hair attracts glares as well as stares!

6.15 Closing diphthongs: summary of key features

The five closing diphthongs are FACE /eɪ/, PRICE /aɪ/, CHOICE /ɔɪ/, GOAT /əʊ/ and MOUTH /aʊ/. Their key features are:

1   They glide towards the close position at the top of the vowel space.

   a)   The fronting diphthongs, FACE /eɪ/, PRICE /aɪ/ and CHOICE /ɔɪ/, glide towards the close front position.

   b)   The backing diphthongs, GOAT /əʊ/ and MOUTH /aʊ/, glide towards the close back position.

2   They are falling diphthongs.
   a)   More time is spent at the start position than gliding.
   b)   The glides rarely reach the close position but finish around close-mid.
3   Diphthongs can also be categorised according to the extent of the glide.
   a)   The narrow diphthongs, FACE /eɪ/ and GOAT /əʊ/, have very short glides.
   b)   The wide diphthongs, PRICE /aɪ/, CHOICE /ɔɪ/ and MOUTH /aʊ/, have longer glides.
4   A schwa /ə/ is often inserted between the closing fronting diphthongs and a following dark /l/ (pre-/l/ breaking).
5   As free vowels, they can appear in syllables with or without a coda.
6   They are of relatively long duration when compared with the checked vowels (and are therefore also *long* vowels).
7   They are shortened when followed by a voiceless consonant in the same syllable (pre-fortis clipping).
   a)   The degree of shortening is as great as that of FLEECE /iː/ and GOOSE /uː/.
   b)   The first part is shortened, causing the glide to begin earlier than in unshortened diphthongs.
   c)   Shortening of vowels is an important cue for identifying whether a following obstruent is voiced or voiceless.

8   The starting position for FACE /eɪ/ is closer than the position for the DRESS /e/ vowel.
9   When followed by dark /l/, GOAT /əʊ/ has the allophone [ɒʊ].

6.16   FACE /eɪ/

Description

Starts below close-mid and moves towards close front. Unrounded throughout.

6.16.1   Spelling

<a + consonant + vowel> lady, change, amazing, nature, space
<ague> = /eɪg/ vague, plague
<ai(gh)> wait, contain, maintain, straight

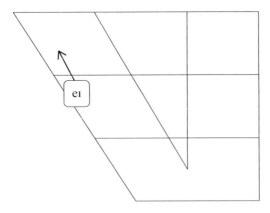

Figure 6.13 The FACE /eɪ/ vowel.

<ay> pay, stay, always
<ei> weigh, eight, beige
<ey> grey, obey, they

Loanwords from French:

ballet, buffet, sachet, café, sauté, puree, foyer, dossier, décor, matinee, suede

Unusual spellings

steak, break, great, gauge, gaol, bass (but the fish is /bæs/)

6.16.2 Full length

a) Open syllables
grey, may, pay, say, spray, they, tray, way/weigh
b) Closed syllables
age, aim, blade, blame, brain, brave, cage, came, cave, chain, change, fade, fame, flame, frame, game, gave, grade, lane, made, main/mane, maze, name, page, paid, pain, rain, same, save, shame, shave, stage, trade, train, vague, wage

6.16.3 Pre-/l/ breaking

mail, rail, sail/sale, snail, tail/tale, fail, nail, dale, frail, gale, jail, pale, prevail, scale, snail, stale, trail

6.16.4 Clipped

ache, bake, base, break, cake, case, chase, date, eight, face, gate, grape, great, hate, lake, late, make, place, plate, race, rate, shake, snake, space, state, straight, take, tape, taste, waist, wait

6.16.5 Full length vs. clipped

fade/fate, phase/face, grade/great, graze/grace, laid/late, made/mate, raise/race, raid/rate, save/safe, trade/trait, trays/trace, wade/wait

6.16.6 Multiple

alienate, aviation, brainwave, database, day-to-day, face-to-face, gateway, mainstay, maintain, make-or-break, mayonnaise, namesake, nation-state, painstaking, payday, playmate, radiator, railway, razor-blade, straightaway, tailor-made, takeaway, wastepaper

6.16.7 Additional words

able, afraid, amazing, apron, arrange, ashamed, awake, baby, bacon, basic, cable, contain, cradle, danger, escape, essay, favour, lady, lazy, major, mistake, nation, nature, paper, station, table, calculate, circulate, decorate, educate, migraine, café

6.16.8 Phrases

a display case, aches and pains, make an accusation, a paper aeroplane, in this day and age, an estate agent, the main aim, stay awake, a naval base, a birthday cake, the brakes failed, lay a cable, bake a cake, an isolated case, a state of chaos, a champagne cocktail, a claim for compensation, face grave danger, at a later date, a grey day, face major delays, a favourite destination, brain drain, make a face, a humiliating failure, his main claim to fame, a naked flame, play a game, the main gates, hate mail, a safe haven, a middle-aged lady, a man-made lake, make a fatal mistake, maiden name, a change of pace, a waste of paper, a famous phrase, a safe place, a railway station, play it safe, at a snail's pace, a faint trace, radioactive waste, take a break, on a case-by-case basis, a radio station

6.16.9 Sentences

 1   The waiter laid eight places at the table.
 2   Don't use spray paint near a naked flame.
 3   We were waiting for the plane to take off.
 4   Wages aren't keeping pace with inflation.
 5   The patients complained of aches and pains.
 6   'The rain in Spain stays mainly in the plain.'
 7   Amy hates changing lanes on the motorway.
 8   Caleb's place is amazingly tastefully decorated.
 9   The stage swayed dangerously under his weight.
10   The translations were displayed on facing pages.
11   The tornado left a trail of devastation in its wake.
12   'See you Later, Alligator' was sung by Bill Haley.
13   David's favourite meal is braised steak with gravy.
14   James was shaking as he made his way to the stage.
15   The wage negotiations will take place later in April.
16   They escaped to a safe haven from a place of danger.
17   The waitress complained about the heavily laden tray.
18   Grace and Jason take their holidays in faraway places.
19   The train was late so we had to wait for ages at the station.
20   The age difference placed a great strain on their relationship.

6.16.10 Dialogues

A: Jane, take a break from saying hateful things for just one day!
B: It's my nature to be straight and to paint things the way they are.
A: But it's plainly a fatal mistake not to refrain from stating to Kate's face that you hate the way she bakes her favourite cake.
B: Is that what made her take the tray of pastries and throw them in my face in that painful way?
A: It may have some relation to the case . . .

A: These cave paintings are in a shameful state.
B: I'm afraid to say *we* may be to blame.
A: We're making the paint fade and flake away?

B: Eighty-eight groups of holidaymakers like us pay to circulate through the caves every day and say what a shame it is that they're obliterating all trace of the famous ancient cave paintings . . .

A: This place makes my favourite gravy.
B: Isn't it strange to rate a café on the taste of their gravy?
A: Wait till you taste the gravy. You'll be grateful we came.
B: If you claim this gravy will amaze me and awaken strange cravings in me, you may be exaggerating.

6.17 PRICE /aɪ/

6.17.1 Description

Starts open central and moves towards close front. Unrounded throughout.

6.17.2 Spelling

<i> climb, kind, find, child, pilot
<i-e> side, time, wise
<ie> die, lie, lies
<igh, ig> high, slight, tight, sign, design
<y> cry, try, why, apply
<ye> eye, bye, dye
<y-e> type, style
<ei> either, neither (both also said with FLEECE), height, feisty
<ui> guide, quite
<uy> buy, guy

Unusual spellings

aisle, isle, island, maestro

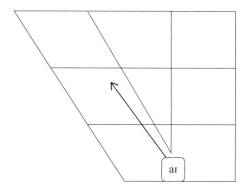

Figure 6.14 The PRICE /aɪ/ vowel.

6.17.3 Full length

a) Open syllables
  buy, cry, die, dry, eye, fly, fry, high, pie, shy, sigh, sky, spy, tie, try, why
b) Closed syllables
  bribe, blind, bride, climb, crime, dive, drive, find, five, guide, hide, kind, line, mind, mine, nine, prize, ride, shine, side/sighed, sign, size, slide, spine, time, wide, wine, wise

6.17.4 Pre-/l/ breaking

aisle, child, file, mild, mile, pile, smile, style, tile, while, wild, agile, compile

6.17.5 Clipped

bike, bite, bright, dice, fight, fright, height, hike, ice, knife, life, light, like, mice, might, nice, night, pipe, price, quite, rice, right, ripe, sight, slice, slight, spike, strike, stripe, tight, twice, type, white, wife, wipe, write

6.17.6 Full length vs. clipped

bride/bright, lies/lice, dies/dice, hide/height, eyes/ice, lied/light, live (adj.)/life, prize/price, rise/rice, ride/right, side/sight, slide/slight, spied/spite, strive/strife, tide/tight, tribe/tripe, tried/trite, wide/white, advise/advice

6.17.7 Multiple

acclimatise, blindside, childlike, childminder, cyanide, dynamite, eyeliner, eyesight, finalise, firefighter, firefly, highflyer, highlight, high-minded, high-profile, hindsight, hypothesise, idealise, identify, lifelike, lifeline, life-size, lifestyle, lifetime, likeminded, likewise, limelight, nightlife, night-light, nighttime, ninety-nine, pile-driver, pipeline, prioritise, privatise, sideline, skydiver, skyline, twilight, typewriter, wide-eyed, wildfire, wildlife

6.17.8 Additional words

appetite, apply, arrive, behind, beside, crisis, cycle, decide, deny, describe, design, despite, divide, exciting, exercise, final, idea, inside, fragile, fertile, missile, pilot, polite, private, provide, qualified, realise, recognise, remind, reply, silence, slice, spider, survive, tidy, tiny, senile, archive, hostile, futile, mobile, camomile, criteria, magpie, multiply, occupy, paradise, paralyse, qualify

6.17.9 Phrases

provide advice, satisfy your appetite, a private archive, ride a bike, turn a blind eye, a bright child, a pint of dry cider, a mild climate, climb high, a minor crime, the life cycle, a tight deadline, try to decide, a slight decline, quite delightful, a stylish design idea, a ninety-nine-mile drive, an exciting enterprise, light exercise, in my mind's eye, a high-fibre diet, a fight for survival, an exciting find, a nice guy, a five-mile hike, a worthwhile idea, a knight in shining armour, a driving licence, a downright lie, in the prime of life, a lightning strike, a slice of lime, a fine line, white mice, a lively enquiring mind, a diamond mine, a guided missile, Friday night, a slice of pie, an airline pilot, write a polite reply, fried white rice, twice the size, high in the sky, the right to strike, time flies, dry white wine, an exercise bike, a crime fighter, a winding tree-lined private drive, reply with a smile

6.17.10 Sentences

1   How time flies!
2   I find my life quite exciting.
3   Heidi's blind in her right eye.
4   Ryan was dying to ride my bike.
5   It's a ninety-mile drive to Brighton.
6   The miners organised a strike in 1999.
7   He couldn't find the Levi's in his size.
8   The flight arrival time is five past nine.
9   The tiny child didn't survive childhood.
10 I'd like to try a slice of your pine nut pie.
11 It reminds me of the time I was in China.
12 It took Isaac quite a while to find his style.
13 I'm not trying to deprive you of your rights.
14 Pineapple with lime ice cream is delightful.
15 Right click on the icon and select 'Hide icon'.
16 I can't specify the time of the crime precisely.
17 My Chinese wife likes to fry white rice with spices.
18 For the first time in my life I realised I was a minority.
19 My wife and I were invited to dine at nine, but declined.
20 Why did you buy that frightful tie with those wide white stripes?

6.17.11 Dialogues

A: It's a kind of time-travelling device. It flies through time.
B: That's nice, Mike. It must be quite a ride.
A: I spy on knights as they fight crime.
B: That's frightfully exciting. Shall we fly the kite once you've finished fighting crime through time?

A: It's not right for Mike to ride his motorbike without a licence.
B: You're quite right. He says riding a motorbike is nothing for a fighter pilot like him.
A: I'd never fly with a pilot like Mike. He rides his motorbike like a suicidal psychopath.
B: He's not quite right in the head. I think he's lying about being an airline pilot. And that diamond mine he acquired as a prize for saving the life of that VIP . . .
A: A qualified fighter pilot or a downright liar?

A: Brian's a nice, bright boy. Always smiling and so polite.
B: Nice? He's vile. I'd like to wipe that smile off his face.
A: Why are you so wildly riled by such a mild child?

B: That nice, bright, polite, mild child is a frighteningly malign, sly, vile child.

A: Brian Price is a frighteningly malign, sly, vile child?

B: Brian Price? No, Brian Price is a nice, bright, polite, mild child. Brian White's a frighteningly malign, sly, vile child.

6.18 CHOICE /ɔɪ/

6.18.1 Description

Starts just below open-mid, back, and moves towards close front. Starts rounded and ends unrounded.

6.18.2 Spelling

<oi> join, moisture, voice, Illinois
<oy> boy, toy, voyage
<uoy> buoy(ant)

Unusual spellings

rooibos, Hawick, Dordogne, Boulogne, Dostoevsky

6.18.3 Full length

a) Open syllables
boy, coy, joy, ploy, toy

b) Closed syllables
coin, groin, join, loin, noise, poise, void

6.18.4 Pre-/l/ breaking

boil, broil, coil, foil, oil, soil, spoil, toil

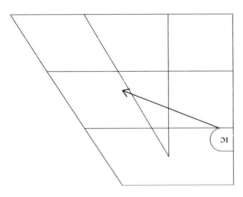

Figure 6.15 The CHOICE /ɔɪ/ vowel.

6.18.5 Clipped

choice, foist, hoist, joint, joist, moist, point, spoilt, voice

6.18.6 Full length vs. clipped

spoiled/spoilt, joined/joint, joys/Joyce, boys/Boyce

6.18.7 Additional words

annoy, appointment, avoid, deploy, destroy, devoid, disappointed, embroider, employ, enjoy, exploit, foible, loiter, moisture, noisy, ointment, oyster, poison, toilet, voyage, alloy, convoy, sirloin, typhoid, android, decoy, paranoid, turmoil, invoice

6.18.8 Phrases

anoint with oil, avoid disappointment, boiling point, hoi polloi, hoity-toity, a loyal employee, moist soil, point-by-point, spoil the enjoyment, voice your disappointment, boiled in oil

6.18.9 Sentences

1   Moira embroidered a doily.
2   That spoilt their enjoyment.
3   The cowboy was held at gunpoint.
4   It was a ploy to poison the playboy.
5   That was a very poignant rejoinder.
6   Our voyage to Hanoi was a real joy.
7   The joiner was employed in Hawick.
8   I had no choice but to pay the invoice.
9   Roy has an annoying adenoidal voice.
10   Rooibos is sweet without being cloying.
11   The hoity-toity try to avoid the hoi polloi.
12   I'm paranoid about catching typhoid fever.
13   We moved from Detroit to Troy in Illinois.
14   The employees voiced their disappointment.
15   Joyce bought the boys toys and the girls toiletries.
16   The original anointing oil was made from olive oil.
17   We went from Croydon to Dordogne via Boulogne.
18   He toiled and toiled, which left his life devoid of any joy.
19   To roister means enjoying oneself in a noisy or boisterous way.
20   He boiled with annoyance when his Rolls Royce was destroyed.

6.18.10 Dialogues

A: I avoid Joyce out of choice.
B: Because she pointed out Roy's playboy ways?
A: It made me paranoid and spoilt our relationship.
B: What a poisonous ploy! The killjoy!

A: You've spoilt my oysters!
B: Olive oil doesn't spoil oysters.
A: Oh boy! You've really destroyed my lovely moist oysters.
B: So avoid the oysters and have the sirloin steak.
A: Have I any choice?

A: Moira's got a new toy boy.
B: What's the point of a toy boy?
A: It's just a foible of hers. She likes to loiter about Croydon with a convoy of toy boys.
B: Don't they exploit her and disappoint her?
A: *She* enjoys exploiting and disappointing *them*!

6.19 GOAT /əʊ/

6.19.1 Description

Starts mid central and moves towards close back. Unrounded, becoming slightly rounded. Before dark /l/, e.g. *coal*, the first element is backer, opener and rounded, [ɒʊ], e.g. *goal, bold*. This started as an allophone in London speech but has now become well established in GB.

6.19.2 Spelling

<o> no, hero, folio, don't, won't
<o-e> zone, those, smoke
<oe> toe, goes
<oa> moan, loan, road
<ow> know, slow, narrow
<olk> = /əʊk/ folk, yolk
<oul> = /əʊl/ shoulder, mould
<ough> though, doughnut

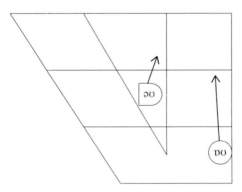

Figure 6.16 The GOAT /əʊ/ vowel, including the pre-dark /l/ allophone [ɒʊ].

Words from French:

<au> or <eau> gauche, mauve, chauffeur, bureau, chateau, Rousseau, Bordeaux, plateau

Unusual spellings

brooch, yeoman

6.19.3 Full length

a) **Open syllables**
blow, crow, flow, go, know/no, low, owe, show, slow, snow, so, though, toe

b) **Closed syllables**
chose, code, drove, froze, hose, load, nose, road, rose, stove, those, bone, comb, flown, foam, groan/grown, home, loan, moan/mown, own, stone, throne/thrown, tone, zone

6.19.4 Retracted before dark /l/

bowl, coal, mole, pole, roll/role, stole, stroll, old, cold, bold, told, gold, fold, sold, hold, mould, bolt, goal, hole/whole, dole, foal, patrol, sole/soul

6.19.5 Clipped

both, broke, choke, cloak, close (adj.), coach, coast, coat, croak, don't, dose, float, folk, ghost, goat, hope, host, joke, loaf, most, note, oak, poke, post, roast, rope, slope, smoke, soak, soap, stroke, throat, toast, vote, woke, won't, wrote

6.19.6 Full length vs. clipped

close (v.)/close (adj.), code/coat, doze/dose, glowed/gloat, grows/gross, mode/moat, node/note, ode/oat, road/wrote, robe/rope, posed/post

6.19.7 Multiple

bronchopneumonia, chromosome, cocoa, cold shoulder, comatose, dodo, goalpost, hobo, hocus-pocus, homeowner, kimono, logo, motorboat, motorhome, mumbo-jumbo, oboe, overcoat, overdose, over-exposure, overflow (v.), overgrown, overload (v.), overshadow, overthrow (v.), ozone, photo, polio, polo, portfolio, postcode, postpone, roadshow, rodeo, roly-poly, Romeo, showboat, slowcoach, soapstone, solo, stone-cold, toad-in-the-hole, towrope, yoyo

6.19.8 Additional words

approach, arrow, awoke, below, bonus, borrow, broken, comb, control, cosy, echo, elbow, emotion, folder, hero, hollow, local, meadow, moment, narrow, ocean, open, over, phone, pillow, pony, potato, radio, shadow, shallow, social, soldier, suppose, swallow, tomato, tomorrow, total, vote, window, yellow, wardrobe, coerce, mango, motto, memo, zero

6.19.9 Phrases

approach slowly, a bow and arrow, a close associate, blow your nose, a bold stroke, bone marrow, a goldfish bowl, stony broke, a flowing cloak, hold close, glowing coals, a coastal road, total control, a low dose, go with the flow, old folk, moan and groan, a local hero, hold your own, a broken home, no hope, a talk-show host, a low-interest loan, a mobile home, slow motion, open to negotiation, a broken nose, no smoking, at a moment's notice, a mobile phone, roast potatoes, a radio programme, slow progress, local radio, a narrow road, a yellow rose, a rowing boat, stone-cold sober, throw stones, vocal folds, a protest vote, a broken window, a bold approach, broken bones, remote control, totally devoted, home-grown, a low profile

6.19.10 Sentences

1   I don't know.
2   Lo and behold!
3   Go with the flow.
4   Don't moan and groan.
5   Growing old's no joke.
6   Show it in slow motion.
7   This is the old coach road.
8   Joan was totally in control.
9   Load the cargo on the boat.
10   My mobile phone's broken.
11   We don't hold out much hope.
12   Hold me close and don't let go.
13   Zoe stood frozen for a moment.
14   Fido swallowed the bone whole.
15   The Rolling Stones stole the show.
16   Keep your nose to the grindstone!
17   Note that this is a no-smoking zone.
18   The hotel is located in Coconut Grove.
19   He wrote both poetry and prose in Polish.
20   Apollo is often shown with a bow and arrow.

6.19.11 Dialogues

A: Don't smoke in the old folks' home.
B: Is that a joke? You know the old blokes there smoke home-grown tobacco?
A: There's no hope for their croaky old throats, but it'd be most social if you quit tomorrow.
B: No, no, no. I don't think so. I won't be coaxed into lowering my dose by those gloating tones.

A: Don't moan. I'm only combing your ponytail.
B: You don't have to poke me with that old comb, you know!
A: Don't groan so much, you old goat. You're almost foaming at the mouth.

B: Since I broke my shoulder bone on that motorboat a week ago, you've grown cold, emotionless and controlling.

A: Is it that I've grown cold, emotionless and controlling, or is it that you've grown stone-cold sober?

A: I've chosen to focus on Polish heroes for my radio programme.

B: Wasn't Chopin, the composer, a Pole?

A: Yes, he wrote mainly solo piano pieces, but also two piano concertos.

B: And Yoko Ono, is she Polish? Or maybe Slovak?

6.20 MOUTH /aʊ/

6.20.1 Description

Starts open central and moves towards close back. Unrounded, becoming slightly rounded.

6.20.2 Spelling

   <ou> house, out, south, ground
   <ow> howl, now, how, down

6.20.3 Full length

a) *Open syllables*
   brow, cow, prow, plough, how, now
b) *Closed syllables*
   blouse, brown, browse, cloud, clown, crowd, crown, down, drown, frown, gown, ground,
     loud, lounge, noun, pound, proud, round, sound, town

6.20.4 Clipped

crouch, doubt, drought, house (n.), mouse, mouth, out, pouch, scout, shout, south, trout

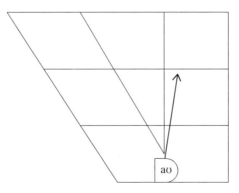

Figure 6.17 The MOUTH /aʊ/ vowel.

6.20.5 Full length vs. clipped

cloud/clout, house (v.)/house (n.), bowed/bout, rowed (argued)/rout, mouth (v.)/mouth (n.), mound/mount, crowd/crouch

6.20.6 Retracted before dark /l/

cowl, foul/fowl, growl, howl, jowl, owl, prowl, scowl

6.20.7 Multiple

countdown, down-and-out, foul-mouthed, housebound, houseproud, loudmouth, power-house, roundabout, sauerkraut, southbound

6.20.8 Additional words

about, account, amount, announce, fountain, mountain, powder, pronounce, scoundrel, sur-round, thousand, trousers, voucher, foundation, eyebrow, discount

6.20.9 Phrases

proud to announce, bring the house down, a countable noun, a county council, crouch down, a discount voucher, go round a roundabout, a house mouse, a loud shout, pronounce a vowel sound, surround sound, without a doubt, without foundation, a council house

6.20.10 Sentences

1   That blouse looks dowdy.
2   It sounds downright lousy.
3   What an astounding discount!
4   He was slouched on the couch.
5   She was bound to be found out.
6   His brows drew down in a scowl.
7   She crouched down beside the cow.
8   The pronoun 'thou' is now outdated.
9   Mount Everest was shrouded in cloud.
10 Howard had no doubts about the outcome.
11 I found trout and flounder at the mouth of the river.
12 How do you pronounce the vowel sounds of Hausa?
13 I shouted out loud when I saw a mouse in the lounge.
14 I could hear the sounds of Strauss in the background.
15 Mr Brown's pronouncements lack a sound foundation.
16 The council houses were built in the outskirts of town.
17 He's now an accountant in his hometown of Hounslow.
18 We built a house down south, close to the county boundary.
19 He has round about a thousand pounds in his bank account.
20 His bowing and kowtowing to the councillors aroused outrage.

6.20.11 Dialogues

A: I doubt that loudmouth clown owns the big town house he's so proud of.

B: That lout spouts a huge amount of nonsense without foundation.

A: The scoundrel belongs in a council house on the outskirts of town.

B: The louse should take his big mouth down south beyond the boundaries of our proud county.

A: I'm proud to announce that I can pronounce all the English vowel sounds.

B: The MOUTH vowel too? Pronounce it out loud.

A: I'll shout it out right now, loudly and proudly: mouth, mouth, mouth!

B: That's without a doubt the loudest MOUTH vowel workout that's ever resounded about this town.

A: Is Brown still walking about town in his doctoral gown?

B: He's very proud of his doctoral gown and won't put it down.

A: How people in town must frown at that clown!

B: They shout, howl and scowl at Brown the clown as he prowls around town in his gown and no trousers.

A: No trousers?! I don't doubt he arouses shouts, howls and scowls. The clown's out of his unsound mind!

6.21 Centring diphthongs: summary of key features

The two centring diphthongs are NEAR /ɪə/ and CURE /ʊə/. Their key features are:

1 They glide towards the schwa /ə/ position at the centre of the vowel space.
2 They are falling diphthongs – more time is spent at the start position than gliding.
3 They are narrow diphthongs – their glides are relatively short.
4 As free vowels, they can appear in syllables with or without a coda.
5 They are of relatively long duration when compared with the checked vowels (and therefore are also *long* vowels).
6 They are shortened when followed by a voiceless consonant in the same syllable (pre-fortis clipping).

   a) The degree of shortening is rather slight, like that of the non-close free monophthongs.
   c) Shortening of vowels is an important cue for identifying whether a following obstruent is voiced or voiceless.

7 The centring diphthongs as a category are in decline.

   a) SQUARE /eə/ has lost its glide and is now classed as a free monophthong.
   b) CURE /ʊə/ is merging with (i.e. being replaced by) THOUGHT.
   c) When not merged with THOUGHT, CURE is often a monophthong [ɵ:], especially after /j/.
   d) NEAR /ɪə/ frequently has a monophthongal realisation – [ɪː].

8 When diphthongs, NEAR and CURE often have closer starting points equivalent to the positions for FLEECE and GOOSE, [iə] and [ʉə].

6.22 NEAR /ɪə/

6.22.1 Description

Starts just above close-mid, front-central and moves towards mid central. Unrounded throughout.

Nowadays, the glide may be absent, so that the vowel sounds like a long KIT vowel. Some speakers have a closer, fronter starting point, resulting in a realisation almost the same as a sequence of FLEECE + schwa.

6.22.2 Spelling

<ear> beard, clear, appear
<eer> beer, cheer, volunteer
<er + vowel> zero, atmosphere, bacteria
<ier> fierce, pier

Unusual spellings

theory, souvenir, weird, weir, idea, theatre

6.22.3 Full length

a) **Open syllables**
   beer, cheer, clear, ear, deer/dear, fear, gear, hear/here, jeer, leer, mere, near, peer/pier, queer, rear, shear/sheer, smear, sneer, spear, sphere, steer, tear (from the eye)/tier, veer, weir, year, appear, atmosphere, career, cashmere, disappear, engineer, inter-fere, persevere, severe, sincere, souvenir, volunteer

b) **Closed syllables**
   beard, beers, cheers, ears, tears (from the eye), years, piers, shears, spears, tiered, weird, cheered, cleared, feared, jeered, leered, neared, peered, reared, sheared, smeared, sneered, speared, steered, veered

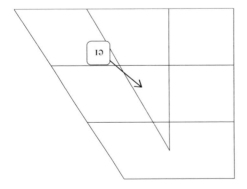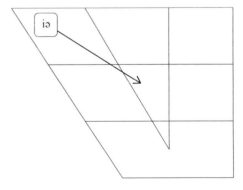

Figure 6.18 The NEAR /ɪə/ vowel. Left: KIT-like starting point. Right: FLEECE-like starting point.

6.22.4 Clipped

fierce, pierce

6.22.5 Full length vs. clipped

fears/fierce, piers/pierce

6.22.6 Before /r/ (medial)

appearance, bleary, cereal/serial, clearance, coherent, delirious, disappearance, dreary, eerie, experience, hero, hysteria, imperial, inferior, interference, material, period, query, series, serious, superior, theory, ulterior, weary, zero

6.22.7 No <r>

idea, theatre

6.22.8 Phrases

appear cheerful, clear the atmosphere, experience fear, steer clear, nearest and dearest, a mysterious disappearance, a dreary atmosphere, a clear idea, seriously interfere, near hysteria, peer-to-peer, pierced ears, a coherent theory, sheer perseverance

6.22.9 Sentences

1   Don't jeer and sneer.
2   He disappeared mysteriously.
3   The material's real cashmere.
4   He's insincere so steer clear of him.
5   Keira had her ears pierced last year.
6   He worked as a volunteer in Liberia.
7   There was a really eerie atmosphere.
8   He realised his theory was incoherent.
9   My fear was turning into near hysteria.
10   The early pioneers travelled to the frontier.
11   The selection criteria appeared to be unclear.
12   Superior mountaineering gear's available here.
13   I like realist painters, but I find surrealists weird.
14   A serious bacterial infection can cause delirium.
15   I saw that revered production of *King Lear* at the theatre.
16   Does he have a clear idea of what engineering involves?
17   She spent the early years of her career at Imperial College.
18   This dreary era of austere budgets was followed by a period of ideals.
19   Our greatest experience in Siberia was seeing herds of reindeer.
20   Cheers! To many more years and many more beers with my peers!

6.22.10 Dialogues

A: See that weird man with the beard?
B: Yes, he's getting nearer and nearer.
A: We'd better steer clear.
B: Too late – he's almost here!

A: It's been a weird year.
B: Clearly a very queer year, my dear.
A: Hysteria, delirium, mysterious appearances and disappearances . . .
B: My dear weird sister, it's been the most superior year, full of fear and fierce good cheer.

A: I had my ears pierced in Siberia last year.
B: That's a serious souvenir!
A: It was a weird experience, but I was fearless.
B: You're my hero! Ear-piercing at zero degrees!

6.23 CURE /ʊə/

6.23.1 Description

Starts just above close-mid, central and moves towards mid central. Slightly rounded, becoming unrounded. In the same way that NEAR has a variant with a closer starting point of the quality of FLEECE, CURE has a variant with a closer starting point of the quality of GOOSE – [uə]. Similar to the monophthonging of the NEAR /ɪə/ vowel, CURE is nowadays often a long monophthong without the glide to schwa /ə/, especially after /j/. For many speakers the THOUGHT /ɔː/ vowel has replaced CURE in high-frequency words, e.g. *sure, your, poor*, and occurs alongside CURE in less common words, e.g. *lure, puerile, spurious*.

6.23.2 Spelling

<ur> cure, curious, plural
<our> dour (also /daʊə/), tour, bourgeois

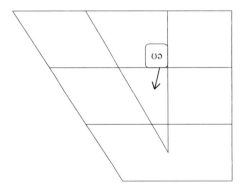 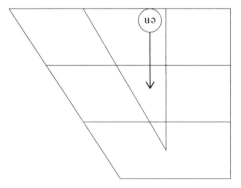

Figure 6.19 The CURE /ʊə/ vowel. Left: FOOT-like starting point. Right: GOOSE-like starting point.

<eur> Europe, liqueur, neural
<oor> moor, boorish

Unusual spellings

puerile

6.23.3 Full length

a) Open syllables

cure, lure, moor, poor, pure, sure, tour, assure, caricature, contour, demure, detour, endure, ensure/insure, liqueur, manicure, mature, obscure, procure, secure

b) Closed syllables

cures, cured, lures, lured, moors, moored, tours, toured

6.23.4 Before /r/

alluring, assurance, bureau, curious, during, endurance, Europe, furious, fury, insurance, jury, lurid, luxurious, neural, plural, puerile, rural, spurious

6.23.5 Phrases

a European tour

6.23.6 Sentences

1   This caricature's infuriating.
2   Their reassurance was premature.
3   Curiouser and curiouser, said Alice.
4   Hike the open moorland of Exmoor.
5   We took a detour through the moors.
6   It was an incurable neural disorder.
7   How do you spell the plural of *bureau*?
8   His behaviour was boorish and immature.
9   Take a tour of the rural areas of Missouri.
10   We toured Dartmoor on our way to Truro.
11   He was furious with the insurance bureau.
12   Where did you procure that alluring mural?
13   I'll have a tournedos followed by a liqueur.
14   He was curious to hear that obscure overture.
15   He was furious with the Eurocentric bureaucrats.
16   This is a chicken tandoori sandwich for gourmets!
17   Despite his bourgeois background he was insecure.
18   Treat yourself to a luxurious manicure and pedicure.
19   The troubadour accompanied himself on the tambour.
20   Even though Muriel's so dour and demure, she's very self-assured.

6.23.7 Dialogue

A: Muriel's in Dartmoor. Or is it Exmoor?

B: That's curious. I thought she'd be touring Europe or would be in some place like Kuala Lumpur.

A: No, she loves dour, rural areas and open moorland.

B: Oh! I imagined she was the bourgeois type lured by a luxurious life.

Chapter 7

Practice
Vowel contrasts

This chapter provides practice in distinguishing between pairs of vowels which learners tend to confuse. The exercise material includes minimal pairs demonstrating the contrast in different phonetic contexts, as well as words, phrases and sentences containing both sounds. The numbers in the table refer to the sections dealing with the contrasts in question.

	ɪ	ʊ	e	ɒ	æ	ʌ	i:	u:	ɜ:	ɑ:	ɔ:	eə	eɪ	aɪ	ɔɪ	aʊ	əʊ	ɪə
ɪ			7.1				7.12											
ʊ								7.13										
e					7.2							7.14	7.25					
ɒ					7.4					7.20	7.19							
æ						7.3				7.15		7.16						
ʌ									7.18	7.17								
i:																		7.21
u:																		
ɜ:										7.6	7.5	7.7					7.23	7.22
ɑ:											7.8							
ɔ:																	7.24	
eə																		7.26
eɪ														7.9				
aɪ															7.10			
ɔɪ																		
aʊ																	7.11	
əʊ																		
ɪə																		

7.1 DRESS /e/ vs. KIT /ɪ/

7.1.1 Minimal pairs

a) *Full length*

   bed/bid, beg/big, dead/did, head/hid, led/lid, red/rid, peg/pig, gem/gym, Ben/bin, den/din, pen/pin, ten/tin, bell/bill, fell/fill, hell/hill, spell/spill, tell/till, well/will

b) *Clipped*

   crept/crypt, bet/bit, let/lit, meant/mint, net/knit, pet/pit, set/sit, wet/wit, belt/built, check/chick, neck/nick, peck/pick, trek/trick, etch/itch, left/lift, bless/bliss, desk/disc, mess/miss, rest/wrist, sense/since

c) *Longer words*

   lesson/listen, letter/litter, medal/middle, petty/pity, possession/position

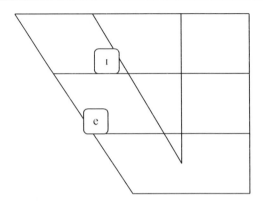

Figure 7.1 DRESS /e/ and KIT /ɪ/.

7.1.2 Words with KIT and DRESS

big-headed, bridgehead, cigarette, disconnect, disrespect, filmset, gingerbread, in-depth, index, influential, influenza, infrared, insect, internet, sickbed, silhouette, acceptability, message, wreckage, engine, epic, ethnic, metric, selfish, spelling, wedding, credit, exit, dentist, tennis, penguin, denim, infect, inspect, instead, intend, intense, invest, academic, aggressive, domestic, energetic, majestic, offensive, membership, dispenser, imperative

7.1.3 Phrases

mental abilities, a desperate bid, a pedal bin, wedded bliss, red bricks, tender chicken breast, a respectable citizen, the city centre, a cliff edge, a committee member, a medical condition, a petty criminal, a sensible decision, a visitor centre, a comprehensive definition, a French dictionary, a special discount, the general drift, a refreshing drink, detective fiction, a legendary figure, an epic film, a freshwater fish, a clenched fist, a wedding gift, terrible guilt, a gentle hint, a chequered history, a head injury, wet ink, insect repellent, a tender kiss, set a limit, a guest list, fresh milk, a mental picture, a feather pillow, immense pity, a steady rhythm, a terrible risk, sick to death, sensitive skin, a generous spirit, spring weather, a length of string, an electric switch, a generous gift, pen and ink, a generous tip, a trick question, a pleasant trip, a regular visitor, a window ledge, a wet winter, an adventure film, no fixed address, a hidden agenda, a king-size bed, fringe benefits, a bread bin, a cement mixer, rigorous checks, a big debt, from beginning to end, energy bills, a significant event, a difficult exercise, a little extra, a picket fence, a hidden gem, a general principle, health issues, fit and healthy, a hedge trimmer, bitterly jealous, a stiff leg, a hidden message, a fishing net, a silly question, a split second, thinly spread, a big step, sweat like a pig, a fitness test, hidden treasure, dripping wet, a good head for figures, an expensive gift, an independent film, a clever trick

7.1.4 Sentences

1   He paid the bill and left a generous tip.
2   I noticed Jim was limping on his left leg.

3   We get fresh milk delivered to our doorstep.
4   It wasn't difficult to get the general drift of it.
5   Neville felt a trickle of sweat drip down his neck.
6   There's definitely no such thing as a silly question.
7   Our best swimmer came in a split second before theirs.
8   We developed some simple exercises to assess his interests.
9   Jenny has excellent business skills and a good head for figures.
10 There are immense differences between printed and electronic texts.

7.2 DRESS /e/ VS. TRAP /æ/

7.2.1 Minimal pairs

a) **Full length**
   bed/bad, dead/dad, head/had, led/lad, said/sad, beg/bag, gem/jam, bend/band, blend/
   bland, lend/land, men/man, pen/pan, send/sand, ten/tan

b) **Clipped**
   bet/bat, met/mat, net/gnat, pet/pat, rent/rant, set/sat, vet/vat, neck/knack, peck/pack,
   trek/track, wreck/rack, guess/gas, flesh/flash

c) **Longer words**
   better/batter, ember/amber, kettle/cattle, letter/latter, phonetic/fanatic, mention/mansion,
   merry/marry, pedal/paddle, perish/parish, celery/salary

7.2.2 Words with DRESS and TRAP

academic, alphabet, ancestor, aspect, asset, benefactor, bedpan, deadpan, democratic, empty-
handed, headband, headlamp, heavy-handed, left-handed, melodramatic, rectangle, stepdad,
stepladder, telegram, telepathic, abject, access, accidental, anorexia, antiseptic, backrest,
blackhead, clarinet, manifesto, apprehend, parallel

7.2.3 Phrases

an American accent, a professional actor, the letters of the alphabet, a red apple, black pepper, an empty can, petty cash, natural selection, excellent value, an aggressive attitude, a

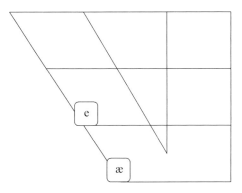

Figure 7.2 DRESS /e/ and TRAP /æ/.

black belt, the best man, bad breath, a chemical reaction, black cherries, the black death, a delicate balance, a black dress, scrambled eggs, a family friend, a leather jacket, capital letters, a negative attitude, a black pen, a pet cat, plan ahead, a chemical reaction, a national treasure, bad weather, well established, catch your breath, black leather, fancy dress, a pet rabbit

7.2.4 Sentences

1   Bury the hatchet.
2   Jack set a trap for Geoff.
3   Larry banged his head again.
4   Get your act together, Gary!
5   Fred acted as if it had never happened.
6   The best man wore a black leather jacket.
7   Bev's pet rabbit bit the hand of a family friend.
8   Frank said the letters of the alphabet backwards.
9   Ben hadn't planned ahead and so met a bad end.
10 Ted has a negative attitude to American accents.

7.3 STRUT /ʌ/ vs. TRAP /æ/

7.3.1 Minimal pairs

a)   **Full length**

cub/cab, dub/dab, grub/grab, stub/stab, bud/bad, dud/dad, mud/mad, bug/bag, drug/drag, hug/hag, rug/rag, tug/tag, budge/badge, crumb/cram, dumb/dam, hum/ham, rum/ram, slum/slam, swum/swam, fun/fan, pun/pan, spun/span, hung/hang, sprung/sprang

b)   **Clipped**

cup/cap, dump/damp, lump/lamp, cut/cat, buck/back, nut/gnat, putt/pat, rut/rat, luck/lack, bunk/bank, drunk/drank, puck/pack, shrunk/shrank, stuck/stack, stunk/stank, truck/track, hutch/hatch, crush/crash, flush/flash, rush/rash, thrush/thrash, slush/slash

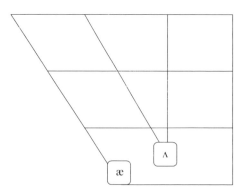

Figure 7.3 STRUT /ʌ/ and TRAP /æ/.

c)   *Longer words*

uncle/ankle, bubble/babble, burrow/barrow, butter/batter, begun/began, compass/campus, courage/carriage, curry/carry, double/dabble, destruction/distraction, flutter/flatter, mutter/matter, puddle/paddle, rubble/rabble, rumble/ramble, rupture/rapture, sudden/sadden, summon/salmon, shutter/shatter

7.3.2 Words with STRUT and TRAP

acupuncture, agriculture, aqueduct, backup, blackcurrant, catapult, dandruff, grandmother, handcuffs, lacklustre, malfunction, maladjusted, malnourished, manhunt, bumbag, comeback, cutback, double-barrelled, dustpan, frontman, hubcap, humpback, hunter-gatherer, moneybag, lumberjack, motherland, mudflap, multinational, muscleman, mustang, nutcracker, punchbag, rubber-stamp, rucksack, stuntman, substandard, suntan, undergraduate, underpants, understand, unhappy, unplanned

7.3.3 Phrases

a blood bank, a plastic bucket, a detached bungalow, rancid butter, pineapple chunks, a fan club, matching colours, a country mansion, a married couple, a drug addict, flood damage, the barrel of a gun, hunger pangs, a panel of judges, a parachute jump, bad luck, a bad mother, muscle spasms, a gas oven, rubbish bags, a mad rush, a damp sponge, stomach cramps, a sun hat, a clap of thunder, a lack of trust, an impulsive act, a splash of colour, a struggling actor, a stuffed animal, apple crumble, back to front, a bloody battle, a rusty can, an introductory chapter, exam results, a rugby fan, a compulsive gambler, a drug habit, hand luggage, plum jam, a panic button, a rabbit hutch, a bundle of rags, a running tap, a travel company, a flat stomach, an animal lover

7.3.4 Sentences

1   It was an impulsive act resulting from frustration and anxiety.
2   My mother's caramel apple crumble is absolutely scrumptious.
3   Samantha's just come back from Falmouth with a lovely suntan.
4   Dustin had a passion for jazz and ended up as a drummer in a jazz club.
5   There were a dozen travel mugs and a stack of plastic cups in the cupboard.
6   The company suffered massive cutbacks due to lack of government funding.
7   My husband wants a cat, but I'm reluctant to have one as I'm not an animal lover.
8   She was worried about her financial troubles but said she'd overcome tougher challenges.
9   I don't understand why they've cancelled the plans for the construction of the new runway.
10 Your tagged luggage will be transferred automatically so you just need to carry your hand luggage.

7.4 LOT /ɒ/ vs. STRUT /ʌ/

7.4.1 Minimal pairs

a)   *Full length*

hob/hub, rob/rub, snob/snub, cod/cud, bog/bug, dog/dug, hog/hug, jog/jug, smog/smug, fond/fund, shone/shun, wan/one, long/lung, wrong/rung, song/sung, strong/strung, tongs/tongues, doll/dull

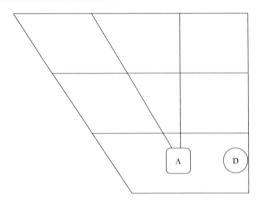

Figure 7.4 LOT /ɒ/ and STRUT /ʌ/.

b)   *Clipped*
   cop/cup, cot/cut, got/gut, hot/hut, knot/nut, pot/putt, shot/shut, dock/duck, lock/luck, mock/muck, sock/suck, stock/stuck, cough/cuff, golf/gulf, boss/bus, lost/lust

c)   *Longer words*
   body/buddy, boggy/buggy, borrow/burrow, collar/colour, dollar/duller, model/muddle, otter/utter, wander/wonder, warrior/worrier

7.4.2 Words with LOT and STRUT

blockbuster, conduct (n.), cross-country, foxglove, godmother, shotgun, bloodshot, butter-scotch, double-cross, gunshot, lunchbox, shuttlecock, sunspot, somewhat, sunblock, underdog

7.4.3 Phrases

a humble apology, a governing body, boxing gloves, a public concert, a troubled conscience, multiple copies, a country cottage, cotton buds, coughing and spluttering, a bumper crop, a dog lover, a sudden drop, a touch of frost, a golf club, chopped nuts, a public holiday, job cuts, a plum job, a sudden longing, blood loss, money problems, a public monument, an odd number, an opera lover, humble origins, bulging pockets, a muddy pond, pop culture, an encouraging response, punk rock, a sudden shock, solve a puzzle, a topic of discussion, a luggage trolley, a dusty volume, a luxury yacht, a drop of blood, a long-lost brother, a mop and bucket, a hot cross bun, a bus stop, a knob of butter, strong colours, a tropical country, a long-lost cousin, a strong current, hot curry, a shocking discovery, a strong drug, a pot of honey, fox hunting, the long jump, junk shop, a love song, a hot lunch, borrow money, strong muscles, mushroom omelette, chopped onions, a rush job, a long-lost son, a strong stomach, a hot summer, a foreign tongue, a public apology, government bonds, a money box, a summer holiday, an opera buff, a duck pond, culture shock, a foreign country, a strong cup of coffee, squander money, a blood clot

7.4.4 Sentences

1   She's not just a dumb blonde.
2   Fox hunting's a horrible blood sport.

3   It'll comfortably accommodate a lot of stuff.
4   The song 'Bus Stop' was sung by the Hollies.
5   A 'hot dog' is a sausage shoved into a crusty bun.
6   We had lots of fun on our summer holiday in Austria.
7   Douglas borrowed large sums of money from Uncle John.
8   Top the chops with mushrooms and onions, and serve hot.
9   I'd love a strong cup of coffee and one of your hot cross buns.
10 I wonder what country that obnoxious shopkeeper comes from.

7.5 THOUGHT /ɔ:/ VS. NURSE /ɜ:/

7.5.1 Minimal pairs

a)   Full length
four/fur, more/myrrh, saw/sir, store/stir, board/bird, hoard/heard, ward/word, form/firm,
   warm/worm, born/burn, lawn/learn, torn/turn, yawn/yearn, all/earl, call/curl, hall/hurl

b)   Clipped
caught/curt, short/shirt, pork/perk, walk/work, porch/perch, course/curse

c)   Longer words
conform/confirm, porpoise/purpose

7.5.2 Words with THOUGHT and NURSE

furthermore, surfboard, workforce, alternative, coursework, foreword, short-term, short-
circuit, skirting-board, workhorse, sportsperson

7.5.3 Phrases

an absurd thought, draw a circle, a cause for concern, draw the curtains, a personal fortune, a
dirty floor, orbit the earth, a first aid course, germ warfare, a gorgeous girl, a quarterly journal, a war of nerves, a normal person, the servants' quarters, a memorial service, a short skirt,

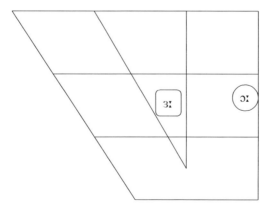

Figure 7.5 THOUGHT /ɔ:/ and NURSE /ɜ:/.

in the short term, a quarter turn, a naughty word, a world war, an airport terminal, burst into applause, a border skirmish, an emergency call, an ordinary person, a courtesy call, a worthy cause, the first course, a football shirt, a reserve force, poor service, a reversal of fortunes, personal glory, the early morning, perfectly normal, a circular orbit, in reverse order, internal organs, earn a reward, the worst sort, the world of sport, my first thought, dirty water, a warm person, in broad terms, a word of caution, further a cause, in normal circumstances

7.5.4 Sentences

1 Herbert's furniture's worth a small fortune.
2 I thought it was the worst sort of boring journalism.
3 Norman taught a first aid course to orphanage workers.
4 She wore short skirts and shirts that showed off her curves.
5 She earned a reward for her extraordinary work as a nurse.
6 George turned up shortly before the first course was served.
7 What were the four most important causes of the First World War?
8 He was a staunch supporter of Spurs and always wore their football shirt.
9 The orchestra's superb performance caused the audience to burst into applause.
10 At first I thought it was going to be a Victorian murder story, but it turned out there was no murder!

7.6 PALM /ɑː/ vs. NURSE /ɜː/

7.6.1 Minimal pairs

a) Full length
bar/burr, car/cur, far/fur, par/purr, spar/spur, star/stir, bard/bird, card/curd, hard/heard, carve/curve, suave/swerve, farm/firm, palm/perm, barn/burn, yarn/yearn

b) Clipped
cart/curt, dart/dirt, heart/hurt, part/pert, lark/lurk, mark/murk, park/perk, larch/lurch, parch/perch, bath/birth, cast/cursed, fast/first, pass/purse

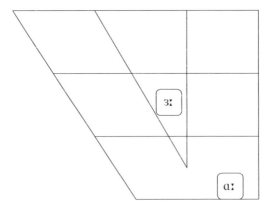

Figure 7.6 PALM /ɑː/ and NURSE /ɜː/.

c) **Longer words**
barley/burly, carnal/colonel, carton/curtain, farmer/firmer, father/further, parson/person, starling/sterling

7.6.2 Words with PALM and NURSE

afterbirth, artwork, barperson, basketwork, hard-working, heartburn, churchyard, surcharge, working-class, birthmark, glasswork, password

7.6.3 Phrases

hard work, early afternoon, the perfect answer, a hurt arm, a commercial artist, perfectly calm, a birthday card, worlds apart, external demands, a first draft, the perfect example, a turkey farm, a herb garden, a cursory glance, a grass verge, the first half, perfect harmony, a heart murmur, burst out laughing, the worst part, a permanent scar, a perfect target, a birthday party, a nasty burn, an impartial observer, dark purple, vast reserves, search far and wide, a smart shirt, a hard word, this part of the world, a superb example, a commercial farm, a furtive glance, heart surgery, a nervous laugh, permanent staff

7.6.4 Sentences

1   Charlotte planted parsley in her herb garden.
2   Margaret hurt her arm at work last Thursday.
3   The churchyard was dark and largely deserted.
4   First-degree burns leave nasty permanent scars.
5   We worked hard to learn the words off by heart.
6   Pearl looked smart in her tartan skirt and black shirt.
7   He cast a furtive glance at the charming girl behind the bar.
8   The carpets were dirty, and the purple curtains looked absurd.
9   We searched far and wide for the perfect card for her birthday.
10   There are some remarkable plants and birds in that part of the world.

7.7 SQUARE /eə/ vs. NURSE /ɜː/

7.7.1 Minimal pairs

a) **Full length**
air/err, bare/burr, blare/blur, care/cur, fair/fur, hair/her, mayor/myrrh, pair/purr, spare/spur, stare/stir, wear/were, cared/curd, haired/heard, bairn/burn
b) **Longer words**
barely/burly, fairness/furnace, fairy/furry

7.7.2 Words with SQUARE and NURSE

earthenware, airworthy, chairperson

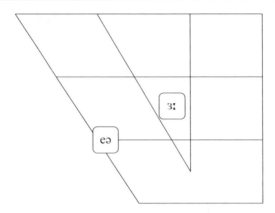

Figure 7.7 SQUARE /eə/ and NURSE /ɜː/.

7.7.3 Phrases

a caesarean birth, urgent repairs, bear a burden, fairly certain, a nightmare journey, curly hair, a stern parent, scarcely deserve, germ warfare, a caring person, a careful search, an aerial survey, a swear word, secretarial work, world affairs, spared the worst, barely worth it, a personal affair, an airport terminal, a research area, emergency care, perfectly fair, return fare, a recurring nightmare, working parents, emergency repairs, surface area

7.7.4 Sentences

1 Claire permed her hair into girlish curls.
2 Mary preferred secretarial work to nursing.
3 I'm preparing a workshop for care workers.
4 Shirley's chairs are in urgent need of repair.
5 He learnt thirty Hungarian swear words and curses.
6 Claire says pairs of canaries are the perfect pet bird.
7 Sarah swears she can draw perfect circles and squares.
8 What's the fare for a return journey from Burnley to Ayr?
9 The passenger service at the airport terminal was virtually deserted.
10 To the despair of his parents he was only concerned with worldly affairs.

7.8 PALM /ɑː/ vs. THOUGHT /ɔː/

7.8.1 Minimal pairs

a) Full length
  bar/bore, car/core, far/four, jar/jaw, par/pour, scar/score, star/store, bard/bored, card/cord, hard/hoard, lard/lord, cars/cause, farm/form, barn/born, darn/dawn, yarn/yawn

b) Clipped
  art/ought, cart/caught, part/port, tart/taught, park/pork, stark/stalk, farce/force, fast/forced

c) Longer words
  martyr/mortar, starry/story

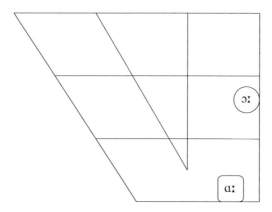

Figure 7.8 PALM /ɑː/ and THOUGHT /ɔː/.

7.8.2 Words with PALM and THOUGHT

afterthought, basketball, carnivore, cardboard, dartboard, passport, tarpaulin, broadcast, court martial, forearm, forecast, forefather, hallmark, short-staffed, wallchart, carport, cart-horse, father-in-law, hardcore, heart-warming, sought-after, scorecard, watermark, warm-hearted

7.8.3 Phrases

a passing thought, a large airport, short grass, a storage jar, a call to arms, sharp claws, an advanced course, an armed escort, a nasty fall, a large hall, a vast fortune, a car horn, a lasting memorial, a portrait artist, tomato sauce, a staff shortage, a snort of laughter, a sports star, a market stall, a charming story, a strawberry plant, a heart-to-heart talk, dark thoughts, a war dance, an enormous advance, a warm afternoon, a cause for alarm, a short answer, a flawed argument, an art historian, a warm bath, a car door, a worn carpet, a sporting chance, a small class, a dance hall, an awful disaster, a courtroom drama, a notorious example, a small farm, an adoring father, a small garden, a glass door, tall grass, a border guard, a warm heart, a jar of marmalade, a forced laugh, a former partner, a glorious past, a task force, claw marks, wall-to-wall carpet

7.8.4 Sentences

1 Charles bought his daughter a fast sports car.
2 It was a glorious afternoon for a walk in the park.
3 Martha's taught art and drama to fourth formers.
4 My aunt Maureen has bought a small farm in Berkshire.
5 My daughter-in-law's cautious, but she has a warm heart.
6 He has a large apartment on the fourteenth floor in New York.
7 There was a notorious shortage of staff in the Law Department.
8 The carpets were worn, and there was water on the floor in the bathroom.
9 Unfortunately, Margaret can't afford her daughter's dancing classes anymore.
10 They all asked for more portions of her mouth-watering strawberry and rhubarb tart.

7.9 PRICE /aɪ/ vs. FACE /eɪ/

7.9.1 Minimal pairs

a) Full length

buy/bay, die/day, high/hay, lie/lay, my/may, pie/pay, sly/slay, sty/stay, try/tray, why/way, bride/braid, glide/glade, ride/raid, wide/wade, prize/praise, rise/raise, climb/claim, lime/lame, mime/maim, time/tame, brine/brain, line/lane, mine/main, pine/pain, spine/Spain, aisle/ale, file/fail, mile/mail, pile/pail, style/stale, tile/tail

b) Clipped

type/tape, white/wait, bite/bait, bike/bake, fight/fate, height/hate, light/late, might/mate, pint/paint, right/rate, like/lake, ice/ace, rice/race, spice/space

c) Longer words

reminder/remainder, viper/vapour

7.9.2 Words with PRICE and FACE

baseline, brainchild, canine, daylight, daytime, drainpipe, grapevine, haywire, ladylike, lakeside, nationwide, playtime, playwright, saline, snakebite, vaporise, waistline, wastepipe, bridesmaid, citation, driveway, eyestrain, fireplace, flypaper, Friday, hibernate, highway, irate, isolate, limescale, microwave, migraine, migrate, primate, sideways, skyscraper, timescale, timetable

7.9.3 Phrases

retirement age, the primary aim, available for hire, wide awake, a slice of bacon, a knife blade, brake lights, a cage fighter, a slice of cake, an isolated case, a bicycle chain, a high-speed chase, the right combination, expiry date, a lively debate, signs of decay, a delayed flight, a minor detail, fail to arrive, widespread dismay, a basic exercise, privately educated, a tight embrace, an essay title, a rival claim, widespread fame, a bright flame, a high grade, blind hatred, a winding lane, a divided nation, white paint, lined paper, the right place at the right time, a railway timetable, a ray of light, razor wire, a sliding scale, a crying shame, stage fright, high stakes, a dining table, break time, a frightening tale, a spicy taste, thriving trade,

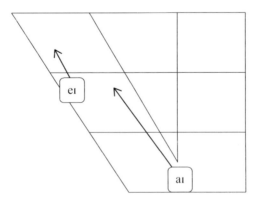

Figure 7.9 PRICE /aɪ/ and FACE /eɪ/.

a train driver, a bridal veil, waist high, a tidal wave, a way of life, arrive late, a racing bike, a grave crisis, a borderline case, a major crisis, a daily cycle, great delight, a failed enterprise, daily exercise, a place of exile, a brave fight, fly spray, a layer of grime, a newspaper head-line, a strange idea, a train line, the fate of mankind, day and night, a faint outline, a great prize, a grain of rice, a sleigh ride, my main rival, a sacred shrine, failing eyesight, in plain sight, an ancient site, a sacred site, shapes and sizes, a range of sizes, a trail of slime, the time of day, a waste of time, a famous writer, a cycle lane, a hiding place, high status, a tiny waist, arrive safely, a grave crime, a great divide, a large-scale enterprise

7.9.4 Sentences

1   Iceland faced a major financial crisis.
2   James remained wide awake until daylight.
3   Ray's wife survived a dangerous snakebite.
4   They engaged in a lively debate on climate change.
5   They denied all accusations of inciting racial hatred.
6   It's a waste of time to try to get Amy to change her mind.
7   Jane regained her eyesight after going blind for five days.
8   I'm terrified of wide open spaces and not being able to escape.
9   We have motorbikes and racing bikes for sale at a range of prices.
10   A survey finds that the privately educated have higher rates of pay than the state-educated.

7.10   PRICE /aɪ/ vs. CHOICE /ɔɪ/

7.10.1 Minimal pairs

a)   **Full length**
     buy/boy, ply/ploy, tie/toy, pies/poise, kind/coined, line/loin, aisle/oil, bile/boil, file/foil, tile/toil
b)   **Clipped**
     pint/point, vice/voice
c)   **Longer words**
     ally/alloy, divide/devoid, imply/employ, lighter/loiter

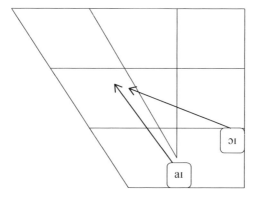

Figure 7.10   PRICE /aɪ/ and CHOICE /ɔɪ/.

7.10.2 Words with PRICE and CHOICE

choirboy, life-buoy, thyroid, viceroy, joyride, moisturise

7.10.3 Phrases

find oil, appoint an adviser, a high voice, a wide choice, a spoilt child, beside the point, the oil crisis, a joint enterprise, moist eyes, a tabloid headline, light soil, lifetime employment, a mind in turmoil, an unspoilt paradise, boiled rice, mildly annoying, fry in oil, slightly annoyed, a bright boy, the right choice, an oil refinery, a full-time employee, a tired voice, derive enjoyment, widely exploited, a final invoice, decide to join, a watertight joint, wild joy, slightly moist, quite noisy, refined oil, precisely pinpoint, the high point, recoil slightly, oil prices, rheumatoid arthritis, fertile soil, an outside toilet, a scientific viewpoint, a fine voice, a joint exercise, a wise choice, quiet enjoyment, his pride and joy, strike oil, emphasise a point, a point in time, dry soil

7.10.4 Sentences

1   Fry the spices in oil and add the rice. Enjoy!
2   He was diagnosed with rheumatoid arthritis of the joints.
3   The cowboys recoiled in surprise at the sight of the python.
4   I enjoy driving my Rolls Royce along the winding coastline.
5   Five boys from Illinois were caught joyriding on motorbikes.
6   The key points were summarised concisely in his PowerPoint slides.
7   She declined point-blank to join him in his voyage to Paradise Island.
8   I was slightly disappointed when Clive decided to employ a full-time driver.
9   What makes one child coy, shy and mild, and another noisy and boisterous?
10 I was annoyed when he arrived late for his appointment without even apologising.

7.11 MOUTH /aʊ/ vs. GOAT /əʊ/

7.11.1 Minimal pairs

a)   *Full length*

bow (bend at the waist)/bow (a knot), how/hoe, now/know, row (an argument)/row (a tier), sow/so, loud/load, house (v.)/hose, clown/clone, crown/crone, drown/drone, town/tone, foul/foal, howl/hole

b)   *Clipped*

flout/float, gout/goat, rout/wrote, stout/stoat, couch/coach, pouch/poach, douse/dose

c)   *Longer words*

arouse/arose, devout/devote

7.11.2 Words with MOUTH and GOAT

boathouse, broken-down, lowbrow, know-how, merry-go-round, overcrowded, pronoun, snowplough, download (n.), houseboat, household, outgoing, outpost, outspoken, powerboat

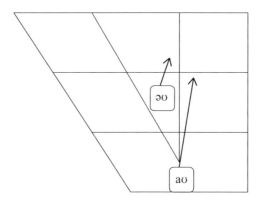

Figure 7.11 MOUTH /aʊ/ and GOAT /əʊ/.

7.11.3 Phrases

a blow-by-blow account, the total amount, a radio announcer, social background, low clouds, the local council, the home counties, crowd control, growing doubts, a close encounter, a foundation stone, low ground, a hotel lounge, a snow-capped mountain, powdery snow, a social outcast, low output, provoke outrage, a social outsider, cocoa powder, a powerful anti-dote, a mouth-watering aroma, a powerful blow, powerful emotions, a loud explosion, a low mountain, a mountain goat, a loud groan, the hero of the hour, a powerful hold, a ghost town, a brown loaf, a proud moment, a five-pound note, a foul odour, a proud owner, a snowbound road, powerful shoulders, a downward slope, brown toast, the power of veto, a low bow, a mountain road, a knock-out blow, a powerful explosion, a mountain slope

7.11.4 Sentences

1   Joe's foul-mouthed outburst provoked the locals.
2   She sold her house in the Home Counties in October.
3   I was dumbfounded at how my hometown had grown.
4   Joan found she couldn't cope with being a social outcast.
5   The bloodhound let out a low growl and pounced on him.
6   All morning mouth-watering aromas wafted from her house.
7   The snowplough was brought out to keep the town's roads open.
8   She told us there was a loud explosion which had blown out the windows.
9   The remote outpost was surrounded by towering, snow-capped mountains.
10 The accountants had growing doubts about the slow progress of the ongoing negotiations.

7.12 FLEECE /iː/ vs. KIT /ɪ/

7.12.1 Minimal pairs

a)   *Full length*
bead/bid, deed/did, greed/grid, heed/hid, lead (v.)/lid, read/rid, leave/live (v.), ease/is, fees/fizz, freeze/frizz, bean/bin, gene/gin, green/grin, seen/sin, sheen/shin, teen/tin, eel/ill, feel/fill, heel/hill, kneel/nil, meal/mill, peel/pill, steal/still, wheel/will

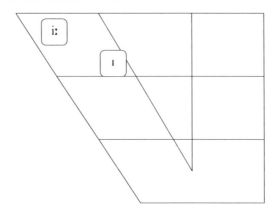

Figure 7.12 FLEECE /iː/ and KIT /ɪ/.

b) *Clipped*

bleep/blip, cheap/chip, heap/hip, leap/lip, sheep/ship, sleep/slip, weep/whip, deep/dip, beat/bit, eat/it, feet/fit, greet/grit, heat/hit, neat/knit, seat/sit, sleet/slit, wheat/wit, cheek/chick, leak/lick, peak/pick, seek/sick, weak/wick, each/itch, peach/pitch, reach/rich, feast/fist

c) *Longer words*

beaker/bicker, beater/bitter, freely/frilly, litre/litter, peeler/pillar, reason/risen, scenic/cynic, sleeper/slipper, treacle/trickle, weaker/wicker

7.12.2 Words with FLEECE and KIT

ceiling, Egypt, scenic, seasick, chickpea, disagree, millimetre, mislead, windscreen, greetings, increase (v.), indeed, intrigue (v.), cleavage, comedic, freakish, hygienic, meaning, meeting, reconsider, sheepish, squeamish, strategic, bittersweet, chimpanzee, displease, sixteen, fifteen, intermediate, intervene, millipede, mincemeat, mistreat, nicotine, evening

7.12.3 Phrases

a key figure, a fridge freezer, a free gift, please give details, the grim reaper, a cheeky grin, grit your teeth, a guilty secret, a history teacher, a complete idiot, an interesting feature, a police interview, a piece of a jigsaw, kidney disease, a field trip, a window cleaner, a kiss on the cheek, a knitting needle, the speed limit, a complete list, a little piece, liver disease, milk teeth, mixed feelings, a complete mystery, Greek myths, pins and needles, pink cheeks, pretty easy, an increased risk, sick leave, a significant increase, skin disease, steeped in history, an evil spirit, a stiff breeze, a bee sting, a piece of string, deep sympathy, the legal system, a cheap thrill, a free ticket, an ego trip, a trivial detail, twigs and leaves, a brief visit, a secret history, a frequent visitor, a bleak winter, Swiss cheese, a written agreement, quick and easy, a string of beads, a mythical beast, a free spirit, a brief history, a chilly breeze, spring cleaning, whipped cream, a business deal, a deep thinker, vivid dreams, an eager listener, greasy skin, a greedy pig, fix a leak, mean-spirited, recent history, visibly relieved, my lips are sealed, a winning streak, a big deal, bits and pieces, finish a meal, an interesting feature, spill the beans

7.12.4 Sentences

1   Jill eats kidney beans.
2   Steve didn't sleep a wink.
3   Keep it simple, quick and brief.
4   Evelyn refilled her beaker with gin.
5   A honey bee's sting kills the bee.
6   Jean's a native speaker of Finnish.
7   Leo makes a pretty decent living.
8   Tim submitted his PhD thesis on the sixth.
9   How can we teach kids the skills they need?
10   There's a bit of minced beef between Jim's teeth.

7.13 GOOSE /uː/ vs. FOOT /ʊ/

7.13.1 Minimal pairs

a)   **Full length**
     cooed/could, who'd/hood, shooed/should, wooed/wood, fool/full, pool/pull
b)   **Clipped**
     Luke/look, suit/soot
c)   **Longer words**
     lucre/looker

7.13.2 Words with GOOSE and FOOT

bullet-proof, footloose, footstool, cuckoo

7.13.3 Phrases

a book review, a cool new look, good news, a do-gooder, a sugar cube, in a good mood, a good view, good value, a good tune, a good loser, too good to be true, put two and two

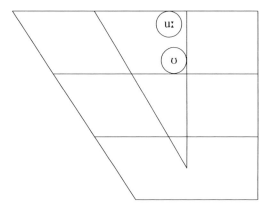

Figure 7.13 GOOSE /uː/ and FOOT /ʊ/.

together, put down roots, book a room, prune bushes, a full moon, a crooked tooth, a wooden spoon, a bullet wound, the school bully, fruit sugar, a beautiful woman, gooseberry juice, a school book

7.13.4 Sentences

1   Sue cooks good food.
2   Julian took a cruise to Acapulco.
3   Hugh looks like a real do-gooder!
4   Julie took a look through the new book.
5   The bully pushed Luke off his scooter.
6   The youth pulled out his crooked tooth.
7   It took some doing before she understood.
8   She took off her shoes and put on her boots.
9   The students put together a news bulletin on the issue.
10 Confused, Andrew shook his head; he knew it couldn't be true.

7.14 DRESS /e/ vs. SQUARE /eə/

7.14.1 Minimal pairs

a)   *Full length*
     bled/blared, dead/dared, fed/fared, fled/flared, head/haired, led/laird, shed/shared, sped/spared, stead/stared, Ben/bairn
b)   *Clipped*
     dent/daren't
c)   *Longer words*
     belly/barely, ferry/fairy, merry/Mary, very/vary

7.14.2 Words with DRESS and SQUARE

airbed, bare-headed, daredevil, farewell, hairdresser, hairnet, stairwell, wherever, deckchair, elsewhere, everywhere, healthcare, menswear, questionnaire, secretarial, setsquare, step-parent, stretcher-bearer, threadbare, vegetarian, welfare

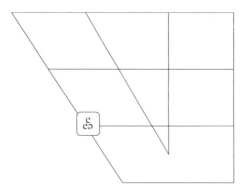

Figure 7.14 DRESS /e/ and SQUARE /eə/.

7.14.3 Phrases

a breath of fresh air, a jet aircraft, a residential area, a leather armchair, intensive care, an empty chair, the depths of despair, a menacing glare, red hair, a terrible nightmare, an aircraft engine, elderly parents, well prepared, a lengthy questionnaire, extensive repairs, dead scared, central square, a steady stare, terribly unfair, leisure wear, a hairpin bend, a careful check, a hairy chest, aircraft wreckage, a glaring error, a rare event, fairly expensive, a fair-weather friend, fairly healthy, hairy legs, air pressure, enemy aircraft, a sensitive area, extra care, essential repairs, scared to death, a set of chairs

7.14.4 Sentences

1   These leather chairs are exceptionally rare.
2   Jeremy has fair hair and a reddish complexion.
3   My elderly parents get the very best healthcare.
4   We went round the hairpin bend as fast as we dared.
5   Take care on each step of those dreadfully steep stairs.
6   They prepared a lengthy questionnaire on leisure wear.
7   They have excellent, if slightly expensive, vegetarian fare.
8   Can you tell me how to get from Edgware to Leicester Square?
9   I had a terrible nightmare yesterday that scared the hell out of me.
10 Ken shared his teddy bear with his friends, and this increased the wear and tear.

7.15 PALM /ɑ:/ vs. TRAP /æ/

7.15.1 Minimal pairs

a)   *Full length*
        bard/bad, card/cad, hard/had, lard/lad, marred/mad, barge/badge, halve/have, jars/jazz, harm/ham, barns/bans
b)   *Clipped*
        aren't/ant, carp/cap, cart/cat, chart/chat, heart/hat, part/pat, bark/back, lark/lack, park/pack, shark/shack, stark/stack, larch/latch, march/match, harsh/hash, marsh/mash
c)   *Longer words*
        auntie/anti, barter/batter, larder/ladder, martyr/matter, varnish/vanish

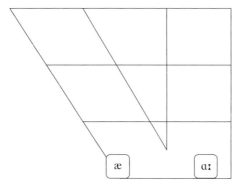

Figure 7.15 PALM /ɑ:/ and TRAP /æ/.

7.15.2 Words with PALM and TRAP

artefact, artisan, barbaric, bathmat, cardiac, carjack, sarcasm, tarmac, abattoir, avatar, bala-clava, barrage, camouflage, flabbergast, grandfather, handicraft, landmark, massage, sand-castle, scrapyard, tap-dance, vanguard, avalanche, avocado, jam-jar, panorama, placard, rampart, sabotage, farmland

7.15.3 Phrases

apple tart, a sandwich bar, a class act, a farm animal, an arson attack, a brass band, the black market, hard cash, a car crash, lasting damage, pass an exam, the hard facts, an armed gang, a gap in the market, a nasty habit, the palm of your hand, a hard hat, barking mad, in a calm manner, a large-scale map, scratch marks, cast a shadow, snap in half, a last stand, a glass tank, a bath tap, car tax, hard to understand, an added advantage, Saturday afternoon, a tal-ented architect, a balanced argument, an art gallery, a snack bar, an absolute bargain, a canal barge, a bank branch, a second-hand car, a pack of cards, a cast of characters, fat chance, a cavalry charge, natural charm, the back of the class, a dance band, a man-made disaster, a classic example, an absent father, damp grass, a cattle market, a narrow path, a man-eating shark, jam tart, the heart of the matter, target practice, a heart attack, a marching band, mark an exam, a natural advantage, graphic art, a salad bar, a shark attack

7.15.4 Sentences

1   His Belfast accent's hard to understand.
2   I had a tomato and basil salad and apple tart.
3   She's married to a talented architect from the Bahamas.
4   Here's a marvellous, large-scale interactive map of Cardiff.
5   Martin passed his exams in banking and finance last March.
6   Amanda practised parking the car in the supermarket car park.
7   The cat gave him a nasty scratch on his arm that left a large scar.
8   Charlie asked if there was a gap in the market for dance magazines.
9   Martha said the Salvation Army brass band were absolutely fantastic.
10 My grandfather went to the National Art Gallery while I ambled round Battersea Park.

7.16 SQUARE /eə/ vs. TRAP /æ/

7.16.1 Minimal pairs

a) *Full length*
    aired/add, bared/bad, cared/cad, chaired/Chad, dared/dad, fared/fad, glared/glad, haired/had, paired/pad, hairs/has, cairn/can
b) *Longer words*
    careless/callous, pharaoh/farrow, hairy/Harry, Mary/marry, rarely/rally

7.16.2 Words with SQUARE and TRAP

airbag, aerobatic, barehanded, whereas, antiquarian, camel-hair, fanfare, grandparents, adversarial, humanitarian, aerodynamic, fairyland, hairband, scaredy-cat

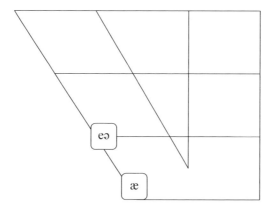

Figure 7.16 SQUARE /eə/ and TRAP /æ/.

7.16.3 Phrases

matching chairs, air travel, an international airport, black hair, apples and pears, bare hands, handle with care, wear a badge, a grand affair, damp air, land an aircraft, a care plan, a plastic chair, a bad fairy, a matching pair, a backlog of repairs, narrow stairs, a blank stare, Gatwick airport, a careless act, animal welfare, a carefree attitude, an aerosol can, a hairline crack, prepare for an exam, scarcely imagine, a fair-haired man, an authoritarian manner, tax affairs, an air crash, standards of care, a padded chair, stand and stare

7.16.4 Sentences

1 The fat mayor staggered to the chair and sat down.
2 Take care to hold the handrail on the narrow stairs.
3 Ann declared the hat was made of camel hair or mohair.
4 Jack compared variables as different as apples and pears.
5 Mary prepared an appetising cabbage salad for her vegetarian pals.
6 We landed at the airport and then shared the taxi fare back to campus.
7 Amanda had black hair and an air of wary carefulness that attracted him.
8 Janet was scared she wasn't adequately prepared for the Italian language exam.
9 The man attacked her in an abandoned warehouse and strangled her with his bare hands.
10 You'll find rare and valuable manuscripts at our stand at the Frankfurt Antiquarian Book Fair.

7.17 PALM /ɑː/ vs. STRUT /ʌ/

7.17.1 Minimal pairs

a) Full length

card/cud, starred/stud, barge/budge, calm/come, charm/chum, harm/hum, psalm/sum, barn/bun, darn/done

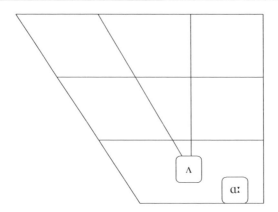

Figure 7.17 PALM /ɑ:/ and STRUT /ʌ/.

b) *Clipped*

carp/cup, cart/cut, heart/hut, part/putt, bark/buck, dark/duck, mark/muck, park/puck, stark/stuck, grant/grunt, branch/brunch, calf/cuff, farce/fuss, pass/pus, task/tusk

c) *Longer words*

barter/butter, drama/drummer, mastered/mustard, martyr/mutter, starter/stutter

7.17.2 Words with PALM *and* STRUT

bathtub, half-brother, stardust, bloodbath, double-park, jump-start, mudbath, mudguard, underclass, underpass, starstruck, junkyard, multi-tasking, sunglasses

7.17.3 Phrases

a summer afternoon, a blunt answer, an art lover, a bargain hunter, bubble bath, a trump card, the front of the class, a dance company, a government department, a rough draft, a touch of drama, a wonderful example, a public garden, coloured glass, lush grass, a bumper harvest, heart trouble, a public park, a bus pass, a colourful past, a blood sample, a sharp tongue, a wonderful start, a nasty stomach bug, a large bunch, the last bus, dark colours, a company car, a faraway country, a half-empty cup, a nasty cut, a startling discovery, hard drugs, half drunk, dust particles, harmless fun, a touch of class, a jar of honey, starving hungry, last month, calf muscles, a bath plug, garden rubbish, a large stomach, asking for trouble, a struggling artist, cut glass, a clump of grass, a country park, a large company

7.17.4 Sentences

1 Get half a dozen jars of honey.
2 Martha has such a sharp tongue.
3 The grass was studded with buttercups.
4 This seminar's a must for all art lovers.
5 Alexander's trump card was his undeniable charm.
6 We jumped on the last bus to Belfast just past midnight.

7   I shoved the charger in the glove compartment of my car.
8   We had a wonderful start to our honeymoon in France last month.
9   She suffered a nasty cut when she was carving the pumpkins for Halloween.
10 He gathered a bunch of dahlias from the garden and put them in a cut-glass vase.

7.18 NURSE /ɜː/ VS. STRUT /ʌ/

7.18.1 Minimal pairs

a) **Full length**
    curb/cub, herb/hub, bird/bud, blurred/blood, curd/cud, spurred/spud, stirred/stud, third/
        thud, burrs/buzz, firs/fuzz, burn/bun, fern/fun, stern/stun, turn/ton, curl/cull, girl/
        gull, hurl/hull

b) **Clipped**
    curt/cut, hurt/hut, pert/putt, shirt/shut, lurk/luck, perk/puck, purse/pus, turf/tough

c) **Longer words**
    curdle/cuddle, hurdle/huddle, murky/mucky, sermon/summon, sturdy/study, circle/
        suckle

7.18.2 Words with NURSE and STRUT

bloodcurdling, bloodthirsty, buzzword, lovebird, mother-of-pearl, multipurpose, suburb,
sunburn, thunderbird, trustworthy, uncertain, underworld

7.18.3 Phrases

a personal budget, a stuffed turkey, a hamburger bun, a suburban bungalow, a bus service, a
double murder, a shirt button, a journey of discovery, eternal love, a first-time mother, public
services, a word puzzle, a Persian rug, firmly shut, a personal touch, earn trust, a flood alert, a
muttered curse, covered in dirt, a lump of earth, a sudden emergency, a young girl, a bunch of
herbs, maternal love, a murder suspect, a bundle of nerves, a subtle perfume, reserve funds,

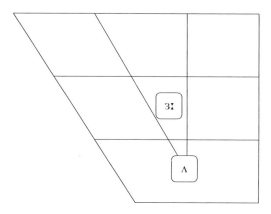

Figure 7.18 NURSE /ɜː/ and STRUT /ʌ/.

an unbuttoned shirt, an oven-ready turkey, a sudden turn, the current version, in other words, blunt words, a tough world, my first love, emergency funds, a murder hunt

7.18.4 Sentences

1 The girl was covered in dirt and dust.
2 Shirley must learn to trust other adults.
3 Why did his blunt words hurt so much?
4 We purchased a dirt-cheap suburban bungalow.
5 The stuffed turkey was served with mushrooms.
6 He looked scruffy in his unbuttoned purple shirt.
7 I'm nervous and worried about my surgery on Monday.
8 After a sudden turn for the worse, my brother succumbed.
9 At first they were unable to adjust to the new circumstances.
10 After working for that company, he'd become allergic to buzzwords.

7.19 LOT /ɒ/ vs. THOUGHT /ɔː/

7.19.1 Minimal pairs

a) Full length
  odd/awed, cod/cord, nod/gnawed, pod/poured, rod/roared, sod/sword, wand/warned, con/corn, don/dawn, swan/sworn

b) Clipped
  cot/caught, pot/port, shot/short, spot/sport, what/wart, fox/forks, stock/stalk

c) Longer words
  coral/choral, knotty/naughty, often/orphan

7.19.2 Words with LOT and THOUGHT

across-the-board, bodywarmer, chloroform, concord, consort, contour, corridor, cosmonaut, encore, foghorn, frogspawn, goddaughter, hobbyhorse, mothball, oddball, offshore,

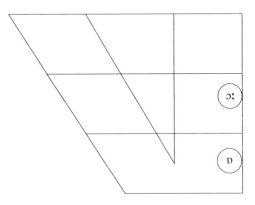

Figure 7.19 LOT /ɒ/ and THOUGHT /ɔː/.

off-the-record, onslaught, popcorn, volleyball, authority, autobiography, autonomy, autopsy, corncob, doorknob, doorstop, horsebox, ornithology, pawnshop, pornography, smallpox, sword-swallower, waterlogged

7.19.3 Phrases

prolonged applause, an anonymous author, a golf ball, a border crossing, a long phone call, strong cord, corn on the cob, a solid core, bottled water, a rotting corpse, a golf course, a squash court, a long-lost daughter, a locked door, a polished floor, a positive force, squander a fortune, a concert hall, a rocking horse, a strong jaw, a frosty morning, chronological order, a long pause, a strong performance, a pork chop, a hospital porter, a popular resort, the top score, boxer shorts, an anonymous source, a popular sport, follow a course, a shop doorway, a tropical storm, a shocking story, a revolving door, a long walk, the horrors of war, hot water, chocolate sauce, coarse cloth, a college course, soft water, the Norman Conquest, an important contract, the overall cost, a small cottage, a poor crop, an important document, a golf tournament, a holiday resort, a hospital ward, a boring job, a long story, a small major- ity, an obstacle course, a formal offer, an ornamental pond, a door knocker, a small profit, a daunting prospect, an enormous quantity, porous rock, pork sausages, an awful shock, a corner shop, a warning shot, a bald spot, an important topic, a sports watch, a horror story, a drop of water, at all costs, a small minority

7.19.4 Sentences

1 Gordon's a sports correspondent in Washington.
2 Does John more often shop online or in normal shops?
3 I got up at four o'clock in the morning to do my chores.
4 Paul was awarded an important contract for an offshore project.
5 George took a course on the Gothic novel when he was at college.
6 Ron and Donna bought a small Victorian holiday cottage in Dorset.
7 My boss and I had morning coffee on the top floor of the tower block.
8 He wanted a job that was less boring and involved more responsibility.
9 The Scott memorial is a Victorian Gothic monument to a famous Scottish author.
10 To cut a long story short, George lost all his confidence after being conned by fraudsters.

7.20 PALM /ɑː/ vs. LOT /ɒ/

7.20.1 Minimal pairs

a) *Full length*
   card/cod, guard/god, balm/bomb
b) *Clipped*
   carp/cop, harp/hop, sharp/shop, cart/cot, dart/dot, heart/hot, part/pot, barks/box, clerk/ clock, dark/dock, mark/mock, shark/shock, calf/cough, laughed/loft, scarf/scoff, glass/gloss, cast/cost, last/lost

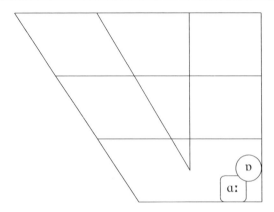

Figure 7.20 PALM /ɑː/ and LOT /ɒ/.

7.20.2 Words with PALM and LOT

bodyguard, bollard, bombard, collage, contrast, godfather, hovercraft, montage, aftershock, archaeology, grasshopper, choreograph, crossbar, oregano, pockmark, top-class, armlock, blast-off, cardiology

7.20.3 Phrases

a positive advantage, tomorrow afternoon, an alarm clock, an honest answer, a logical argument, cross your arms, a coffee bar, a shopping basket, a hot bath, polished brass, a model car, top of the class, modern dance, a costume drama, a concrete example, a model farm, a foster father, a rock garden, garlic sausage, a glass bottle, a strong grasp, a guard dog, from the bottom of my heart, at long last, a hollow laugh, a well-trodden path, an exotic plant, a long scarf, a soft target, a heartfelt apology, starting blocks, parts of the body, dark chocolate, armed combat, a marked contrast, a master copy, a charming cottage, a nasty cough, a sharp drop, an advanced economy, a dark forest, a sharp frost, a disastrous holiday, the job market, a sharp knock, vast knowledge, a large monster, a lasting monument, a passing nod, a hardback novel, a garden pond, a large profit margin, a large quantity, a car wash, a hot afternoon, the wrong answer, a guard of honour, a heart problem, a bar of chocolate, a demanding job

7.20.4 Sentences

1 Barbara had a nasty chronic cough.
2 *Gosford Park* is a marvellous costume drama.
3 The guard dog on the property barked non-stop.
4 He got some exotic tropical plants for his garden.
5 Dr Parker has a vast knowledge of modern drama.
6 It's a charming cottage in the heart of the Cotswolds.
7 We had garlic sausages followed by coffee and dark chocolate.
8 We were asked to submit an electronic and a hard copy of the article.
9 Charlotte wants to be a doctor, and Charles wants to be an army officer.
10 My aunt started a demanding part-time job in March but lost it the following October.

7.21 FLEECE /iː/ vs. NEAR /ɪə/

7.21.1 Minimal pairs

Full length

bee/beer, D/dear, E/ear, fee/fear, G/jeer, he/hear, me/mere, knee/near, pea/peer, she/sheer, tea/tear (from the eye), V/veer, we/weir, bead/beard, feed/feared, need/neared, lead/leered, read/reared, speed/speared, steed/steered, weed/weird, ease/ears, cheese/cheers, sneeze/sneers, tease/tears (from the eye)

7.21.2 Words with FLEECE and NEAR

cheerleader, earpiece, dematerialise, reappear

7.21.3 Phrases

a yearly fee, an experienced teacher, a brief appearance, steal an idea, free beer, a brief career, a recent experience, beneath the exterior, deep fear, a piece of material, nearly asleep, a brief period, a TV series, extremely serious, a steering wheel, a feeling of superiority, a tear-stained cheek, speak from experience, street theatre, clear reasons, repeat an experience, keep clear, a weird feeling, in recent years, a weird dream, searing heat, a key idea, an ear-piercing scream, meet the criteria, completely disappear, an appeal for volunteers, pleased to hear it, keep up appearances, previous experience, reading material, a leap year, sheep shearing

7.21.4 Sentences

1 Pete's at the peak of his career as an engineer.
2 I can't believe my ears when I hear his squeaky speech.
3 The people who adhere to these theories are pure believers.
4 I'm sincerely pleased to hear you appreciated the experience.
5 It appears the reading material for the next three weeks has been deleted.

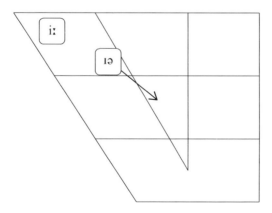

Figure 7.21 FLEECE /iː/ and NEAR /ɪə/.

6   The teacher's ill-concealed feeling of superiority did not endear him to his trainees.
7   The BBC has created some of the most appealing miniseries and period pieces I've seen.
8   Experienced shearers can shear a sheep in three minutes and remove the fleece in one piece.
9   We didn't hear from him for years, but he was recently seen by my niece in Tyne and Wear.
10   With a piercing scream she released the steering wheel and crashed into the preceding vehicle.

7.22 NURSE /ɜ:/ vs. NEAR /ɪə/

7.22.1 Minimal pairs

a)   Full length
    err/ear, burr/beer, fur/fear, her/hear, myrrh/mere, purr/peer, spur/spear, stir/steer, were/weir, bird/beard, gird/geared, word/weird
b)   Clipped
    purse/pierce

7.22.2 Words with NURSE and NEAR

persevere, world-weary, tearjerker

7.22.3 Phrases

clearly absurd, a serious alternative, severe burns, a worthwhile idea, a theatre curtain, clearly determined, a serious emergency, first-hand experience, period furniture, on the verge of tears, an experienced observer, reverse gear, a word in your ear, the germ of an idea, the material world, a personal appearance, a turbulent career, perfectly clear, seriously hurt, a nerve-racking experience, on the verge of hysteria, an alternative idea, burning tears, a volunteer worker, a serious concern, personal experience

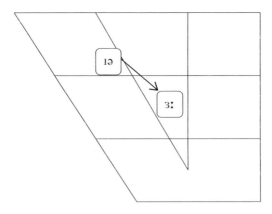

Figure 7.22 NURSE /ɜ:/ and NEAR /ɪə/.

7.22.4 Sentences

1 It's his first personal appearance here.
2 He selected reverse gear instead of first gear.
3 We'll alert you if a serious emergency occurs.
4 It appears Gertrude's worst fears were confirmed.
5 Pearl burst into tears when she heard that he'd disappeared.
6 The volunteers clearly preferred turkey burgers to beef burgers.
7 The first turtles appeared on earth nearly 230 million years ago.
8 Vernon's had a turbulent career as a pioneer in nursing research.
9 The girls with the pierced ears purchased sterling silver earrings.
10 They cheerfully returned to work after a period of fearful uncertainty.

7.23 NURSE /ɜː/ vs. GOAT /əʊ/

7.23.1 Minimal pairs

a) Full length
blur/blow, err/owe, her/hoe, fur/foe, sir/so, slur/slow, curd/code, curve/cove, firm/foam, earn/own, burn/bone, fern/phone, learn/loan, stern/stone, turn/tone, curl/coal, girl/goal, hurl/hole, pearl/pole

b) Clipped
blurt/bloat, curt/coat, dirt/dote, flirt/float, weren't/won't, jerk/joke, perk/poke, smirk/smoke, work/woke, perch/poach, burst/boast, cursed/coast

c) Longer words
turtle/total

7.23.2 Words with NURSE and GOAT

coercion, glowworm, ergo, roadworks, churchgoer, furthermost, inferno, turbo, workload, wormhole, turncoat, co-worker, homework, loanword, noteworthy, overt, overturn, overwork, slowworm, soul-searching, stonework

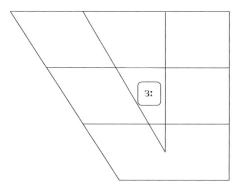 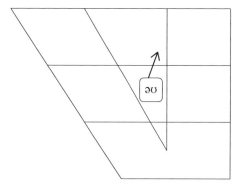

Figure 7.23 Left: NURSE /ɜː/. Right: GOAT /əʊ/.

7.23.3 Phrases

a golden wedding anniversary, know for certain, shoulder a burden, bold words, the local church, a close social circle, commercial radio, a dirt road, upholstered furniture, a coal merchant, a cold-blooded murderer, a homeless person, the sole purpose, low gold reserves, search high and low, a devoted servant, the postal service, a polo shirt, a colloquial term, a frozen turkey, work in progress, the known world, an alternative approach, permanent closure, maternity clothes, a coach journey, a fur coat, a surface coating, a university diploma, social work, a personal goal, slow customer service, a firm hold, a permanent home, eternally hopeful, a dirty joke, a personal loan, the perfect moment, a circular motion, an absurd notion, early parole, the spoken word, the learning process, further progress, a controversial proposal, turn on the radio, words of reproach, role reversal, rote learning, dirty windows, a reserve goalkeeper, social services, in glowing terms, roast turkey, a code word, in a world of your own, dirty clothes, a nursing home

7.23.4 Sentences

1 Percy yearned to own a boat and see the world.
2 There are loads of English loanwords in German.
3 Joe's controversial proposal was deferred until October.
4 Earl confirmed that the show on Thursday's almost sold out.
5 There's a superb coach service from Heathrow to Birmingham.
6 Our goal is to promote the motivation to learn in the workplace.
7 She observed that the girls had made slow but noticeable progress.
8 My only concern was how to cope with the journey to and from work.
9 Tony was searching for the perfect moment to propose to his girlfriend.
10 We're virtually certain it's Roland and Joan's golden wedding anniversary on the thirty-first.

7.24 THOUGHT /ɔː/ vs. GOAT /əʊ/

7.24.1 Minimal pairs

a) *Full length*
    bore/bow (a knot), door/dough, flaw/flow, law/low, more/mow, gnaw/know, saw/so, shore/show, snore/snow, tore/toe, cord/code, lord/load, clause/close, pause/pose, form/foam, norm/gnome, born/bone, corn/cone, drawn/drone, horn/hone, lawn/loan, torn/tone, stall/stole, bald/bold, call/coal, hall/hole

b) *Clipped*
    ought/oat, caught/coat, daunt/don't, vault/volt, chalk/choke, cork/coke, fork/folk, walk/woke, porch/poach

c) *Longer words*
    mortar/motor, quarter/quota, portion/potion

7.24.2 Words with THOUGHT and GOAT

blowtorch, clotheshorse, cold-call, coleslaw, folklore, notice-board, notorious, overall, overawe, overboard, post-mortem, snowball, snowstorm, audio, auto, cornerstone,

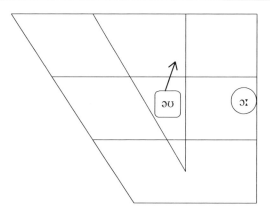

Figure 7.24 THOUGHT /ɔ:/ and GOAT /əʊ/.

hormone, jawbone, moreover, porthole, thought-provoking, tornado, torpedo, torso, also, almost, doorpost

7.24.3 Phrases

an orthodox approach, a bowl of water, a charcoal drawing, a short solo, formal clothes, a coach and horses, Morse code, border control, a small dose, an enormous ego, raw emotion, water flow, ordinary folk, a ghost story, a warm glow, a social call, growth hormone, a fallen hero, an awkward moment, a small nose, a short note, the former owner, a border patrol, the overall score, a phone call, a straw poll, a stone wall, a progress report, a lonely road, a moment's thought, broad shoulders, a talk show, a show of force, soap and water, a stone floor, a short stroll, a sore throat, walk on tiptoe, tomato sauce, a dormant volcano, at short notice, a local airport, an open border, a local call, a cold morning, a noble cause, household chores, a grown-up daughter, a gross distortion, an open door, a border post, a motorcycle escort, a warning notice, a polar explorer, local folklore, a potent force, a toasting fork, hold the fort, a moment of glory, a cold hall, an old haunt, blow a horn, a broken jaw, an overgrown lawn, an organ donor, a morning stroll, roast pork, a local reporter, a low score, golden shores, motor sport, an unspoken thought, the thought process, emotional trauma, a slow walk, a low wall, a war zone, cold water, approach with caution, warm clothes, an enormous explosion, the lawful owner, a hoax call, a closed door, tomorrow morning

7.24.4 Sentences

1   We ordered tortellini with home-made gorgonzola sauce.
2   Paula opened the wardrobe door and chose an outdoor coat.
3   He owns a gorgeous charcoal drawing of a horse-drawn coach.
4   They were flown from their local airport to a resort in Arizona.
5   Tomorrow they've forecast a snowstorm off the coast of Cornwall.
6   We had slowly roasted shoulder of pork with potatoes and port sauce.
7   If you have a sore throat and can't swallow, gargle some warm salty water.
8   Tomorrow morning I'm going to do the laundry and mow this overgrown lawn.

9   Did you know that George Orwell wrote *1984* as a warning after World War II?

10 Fortunately, his thought-provoking report on the dangers of smoking tobacco wasn't ignored by the authorities.

7.25 DRESS /e/ vs. FACE /eɪ/

7.25.1 Minimal pairs

a) *Full length*

bread/braid, shed/shade, edge/age, men/main, pen/pain, fell/fail, gel/jail, sell/sail, tell/tail

b) *Clipped*

bet/bait, get/gate, sent/saint, chess/chase, chest/chased, less/lace, pest/paste, test/taste, west/waste

c) *Longer words*

letter/later, pepper/paper, cellar/sailor

7.25.2 Words with DRESS and TRAP

accelerate, breathtaking, celebration, demonstration, education, essay, hesitation, investigate, lemonade, anyway, beret, commemorate, decimate, decorate, dedicate, destination, devastate, entertain, featherweight, generate, headache, meditate, penetrate, regulation, renovate, speculate

7.25.3 Phrases

a change of address, a great adventure, a display of affection, a dangerous bend, a major benefit, make a bet, stale bread, save your breath, dangerous chemicals, a game of chess, credit rating, a dreadful taste, a faint echo, a wasted effort, creative energy, the main entrance, a fatal error, a chain of events, stay fresh, a safe guess, a shake of the head, health and safety, weights and measures, a straight question, red in the face, fail a test, rented accommodation,

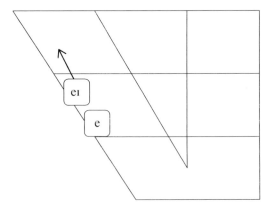

Figure 7.25 DRESS /e/ and FACE /eɪ/.

friends and acquaintances, aims and objectives, readily available, a healthy baby, an intense blaze, a wedding cake, a fresh face, a metal gate, a pet hate, a pen name, wet paint, an empty plate, heavy rain, a deadly snake, an endless wait, freshly baked bread, a waste of energy

7.25.4 Sentences

1 James went red in the face with rage.
2 State your name and address in your letter.
3 Making empty threats is a waste of energy.
4 What are the aims and objectives of Fred's paper?
5 We failed to make the deadline on September the eighth.
6 The wedding cake tasted great, but it was terribly expensive.
7 To save space, you can compress sentences into brief phrases.
8 With a shake of the head, he said, 'I don't remember the date'.
9 He held a reception for friends and acquaintances in the Croatian embassy.
10 First they played table tennis, and then they settled down to a game of chess.

7.26 NEAR /ɪə/ VS. SQUARE /eə/

7.26.1 Minimal pairs

a) **Full length**
ear/air, beer/bear, cheer/chair, clear/Claire, dear/dare, fear/fair, here/hair, leer/lair, mere/mayor, pier/pair, rear/rare, sheer/share, sneer/snare, spear/spare, steer/stare, tear (from the eye)/tear (rip), weir/ware, beard/bared, leered/laird

b) **Longer words**
weary/wary

7.26.2 Phrases

clear air, a fierce glare, years of wear, appear from nowhere, a rarefied atmosphere, a varied career, fairly cheerful, a shared experience, impaired hearing, fairly serious, a volunteer carer, clear the area, stare fiercely, a rare appearance

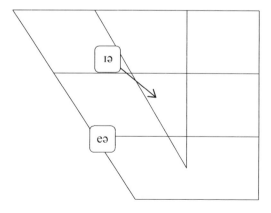

Figure 7.26 NEAR /ɪə/ and SQUARE /eə/.

7.26.3 Sentences

1 Claire scarcely ever interferes in my affairs.
2 The mayor's hearing was seriously impaired.
3 He was the airline's chairman for nearly ten years.
4 Mary said getting her ears pierced was a nightmare.
5 The millionaire made a rare appearance at the theatre.
6 Take care shearing the mohair and cashmere goats this year.
7 Mr Baird's fair-haired, so wearing a beard makes him look weird.
8 He had a varied career in theoretical engineering and aircraft repair.
9 The mountaineer was a fearless daredevil drawn to scary experiences.
10 Nothing compares with experiencing Shakespeare at an open air theatre.

Chapter 8

Weak vowels and weak forms

8.1 Weak vowels

A small set of vowels (see Figure 8.1), known as the **weak vowels**, predominate in unstressed syllables:

- schwa /ə/: *banana, computer, surprise, hazardous, policeman*
- weak KIT /ɪ/: *ignore, damage, wanted, churches*
- weak FLEECE [i]: *happy, money, coffee, area, react*
- weak GOOSE [u]: *continuous, reputation*
- weak FOOT /ʊ/: *accurate, regular*

8.1.1 Schwa /ə/

Schwa is the pre-eminent weak vowel because it appears exclusively in unstressed syllables. In contrast, the remaining weak vowels belong to both the strong and the weak vowel sets, and thus are found in the stressed syllables of numerous words besides their use as weak vowels in unstressed syllables. Due to its occurrence in weak syllables, schwa is the most common vowel and the most common phoneme in the language. Note that schwa can be spelt with any vowel letter, with or without a following <r>, e.g. *about, collar, system, better, theatre, ability, Hampshire, pilot, forget, famous, colour, bonus, murmur, Pennsylvania, martyr.*

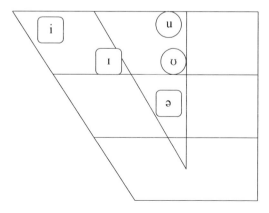

Figure 8.1 Weak vowels.

8.1.2 Weak KIT /ɪ/

Weak KIT continues to be the most common weak vowel after schwa, but in contemporary GB it isn't as frequent as it formerly was. Firstly, in certain syllable-final positions it has developed into weak FLEECE (see sections 5.2.1 and 8.1.3), and, secondly, in many words schwa has replaced weak KIT (e.g. *chocol<u>a</u>te*) or is a more frequent variant alongside it (-*l<u>e</u>ss*, -*n<u>e</u>ss*). Although schwa is frequently an alternative to weak KIT, there are many words where only weak KIT is a possibility in the GB accent (e.g. *pock<u>e</u>t*, *cabb<u>a</u>ge*). When the -**s** and -**ed** inflections contain a vowel, weak KIT is the norm (see section 2.15), and the distinction between such pairs as *centred* /'sentəd/ vs. *scented* /'sentɪd/, *bordered* /'bɔːdəd/ vs. *boarded* / 'bɔːdɪd/, and *losers* /'luːzəz/ vs. *loses* /'luːzɪz/ is maintained.

8.1.3 Weak FLEECE [i] and GOOSE [u]

Weak FLEECE and GOOSE have special symbols to distinguish them from their strong counterparts, but this doesn't mean that they are different phonemes or sound different from strong FLEECE and GOOSE. Naturally, weak FLEECE and GOOSE tend to be shorter because they occur only in unstressed syllables, but strong FLEECE and GOOSE can also be short depending on the phonetic environment. Different symbols are used because these two weak vowels were formerly identical with weak KIT and FOOT, but gradually split from them during the course of the twentieth century. Consequently, during the latter half of the twentieth century, older speakers tended to use weak KIT and FOOT where younger speakers tended to use weak FLEECE and GOOSE, and some speakers varied. In response to this, phoneticians started to use the non-phonemic [i] and [u] symbols to cover both possibilities. Over the following decades, however, the use of weak FLEECE and GOOSE has become practically universal, and these special symbols are no longer strictly required, although we use them in this work for the sake of consistency with other published materials. To use weak KIT or FOOT in place of weak FLEECE or GOOSE would now be characteristic of old-fashioned Received Pronunciation (RP) or of certain regional accents.

Both weak FLEECE and GOOSE occur before vowels (*glorious*, *stren<u>u</u>ous*), while weak FLEECE is also common at the end of words (*happ<u>y</u>*) and morphemes (*sem<u>i</u>-*). In word-initial **be-** (*become*), **de-** (*decide*), **e-** (*enough*), **pre-** (*prefer*) and **re-** (*relax*), weak FLEECE is increasingly found as an alternative to variants with weak KIT or schwa.

Some speakers alternate between weak FLEECE in word-final position (*city*, *marry*) and weak KIT in inflected forms when a consonant immediately follows (*cities*, *married*). It's not necessary to adopt this patterning because using weak FLEECE in both positions is always acceptable.

8.1.4 Weak FOOT /ʊ/

Weak FOOT is nowadays only a very marginal member of the weak vowel set. It's more typical of old-fashioned usage and can always be replaced by weak GOOSE or schwa.

8.2 Syllabic consonants

One notable characteristic of weak syllables is that in certain circumstances they can have a consonant as their nucleus. Strong syllables, on the other hand, must always centre around a vowel. Syllabic consonants develop out of sequences of schwa and a sonorant, the more vowel-like type of consonant. When these sequences are preceded by particular consonants, the articulators can move directly from the consonant to the sonorant, skipping the schwa altogether. In such cases, the syllabicity (i.e. the syllable-forming capability) of the vowel is taken up by the sonorant, and the overall number of syllables in the word remains the same. Although syllabic consonant formation isn't completely obligatory, it's very common, and to never use syllabic consonants would be very unusual.

The most common syllabic consonants are /l/ and /n/. Syllabic /m/ is less usual because there are few words which provide the appropriate phonetic context, and syllabic /ŋ/ occurs only as a result of assimilation (see section 12.3.1). While the occasional syllabic /r/ can be heard (e.g. sometimes in a word like *camera* /ˈkæmr̩ə/), this sound is unstable in the non-rhotic GB accent and can be ignored for practical purposes.

8.2.1 Syllabic /l/

Syllabic /l/ freely occurs after:

- **plosives**: /p/ *apple*, /b/ *bubble*, /t/ *bottle*, /d/ *middle*, /k/ *tackle*, /g/ *haggle*
- **affricates**: /ʧ/ *satchel*, /ʤ/ *angel*
- **nasals**: /m/ *normal*, /n/ *final*
- **fricatives**: /f/ *trifle*, /v/ *devil*, /θ/ *lethal*, /ð/ *betrothal*, /s/ *parcel*, /z/ *nasal*, /ʃ/ *special*

but is less usual after /r/ *moral*, and doesn't occur after the remaining approximants, /l/, /j/ and /w/.

8.2.2 Syllabic /n/

There are more restrictions on syllabic /n/ than on syllabic /l/. A notable change that has occurred in recent decades is that where formerly syllabic /n/ was almost compulsory after /t/ and /d/, there is now far more variation and many speakers prefer the variant with schwa when speaking emphatically or distinctly, especially after /t/.

Syllabic /n/ freely occurs after

- **alveolar plosives**: /t/ *button*, /d/ *sadden*
- **fricatives**: /f/ *soften*, /v/ *oven*, /θ/ *python*, /ð/ *southern*, /s/ *lesson*, /z/ *dozen*, /ʃ/ *mission*, /ʒ/ *vision*

and is less usual after:

- **non-alveolar plosives**: /p/ *weapon*, /b/ *ribbon*, /k/ *token*, /g/ *dragon*
- **affricates**: /ʧ/ *question*, /ʤ/ *region*
- /r/: *barren*

and doesn't occur after:

- **nasals**: /m/ *lemon*, /n/ *cannon*

- **approximants (except /r/)**: /l/ *melon*, /j/ *canyon*, /w/ *frequent*

There are further limitations on syllabic /n/ after alveolar plosives. Syllabic /n/ rarely occurs when /t/ or /d/ are preceded by:

- **a nasal**: *abandon, abundant, dependent, descendent, despondent, pendant, redundant, tendon, attendant, accountant, acquaintance, lantern, repentant, sentence, wanton, London, Paddington, Camden*
- **a plosive**: *disinfectant, lectern, plankton, expectant, reluctant, acceptance*
- **alveolar fricative /s/**: *cistern, constant, instance, instant, western, assistant, consistent, contestant, distance, distant, eastern, existence, insistent, persistent, Protestant, resistance, resistant, substance*
- **an unstressed syllable**: *accident, coincidence, confidence, confident, evidence, evident, incident, president, resident, skeleton*

8.2.3 Syllabic /m/

Syllabic /m/ can be heard after fricatives in a small number of words, notably in the suffix **-ism**:

- *ransom, awesome, gruesome, handsome, blossom*
- *chasm, prism, sarcasm, spasm, communism, journalism, organism, tourism*
- *anthem*
- *fathom, algorithm, rhythm*

8.2.4 De-syllabification

When a suffix beginning with a weak vowel is added to a word ending in a syllabic consonant, the consonant can lose its syllabicity. This is termed **de-syllabification**. The more common the word is, the more likely this is to occur.

bubbling may be /ˈbʌbəlɪŋ/ (three syllables), /ˈbʌbl̩ɪŋ/ (three syllables) or /ˈbʌblɪŋ/ (two syllables)
poisonous may be /ˈpɔɪzənəs/, /ˈpɔɪzn̩əs/ or /ˈpɔɪznəs/
ticklish may be /ˈtɪkəlɪʃ/, /ˈtɪkl̩ɪʃ/ or /ˈtɪklɪʃ/
pensioner may be /ˈpenʃənə/, /ˈpenʃn̩ə/ or /ˈpenʃnə/
vandalise may be /ˈvændəlaɪz/ or /ˈvændl̩aɪz/, but not */ˈvændlaɪz/
modernise may be /ˈmɒdənaɪz/ or /ˈmɒdn̩aɪz/, but not */ˈmɒdnaɪz/

8.2.5 Sequences of syllabic consonants

Sequences of syllabic consonants are also possible, but only in the order /n/ + /l/ because syllabic /n/ doesn't occur after /l/. Since syllabic /l/ is a variant of /əl/, and a syllabic consonant can lose its syllabicity when followed by a suffix beginning with a weak vowel, the syllabicity of /n/ can be lost in such sequences. The more common the word is, the more likely this is to happen:

national /ˈnæʃn̩l̩/ can become /ˈnæʃnl̩/
occasional /əˈkeɪʒn̩l̩/ can become /əˈkeɪʒnl̩/

personal /ˈpɜːsn̩l/ can become /ˈpɜːsn̩l/
professional /prəˈfeʃn̩l/ can become /prəˈfeʃn̩l/
rational /ˈræʃn̩l/ can become /ˈræʃn̩l/
emotional /ɪˈməʊʃn̩l/ can become /ɪˈməʊʃn̩l/
traditional /trəˈdɪʃn̩l/ can become /trəˈdɪʃn̩l/

8.2.6 Transcription of syllabic consonants

As we have seen, the phonetic symbol used to show that a consonant is syllabic is a small vertical stroke under the consonant – [l̩], [n̩]. Strictly speaking, the syllabic consonant diacritic isn't a phonemic symbol because syllabic consonants are not separate phonemes, but only a special way of realising the sequence of schwa plus a consonant. In many cases, it's possible not to mark consonant syllabicity explicitly. When *juggle* and *garden* are transcribed /ˈdʒʌgl/ and /ˈgɑːdn/, for example, because of the structure of the English syllable, the final /l/ and /n/ could only be syllabic. However, when a vowel follows, it is necessary to use the syllabic consonant diacritic because the consonant could be either syllabic or non-syllabic, as in *juggler* /ˈdʒʌgl̩ə/ or /dʒʌglə/, and *gardening* /ˈgɑːdn̩ɪŋ/ or /ˈgɑːdnɪŋ/ (see section 8.2.4).

For the sake of convenience and clarity, we will use phonemic bracketing with syllabic consonants in order to avoid constantly switching between slanted (phonemic) and square (phonetic) brackets, and we will always use the syllabic consonant diacritic, even when it isn't strictly necessary.

8.3 Strong forms and weak forms

A number of high-frequency grammatical words (i.e. auxiliary verbs, prepositions, pronouns, conjunctions and determiners) have more than one pronunciation. The **strong form** is the pronunciation used when the word is stressed, as when citing it in isolation or giving it special emphasis in a sentence. The **weak form** is the pronunciation the word has when it's unstressed.

Although we are typically more conscious of the strong forms of words than the weak forms, the weak forms are actually more common because grammatical words are usually unstressed, in contrast to lexical words (i.e. nouns, main verbs, adjectives and adverbs), which are typically stressed. (Note that grammatical words are sometimes termed *form* or *function* words, and lexical words may also be called *content* words.) Table 8.1 provides a list of the most important grammatical words taking a weak form. Note that a number of grammatical words do not take a weak form, e.g. *in, if, it, on, they.*

8.4 The use of strong forms

As stated above, these words normally appear in their weak forms because it is usual for them to be unstressed. Note, however, that there are contexts in which these words are stressed and their strong forms used. Strong forms are used in the following contexts:

1   When a word is stressed for emphasis, the strong form is used:
*I didn't tell **him**, I told **her*** /aɪ ˈdɪdnt ˈtel ˈhɪm aɪ ˈtəʊld ˈhɜː/
*he **had** seen her (even though he denied it)* /hi ˈhæd ˈsiːn ə/
*it's **from** John, not **for** John* /ɪts ˈfrɒm ˈdʒɒn ˈnɒt ˈfɔː ˈdʒɒn/

Table 8.1 The most important weak form words: weak vs. strong forms

Word	Weak form	Strong form	Word	Weak form	Strong form
am	/əm/	/æm/	for	/fə/	/fɔː/
are	/ə/	/ɑː/	to	/tə/	/tuː/
was	/wəz/	/wɒz/	he	/i/	/hiː/
were	/wə/	/wɜː/	him	/ɪm/	/hɪm/
have	/əv, həv/	/hæv/	his	/ɪz/	/hɪz/
has	/əz, həz/	/hæz/	them	/ðəm/	/ðem/
had	/əd, həd/	/hæd/	us	/əs/	/ʌs/
there	/ðə/	/ðeə/	her	/ə, ɜː, hə/	/hɜː/
do	/də/	/duː/	a	/ə/	/eɪ/
does	/dəz/	/dʌz/	an	/ən/	/æn/
would	/əd, wəd/	/wʊd/	the	/ðə/	/ðiː/
will	/əl/	/wɪl/	some	/səm/	/sʌm/
can	/kən/	/kæn/	and	/ən, ənd/	/ænd/
must	/məst/	/mʌst/	but	/bət/	/bʌt/
shall	/ʃəl/	/ʃæl/	as	/əz/	/æz/
at	/ət/	/æt/	than	/ðən/	/ðæn/
from	/frəm/	/frɒm/	that	/ðət/	/ðæt/
of	/ə(v)/	/ɒv/			

2 The strong form is used when prepositions are separated from the noun phrases they relate to:
What are you looking at? /ˈwɒt ə ju ˈlʊkɪŋ ˈæt/
He was sent for at once /hi wəz ˈsent ˈfɔːr ət ˈwʌns/
the one that I'd heard of /ðə ˈwʌn ðət aɪd ˈhɜːd ˈɒv/

3 When auxiliary verbs are used without their main verb, the strong form is used:
You can swim, and I can too /ˈjuː kən ˈswɪm ən ˈaɪ ˈkæn ˈtuː/
I've seen it, you know I have /aɪv ˈsiːn ɪt ju ˈnəʊ aɪ ˈhæv/
Are you here? Yes, I am /ə ju ˈhɪə ˈjes aɪ ˈæm/
Note that *have* is weak when preceded by a modal auxiliary:
I didn't do it, but I should've /aɪ ˈdɪdn̩ ˈduː ɪt bət aɪ ˈʃʊd əv/
He did it? He couldn't have /hi ˈdɪd ɪt hi ˈkʊdn̩ əv/

4 At the ends of sentences, preposition + pronoun sequences tend to have a weak preposition if a stressed syllable precedes, and a strong preposition if one or more unstressed syllables precede:
Look at him! /ˈlʊk ət ɪm/
I took all of them /aɪ ˈtʊk ˈɔːl ə ðəm/
He repeated it for me /hi rɪˈpiːtɪd ɪt ˈfɔː mi/
They borrowed some furniture from us /ðeɪ ˈbɒrəʊd səm ˈfɜːnɪtʃə ˈfrɒm əs/

5 When speaking more slowly and deliberately, auxiliary verbs tend to be stressed and have a strong form in yes/no questions:
Are we there yet? /ˈɑː wi ˈðeə ˈjet/
Was he awake? /ˈwɒz i əˈweɪk/

Have they done it? /ˈhæv ðeɪ ˈdʌn ɪt/
Had they left? /ˈhæd ðeɪ ˈleft/
Does it matter? /ˈdʌz ɪt ˈmætə/
Can you repeat that? /ˈkæn ju rɪˈpiːt ˈðæt/

8.5 Contractions

A number of weak forms combine with words which precede them to form **contractions** and are represented in the orthography by means of an apostrophe. These are of three types: (1) those where the weak form is reduced to a consonant, which therefore can't stand alone as a syllable and attaches itself to the preceding word (e.g. *they've* /ðeɪv/); (2) those where the weak form is reduced to a vowel, which combines with the vowel in the preceding word to form a different vowel (e.g. *they're* /ðeə/); and (3) those involving *not*. See Table 8.2.

8.6 Forms of *BE* (main verb and auxiliary)

8.6.1 AM *and* ARE

Am and *are* have contracted forms when they follow certain personal pronouns. The contraction *you're* is homophonous with *your*, and both words can be further reduced to /jə/ in more casual speech (as can *you* before consonants). For some speakers *we're* is pronounced /weə/, homophonous with *where*.

Table 8.2 The most important contractions

Contraction	Pronunciation	Contraction	Pronunciation
I'm	/aɪm/	he'll	/hil/
you're	/jɔː/	she'll	/ʃil/
we're	/wɪə/	we'll	/wil/
they're	/ðeə/	they'll	/ðeɪl/
's (is)	/s, z/	there'll	/ðəl/
I've	/aɪv/	isn't	/ˈɪzn̩t/
you've	/juv/	aren't	/ɑːnt/
we've	/wiv/	wasn't	/ˈwɒzn̩t/
they've	/ðeɪv/	weren't	/wɜːnt/
's (has)	/s, z/	don't	/dəʊnt/
I'd (had/would)	/aɪd/	doesn't	/ˈdʌzn̩t/
you'd	/jud/	didn't	/ˈdɪdn̩t/
he'd	/hid/	haven't	/ˈhævn̩t/
she'd	/ʃid/	hasn't	/ˈhæzn̩t/
we'd	/wid/	hadn't	/ˈhædn̩t/
they'd	/ðeɪd/	won't	/wəʊnt/
who'd	/hud/	can't	/kɑːnt/
there'd	/ðəd/	shouldn't	/ˈʃʊdn̩t/
I'll	/aɪl/	couldn't	/ˈkʊdn̩t/
you'll	/jul/	wouldn't	/ˈwʊdn̩t/

Orthographic form	Pronunciation	Example	
I'm	/aɪm/	*I'm fine.*	/aɪm ˈfaɪn/
you're	/jɔː/ (or /jə/)	*You're late.*	/jɔː ˈleɪt/
we're	/wɪə/ (or /weə/)	*We're lost.*	/wɪə ˈlɒst/
they're	/ðeə/	*They're safe.*	/ðeə ˈseɪf/

In other positions, *am* and *are* are /əm/ and /ə/:

Orthographic form	Pronunciation	Example	
am	/əm/	*Am I right?*	/əm aɪ ˈraɪt/
are	/ə/	*Are you here?*	/ə ju ˈhɪə/
		Are we home?	/ə wi ˈhəʊm/
		Are they mine?	/ə ðeɪ ˈmaɪn/
		The doors are locked.	/ðə ˈdɔːz ə ˈlɒkt/

8.6.2 IS

Is forms a contraction with a word it follows. Like the plural, third person singular and possessive endings (see section 2.15), the contraction of *is* agrees in voicing with the final sound of the word it attaches to and is therefore /z/ after voiced sounds and /s/ after voiceless sounds.

Orthographic form	Pronunciation	Example	
's	/z/	*He's sad.*	/hiz ˈsæd/
		She's dull.	/ʃiz ˈdʌl/
		His dog's brown.	/hɪz ˈdɒgz ˈbraʊn/
		My car's new.	/maɪ ˈkɑːz ˈnjuː/
	/s/	*It's good.*	/ɪts ˈgʊd/
		This knife's blunt.	/ðɪs ˈnaɪfs ˈblʌnt/
		The cap's off.	/ðə ˈkæps ˈɒf/

In other positions and when the preceding word ends in a sibilant, i.e. /s z ʃ ʒ tʃ dʒ/, *is* is pronounced /ɪz/, i.e. identically with the strong form:

Orthographic form	Pronunciation	Example	
is	/ɪz/	*Is it right?*	/ɪz ɪt ˈraɪt/
		This is it.	/ðɪs ɪz ˈɪt/
		Hers is best.	/ˈhɜːz ɪz ˈbest/
		The dish is hot.	/ðə ˈdɪʃ ɪz ˈhɒt/
		My watch is slow.	/maɪ ˈwɒtʃ ɪz ˈsləʊ/
		The bridge is closed.	/ðə ˈbrɪdʒ ɪz ˈkləʊzd/

8.6.3 WAS *and* WERE

Was and *were* are /wəz/ and /wə/ respectively:

Orthographic form	Pronunciation	Example	
was	/wəz/	I was waiting.	/aɪ wəz 'weɪtɪŋ/
		Was I seen?	/wəz aɪ 'siːn/
		He was ready.	/hi wəz 'redi/
		Was he there?	/wəz i 'ðeə/
		She was fine.	/ʃi wəz 'faɪn/
		Was she told?	/wəz ʃi 'təʊld/
		It was easy.	/ɪt wəz 'iːzi/
		Was it hot?	/wəz ɪt 'hɒt/
were	/wə/	You were tired.	/ju wə 'taɪəd/
		Were you pleased?	/wə ju 'pliːzd/
		We were leaving.	/wi wə 'liːvɪŋ/
		Were we noticed?	/wə wi 'nəʊtɪst/
		They were free.	/ðeɪ wə 'friː/
		Were they here?	/wə ðeɪ 'hɪə/

8.7 Forms of *HAVE* (auxiliary)

8.7.1 HAVE

Auxiliary *have* forms contractions with personal pronouns:

Orthographic form	Pronunciation	Example	
I've	/aɪv/	I've won.	/aɪv 'wʌn/
you've	/juv/	You've done it.	/juv 'dʌn ɪt/
we've	/wiv/	We've left.	/wiv 'left/
they've	/ðeɪv/	They've gone.	/ðeɪv 'gɒn/

In other contexts, auxiliary *have* is pronounced /əv/ or, after a pause, /həv/.

Orthographic form	Pronunciation	Example	
have	/əv/	My friends have gone.	/maɪ 'frendz əv 'gɒn/
		The rest have left.	/ðə 'rest əv 'left/
		The leaves have turned brown.	/ðə 'liːvz əv 'tɜːnd 'braʊn/
have	/həv/	Have I passed?	/həv aɪ 'pɑːst/
		Have you seen it?	/həv ju 'siːn ɪt/
		Have we won?	/həv wi 'wɒn/
		Have they finished?	/həv ðeɪ 'fɪnɪʃt/
		Have the keys been found?	/həv ðə 'kiːz biːn 'faʊnd/

8.7.2 HAS

Like *is*, auxiliary *has* forms contractions with the word it follows, and its form depends on the voicing of the preceding sound.

Orthographic form	Pronunciation	Example	
's	/z/	He's gone away.	/hiz 'gɒn ə'weɪ/
		She's broken it.	/ʃiz 'brəʊkən ɪt/
		My arm's gone numb.	/maɪ 'ɑːmz gɒn 'nʌm/
		The car's been stolen.	/ðə 'kɑːz biːn 'stəʊlən/
	/s/	It's been found.	/ɪts biːn 'faʊnd/
		My wife's left me.	/maɪ 'waɪfs 'left mi/
		The cat's made a mess.	/ðə 'kæts 'meɪd ə 'mes/

Also like *is*, auxiliary *has* doesn't form contractions when preceded by sibilants, /s z ʃ ʒ tʃ dʒ/:

Orthographic form	Pronunciation	Example	
has	/əz/	My boss has been fired.	/maɪ 'bɒs əz biːn 'faɪəd/
		The rose has wilted.	/ðə 'rəʊz əz 'wɪltɪd/
		My wish has come true.	/maɪ 'wɪʃ əz kʌm 'truː/
		The branch has snapped.	/ðə 'brɑːntʃ əz 'snæpt/
		The badge has fallen off.	/ðə 'bædʒ əz 'fɔːlən 'ɒf/

After a pause, *has* is pronounced /həz/.

Orthographic form	Pronunciation	Example	
has	/həz/	Has he read it?	/həz i 'red ɪt/
		Has she tried it?	/həz/ ʃi 'traɪd ɪt/
		Has it happened?	/həz ɪt 'hæpənd/
		Has the film started?	/həz ðə 'fɪlm 'stɑːtɪd/

8.7.3 HAD

Auxiliary *had* forms contractions with personal pronouns:

Orthographic form	Pronunciation	Example	
I'd	/aɪd/	I'd finished.	/aɪd 'fɪnɪʃt/
you'd	/jud/	You'd left.	/jud 'left/
he'd	/hid/	He'd gone.	/hid 'gɒn/
she'd	/ʃid/	She'd arrived.	/ʃid ə'raɪvd/
we'd	/wid/	We'd eaten.	/wid 'iːtn̩/
they'd	/ðeɪd/	They'd spent it.	/ðeɪd 'spent ɪt/

In other contexts, auxiliary *had* is pronounced /əd/ or, after a pause, /həd/.

Orthographic form	Pronunciation	Example	
had	/əd/	The doors had been closed.	/ðə 'dɔːz əd biːn 'kləʊzd/
		I wish my team had won.	/aɪ 'wɪʃ maɪ 'tiːm əd 'wʌn/
	/həd/	Had I missed it?	/həd aɪ 'mɪst ɪt/
		Had you read it?	/həd ju 'red ɪt/
		Had he gone?	/həd i 'gɒn/
		Had she left?	/həd ʃi 'left/
		Had we landed?	/həd wi 'lændɪd/
		Had they promised?	/həd ðeɪ 'prɒmɪst/

8.8 *THERE*

Existential *there* has the weak form /ðə/. The adverb *there* doesn't have a weak form (e.g. *I work there* /ðeə/).

Orthographic form	Pronunciation	Example	
there	/ðə/	There's another way.	/ðəz ə'nʌðə 'weɪ/
		There are many more.	/ðər ə 'meni 'mɔː/
		There's been a mistake.	/ðəz 'biːn ə mɪ'steɪk/
		There've been a few.	/ðəv 'biːn ə 'fjuː/
		There was a problem.	/ðə wəz ə 'prɒbləm/
		There were plenty.	/ðə wə 'plenti/
		There'd been a mix-up.	/ðəd 'biːn ə 'mɪksʌp/

8.9 Forms of *DO* (auxiliary)

Auxiliary *does* has the weak form /dəz/. Before consonants auxiliary *do* has the weak form /də/, while before vowels it's /du/ and therefore phonemically the same as the strong form.

Orthographic form	Pronunciation	Example	
do	/də/	Where do we wait?	/'weə də wi 'weɪt/
		Do they know?	/də ðeɪ 'nəʊ/
	/də/ (or /dʒu/ or /dʒə/)	Do you like it?	/də ju 'laɪk ɪt/
	/du/	Where do I go?	/'weə du aɪ 'gəʊ/
		Do animals dream?	/du 'ænəmḷz 'driːm/
does	/dəz/	Does he drink?	/dəz i 'drɪŋk/
		Does she smoke?	/dəz ʃi 'sməʊk/
		Does it work?	/dəz ɪt 'wɜːk/

8.10 Modal verbs

8.10.1 WOULD

Like *had*, *would* forms contractions with personal pronouns:

Orthographic form	Pronunciation	Example	
I'd	/aɪd/	I'd buy one.	/aɪd 'baɪ 'wʌn/
you'd	/jud/	You'd like it.	/jud 'laɪk ɪt/
he'd	/hid/	He'd do it.	/hid 'duː ɪt/
she'd	/ʃid/	She'd see it.	/ʃid 'siː ɪt/
we'd	/wid/	We'd get better.	/wid 'get 'betə/
they'd	/ðeɪd/	They'd help.	/ðeɪd 'help/

In other contexts, *would* has the uncontracted form /əd/ or, after pauses, /wəd/ (or /wʊd/).

Orthographic form	Pronunciation	Example	
'd	/əd/	It'd work.	/ɪt əd 'wɜːk/
would		The boss would hate it.	/ðə 'bɒs əd 'heɪt ɪt/
		The top would fall off.	/ðə 'tɒp əd 'fɔːl 'ɒf/
	/wəd/ (or /wʊd/)	Would I do it?	/wəd aɪ 'duː ɪt/
		Would you like one?	/wəd ju 'laɪk 'wʌn/
		Would he try?	/wəd i 'traɪ/
		Would she help?	/wəd ʃi 'help/
		Would it matter?	/wəd ɪt 'mætə/
		Would we win?	/wəd wi 'wɪn/
		Would they come?	/wəd ðeɪ 'kʌm/

8.10.2 WILL

Will forms contractions with personal pronouns:

Orthographic form	Pronunciation	Example	
I'll	/aɪl/	I'll ask.	/aɪl 'ɑːsk/
you'll	/jul/	You'll see.	/jul 'siː/
he'll	/hil/	He'll wait.	/hil 'weɪt/
she'll	/ʃil/	She'll leave.	/ʃil 'liːv/
we'll	/wil/	We'll go.	/wil 'gəʊ/
they'll	/ðeɪl/	They'll finish.	/ðeɪl 'fɪnɪʃ/

In other contexts, the weak form of *will* is /əl/ or, after pauses, /wɪl/ (i.e. the strong form):

Orthographic form	Pronunciation	Example	
'll	/əl/	It'll work.	/ɪt əl 'wɜːk/
will		That will do.	/'ðæt əl 'duː/
		Mike will go.	/'maɪk əl 'gəʊ/
	/wɪl/	Will you help?	/wɪl ju 'help/
		Will he say?	/wɪl i 'seɪ/
		Will she ask?	/wɪl ʃi 'ɑːsk/
		Will they leave?	/wɪl ðeɪ 'liːv/

8.10.3 CAN, MUST and SHALL

The weak forms of *can*, *must* and *shall* are /kən/, /məst/ and /ʃəl/:

Orthographic form	Pronunciation	Example	
can	/kən/	Tom can drive.	/'tɒm kən 'draɪv/
		You can try.	/ju kən 'traɪ/
		Can you come?	/kən ju 'kʌm/
must	/məst/	This must be wrong.	/'ðɪs məst bi 'rɒŋ/
		Paul must be mad.	/'pɔːl məst bi 'mæd/
shall	/ʃəl/	Shall I help?	/ʃəl aɪ 'help/

8.11 Prepositions

8.11.1 AT, FROM and FOR

The weak forms of *at*, *from* and *for* are /ət/, /frəm/ and /fə/.

Orthographic form	Pronunciation	Example	
at	/ət/	Look at that.	/'lʊk ət 'ðæt/
		At long last.	/ət 'lɒŋ 'lɑːst/
from	/frəm/	You can walk from here.	/ju kən 'wɔːk frəm 'hɪə/
		From time to time.	/frəm 'taɪm tə 'taɪm/
for	/fə/	He took it for granted.	/hi 'tʊk ɪt fə 'grɑːntɪd/
		For hire.	/fə 'haɪə/

8.11.2 TO and OF

Before consonants, the weak form of *to* is /tə/, both as a preposition and as the *to*-infinitive. Before vowels, the weak form of *to* is /tu/, and therefore phonemically the same as the strong form. The weak form of *of* is /əv/. When a consonant follows, the /v/ is often dropped, especially in high-frequency phrases and when the following word begins with /ð/ (e.g. *the*, *this that*, *these*, *those*, *them*).

Orthographic form	Pronunciation	Example	
to	/tə/	I go to work to make money.	/aɪ 'gəʊ tə 'wɜːk tə 'meɪk 'mʌni/
		I told him to go to hell.	/aɪ 'təʊld ɪm tə 'gəʊ tə 'hel/
of	/əv/	A piece of advice.	/ə 'piːs əv əd'vaɪs/
		The capital of Spain.	/ðə 'kæpɪtl̩ əv 'speɪn/
	/ə/ (or /əv/)	A cup of coffee.	/ə 'kʌp ə 'kɒfi/
		All of them.	/'ɔːl ə ðəm/
		The best of the best.	/ðə 'best ə ðə 'best/

8.12 Pronouns

8.12.1 HE, HIM and HIS

He, *him* and *his* have the weak forms /i/, /ɪm/ and /ɪz/. When they occur after a pause, forms with initial /h/ are used which are indistinguishable from the strong form. *His* has a weak form only as a determiner (e.g. *I've read his book*) but not as a pronoun (e.g. *I've read his*).

Orthographic form	Pronunciation	Examples	
he	/i/	I know he thinks so.	/aɪ 'nəʊ i 'θɪŋks səʊ/
		They said he left.	/ðeɪ 'sed i 'left/
	/hi/	He thinks so.	/hi 'θɪŋks səʊ/
		He left.	/hi 'left/
him	/ɪm/	Tell him.	/'tel ɪm/
		They made him leave.	/ðeɪ 'meɪd ɪm 'liːv/
his	/ɪz/	I took his watch.	/aɪ 'tʊk ɪz 'wɒtʃ/
		They know his name.	/ðeɪ 'nəʊ ɪz 'neɪm/
	/hɪz/	His watch was stolen.	/hɪz 'wɒtʃ wəz 'stəʊlən/
		His name was known.	/hɪz 'neɪm wəz 'nəʊn/

8.12.2 THEM, US and HER

Them and *us* have the weak forms /ðəm/ and /əs/. The weak form of *her* can be /ə/ or /ɜː/. When *her* is a pronoun (e.g. *I know her*), /ə/ is more common than /ɜː/, but when *her* is a determiner (e.g. *I know her name*), /ɜː/ is more common than /ə/. After a pause, *her* has an initial /h/ and is therefore identical with the strong form.

Orthographic form	Pronunciation	Example	
them	/ðəm/	I saw them.	/aɪ 'sɔː ðəm/
us	/əs/	Tell us everything.	/'tel əs 'evriθɪŋ/
her	/ə/ (or /ɜː/)	I've never met her.	/aɪv 'nevə 'met ə/
		Give her the book.	/'gɪv ə ðə 'bʊk/
	/ɜː/ (or /ə/)	I've met her mother.	/aɪv 'met ɜː 'mʌðə/
		I've read her book.	/aɪv 'red ɜː 'bʊk/
	/hɜː/ (or /hə/)	Her book's good.	/hɜː 'bʊks 'gʊd/
		Her dog died.	/hɜː 'dɒg 'daɪd/

8.13 Determiners

8.13.1 A, AN, THE and SOME

The weak forms of *a* and *an* are /ə/ and /ən/. Before a consonant, *the* has the weak form /ðə/, but before a vowel it's /ði/ and therefore phonemically the same as the strong form. When *some* is a determiner (not a pronoun) meaning 'an unspecified quantity or amount', it has the weak form /səm/.

Orthographic form	Pronunciation	Example	
a	/ə/	A banana.	/ə bə'nɑːnə/
an	/ən/	An orange.	/ən 'ɒrɪndʒ/
the	/ðə/	The police.	/ðə pə'liːs/
some	/səm/	Take some nuts.	/'teɪk səm 'nʌts/
		Have some water.	/'hæv səm 'wɔːtə/

8.14 Conjunctions

8.14.1 AND, BUT, AS, THAN and THAT

But, than and *as* have the weak forms /bət/, /ðən/ and /əz/. It's sometimes said that the weak form of *and* is /ən/ before a consonant and /ənd/ before a vowel, but this isn't true – the form without /d/ is much more common no matter what follows. *That* has the weak form /ðət/ when it's a conjunction or relative pronoun, but not when it's a determiner (e.g. *I know that* /ðæt/ *man*) or demonstrative pronoun (e.g. *I know that* /ðæt/).

Orthographic form	Pronunciation	Examples	
and	/ən/ (or /ənd/)	A cup and saucer.	/ə 'kʌp ən 'sɔːsə/
but	/bət/	Last but not least.	/'lɑːst bət 'nɒt 'liːst/
as	/əz/	As old as the hills.	/əz 'əʊld əz ðə 'hɪlz/
than	/ðən/	He left earlier than I did.	/hi 'left 'ɜːliə ðən 'aɪ dɪd/
that	/ðət/	I know that it's wrong.	/aɪ 'nəʊ ðət ɪts 'rɒŋ/
		The dog that bit me.	/ðə 'dɒg ðət 'bɪt mi/
		The man that I saw.	/ðə 'mæn ðət aɪ 'sɔː/

8.15 Contractions with NOT

The weak form of *not* differs from other weak forms in two important ways: (1) it appears only in contractions, and (2) these contractions are usually stressed.

The final /t/ of *not* contractions occurs regularly only before a pause. In other contexts /t/ is frequently dropped, especially in the case of the disyllabic contractions, e.g. *I didn't know.*

When *not* contracts with a word ending in a sonorant, it has the form /nt/. In the case of *do* /duː/, *can* /kæn/ and *will* /wɪl/, a change of vowel is also involved.

Orthographic form	Pronunciation	Example	
aren't	/ɑːnt/	We aren't ready.	/wi 'ɑːnt 'redi/
		Aren't they here?	/'ɑːnt ðeɪ 'hɪə/
weren't	/wɜːnt/	They weren't home.	/ðeɪ 'wɜːnt 'həʊm/
		Weren't we invited?	/'wɜːnt wi ɪn'vaɪtɪd/
won't	/wəʊnt/	I won't say.	/aɪ 'wəʊnt 'seɪ/
don't	/dəʊnt/	They don't care.	/ðeɪ 'dəʊnt 'keə/
can't	/kɑːnt/	He can't swim.	/hi 'kɑːnt 'swɪm/

When *not* contracts with a word ending in an obstruent, it has the form /ənt/, which readily forms a syllabic /n/.

Orthographic form	Pronunciation	Example	
isn't	/'ɪzn̩t/ (or /'ɪzn̩/)	*It isn't right.*	/ɪt 'ɪzn̩t 'raɪt/
wasn't	/'wɒzn̩t/ (or /'wɒzn̩/)	*I wasn't there.*	/aɪ 'wɒzn̩t 'ðeə/
haven't	/'hævn̩t/ (or /'hævn̩/)	*We haven't done it.*	/wi 'hævn̩t 'dʌn ɪt/
hasn't	/'hæzn̩t/ (or /'hæzn̩/)	*It hasn't worked.*	/ɪt 'hæzn̩t 'wɜːkt/
hadn't	/'hædn̩t/ (or /'hædn̩/)	*They hadn't left.*	/ðeɪ 'hædn̩t 'left/
doesn't	/'dʌzn̩t/ (or /'dʌzn̩/)	*He doesn't smoke.*	/hi 'dʌzn̩t 'sməʊk/
didn't	/'dɪdn̩t/ (or /'dɪdn̩/)	*She didn't leave.*	/ʃi 'dɪdn̩t 'liːv/
shouldn't	/'ʃʊdn̩t/ (or /'ʃʊdn̩/)	*I shouldn't say.*	/aɪ 'ʃʊdn̩t 'seɪ/
couldn't	/'kʊdn̩t/ (or /'kʊdn̩/)	*They couldn't help.*	/ðeɪ 'kʊdn̩t 'help/
wouldn't	/'wʊdn̩t/ (or /'wʊdn̩/)	*I wouldn't go.*	/aɪ 'wʊdn̩t 'gəʊ/

8.16 Obsolete weak forms

Our transcription system distinguishes between stressed *be* /biː/ and unstressed *be* /bi/, and between stressed *you* /juː/ and unstressed *you* /ju/. This reflects the fact that weak FLEECE /i/ and weak GOOSE /u/ developed out of weak KIT /ɪ/ and weak FOOT /ʊ/. Whereas formerly the difference between stressed *be* and unstressed *be* was the difference between the phonemes FLEECE and KIT, and the difference between stressed *you* and unstressed *you* was the difference between the phonemes GOOSE and FOOT, the difference now is between different categories, strong and weak, of the same phoneme. The same difference is found between stressed *is* /ɪz/ and the unstressed *is* /ɪz/ which occurs after a pause or sibilant /s z ʃ ʒ tʃ dʒ/, but in the case of KIT, the same symbol is used for both categories. Therefore, for practical purposes the distinction can be ignored, and it's not necessary to consider *be* or *you* to have weak forms based on the strong/weak distinction. We continue to make the distinction in transcriptions, however, in order to be consistent with other published materials.

The following is a list of obsolete weak forms:

Orthographic form	Strong form	Present weak form	Former weak form
be	/biː/	/bi/	/bɪ/
she	/ʃiː/	/ʃi/	/ʃɪ/
me	/miː/	/mi/	/mɪ/
we	/wiː/	/wi/	/wɪ/
he	/hiː/	/hi/ (after a pause)	/hɪ/
the	/ðiː/	/ði/ (before vowels)	/ðɪ/
you	/juː/	/ju/	/jʊ/
do	/duː/	/du/ (before vowels)	/dʊ/
to	/tuː/	/tu/ (before vowels)	/tʊ/

8.17 Weak forms and connected speech

The above weak forms have been given in their most neutral forms, but it's common for such high-frequency words to appear in phonetic contexts which alter their phonetic structure.

Since *and*, *an* and *will* have the weak forms /ən/ and /əl/, these can form syllabic consonants more or less readily depending on the final consonant of the preceding word (see section 8.2). The weak form of *some* contains /əm/ preceded by /s/, and that of *shall* has /əl/ preceded by /ʃ/, which are contexts in which /m/ and /l/ can become syllabic.

Orthographic form	Pronunciation	Example	
and	/ən/ → /n̩/	*Fish and chips.*	/ˈfɪʃ n̩ ˈtʃɪps/
		Knife and fork.	/ˈnaɪf n̩ ˈfɔːk/
		Bought and sold.	/ˈbɔːt n̩ ˈsəʊld/
an	/ən/ → /n̩/	*I had an answer.*	/aɪ ˈhæd n̩ ˈɑːnsə/
		Cause an accident.	/ˈkɔːz n̩ ˈæksədənt/
		Eat an orange.	/ˈiːt n̩ ˈɒrɪndʒ/
'll	/əl/ → /l̩/	*That'll do.*	/ˈðæt l̩ ˈduː/
		Help'll come.	/ˈhelp l̩ ˈkʌm/
		Time'll tell.	/ˈtaɪm l̩ ˈtel/
some	/səm/ → /sm̩/	*Take some sugar.*	/ˈteɪk sm̩ ˈʃʊgə/
shall	/ʃəl/ → /ʃl̩/	*What shall we do?*	/ˈwɒt ʃl̩ wi ˈduː/

The weak forms of *are*, *were*, *there*, *for* and *her* and the contractions *you're*, *we're* and *they're* end in vowels, which leads to /r/-liaison (see section 12.4) when a vowel immediately follows.

Orthographic form	Pronunciation	Example	
are	/ə/ → /ər/	*Are all swans white?*	/ər ˈɔːl ˈswɒnz ˈwaɪt/
you're	/jɔː/ → /jɔːr/	*You're awful.*	/jɔːr ˈɔːfl̩/
we're	/wɪə/ → /wɪər/	*We're away.*	/wɪər əˈweɪ/
they're	/ðeə/ → /ðeər/	*They're empty.*	/ðeər ˈempti/
were	/wə/ → /wər/	*You were out.*	/ju wər ˈaʊt/
there	/ðə/ → /ðər/	*There are lots.*	/ðər ə ˈlɒts/
for	/fə/ → /fər/	*A free-for-all.*	/ə ˈfriː fər ˈɔːl/
her	/ə/ → /ər/	*I met her again.*	/aɪ ˈmet ər əˈgen/
	/ɜː/ → /ɜːr/	*I found her office.*	/aɪ ˈfaʊnd ɜːr ˈɒfɪs/

Chapter 9

Practice

Weak vowels and weak forms

9.1 Weak vowels: practice

This section provides practice in pronouncing the English weak vowels in different phonetic contexts, in words and phrases, and in sentences. Because of its high frequency, schwa /ə/ in particular is practised in a wide variety of contexts and combinations.

9.2 Schwa /ə/

9.2.1 Description

Mid, central, unrounded. Schwa tends to be opener, i.e. open-mid, in final position before a pause. Although schwa appears almost exclusively in unstressed syllables, it can be found exceptionally in the stressed syllable of a very small number of words, principally *because* /bɪˈkəz/.

9.2.2 Final syllable

a) <-er>

anger, answer, border, brother, butter, chapter, clever, corner, cover, danger, daughter, dinner, eager, enter, father, feather, fever, filter, finger, folder, ginger, hammer, hamster, hover, hunger, ladder, leather, letter, linger, manner, matter, member, meter,

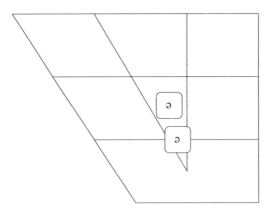

Figure 9.1 Allophones of schwa: an open-mid vowel in final position before a pause and a mid vowel in other contexts.

monster, mother, murder, number, offer, order, oyster, paper, partner, pepper, poster, powder, quarter, rather, river, shoulder, silver, sister, slender, snooker, sober, soldier, spider, stranger, summer, temper, tender, thunder, tiger, timber, wander, water, weather, winter, wonder

b)   **<-or, -ure, -a, -ar, -ard>**

actor, anchor, author, doctor, error, horror, major, minor, mirror, motor, razor, sailor, terror, tractor; capture, creature, culture, failure, feature, figure, future, injure, lecture, leisure, measure, mixture, nature, picture, pleasure, pressure, structure, treasure; asthma, china, comma, data, drama, extra, panda, pasta, pizza, quota, sauna, sofa, zebra; beggar, burglar, cellar, collar, dollar, grammar, sugar, vulgar; awkward, backward, forward, orchard, standard, leopard, hazard, mustard, lizard, blizzard

c)   **<-our, -re, -us, -ous>**

armour, colour, favour, flavour, glamour, harbour, honour, humour, labour, neighbour, rumour, vapour; acre, centre, fibre, litre, metre, theatre; cactus, campus, chorus, circus, citrus, focus, foetus, fungus, minus, virus, versus; cautious, conscious, famous, gorgeous, gracious, jealous, spacious, precious, vicious, nervous

d)   ***Various other spellings***

cheetah, murmur, sulphur, thorough, atlas, August, ballot, barracks, bishop, breakfast, buttock, canvas, carrot, Christmas, comfort, compass, concert, cupboard, effort, gallop, hammock, locust, martyr, mattress, method, monarch, parrot, pilot, purpose, salad, shepherd, stomach, syrup, system, tortoise, yoghurt

9.2.3 Phrases

bitter anger, an instant answer, border control, elder brothers and sisters, bumper to bumper, cancer treatment, a pressure cooker, constant danger, a sumptuous dinner, a learner driver, a father figure, a feather duster, scarlet fever, a water heater, nervous laughter, an advanced learner, a silent letter, a cigarette lighter, a master craftsman, a founder member, a water meter, a random number, a painter and decorator, a ballot paper, talcum powder, a swollen river, a snooker tournament, a complete stranger, suffer in silence, a vicious temper, water vapour, a character actor, human error, a complete and utter failure, a permanent feature, an obscene gesture, a lecture theatre, a treasure hunter, accurate data, a Roman villa, a computer virus, a jealous husband, a proper breakfast, creature comforts, an amateur painter

9.2.4 Sentences

1   My elderly mother favours sombre colours.
2   Martha met a famous footballer in London.
3   Silent letters often pose problems for learners.
4   Her husband's jealous and has a vicious temper.
5   Anna ordered a tuna salad, and I had pasta with salmon.
6   The youngster had fallen in the water but wasn't injured.
7   Trevor was tortured by inner demons, but suffered in silence.
8   This is a common feature of both human and animal behaviour.
9   He discovered to his horror that the secret document had been stolen.
10   In motor insurance, accidents by a learner driver are normally covered.

9.2.5 First syllable

about, above, across, address, adore, advance, advice, afford, afraid, agree, alarm, alive, allow, alone, amount, announce, appear, arrange, arrive, asleep, attack, avoid, awake, balloon, canal, career, collect, compare, complain, complete, concerned, conclude, confirm, confused, connect, contain, continue, convince, correct, forget, forgive, machine, observe, occur, offend, parade, patrol, perform, perhaps, persuade, police, polite, possess, produce, promote, propose, protect, provide, success, suggest, supply, support, suppose, surprise, surround, survive

9.2.6 Word-medial syllable

acrobat, advertise, aeroplane, alcohol, alphabet, analyse, astronaut, atmosphere, aubergine, autograph, avalanche, caravan, compromise, crocodile, decorate, demonstrate, devastate, dinosaur, diplomat, dynamite, exercise, generate, hibernate, horoscope, interview, kilogram, liberate, memorise, microphone, microscope, nicotine, operate, organise, parachute, paradise, paragraph, parallel, paralyse, photograph, recognise, reservoir, Saturday, somersault, suffocate, supervise, sympathise, tolerate, vandalise, yesterday; contradict, entertain, guarantee, immature, interfere, interrupt, introduce, kangaroo, lemonade, magazine, margarine, recommend, referee, reproduce, understand, volunteer

9.2.7 Two schwas

a)   *Medial and final syllable*
     adequate, afterwards, algebra, bachelor, calendar, character, conjuror, customer, foreigner, hazardous, permanent, popular, signature, singular, syllabus, amateur, ignorance, ignorant, vigorous, miniature

b)   *Initial and final syllable*
     adventure, agenda, announcer, another, arena, attacker, banana, cathedral, collector, composer, computer, conductor, consumer, container, ferocious, forever, gorilla, performer, producer, professor, projector, propeller, saliva, supporter, suspicious, together, vanilla, veranda, consider, contagious

c)   *Second and final syllable*
     ballerina, disagreement, disappointment, entertainment, European, caterpillar, commentator, escalator, generator

9.2.8 Three schwas

accelerator, asparagus, astronomer, photographer, hippopotamus

9.2.9 Phrases

an abuse of power, current affairs, a burglar alarm, an alleged assault, a major award, careers advice, a major concern, forgive and forget, a minor offence, a police patrol, a regular supply, a surprise announcement, a paper aeroplane, the letters of the alphabet, a retired diplomat, a Christmas pantomime, a colour photograph, an underground reservoir, tomorrow afternoon, a volunteer worker, a confirmed bachelor, a suspicious character, a regular customer, a secret agenda, a collector's item, a famous composer, an amateur performer, a water container, a bitter disagreement, a power generator, an amateur photographer, a matter of concern

9.2.10 Sentences

1 Jonathan, a confirmed bachelor, had a secret admirer.
2 Numerous universities award extra-curricular scholarships.
3 Our oldest daughter's obsessed with dinosaurs and dragons.
4 Rebecca was completely incapable of forgiving and forgetting.
5 Nicholas observed a suspicious character in the neighbourhood.
6 Elizabeth was apparently a tremendous disappointment to her parents.
7 Yesterday a woman was attacked by a ferocious gorilla in the Netherlands.
8 An amateur photographer took some amazing pictures of Canterbury Cathedral.
9 He's a terrific commentator – knowledgeable, articulate, perceptive and passionate.
10 Christopher was in the entertainment business as a theatre producer, concert agent and general manager.

9.3 Vowel plus schwa

9.3.1 PRICE /aɪ/ + /ə/

acquire, admire, amplifier, aspire, attire, buyer, choir, conspire, desire, empire, enquire, entire, fire, hire, iron, liar, pliers, require, retire, satire, spire, tired, tyre, umpire, vampire, wire, dire, expire, inspire, lyre, mire, prior, pyre, sapphire, alliance, anxiety, appliance, bias, Brian, certifiable, client, compliant, cyanide, dandelion, defiant, denial, diabetes, diagnose, diagram, dialect, dialogue, diaphragm, diarrhoea, diary, diet, giant, liable, lion, quiet, riot, trial, variety, violence, violent, iodine, maniacal, pariah, pious, reliable, science, society, triumph, violin

9.3.2 MOUTH /aʊ/ + /ə/

coward, flour/flower, hour, power, sour, tower, cower, devour, Howard, scour, shower, nowadays, towel, vowel, allowance, bowel, trowel

9.3.3 FACE /eɪ/ + /ə/

layer, player, surveyor, bayonet, betrayal, mayonnaise

9.3.4 CHOICE /ɔɪ/ + /ə/

employer, lawyer, destroyer, annoyance, disloyal, loyal, royal, buoyant, clairvoyant, flamboyant

9.3.5 GOAT /əʊ/ + /ə/

lower, mower, grower, rower, coalesce, coalition

9.3.6 GOOSE /uː/ + /ə/

brewer, steward, cruel, dual/duel, fluent, fuel, truant, gruel, jewel

9.3.7 FLEECE /iː/ + /ə/

European, leotard, reassure, Caribbean, agreeable, geographic, herculean, museum, pianist, vehement

9.3.8 Phrases

a secret admirer, an anxiety attack, a domestic appliance, a power failure, a cathedral choir, a prospective client, a vehement denial, a standard dialect, acute diarrhoea, a secret diary, a balanced diet, a murder enquiry, a fire fighter, corrugated iron, a compulsive liar, a lion tamer, surplus to requirements, riot police, trial and error, tyre pressure, a tremendous variety, random violence, razor wire, a science museum, a secret society, a major triumph, autumn flowers, enormous power, a clever lawyer, a truant officer, a precious jewel

9.3.9 Sentences

1   The steward was fluent in Korean.
2   Brian left the towels in the shower.
3   He inspired loyalty in his employees.
4   Howard was diagnosed with diabetes.
5   He's an annoying, disagreeable tyrant.
6   She hired a lawyer to conspire against her client.
7   All the flowers, except for the dandelions, have expired.
8   Nowadays he spends hours and hours playing the violin.
9   Brian's employer reassured him that he would not be fired.
10   The dialect he speaks is a variety of Caribbean English Creole.

9.4 Weak KIT /ɪ/

9.4.1 Description

Just above close-mid, front-central, unrounded. KIT is also a member of the strong vowel set.

9.4.2 Final syllable

Weak KIT frequently occurs in word-final syllables, notably in syllables realising the <-s> and <-ed> inflections.

9.4.3 In inflections (/ɪz/ after sibilants /s z ʃ ʒ tʃ dʒ/, /ɪd/ after /t d/)

a)   Following /z/
      Ambrose's, Charles's, Dez's, Giles's, James's, Liz's, Rose's; blouses, breezes, bruises, cruises, diseases, disguises, fuses, hoses, mazes, noises, noses, phases, phrases,

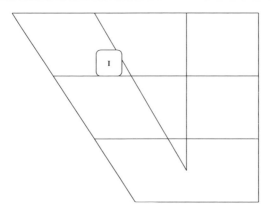

Figure 9.2 Weak KIT /ɪ/.

prizes, roses, sizes, vases; accuses, advises, amuses, analyses, apologises, browses, chooses, closes, confuses, criticises, despises, fizzes, freezes, gazes, pleases, proposes, refuses, seizes, teases

b) *Following /s/*

Alex's, Alice's, Angus's, Bruce's, Joyce's, Max's, Thomas's; addresses, axes, bonuses, bosses, boxes, buses, businesses, cases, chances, choices, classes, courses, differences, faces, fences, foxes, horses, mattresses, offices, pieces, prices, purses, spaces, taxes; announces, bounces, ceases, chases, collapses, commences, confesses, dances, embarrasses, expresses, fixes, grimaces, hisses, misses, mixes, pierces, presses, relaxes

c) *Following /ʃ/*

Josh's, Hamish's, Trish's; ashes, bushes, dishes, marshes, blemishes, brushes, leashes, niches, rashes; astonishes, banishes, bashes, cherishes, crashes, crushes, demolishes, flourishes, furnishes, nourishes, perishes, punishes, pushes, relishes, smashes, squashes, vanishes, washes, wishes

d) *Following /tʃ/*

Rich's, Mitch's; batches, beaches, benches, branches, brooches, churches, ditches, peaches, pouches, ranches, riches, speeches, trenches; attaches, catches, clenches, crouches, crunches, drenches, fetches, itches, punches, reaches, snatches, stretches, teaches, touches, watches

e) *Following /dʒ/*

Reg's, George's, Madge's; advantages, badges, bandages, barges, bridges, cabbages, cages, carriages, colleges, cottages, edges, fridges, hedges, hinges, images, languages, marriages, messages, oranges, pages, passages, sausages, sponges, villages; acknowledges, arranges, changes, cringes, damages, discourages, dodges, emerges, engages, indulges, manages, nudges, ravages, scavenges, surges

f) *Following /t/*

arrested, attracted, boasted, chatted, cheated, collected, commented, committed, completed, consulted, corrected, counted, created, debated, delighted, devoted, donated, drifted, elected, fainted, hunted, insisted, lifted, melted, painted, pointed, posted, predicted, prevented, printed, protected, regretted, rejected, rented, repeated, reported, respected, rested, selected, shouted, spotted, started, tested, treated, trusted, wanted

g)   Following /d/

avoided, awarded, bonded, blended, concluded, decided, defended, demanded, divided, ended, faded, flooded, guarded, guided, handed, headed, included, intended, mended, needed, nodded, pleaded, raided, regarded, shielded, skidded, sounded, traded

9.4.4 Weak KIT in other word endings

a)   <-age, -et, -ed>

baggage, bandage, cabbage, cottage, courage, image, luggage, marriage, message, mortgage, package, passage, postage, sausage, shortage, village, voyage, wreckage, damage, language, hostage; blanket, bracket, bucket, budget, carpet, comet, cricket, jacket, market, packet, planet, pocket, puppet, rocket, target, ticket, socket; crooked, jagged, rugged, wicked, naked

b)   <-ic, -ish, -ive>

attic, basic, classic, clinic, critic, fabric, garlic, graphic, hectic, lyric, magic, mimic, music, panic, picnic, plastic, public, topic, toxic, traffic, tragic, comic; childish, finish, foolish, furnish, publish, punish, rubbish, selfish, vanish, English, polish; active, captive, native, motive, passive, massive

c)   <-ing, -it, -ist, -id, -is, -in>

building, ceiling, clothing, darling, during, evening, greeting, morning, nothing, wedding, drawing; bandit, credit, exit, habit, limit, permit (n.), profit, rabbit, spirit, unit, visit, vomit; artist, cyclist, dentist, florist, tourist, typist; vivid, valid, timid, stupid, solid, rigid, rapid, humid, fluid, liquid; basis, crisis, tennis; cabin, coffin, dolphin, Latin, margin, penguin, pumpkin, robin, ruin, satin, napkin

d)   Various other spellings

biscuit, engine, famine, knowledge, linen, minute (n.), spinach, college, addict, denim, district, gossip, instinct, notice, office, olive, ostrich, physics, porridge, practice, promise, province, sandwich, service, tulip, turnip, verdict, victim, worship

9.4.5 Initial syllable

dictate (v.), dislike, dismiss, display, ignore, imply, impress, improve, include, indeed, infect, inflate, inform, inhale, inject, insert, insist, inspect, instead, instruct, insure, intend, intense, invade, invent, invest, invite, involve

9.4.6 Words with schwa /ə/ and weak KIT /ɪ/

abolish, academic, accomplish, advantage, aggressive, allergic, astonish, atomic, attractive, automatic, comparative, conservative, democratic, diplomatic, disappointed, domestic, dramatic, emphasis, energetic, fanatic, majestic, membership, negative, offensive, opposite, partnership, pathetic, pharmacist, photographic, productive, pyramid, statistics, sympathetic, talkative, vitamin, dictator, imperative, improvement, indignant, infectious, informative, inspector, instalment, instructor, insurance, intruder

9.4.7 Phrases

a derelict cottage, a vivid image, a cryptic message, postage and packing, garlic sausage, a chronic shortage, an epic voyage, twisted wreckage, extensive damage, offensive language, an electric blanket, a plastic bucket, a limited budget, fitted carpet, a denim jacket, a ticket inspector, a packet of biscuits, limited knowledge, a music critic, a last-minute panic, a picnic basket, congested traffic, a thrilling finish, a dramatic flourish, domestic rubbish, a public building, a painted ceiling, a credit limit, an eccentric habit, a basic unit, a flying visit, a gifted artist, a growing crisis, a primitive instinct, a linen napkin, an office building, atomic physics, an unsuspecting victim, an intense dislike, an attractive display, a distinct advantage, a chronic alcoholic, advantages and disadvantages, a valid ticket

9.4.8 Sentences

1   Alison's knowledge of music is encyclopaedic.
2   The editor encouraged me to publish my article.
3   Dennis insisted on my wearing a bicycle helmet.
4   This artist intensely dislikes anything asymmetrical.
5   The initial experiments led to some interesting findings.
6   Alice explained the advantages of outsourcing medical services.
7   David rented a charming cottage in a pretty little village in Dorset.
8   These restrictions resulted in a chronic shortage of nurses in England.
9   He finished the packet of digestive biscuits he'd discovered in the kitchen.
10   It's estimated that eleven per cent of the passengers were travelling without a valid ticket.

9.5 Weak FLEECE [i]

9.5.1 Description

A little lower than close, a little backer than front, unrounded. FLEECE is also a member of the strong vowel set.

9.5.2 Word-final

a)   <-y>
   angry, any, army, baby, beauty, body, bully, bumpy, bury, busy, carry, cheeky, cherry, chilly, city, clumsy, copy, country, crazy, curry, dirty, dizzy, dummy, dusty, duty,

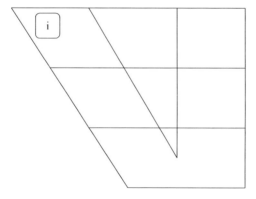

Figure 9.3 Weak FLEECE [i].

early, easy, empty, entry, envy, fancy, faulty, ferry, filthy, fizzy, fluffy, friendly, funny, fussy, gloomy, glory, greasy, greedy, guilty, happy, heavy, hungry, hurry, ivy, jelly, juicy, lady, lazy, lucky, many, marry, merry, nasty, naughty, only, party, pity, plenty, pretty, ready, silly, sorry, story, study, tidy, very, worry

b) *Various other spellings* <ey, i, ee, ie, e>

abbey, alley, barley, chimney, donkey, hockey, honey, jersey, jockey, journey, kidney, money, monkey, trolley, turkey, valley; chilli, khaki, muesli, taxi; coffee, toffee; cookie, genie, movie; acne

9.5.3 Pre-vocalic

abbreviate, aerial, alien, appreciate, aquarium, area, audience, audio, bacteria, barrier, burial, cereal, civilian, comedian, convenient, curious, embryo, encyclopaedia, enthusiastic, envious, experience, exterior, familiar, furious, genius, glorious, guardian, hideous, historian, idiom, idiot, industrial, inferior, ingredient, interior, librarian, luxurious, malaria, material, media, mediaeval, medium, memorial, millennium, mysterious, notorious, nuclear, nucleus, obedient, oblivious, obvious, patio, peculiar, pedestrian, period, pneumonia, previous, radiator, radio, radius, serious, stadium, stereo, studio, superior, tedious, trivial, various, vegetarian, victorious, video, create, deodorant, geography, geology, geometry, piano, react, reality, archaeology, liaison, meander, mediocre, theatrical

9.6 Weak GOOSE [u]

9.6.1 Description

Close, central, weakly rounded.

9.6.2 Pre-vocalic

actual, annual, casual, constituency, continual, continuous, estuary, evacuate, eventual, genuine, gradual, graduate (v.), individual, influence, intellectual, jaguar, January, manual, punctual, punctuate, situate, spiritual, usual, virtual, visual

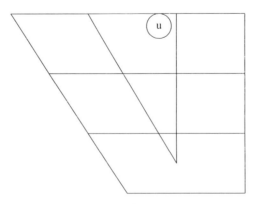

Figure 9.4 Weak GOOSE [u]. GOOSE is also a member of the strong vowel set.

9.6.3 Phrases with weak FLEECE [i] and weak GOOSE [u]

a radio aerial, totally alien, deeply appreciate, an area of difficulty, an enthusiastic studio audience, a burial ceremony, extremely convenient, deeply curious, an encyclopaedia entry, incredibly enthusiastic, slightly envious, money worries, previous experience, strangely familiar, absolutely furious, a creative genius, a military historian, a silly idiot, socially infe-rior, a gloomy interior, a university librarian, positively luxurious, industrial materials, a memorial ceremony, negotiate successfully, completely oblivious, blatantly obvious, a happy period, community radio, deadly serious, a movie studio, numerically superior, a monetary union, vegetarian cookery, ultimately victorious, react badly, daily reality, a mighty army, a tiny baby, a healthy body, a juicy cherry, a friendly country, slightly crazy, pretty creepy, heavy duty, pretty gloomy, truly happy, fairly healthy, ravenously hungry, an elderly lady, dirty laundry, desperately lonely, a fancy-dress party, flaky pastry, potentially risky, extremely silly, a conspiracy theory, a serious worry, a vicarious experience

9.6.4 Sentences

1   His military experience was invaluable.
2   Olivia has a degree in industrial psychology.
3   Lilian's a historian, and Marion's a librarian.
4   Gillian's baby was tiny but perfectly healthy.
5   Gabriel wasn't familiar with this unusual idiom.
6   I had a juicy kiwi and some succulent strawberries.
7   It became obvious that Victoria was a creative genius.
8   Jamie recently graduated from an Australian university.
9   The documentary received enthusiastic reviews in the media.
10 The committee's activities are described in the annual report.

9.7 Syllabic consonants: practice

This section provides practice in pronouncing syllabic consonants in the phonetic contexts which favour their use. The exercise material includes the target sounds in words, phrases and sentences.

9.8 Syllabic /l/

9.8.1 Words

a)   /pl̩/, /bl̩/

apple, chapel, couple, example, nipple, opal, people, pupil, purple, ripple, sample, simple, scalpel, staple, triple, cripple, principal/principle; bubble, cable, crumble, double, gamble, global, herbal, humble, marble, mumble, noble, pebble, ramble, rubble, stable, stumble, table, tremble, trouble, label, rebel (n.), rumble, probable, reliable, respectable, syllable, impossible, invisible, responsible, sensible, incred-ible, cannibal, horrible, resemble, terrible

b)   /tl̩/, /dl̩/

battle, beetle, bottle, brutal, cattle, crystal, dental, fatal, gentle, hostel, kettle, little, men-tal, metal, nettle, petal, pistol, postal, rattle, settle, shuttle, startle, subtle, title, total, turtle, vital, capital, gentleman, settlement; bundle, bridal, candle, cradle, cuddle, doodle, fiddle, handle, huddle, idol/idle, ladle, medal, middle, model, muddle, needle, paddle, pedal/peddle, puddle, riddle, saddle, sandal, scandal, vandal

c) /kl̩/, /gl̩/, /tʃl̩/, /dʒl̩/

ankle, buckle, circle, crackle, cycle, difficult, fickle, freckle, knuckle, snorkel, sparkle, sprinkle, tickle, trickle, twinkle, wrinkle, local, uncle, vocal, article, chemical, classical, hysterical, icicle, identical, logical, magical, mechanical, medical, miracle, musical, obstacle, practical, sceptical, technical; angle, bangle, burgle, eagle, gargle, giggle, haggle, jingle, juggle, jungle, legal, mingle, single, smuggle, squiggle, strangle, struggle, tangle, tingle, wiggle, wriggle, rectangle; satchel, Rachel; angel, cudgel

d) /ml̩/, /nl̩/

camel, dismal, formal, mammal, normal, thermal, animal, simultaneous; channel, colonel, final, funnel, journal, kennel, panel, signal, tunnel, criminal, eternal, external, internal, maternal, paternal, terminal, penalty

e) /fl̩/, /vl̩/, /θl̩/, /ðl̩/

baffle, muffle, stifle, trifle, waffle, raffle, rifle, shuffle, awful, cheerful, hopeful, useful; civil, devil, drivel, evil, gravel, grovel, hovel, level, naval/navel, novel, oval, rival, shovel, shrivel, travel, approval, arrival, carnival, disapproval, festival, interval, removal; lethal, brothel; betrothal

f) /sl̩/, /zl̩/, /ʃl̩/

axle, bristle, cancel, castle, council, fossil, gristle, hassle, muscle/mussel, parcel, pencil, rustle, stencil, thistle, whistle, wrestle, rehearsal, universal; chisel, dazzle, drizzle, diesel, easel, fizzle, measles, nasal, nozzle, puzzle, sizzle, weasel, proposal, refusal, hazelnut; crucial, partial, social, special, artificial, commercial, controversial, essential, financial, influential, initial, official, potential, residential

9.8.2 Phrases

financial difficulty, a social animal, universal approval, a controversial article, a provincial capital, harmful chemicals, a professional criminal, social disapproval, the local hospital, an impossible obstacle, a controversial proposal, a little puzzled, the local council, facial muscles, normal levels, a historical novel, a political rival, international travel, official channels, a journal article, verbal signals, a nocturnal mammal, a little angel, stifle a giggle, a tropical jungle, a political struggle, unravel a tangle, social circles, a skilful tackle, a little tickle, a statistical model, a financial muddle, a bicycle pedal, a political scandal, a legal battle, a little startled, the final total, a political gamble, a trestle table, a beautiful couple, a typical example, local people, an able pupil, a little ripple, a classical temple, official approval

9.8.3 Sentences

1 I was a trifle puzzled by his refusal.
2 Rachel was unable to stifle a giggle.
3 She made a simple but special apple crumble.
4 He feels comfortable in multiple social circles.
5 It's an unmistakable signal of financial trouble.

6   My uncle wobbled home on his unstable bicycle.
7   The title of his article was 'The Maximal Syllable'.
8   It was crucial to get approval from the local council.
9   Our principal is responsible, respectable and reliable.
10 The pupils found it difficult to give examples of ethical principles.

9.9 Syllabic /n/

9.9.1 Words

a) /tṇ/, /dṇ/

bitten, brighten, button, carton, certain, cotton, curtain, fatten, flatten, frighten, glutton, kitten, lighten, mitten, mutton, pattern, rotten, shorten, straighten, tartan, threaten, tighten, whiten, important; burden, garden, harden, modern, pardon, sudden, warden, widen, wooden, rodent, student, couldn't, shouldn't, didn't, wouldn't, hadn't, guidance

b) /fṇ/, /vṇ/, /ðṇ/, /θṇ/

deafen, hyphen, often, orphan, soften, stiffen, toughen, infant; cavern, driven, even, given, govern, heaven, liven, oven, proven, raven, seven, servant, eleven; northern, southern; strengthen, lengthen, python

c) /sṇ/, /zṇ/

arson, basin, fasten, glisten, lessen/lesson, listen, loosen, person, vixen, decent, recent, comparison, adolescent; chosen, cousin, crimson, dozen, frozen, poison, prison, raisin, reason, risen, season, treason, crescent, doesn't, isn't, peasant, present, presence, horizon

d) /ʃṇ/, /ʒṇ/

caution, cushion, fashion, lotion, mission, motion, nation, ocean, passion, portion, session, station, action, fiction, option, section, patient, pension, mention, mansion, conscience, function, profession, operation, information, foundation, education, creation, accommodation, tradition, position, ambition, condition, revolution, politician, magician, musician, technician, attention, attraction, collection, description, election, instruction, introduction, protection, reception, sufficient, efficient, emotion, solution, suspicion; version, vision, revision, provision, division, collision, decision, conclusion, confusion, illusion, conversion, diversion, excursion, occasion, invasion, persuasion, explosion

9.9.2 Phrases

fasten a button, a prison warden, student accommodation, modern fashion, the Southern Ocean, a session musician, modern fiction, a television licence, heightened tension, pension contributions, an important function, my chosen profession, a sudden resignation, tighten regulations, a pleasant sensation, an unpleasant situation, the situation worsened, a student organisation, sudden inspiration, a written examination, a student demonstration, pleasant associations, an important collection, a wooden construction, written instructions, a television production, a sudden vision, pension provision, an important decision, a sudden conversion, a population explosion, an important lesson, listen patiently, a decent person

9.9.3 Sentences

1   Jason met his relations at Luton Station.
2   Read this important information about depression medication.
3   He studied the representation of adolescence in modern fiction.
4   Gordon listened in growing confusion to his cousin's objections.
5   Seven patients developed infections and required hospitalisation.
6   There was a population explosion due to immigration and urbanisation.
7   His frightened expression strengthened my impression of his innocence.
8   Nathan's dedication to his chosen profession is an inspiration to all of us.
9   Information about my former positions is given in the written application.
10   What expectations does the present generation of students have from education?

9.10 Weak forms and contractions: practice

This section provides practice in using English weak forms and contractions in short phrases and sentences.

9.11 Forms of BE (main verb and auxiliary)

9.11.1 AM and ARE

a)   /aɪm/

I'm fine. I'm lost. I'm tired. I'm leaving. I'm busy. I'm having dinner. I'm waiting. I'm taking my time. I'm seeing John later. I'm doing my best. I'm drowning. I'm trying. I'm worn out. You know I'm right.

b)   /əm/

Am I late? Am I right? Am I wrong? Am I winning? Am I under arrest? Am I boring you? Am I making myself clear? What am I waiting for? Where am I going? Who am I talking to? How am I doing? When am I expected?

c)   /jɔː/

You're wonderful. You're learning. You're a real friend. You're forgetting something. You're a star. You're almost there. You're doing well. You're close. You're getting better. You're being silly. You're seeing things. You're annoying me. You're making a mistake. You're breaking the law. You're late. You're very brave. Now you're talking. If you're interested . . . When you're in the area . . . Because you're a friend . . . I think you're great. I know you're busy. He said you're trying hard. She knows you're interested. We believe you're cheating.

d)   /wɪə/

We're coming. We're running late. We're getting along well. We're making good progress. We're finding it difficult. We're making good time. We're having problems. We're leaving soon. We're thinking about it. We're doing it again. We're meeting later. We're happy together. We're staying nearby. If we're successful . . . When we're at home . . . When we're out shopping . . . When we're hungry . . . He knows we're here. She thinks we're a couple. They said we're allowed.

e) /ðeə/

They're awful. They're here. They're on their way. They're taking it easy. They're nearly there. They're plotting. They're out. They're starting. They're playing chess. They're both teachers. They're difficult. They're gone. If they're still waiting . . . When they're in a good mood . . . If they're good enough . . . When they're ready . . . She said they're coming. He knows they're cheating. They think they're special. It sounds like they're serious.

f) /ə/

Are you ready? Are you there? Are you mad? Are you sure? Are you all right? Are you comfortable? Are you joking? Are we sinking? Are they hiding? Are they lost? What are you waiting for? What are you doing? What are you trying to say? What are you looking at? What are you talking about? Where are you going? Where are you from? Where are they kept? Where are they made? Where are we staying? When are we going? When are you leaving? When are they arriving? When are we meeting? When are you getting up? When are they having dinner? Why are you angry? Why are they broken? Why are we waiting? Why are they laughing? Why are we arguing? Why are you smiling? Why are they complaining? What are they eating? What are you carrying? What are they hiding? What are we doing?

9.11.2 IS

a) /z/

The job's easy. His dad's rich. This bag's heavy. The cave's very dark. This scythe's blunt. The game's over. The gun's loaded. This ring's very expensive. The bill's wrong. My knee's aching. The glue's drying. Who's there? His fur's falling out. My car's outside. The door's locked. My pay's too low. Why's that? My toy's better. My toe's hurting. Now's the time. Here's an idea. This chair's reserved. Where's Tom?

b) /s/

The tap's leaking. The shop's closed. The ship's sinking. The cat's sleeping. That's incredible. His flat's very big. What's the problem? My back's itching. This cake's too sweet. This lock's useless. This fork's bent. My life's amazing. My cough's getting worse. This knife's very sharp. That tooth's rotten.

c) /ɪz/

This is it. The bus is late. The case is closed. Chess is boring. The choice is yours. The course is ending. My dress is new. The horse is limping. The house is for sale. This place is awful. His voice is breaking. Hers is better. His is worse. The news is exciting. That blouse is nice. My bruise has gone. The cause is unknown. This cheese is very smelly. That disease is rare. The hose is leaking. My nose is bleeding. The prize is pathetic. The quiz is too difficult. The brush is dirty. English is fun! This fish is rotten. The varnish is still wet. Beige is my favourite colour. This batch is faulty. The beach is empty. Bleach is dangerous. The branch is breaking. Your brooch is lovely. The patch is coming off. This peach is very sweet. This torch is useless. My watch is very old. That badge is a classic. My luggage is heavy. The bridge is collapsing. That cabbage is huge. The cage is open. College is exciting. The damage is done. The hedge is overgrown. This language is easy. The last page is missing. This sausage is tasty. The village is empty.

9.11.3 WAS and WERE

a)   /wəz/

He was drunk again. I was on time. It was a shame. She was lonely. The door was open. The lock was broken. The time was right. His advice was pointless. The book was too long. The boss was leaving. I was making dinner. That was that. Was John there? Was I right? Who was driving? It was better. Was Monday a success? Was that the answer? Was it working? Was the pilot sober? Where was the teacher? When was the party? Who was the leader? That was a bad start. It was a boring film. She was sleeping. I was alone.

b)   /wə/

We were tricked. They were criminals. You were working. The boys were playing. The men were talking. The women were waiting. The schools were closed. The soldiers were marching. The walls were uneven. The scissors were sharp. We were joking. You were slow. The girls were hiding. The men were fighting. They were outside. Were those okay? Were these the ones? Where were the police? When were they last seen? Who were they waiting for? Where were they going? Who were they meeting?

9.12 Forms of *HAVE* (auxiliary)

9.12.1 HAVE

a)   /aɪv/

I've seen it. I've finished. I've done it. I've been waiting all day. I've been robbed. I've made dinner. I've been there. I've found it. I've had enough. I've done my best. I've had a try. I've had a shower. You know I've tried.

b)   /juv/

You've broken it. You've made a mess. You've succeeded. You've made it. You've taken too long. You've missed one. You've spilt some. You've dropped something. You've said that before. You've lost. I think you've had enough.

c)   /wiv/

We've never met. We've arrived. We've changed. We've prepared everything. We've done our best. We've had it fixed. We've worn it out. We've turned it off. We've given up. We've bought a new one. You think we've cheated?

d)   /ðeɪv/

They've got it all wrong. They've left. They've done it before. They've made a mistake. They've already eaten. They've got lost. They've been stolen. They've been welcomed. They've split up. I bet they've gone.

e)   /əv/

People have complained. The fish have swum away. The sheep have wandered off. The children have gone to bed. The men have been arrested. The women have vanished. My feet have got wet. His teeth have fallen out. The geese have flown away. The mice have eaten all the cheese. The police have been asking about you. My parents have gone on holiday. Ten cars have been stolen. Where have you been? It might have happened. What have you done? You shouldn't have left.

f)   /həv/

Have I missed something? Have you noticed anything? Have we won? Have they replied? Have the kids come home? Have you finished? Have the police been called? Have we passed the exam? Have you seen it?

9.12.2 HAS

a)   /z/

The job's been done. The bread's gone mouldy. The dog's died. My glove's disappeared. My scythe's been stolen. A crime's been committed. The machine's stopped working. The building's fallen down. The well's run dry. His knee's got worse. My coffee's gone cold. Who's bought one? Its fur's fallen out. The car's broken down again. The floor's been polished. My pay's disappeared. The sky's got darker. The joy's gone out of it. The snow's all melted. The cow's been milked. This year's been great. My hair's changed colour. Trevor's struck gold. Lucy's worked hard.

b)   /s/

My zip's got stuck. The group's fallen apart. The cat's been run over. A jet's just crashed. My snake's shed its skin. The chalk's run out. My wife's left me. The roof's collapsed. The new bath's been installed. My rotten tooth's been pulled out. Ruth's left.

c)   /əz/

The address has changed. The bus has broken down. The vase has been replaced. My nose has been itching all day. My wish has come true. The bush has grown too big. The camouflage has fooled them. The barrage has started. My watch has stopped. Your brooch has fallen off. The cottage has burnt down. The urge has passed.

d)   /həz/

Has it worked? Has she left? Has he done it? Has the train arrived yet? Has your headache gone? Has my mother called? Has the baby gone to sleep? Has the traffic got worse? Has the rain stopped? Has it all made sense? Has it helped?

9.12.3 HAD

a)   /aɪd/

I'd already finished. I'd done all I could. I wish I'd told him. I'd already left. I'd seen it before. I'd better go. If only I'd known. He said I'd spoilt it. She thought I'd taken it. I knew I'd made a mistake. I'd wrecked it.

b)   /jud/

You'd been before. You'd never seen it. I wish you'd come earlier. If only you'd said. You'd made a mess. She said you'd left. I thought you'd finished. I knew you'd been tricked. You'd already eaten it.

c)   /hid/

He'd already gone. He'd left. He'd seen it. He'd been there before. He'd hardly started. He'd done it again. He'd spoilt it. He'd already bought it. He'd crashed the car. He'd lost it. He'd fallen over.

d)   /ʃid/

She'd said everything. She'd been there all day. She'd already finished. I wish she'd done better. If only she'd listened. She'd given up. She'd arrived early. I knew she'd failed. I thought she'd done better.

e)   /wid/

We'd better leave. We'd finished early. We'd taken a long time. We'd already opened it. I wish we'd tried that first. If only we'd met ten years ago. I thought we'd passed. I knew we'd gone too far. We'd missed it.

f)   /ðeɪd/

They'd broken it. They'd done it before. They'd tried their best. They'd broken new ground. They'd set a new record. If only they'd said so. I wish they'd left earlier. They said they'd been invited. I thought they'd gone.

g)   /əd/ *(after consonants)*

The gap had widened. The job had got worse. It had broken down. The fad had passed. The sack had torn. The dog had run off. The coach had gone home. The bridge had been strengthened. His cough had cleared up. The love had gone. The myth had grown. The scythe had rusted. The boss had left. The prize had been won. My wish had been granted. Its prestige had lessened. The dam had been built. The phone had been ringing. The song had finished. The bill had arrived.

h)   /əd/ *(after /r/-liaison vowels)*

The bar had closed. The door had been locked. His fur had got wet. The beer had run out. The bear had returned. The weather had changed.

i)   /əd/ *(after other vowels)*

The sea had been polluted. My money had run out. The zoo had closed down. The day had gone well. The lie had been discovered. The toy had broken. The plough had rusted. The show had finished.

j)   /həd/

Had she already left? Had it been going on long? Had it been a success? Had they tidied up? Had they done it before? Had it been prepared? Had you been there before? Had it worked? Had it been stolen?

9.13 *THERE*

a)   /ðə/

There's a problem. There are too many. There's been a mix up. There've been lots. There was no point. There were lots more. There'd been a complaint.

9.14 *DO* (auxiliary)

a)   /də/

Do they know? Do we park here? Do people like that? Do pandas eat meat? Do rabbits hibernate? Where do penguins live? How do birds fly? When do babies start talking? Which do they like? What do the police want?

b)   /du/

Do ants sleep? Do apples grow on trees? Do elephants really never forget? Do onions make you cry? Do old people sleep more? Where do Ann's parents live? When do I start? What do owls eat?

c)   /dəz/

Does anybody care? Does it work? Does she like it? Does it matter? Does the tap leak? Where does Tom live? What does it do? When does it start? Who does it concern? How does it work? What does it mean? Where does he come from?

9.15 Modal verbs

9.15.1 WOULD

a)   /aɪd/

I'd like to go. I'd enjoy it. I'd do it. I'd have a go. I'd open it. I'd take one. I'd like one. I'd win easily. I'd eat it all. I'd laugh my head off. I'd leave it alone. I'd love to come. I'd make a difference. You know I'd love it.

b)   /jud/

You'd find it difficult. You'd notice the difference. You'd get it wrong. You'd eat it all. You'd spoil it. You'd easily win. You'd never finish in time. You'd never understand. You'd love it. I think you'd like it.

c)   /hid/

He'd steal it. He'd never do it. He'd waste our time. He'd make a mess. He'd work it out. He'd take a long time. He'd help. He'd have a go. He'd make you proud. He'd drive you crazy. He'd buy it all.

d)   /ʃid/

She'd get angry. She'd see the funny side. She'd throw it away. She'd lose it. She'd take it all. She'd take it home. She'd make a fortune. She'd say what she thinks. She'd like to keep it. She'd like one. I think she'd hate it.

e)   /wid/

We'd break the record. We'd have a great time. We'd like to join you. We'd get lost. We'd be wasting our money. We'd win. We'd get away with it. We'd be rich. We'd be able to do it. We'd enjoy it. I know we'd do well.

f)   /əd/ *(after consonants)*

The top would fall off. The lab would close down. The debt would increase. The bed would be too big. The itch would get worse. The cage would rust. The knife would be found. The drive would be tiring. The myth would grow. The scythe would be dangerous. A kiss would be nice. A snooze would be good. I wish this rash would go. Beige would look nice. I said Pam would do it. The bone would break. The ring would get lost. The coal would run out.

g)   /əd/ *(after /r/-liaison vowels)*

Its fur would fall out. The car would break down. A war would be terrible. A year would be enough. A spare would be a good idea. If only my mother would leave.

h)   /əd/ *(after other vowels)*

The tea would go cold. A party would be great. A few would be enough. That way would be quicker. A pie would be too much. That boy would be suitable. If only the snow would melt. I wish that cow would move.

9.15.2 WILL

a)   /aɪl/, /jul/, /(h)il/, /ʃil/, /wil/, /ðeil/

I'll let you know. I think I'll leave. You'll understand. I know you'll do well. He'll never admit it. I think he'll leave early. She'll never know. Now she'll feel better. We'll work it out. I know we'll manage. They'll never find it. I think they'll stop looking.

b) /l̩/ *(after consonants)*

The top'll break. A cab'll stop. That'll do. It'll never work. The mood'll change. The park'll close. The egg'll break. Which'll fit? The bridge'll collapse. Crime'll increase. When'll that happen? Half'll be enough. The cave'll be dark. Your teeth'll rot. The scythe'll be blunt. The bus'll be late. The surprise'll kill him. My cash'll run out. Sabotage'll work. This one'll do. My room'll be big enough. The string'll snap.

c) /əl/ *(after /l/)*

The bill will be high. The bell will ring soon. The fool will get hurt. The smell will get worse. The wall will be demolished. The wheel will fall off.

d) /əl/ *(after /r/-liaison vowels)*

The car will break down. The bar will be closed. The star will explode. The jar will crack. The tar will melt. The scar will fade. My guitar will sound great. Its fur will fall out. The blur will spoil the pictures. A short stir will do. The door will creak. The floor will be cold. Four will do. The score will change. The war will end. My ear will get better. The deer will be frightened. The pier will close down. Next year will be a leap year. The atmosphere will be amazing. The engineer will know. A volunteer will do it. The fresh air will do you good. The bear will hibernate. This chair will fall apart. Your hair will go grey. The millionaire will pay. The questionnaire will only take a minute. The butter will melt. His brother will help. The colour will fade. The rumour will spread.

e) /əl/ *(after other vowels)*

That bee will sting you. The sea will be cold. The key will fit. The tea will arrive soon. Three will be enough. My knee will start hurting. The fee will be high. The crew will help. The glue will dry quickly. The queue will start moving soon. That screw will be too short. The zoo will be closed. The tray will be too heavy. My essay will be a success. This hairspray will work. The day will fly by. Your eye will get better. This pie will taste great. The sky will clear up. My reply will be brief. This guy will know. This lie will work. That toy will break. The joy will fade. That boy will do well. The snow will soon melt. Your toe will only get worse. I'm sure the show will be great. The window will get dirty. Now will be fine. The baby will stop crying. This coffee will give me a headache. My new hobby will last forever. This money will last about a week. This movie will be great.

f) /wɪl/

Will you give it a go? Will it work? Will she make it? Will they do it? Will it be enough? Will that do?

9.15.3 CAN, MUST *and* SHALL

a) /kən/

I can swim. You can try. Can they see it too? It can wait. I can tell. Dave can do it. Can we go? Jack can take the train. The neighbours can hear you. Can you say that again? Where can I park? What can I say? Who can it be? Which can I take? When can I call round? You can say that again! As far as I can see. I can barely hear myself think. I can live with it. I can take it or leave it. I've bitten off more than I can chew.

b) /məst/

The show must go on. That car must be worth a fortune. That must be painful. This must be it.

c) /ʃəl/

Where shall I go? What shall I do? Who shall I ask? When shall I leave? I shall try. I shall leave.

9.16 Prepositions

9.16.1 AT, FROM *and* FOR

a) /ət/

clutch at straws, asleep at the wheel, young at heart, choose at random, talk at length, take something at face value, burn the candle at both ends, fall at the first hurdle, howl at the moon, ill at ease, at short notice, weak at the knees, at the drop of a hat, in the right place at the right time

b) /frəm/

from A to Z, live from hand to mouth, miles from nowhere, fade from view, fall from grace, a home from home, a bolt from the blue, cut from the same cloth, start from scratch, go from rags to riches, a blast from the past, go from door to door, straight from the horse's mouth, go from strength to strength

c) /fə/

one for luck, for the sake of argument, a recipe for disaster, word for word, for better or for worse, good for nothing, lost for words, spoilt for choice, food for thought, a cry for help, take for granted, a sight for sore eyes, an A for effort, a man for all seasons, money for old rope, tit for tat, a free-for-all, once and for all

9.16.2 TO *and* OF

a) /tə/

a hard nut to crack, a tough act to follow, back to square one, up to date, a score to settle, agree to disagree, back to basics, close to home, a bitter pill to swallow, bored to tears, a shoulder to cry on, raring to go, too hot to handle, A to Z, day to day, man to man, well to do, a bride to be, face to face, head to head, a mother to be, wall to wall, door to door, ready to wear, true to love, heart to heart

b) /tu/

a bite to eat, a means to an end, afraid to ask, end to end, down to earth, made to order, a call to action

c) /ə(v)/ *(before consonants)*

fifteen minutes of fame, a bag of nerves, a beast of burden, a can of worms, a clean bill of health, a fish out of water, a labour of love, a meeting of minds, a piece of cake, a rule of thumb, a safe pair of hands, a war of words, ahead of the game, a thing of the past, out of the way, out of business, a bag of bones, a bed of roses, a fact of life, a pack of lies, a waste of breath, the back of beyond, a figure of fun, a stroke of luck, a sign of the times *d)* /əv/ *(before vowels)*

a jack of all trades, a matter of opinion, a mine of information, out of order, all of a sudden, at the drop of a hat, a maid of honour, a work of art, a figure of eight, a point of order, a comedy of errors

9.17 Pronouns

9.17.1 HE, HIM *and* HIS

a) /i/

So he knows, does he? Has he seen it? Will he know? Can he help? Where did he go? What does he want? Should he try? Could he answer? I know he does. She said he did. I thought he knew.

b) /hi/

He told us everything. He knows a lot. He ran off. He did it well. He told me so. He thought about it.

c) /ɪm/

Help him. Don't rob him. We've got him. They hated him. I woke him up. They had to drag him. I can't reach him. They didn't charge him anything. It drove him mad. He said it was beneath him. She tried to soothe him. I don't miss him. It didn't faze him. Please don't push him. I can't name him. I'll phone him later. Sing him a song. Let's call him. I can see him. They adore him.

d) /ɪz/

I know his mother. I caught his cold. She took his details. I believed his story. It's near his house. Can you see his car? Has he learnt his lesson? Does his brother live there? They took his keys. Give me his stuff.

e) /hɪz/

His coat's wet. His car's gone. His mother called. His house is on fire. His brother took it. His wife left.

9.17.2 THEM, US *and* HER

a) /ðəm/

Help them. Nobody mentioned them. I know them. Jack found them. Show them again. I took them home. He broke them. Put them over there. Can I borrow them? Will you look after them? He stood behind them.

b) /əs/

Tell us everything. Take us there. They're following us. He made us wait. They hardly know us. She bought us a treat. Remind us later. They've seen us. They'll just ignore us. He promised us.

c) /ə/

I can't find her. Just ask her. They gave her a prize. I'll phone her later. He met her. Tell her again. She said she'll miss her. I hardly know her. I bought her one. I can see her.

d) /ɜː/

What's her name? Take her bag. I found her number. Will her brother come? Is her mother okay? I know her aunt. I've read her book. She took her time. Someone took her coat.

e) /hɜː/

Her mother left. Her bag's over there. Her brother said so. Her finger's swollen. Her car's been stolen.

9.18 Determiners

9.18.1 A, AN, THE *and* SOME

a) /ə/ *(in short phrases)*

a pocket, a bin, a table, a dog, a coat, a guess, a cheat, a joke, a farm, a vote, a thing, a sock, a zoo, a shop, a genre, a hobby, a minute, a note, a letter, a robot, a university, a unit, a uniform, a yacht, a window

b) /ə/ *(in longer phrases)*

a proud father, a big decision, a tricky question, a dirty mind, a close shave, a good time, a cheap ticket, a gentle breeze, a frank answer, a vulgar attitude, a thin line, a soft landing, a zany idea, a short walk, a hot drink, a misty morning, a naughty child, a loud bang, a rough plan, a useful tip, a united country, a unique situation, a universal truth, a young man, a one-eyed dog, a wonderful achievement

c) /ən/ *(in short phrases)*

an idiot, an elephant, an animal, an uncle, an offer, an eagle, an urn, an answer, an author, an airport, an alien, an item, an oyster, an ocean, an hour, an ear

d) /ən/ *(in longer phrases)*

an interesting story, an envious friend, an angry stranger, an understandable mistake, an odd couple, an easy task, an early start, an artistic endeavour, an ordinary day, an aerial photograph, an aching back, an idle moment, an oily rag, an open door, an outdoor swimming pool, an eerie silence

e) /ðə/

the police, the beach, the Thames, the kitchen, the ground, the champion, the gym, the French, the Vatican, the thirties, the sky, the zoo, the shower, the heart, the moon, the knowledge, the last, the radio, the United States, the world

f) /ði/

the internet, the entrance, the attic, the others, the office, the East, the Earth, the Arctic, the audience, the aeroplane, the eighties, the ice caps, the oil crisis, the owner, the outback

g) /səm/

I need some fresh air. I'll make some tea. Here's some advice. I've made some changes. Take some sweets. I've got some bad news. Lend me some money. He bought some chocolate. I drank some milk.

9.19 Conjunctions

9.19.1 AND, BUT, AS, THAN *and* THAT

a) /ən/

up and down, ebb and flow, cat and dog, food and drink, through thick and thin, big and bold, coach and horses, sausage and mash, knife and fork, alive and well, north and south, smooth and silky, this and that, his and hers, flesh and blood, an arm and a leg, again and again, willing and able, all and sundry, free and easy, few and far between, from far and wide, war and peace, day and night, high and dry, slow and steady, now and again, clear and concise, wear and tear

b)   /bət/

slow but steady, gone but not forgotten, last but not least, slowly but surely, poor but happy

I'll do it, but not now. He visits, but not often. They like it, but not much. I can swim, but not very well.

c)   /əz/

as far as the eye can see, as old as the hills, as soon as possible, as clean as a whistle, as bright as a button, as good as new, as smooth as silk, as cold as ice, as fit as a fiddle, as light as a feather, as gentle as a lamb, as busy as a bee, as dry as a bone, as flat as a pancake, as quiet as a mouse, as strong as an ox, as white as snow

d)   /ðən/

larger than life, more trouble than it's worth, better than nothing, a fate worse than death, better safe than sorry, larger than life, rather you than me, easier said than done, more often than not, better late than never, His bark's worse than his bite.

e)   /ðət/

I know that he did it. He said that she knew. They agreed that it was wrong. She claimed that she understood. They pretended that they were working. They hoped it was true.

the man that they saw, the meal that they had, a question that they answered, the man that lives next door, the woman that found it, the boy that left early, the girl that works there, the people that made it

Chapter 10

Consonant clusters

10.1 Consonant clusters vs. consonant sequences

English consonants can occur in groups, known as **consonant clusters**. For example, there are consonant clusters at the beginning of the words *float*, *cream*, *sprout* and *stream*, and at the end of the words *bank*, *past*, *wasps* and *instincts*. Words such as *sing*, *knife*, *gnome* and *receipt*, of course, don't contain consonant clusters because clusters are a matter of pronunciation, not spelling. Groups of consonants occurring between words also don't count as consonant clusters. For example, the /st/ of *past* is a cluster, while the /st/ of *this time* isn't, because the /s/ and the /t/ belong to different words and therefore to different syllables. The consonants of a true cluster must belong to the same syllable. Consonants which are merely adjacent to each other with a syllable boundary between them are known as consonant **sequences**. This is why /st/ in *disturb*, where the syllable boundary is before /st/, is a cluster, while /st/ in *mistime*, where the syllable boundary is between /s/ and /t/, is a sequence.

The clusters permissible in English differ according to whether they are at the beginning of a syllable or the end of a syllable.

What follows is a summary of the clusters commonly found in the core vocabulary of English. Further clusters would be possible if we included minority pronunciations (/slj/ in *sluice*), foreign borrowings (/ʃm/ in *schmuck*), rare words (word-initial /θj/ in *thew*), technical words (/skl/ in *sclerosis*), onomatopoeic words (/vr/ in *vroom*) or proper nouns (word-initial /gw/ in *Gweek*, /ʃl/ in *Shlaen*), but for practical purposes we exclude these.

10.2 Initial clusters

Initial two-consonant clusters are of three main types:

1   A plosive followed by an approximant:

	/p/	/b/	/t/	/d/	/k/	/g/
/j/	/pj/ *pure*	/bj/ *beauty*	/tj/ *tune*	/dj/ *duty*	/kj/ *cute*	
/w/			/tw/ *twice*	/dw/ *dwell*	/kw/ *quick*	
/r/	/pr/ *price*	/br/ *bright*	/tr/ *try*	/dr/ *drive*	/kr/ *cry*	/gr/ *grow*
/l/	/pl/ *play*	/bl/ *blue*			/kl/ *clock*	/gl/ *glad*

Note that /gj/ occurs word-internally (*singular* /ˈsɪŋgjələ/), and /gw/ occurs initially in Welsh (*Gwen* /gwen/) and foreign borrowings (*guava* /ˈgwɑːvə/), as well as word-internally (*anguish* /ˈæŋgwɪʃ/).

2   A fricative followed by an approximant:

	/f/	/v/	/θ/	/ð/	/s/	/z/	/ʃ/	/ʒ/	/h/
/j/	/fj/ few	/vj/ view							/hj/ hue
/w/					/sw/ swim				
/r/	/fr/ fry		/θr/ throw				/ʃr/ shred		
/l/	/fl/ fly				/sl/ slip				

Note that /θw/ occurs initially in *thwart*, and /θj/, /sj/ and /zj/ occur word-internally – *enthuse* /ɪn'θjuːz/, *assume* /ə'sjuːm/, *presume* /prɪ'zjuːm/.

3   /s/ followed by a plosive or a nasal:

	/p/	/b/	/t/	/d/	/k/	/g/	/m/	/n/
/s/	/sp/ spot		/st/ stop		/sk/ skip		/sm/ small	/sn/ snow

Initial three-consonant clusters are a combination of the first and third types of two-consonant clusters: a plosive preceded by /s/ and followed by an approximant.

		/p/	/t/	/k/
	/j/	/spj/ spew	/stj/ stew	/skj/ skew
/s/	/w/			/skw/ square
	/r/	/spr/ spring	/str/ street	/skr/ scratch
	/l/	/spl/ splash		

10.3 Final clusters

Final two-consonant clusters are of three types: (1) obstruent + obstruent, (2) sonorant + obstruent and (3) sonorant + sonorant.

Obstruent	**Obstruent**	
plosive	plosive	/kt/ *act*, /pt/ *accept*
plosive	fricative	/ps/ *collapse*, /ts/ *quartz*, /dz/ *towards*, /dθ/ *width*, /ks/ *axe*
fricative	plosive	/sp/ *wasp*, /sk/ *mask*, /st/ *list*, /ft/ *left*
Sonorant	**Obstruent**	
nasal	stop	/mp/ *dump*, /nt/ *hint*, /nd/ *hand*, /ŋk/ *thank*, /ntʃ/ *lunch*, /ndʒ/ *sponge*
nasal	fricative	/mf/ *lymph*, /nθ/ *month*, /ns/ *once*, /nz/ *lens*
approximant	stop	/lp/ *help*, /lb/ *bulb*, /lt/ *tilt*, /ld/ *cold*, /lk/ *milk*, /ltʃ/ *belch*, /ldʒ/ *bulge*
approximant	fricative	/lf/ *golf*, /lv/ *solve*, /lθ/ *health*, /ls/ *false*
Sonorant	**Sonorant**	
approximant	nasal	/lm/ *film*

Note that /pθ/ occurs in *depth*, /mθ/ in *warmth*, /ŋθ/ in *strength* and *length*, /lʃ/ in *Welsh* and /ln/ in *kiln*.

Three-consonant clusters are of two types: (1) obstruent + obstruent + obstruent and (2) sonorant + obstruent + obstruent.

Obstruent	Obstruent	Obstruent	
plosive	fricative	plosive	/kst/ *text*

Sonorant	Obstruent	Obstruent	
nasal	plosive	plosive	/mpt/ *prompt*, /ŋkt/ *instinct*
nasal	plosive	fricative	/mps/ *glimpse*, /ŋks/ *lynx*

The medial plosives of /mpt/, /mps/, /ŋkt/ and /ŋks/ are often not pronounced. A number of clusters occur only in one or a very small group of words: /lpt/ *sculpt*, /lst/ in *whilst*, /lts/ in *waltz* (which has an alternative pronunciation with /ls/), /dst/ in *amidst*, /nst/ in *against* and /ŋst/ in *amongst*.

The addition of the <-s>, <-ed> and <-th> endings to words increases the number of cluster possibilities. The following two-consonant clusters occur only when an inflectional ending is added. The only new type of cluster that this produces is fricative + fricative:

Obstruent	Obstruent	
stop	plosive	/gd/ *jogged*, /bd/ *robbed*, /tʃt/ *watched*, /dʒd/ *charged*
stop	fricative	/bz/ *robs*, /gz/ *bags*
fricative	plosive	/θt/ *frothed*, /ðd/ *bathed*, /vd/ *lived*, /zd/ *gazed*, /ʃt/ *wished*
fricative	fricative	/fs/ *cliffs*, /vz/ *gives*, /θs/ *myths*, /ðz/ *breathes*

Sonorant	Obstruent	
nasal	plosive	/md/ *blamed*, /ŋd/ *pinged*
nasal	fricative	/mz/ *times*, /ŋz/ *sings*, /nθ/ *ninth*
approximant	fricative	/lz/ *falls*

Note that /tθ/ appears in *eighth* and /fθ/ in *fifth*.

The following three-consonant clusters (e.g. /pst/, /nts/, /lps/) occur only when an inflectional ending is added to a two-consonant cluster:

Obstruent	Obstruent	Obstruent	
plosive	fricative	stop	/pst/ *lapsed*

Sonorant	Obstruent	Obstruent	
nasal	stop	plosive	/ntʃt/ *wrenched*, /ndʒd/ *lunged*
nasal	stop	fricative	/nts/ *hunts*, /ndz/ *hands*
approximant	stop	plosive	/ltʃt/ *squelched*, /ldʒd/ *indulged*
approximant	plosive	fricative	/lps/ *helps*, /ldz/ *fields*, /lks/ *milks*
approximant	fricative	plosive	/lvd/ *revolved*

Note that /nzd/ occurs in *cleansed*, /ŋst/ in *amongst* and *angst*, /ndθ/ in *thousandth*, /lbz/ in *bulbs* and /lst/ in *whilst*.

The following three-consonant cluster *types* (e.g. plosive + plosive + fricative, nasal + fricative + fricative) occur only when an inflectional ending is added to a two-consonant cluster:

Obstruent	**Obstruent**	**Obstruent**	
plosive	plosive	fricative	/pts/ *accepts*, /kts/ *rejects*
fricative	plosive	fricative	/sps/ *gasps*, /sts/ *fists*, /sks/ *risks*, /fts/ *lifts*
fricative	plosive	plosive	/spt/ *grasped*, /skt/ *tasked*
Sonorant	**Obstruent**	**Obstruent**	
nasal	fricative	fricative	/mfs/ *triumphs*, /nθs/ *tenths*
approximant	fricative	fricative	/lvz/ *involves*
approximant	nasal	fricative	/lmz/ *films*

Note that /lmd/ occurs in *filmed* and *overwhelmed*, /lnz/ in *kilns*, /lfθ/ in *twelfth*, /lfs/ in *gulfs*, /ŋθs/ in *lengths* and *strengths*, /fθs/ in *fifths*, /ksθ/ in *sixth*, /dθs/ in *widths* and *breadths*, /tθs/ in *eighths* and /pθs/ in *depths*.

All four-consonant final clusters require one or more inflectional endings, and only /ŋkts/ occurs in more than a single word (*instincts*, *precincts*, *adjuncts*, *conjuncts*, *subjuncts*). /ksts/ is found in *texts*, /ksθs/ in *sixths*, /ŋkst/ in *jinxed*, /ndθs/ in *thousandths*, /lpts/ in *sculpts* and /lfθs/ in *twelfths*.

10.4 Elision

A number of syllable-final clusters can be simplified through the process of **elision** described in section 12.2. The /t/ can be elided from /pts/, /kts, /sts/, /fts/, /ksts/, /ŋkts/, /ŋsts/ and /lpts/; the /d/ elided from /ndz/, /ndθ/, /ldz/ and /ndθs/; and the /k/ elided from /skt/. When immediately followed by a word beginning with a consonant, /t d/ can be elided from all clusters in which they appear in final position (except for /lt/ and /nt/), and /k/ elided when it's preceded by /s/.

10.5 Epenthesis

Sounds can also be inserted into clusters, a phenomenon known as **epenthesis**. This usually involves the insertion of a voiceless plosive (/p/, /t/ or /k/) between a nasal and a following

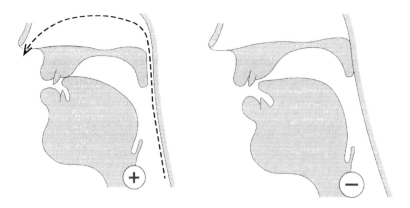

Figure 10.1 Transition from English /n/ (left) to /s/ (right). The arrow indicates the escape of the airstream through the nose.

voiceless fricative. It happens for straightforward articulatory reasons. Figure 10.1 shows that three changes have to be made simultaneously when moving from the position for /n/ to that for /s/: (1) vocal fold vibration stops; (2) the soft palate rises, closing off the nasal cavity; and (3) the closure between the tip of the tongue and the alveolar ridge opens into a narrow gap. If steps 2 and 3 aren't carried out at precisely the same moment, and step 3 lags behind, then pressure builds up in the oral cavity and when the alveolar closure is released, a plosive /t/ occurs. Note that the epenthetic voiceless plosive occurs at the same place of articulation as the nasal, and so when the nasal is bilabial /m/, the plosive is bilabial /p/, and when the nasal is velar /ŋ/, the plosive is velar /k/.

- Epenthetic /p/: /mf/ becomes /mpf/ in *lymph*; /mfs/ becomes /mpfs/ in *triumphs*; /mθ/ becomes /mpθ/ in *warmth*.
- Epenthetic /t/: /ns/ becomes /nts/ in *once*; /nst/ becomes /ntst/ in *against*; /nθ/ becomes /ntθ/ in *month*; /nθs/ becomes /ntθs/ in *tenths*.
- Epenthetic /k/: /ŋθ/ becomes /ŋkθ/ in *length*; /ŋθs/ becomes /ŋkθs/ in *strengths*; /ŋsts/ becomes /ŋksts/ in *angsts*.

Epenthesis with /t/ is more common than with /p/ or /k/ because there are more words with the /ns/ cluster, and these words also tend to be in more frequent use. This leads to *prince* being pronounced like *prints*, *sense* like *scents*, *chance* like *chants*, and *dense* like *dents*.

Chapter 11

Practice

Consonant clusters

The following sections provide practice in pronouncing initial and final English consonant clusters. The clusters have been combined into larger groups and are practised in words, phrases and sentences. The initial clusters are presented in the following order: (1) clusters ending in /j/, (2) clusters ending in /w/, (3) clusters ending in /l/, (4) clusters ending in /r/ and (5) clusters beginning with /s/. In the practice sentences at least one occurrence of the cluster dealt with in a particular section is combined with other clusters.

11.1 Initial clusters ending in /j/

11.1.1 /pj/, /spj/, /bj/, /tj/, /stj/, /dj/, /kj/, /skj/

Note that /tj/ and /dj/ are often replaced by /ʧ/ and /ʤ/ (yod-coalescence; see section 2.14.9).

a) **Words**

pew, pewter, puberty, puce, puerile, puny, pupil, pure, putrid; spew, spume, spurious, sputum; beautiful, beauty, bugle, bureaucrat; tube, Tuesday, tuition, tulip, tumour, tuna, tune, tunic, tutor; stew, steward, studio, student, stupefy, stupendous, stupid; dew/due, dual/duel, dubious, duet, duke, dune, duo, duplicate (v.), during, durable, duration, duress, duty; cube, cucumber, cue/queue, cumulative, cumin, cure, curious, cute, skew, skewer

b) **Phrases**

a bright pupil, beauty treatment, the student population, a tube station, private tuition, a beauty contest, a student grant, a stupid act, dew drops, suspended from duties, a miraculous cure, discover a cure, genuinely curious, jump the queue, skewed results, the star pupil, breathtaking beauty, travel by tube, language tuition, a brilliant student, plain stupid, an instant cure

c) **Sentences**

1 It wasn't a blunder; it was plain stupidity.
2 He practically accused me of being a traitor.
3 The six students contributed equally to the project.
4 Botswana's an extremely sparsely populated country.
5 The tournament was a true test of endurance and skill.
6 Switzerland's a small country of breathtaking beauty.
7 He was suspended from his duties as museum curator.
8 Three people jumped the queue when I was at the bank.

9   It was claimed to be a miraculous cure for rheumatism.

10 I cooked a shrimp and crab stew with boiled eggs last Friday.

11 Professor Smith introduced the guest speaker to the audience.

12 The three gangs have been engaged in a long-standing dispute.

13 A degree in health science gives access to a broad range of occupations.

14 There are numerous genuinely curious questions you can ask your clients.

15 In desperation, Bruce switched off the computer and started from scratch.

16 He explained that he felt it was important to treat his students as his equals.

17 We are continuously preoccupied with creating and promoting new products.

18 France has acquired a fantastic reputation for producing quality walnuts and plums.

19 The monument's a lasting tribute to those who sacrificed their lives for our country.

20 During our stay my travelling companion broke her ankle and required hospitalisation.

21 This module's compulsory for students on the electrical engineering degree programmes.

22 Most interpreters have acquired their extensive vocabulary through professional experience.

23 She prepared a first draft of the document which was subsequently distributed for comments.

24 Health foods have recently experienced a considerable increase in popularity among consumers.

11.1.2 /fj/, /vj/, /mj/, /nj/, /hj/

a) Words

feud, feudal, few, fuchsia, fuel, fume, funeral, furious, fury, fuse, futile, future; view; mews/muse, muesli, mule, mural, museum, music, mute, mutilate, mutiny, mutual; neurotic, neutral, new, nuance, nuclear, nude, numerous, nutrition, pneumonia; hue, huge, human, humid, humiliate, humility, humour

b) Phrases

a long-standing feud, the distant future, a breathtaking view, as stubborn as a mule, a museum curator, a music stand, stay neutral, brand new, break the news, slapstick humour, predict the future, classical music, spread the news

c) Sentences

1   The news spread like wildfire.

2   We strolled down a tree-lined avenue.

3   Even celebrities aren't immune to criticism.

4   The soft background music made her feel sleepy.

5   Trevor was humiliated in front of his schoolmates.

6   Our assistance in this crisis is purely humanitarian.

7   The grammatical mistakes are too numerous to count.

8   We adopted a heuristic approach to solve the problem.

9   My uncle's as stubborn as a mule and refuses treatment.

10 He refused point-blank to accept the terms of the compromise.

11 John's stepson has developed impressive communication skills.

12 Samuel felt a glimmer of amusement at the proprietor's response.

13 Hugh can't stand slapstick humour as he thinks it's too predictable.

14   Three of my friends were granted refugee status in Britain last August.
15   Gabriel disagreed with the prevailing view held by scholars in the field.
16   A question mark hangs over the future of the bank where she's employed.
17   This review provides an overview of the available literature on speech acts.
18   Tabloid newspapers are sometimes accused of having sensationalist stories.
19   A recently published study revealed that there's widespread confusion over state pensions.

11.2 Initial clusters ending in /w/

11.2.1 /tw/, /dw/, /kw/, /skw/, /sw/

a) Words

twaddle, twang, tweak, tweed, tweet, tweezers, twelve, twice, twiddle, twig, twilight, twin, twinkle, twirl, twist; dwarf, dwell, dwindle; quack, quaint, qualify, quality, quantity, quarrel, quarry, queen, queer, query, quest, question, quick, quiet, quilt, quit, quite, quiver, quiz, quota, quote, choir, cuisine; squabble, squad, squalid, squander, square, squash, squat, squeak, squeal, squeeze, squelch, squid, squiggle, squint, squirm, squirrel, squirt; suede, swagger, swallow, swamp, swan, swap, sway, swear, sweat, sweep, sweet, swell, swerve, swift, swim, swine, swing, swipe, switch

b) Phrases

a slight twang, a dry twig, sweat profusely, twin brother, a strange twist, a slum dweller, a school choir, French cuisine, quality control, a long-standing quarrel, a probing question, complete a questionnaire, strangely quiet, try to quit, a quiz programme, a squeak of surprise, the squeal of brakes, freshly squeezed orange juice, a grey squirrel, a black swan, a straight swap, the smell of stale sweat, a quick swig, the flick of a switch, an unexpected twist, a private dwelling, an awkward question, blissfully quiet, threaten to quit, break into a cold sweat, switch places

c) Sentences

1   Brian swallowed his pride and asked for help.
2   A quarrel broke out between the three brothers.
3   A strong earthquake struck Pakistan last Friday.
4   Be prepared for a dramatic swing in temperatures!
5   Grace watched the squirrel scamper across the fence.
6   Chloe drank a glass of freshly squeezed orange juice.
7   Craig twisted himself free from his opponent's grasp.
8   The population dwindled to a fraction of what it used to be.
9   Mr Sweeney started in English but then switched to Swahili.
10   There was a clear blue sky, and the trees swayed in the breeze.
11   Drew spoke with a faint lisp coupled with a slight Oklahoma twang.
12   Drain off the liquid and brush off any excess salt from the cucumbers.
13   Beautiful black swans were swimming close to the bank of the Thames.
14   Mature applicants don't always have the appropriate entry qualifications.
15   Steven works as an accountant, and his twin brother, Clement, is a historian.
16   You are required to produce evidence of having completed appropriate training.

17   I asked my friends and acquaintances to help me find the best specialist possible.

18   The programme included special guest speakers and a spectacular performance by the school choir.

19   These scholars made a valuable contribution to the integration of qualitative and quantitative methods.

20   The respondents were asked to complete the questionnaire and comment on words that were difficult to understand.

11.3   Initial clusters ending in /l/

11.3.1   /pl/, /spl/, /bl/

a)   *Words*

place, plain, plan, planet, plank, plant, plaster, plastic, plate, play, pleasant, please, pleasure, plenty, plot, plough, plug, plum, plumber, plump, plural, plus; splash, splay, spleen, splendid, splice, splinter, split, splutter; black, blade, blame, blank, blanket, blast, blatant, blaze, bleach, bleak, bleed, blend, blind, blink, bliss, blister, block, blonde, blood, blouse, blow, blue, blunt, blush

b)   *Phrases*

future plans, a spy plane, a brass plaque, a blood clot, clear plastic, swap places, a strange blend, the proper place, a crippling blow, stick to the plan, a plane crash, tropical plants, a clean plate, a sleeveless blouse, a brilliant player, a school playground, plead guilty, the pleasures of the flesh, a clever plot twist, strategically placed, a clever ploy, a three-pin plug, glorious splendour, a glass splinter, blood pressure, breeze blocks, a slight blemish, a stone block, a thriving black market, a blunt blade, a huge blast, a curious blend, a drop of blood, a frilly blouse, strike a blow, a prominent place, strawberry plants

c)   *Sentences*

1   A huge stone block dropped off the trailer.

2   This is a gross simplification of the facts.

3   Crews rushed to the spot and extinguished the blaze.

4   His comments were greeted with applause by the crowd.

5   He's one of Australia's most outstanding cricket players.

6   The world's growing population has exacerbated the problem.

7   Language skills help improve students' employment prospects.

8   Most cathedrals were built as an ostentatious display of wealth.

9   His works had sunk into oblivion but were recently rediscovered.

10   Nutritional supplements are among the safest products in existence.

11   Brenda interpreted her friend's words as a double-edged compliment.

12   The soles of my boots split clean across the middle within six months.

13   He was unable to provide a credible explanation for his strange request.

14   They trained their staff to respond to customers' complaints and enquiries.

15   Christopher's views represented a curious blend of traditional and progressive values.

16   Increased agricultural production has resulted in a population explosion in some countries.

11.3.2 /kl/, /gl/

a) **Words**

claim, clap, class, claw, clay, clean, clear, clever, click, client, cliff, climate, climax, clinic, clip, cloak, clock, cloth, clothes, cloud, clover, clown, club, clue, clutter; glad, glade, glamour, glance, glare, glass, glaze, gleam, glee, glen, glide, glimpse, glint, glisten, glitter, gloat, globe, gloom, glory, glove, glow, glue, glum

b) **Phrases**

a strong claim, broken glass, a slow clap, provide clarification, scrape clean, slum clearance, a grandfather clock, black clouds, a cryptic clue, a broad classification, crystal clear, a tropical climate, a thrilling climax, a blood clot, a scrap of cloth, a sports club, a brief glance, frosted glass, a brief glimpse, a fleeting glance, swollen glands, flying glass, travel the globe, shrouded in gloom, a blaze of glory, protective gloves, the present climate, a floor cloth

c) **Sentences**

1   Constance threw her uncle an angry glance.
2   Stephanie sank into gloom and despondency.
3   Fred grossly neglected his duties for months on end.
4   Adrian stated he wouldn't respond to unsubstantiated claims.
5   Frida used fingerless gloves to conceal the scars on her hands.
6   Stella seemed extremely rushed and kept glancing at the clock.
7   The construction industry has experienced a dramatic decline over the past months.
8   Patrick was the best player in the tournament and truly deserved his moment of glory.
9   The process was drawn out due to a controversy about the inclusion of an opt-out clause in the agreement.

11.3.3 /fl/, /sl/

a) **Words**

flag, flame, flap, flare, flash, flat, flatter, flavour, flaw, flea, flexible, flick, flight, flimsy, flinch, flint, flip, flirt, flock, flood, floor, flour/flower, flow, flu, fluent, fluid, fly; slap, sleek, sleep, sleet, sleeve, slender, slice, slide, slight, slim, slime, slip, slogan, slope, sloppy, slot, slouch, slow, slum, slump, slur, slush, sly

b) **Phrases**

a glass flask, a pleasant flavour, a flame thrower, a critical flaw, a slippery slope, flesh and blood, flash floods, squeaky floorboards, plain flour, fresh flowers, a flag fluttering in the breeze, flickering flames, the quick flick of a switch, a flight of stairs, clean the floor, beauty sleep, a snappy slogan, a steep slope, a strong flavour, human flesh, bright flames, scrub the floor

c) **Sentences**

1   He wiped the slate clean and started afresh.
2   The French flag was fluttering in the breeze.
3   Drink plenty of fluids when you have a cold.
4   I tried desperately to staunch the flow of blood.

5   Our lives changed at the flick of a switch last April.
6   Andrew pointed out a crucial flaw in the argument.
7   Their speech contained numerous slang expressions.
8   Alex was fast asleep when we arrived at the playground.
9   My brother acquired a degree of fluency in spoken Swedish.
10   He was scared stiff at the prospect of flying in that flimsy plane.
11   These suede slippers are lined with luxurious Australian lambswool.
12   My husband sent me a beautiful bunch of flowers to celebrate the event.

11.4 Initial clusters ending in /r/

11.4.1 /pr/, /spr/, /br/

a)   *Words*

precious, precise, predict, prefer, present (n.), press, pretty, price, pride, print, prison, prize, problem, profit, promise, proof, proper, protect, provide, practice; sprain, sprawl, spray, spread, spring, sprinkle, sprint, sprout, spruce; brain, brave, bread, break, breath, breeze, brick, bride, bridge, brief, bright, bring, brother, brown, bruise, brush, brutal

b)   *Phrases*

standard practice, gloomy predictions, three months pregnant, blind prejudice, specially prepared, a strong presence, sliced bread, the bride and groom, presentation skills, crime prevention, professional pride, prim and proper, the crux of the problem, a gradual process, fresh produce, a quality product, growing profits, steady progress, break a promise, pronounce clearly, a Christmas present, a clear preference, prescription drugs, a press statement, a special prize, stolen property, spring cleaning, fly spray, create a spreadsheet, a crime spree, a quick sprint, front brakes, a drunken brawl, fresh bread, a crucial breakthrough, a stone bridge, square brackets, brains and brawn, plum brandy, a clean break, a stiff breeze, a beautiful bride, blood brothers, drab brown, a scrubbing brush, swallow your pride, the scale of the problem, steel production, swift progress, pronunciation drills, a brain scan, a stiff brandy, crusty bread, a fresh breeze, pronunciation practice

c)   *Sentences*

1   The classes are spread over six weeks.
2   Her breadth of experience is unrivalled.
3   His predictions proved unduly pessimistic.
4   Brian quoted a brief extract from the preface.
5   At daybreak we had a stiff breeze from the west.
6   His expression betrayed no trace of apprehension.
7   Elspeth started her annual spring cleaning last month.
8   The new project was launched on the tenth of April.
9   They discussed the risks and threats to global security.
10   The students demonstrated proficiency in English language skills.
11   It's difficult to provide conclusive proof for or against his claims.
12   A lunch break improves productivity and creativity in the workplace.
13   Under the circumstances, I can't blame Christine for breaking her promise.

14   You should not employ angle brackets or square brackets in the translated text.
15   We have implemented strict quality control procedures in our production processes.
16   Employees were expected to embrace the library's values and standards of behaviour.

11.4.2 /tr/, /str/, /dr/

a) Words

track, trade, traffic, train, trap, tray, treasure, treat, tree, trick, trip, trouble, trousers, truck, true, trumpet, trunk, trust, truth, try; straight, strain, strand, strange, strangle, strap, straw, stream, street, strength, stress, stretch, strict, strike, string, stripe, strong, structure, struggle; drag, dragon, drain, drama, draw, dread, dream, drench, dress, drift, drill, drink, drive, drop, drown, drug, drum, dry

b) Phrases

a proven track record, drinking and driving, a breach of trust, a skilled trade, special training, a breakfast tray, a cruel trick, a sports trophy, thriving trade, drink and drugs, a crowded train, a priceless treasure, a dream come true, a special treat, preferential treatment, plant a tree, a trial of strength, a stupid trick, a steady trickle, frequent trips, stay out of trouble, play truant, blind trust, a grain of truth, stresses and strains, a stubborn streak, a fast-flowing stream, a blocked drain, a strange dream, a sleeveless dress, a strong drink, a draft proposal, a gritty drama, a beautiful dress, the tricks of the trade, trials and tribulations, tried and trusted, a quick drink, brisk trade, a school trip

c) Sentences

1   He clenched his fists in frustration.
2   Tracy's kids drive me to distraction.
3   Huge crowds make me claustrophobic.
4   It was a true test of strength and stamina.
5   She blew the smoke through her nostrils.
6   He illustrated his point with three examples.
7   Greg was a complete stranger to these parts.
8   How do you construct an equilateral triangle?
9   Change to the express train bound for Brussels.
10   He promised to do his best to stay out of trouble in future.
11   Gwyneth claimed the results were beyond her wildest dreams.
12   Douglas found a small black box in the secret drawer in the desk.
13   She tried to escape from the stresses and strains of the workplace.
14   The escaped prisoners lived in constant dread of being discovered.
15   There was a steady trickle of customers throughout the afternoon.
16   Gusty winds left a trail of destruction along the east coast of Scotland.
17   Alastair played the bagpipes in traditional Scottish dress including kilt.
18   Gwen and Chris spend most weekends at their country retreat in Wales.
19   Three countries threatened to withdraw their athletes from the Olympics.
20   The manuscript was lost but was subsequently painstakingly reconstructed.
21   Frank needs an experienced driver to distribute goods promptly to his customers.
22   His structured approach stood in stark contrast to the intuitive viewpoints of his predecessors.
23   Click here if you require step-by-step instructions for completing your exam registration forms.

11.4.3 /kr/, /skr/, /gr/

a) Words

crab, crack, craft, crash, cream, crease, credit, creep, crew, crime, crisis, critic, cross, crowd, crude, crumb, cry, crystal; scrap, scrape, scratch, scrawl, scream, screen, screw, scribble, script, scroll, scrounge, scrub, scruffy, scruple, scrutiny; grab, grade, grain, grammar, grand, grape, grasp, grave, gravy, grease, great, green, grid, grin, grip, groan, ground, group, grow, growl, grudge, grumpy

b) Phrases

stomach cramps, fresh clotted cream, play cricket, stand out from the crowd, a primitive creature, credit where credit's due, a skeleton crew, a brutal crime, a growing crowd, a pleasure cruise, bread crumbs, quartz crystals, a shrill scream, stars of stage and screen, close scrutiny, a small scratch, a blank screen, green grapes, break new ground, a splinter group, a pressure group, grunt and groan, a skin graft, a broad grin, a slight gradient, green grass, pure greed, a smug grin, stifle a groan

c) Sentences

1. Please stack the crates on the floor.
2. They promised to stick to the agreement.
3. A sixth of the population was employed in agriculture.
4. The gnarled tree trunks creaked and groaned in the wind.
5. We had scones and fresh strawberries with clotted cream.
6. We scrimped and scraped to put our girls through school.
7. James and Brenda went on a pleasure cruise to Greenland.
8. I just kept staring at the blank screen but found no inspiration.
9. She felt a twinge of regret for drawing such hasty conclusions.
10. These countries experienced a slight increase in unemployment.
11. The fruit bowls were filled with bunches of green and black grapes.
12. Her bloodstained footprints left a trail across the freshly scrubbed floor.
13. The volume includes a comprehensive bibliography and a detailed index.
14. Graham applied for a grant and to his surprise received twelve thousand pounds.
15. The population continued to practise traditional crafts such as producing sealskin boots and gloves.

11.4.4 /fr/, /θr/

a) Words

fraction, fragile, fragrant, frail, frame, fraud, free, freeze, frequent (adj.), fresh, friction, fridge, friend, frog, front, frost, fruit, fry; thrash, thread, threat, three, thresh, threshold, thrifty, thrill, thriller, thrive, throat, throb, throne, throttle, through, throw, thrush, thrust

b) Phrases

fragrant flowers, break free, a mutual friend, tremble with fright, a true friend, fresh fruit, a small fraction, a pleasant fragrance, a close friend, French fries, cross the threshold, clear your throat, a school friend

c) Sentences

1. The artist's hands were crippled with arthritis.
2. My computer freezes with increasing regularity.

3   He pretended to be an expert on cultural anthropology.
4   The slimy green frog croaked and jumped into the pond.
5   He found it difficult to swallow and felt a lump in his throat.
6   Craig was the latest in her string of questionable boyfriends.
7   My grandfather felt too old and frail to travel such distances.
8   Oscar lent me a fast-paced gripping thriller filled with suspense.
9   They're anxious to promote friendship between the two countries.
10 The belt is exquisitely embroidered in threads of silver, blue, grey and gold.
11 The struggle against discrimination was constantly at the forefront of his mind.
12 Approximately twenty per cent of the plants in the world are threatened with extinction.

11.5 Initial clusters beginning with /s/

11.5.1 /sp/, /st/, /sk/

a) *Words*

space, spade, spare, speak, special, speech, speed, spell, spend, spice, spider, spill, spin, spine, spirit, spit, spoil, sponge, spoon, sport, spot, spout, spy; stab, stable, staff, stage, stain, stair, stamp, stand, star, start, state, station, stay, steal, step, stick, stiff, still, stomach, stone, stop, storm, story, study, stuff, style; scan, scar, scare, scheme, school, score, scout, sketch, ski, skid, skill, skim, skin, skirt, skull, skunk, sky

b) *Phrases*

storage space, flying sparks, a dramatic spectacle, a grim spectre, a broad spectrum, slurred speech, ground spices, a huge spider, pure spite, stare into space, a fluent speaker, clear speech, trouble spots, skilled staff, a stubborn stain, steep stairs, a spiral staircase, a flower stall, a strong start, a sweeping statement, space flight, a place to stay, grilled steak, a true story, stage fright, stale bread, stand up straight, bright stars, a fresh start, a state school, stainless steel, stand stock-still, throw stones, storm clouds, a study group, a stumbling block, a blind spot, a spectacular stunt, a scale drawing, a flaky scalp, a brain scan, a crazy scheme, a human skeleton, a sliding scale, scared stiff, fractured skull, cloudless skies, a bright sky, clear skin, a blank space, study skills

c) *Sentences*

1   The results are consistent across the studies.
2   The team stuck to a tried and tested formula.
3   Skiing equipment is very expensive to replace.
4   The troops stumbled blindly through the forest.
5   Property prices are currently prohibitively expensive.
6   These quaint customs still prevail in parts of the country.
7   The criminal was imprisoned for the space of six months.
8   He managed to escape the clutches of a bloodthirsty cult.
9   He smiled at her from behind his gold-rimmed spectacles.
10 She was dressed in a quilted vest and an ankle-length skirt.
11 They were attacked by a swarm of mosquitoes and black flies.
12 She claimed that the documentary was a gross distortion of the truth.

13   She works as a speech therapist with children on the autism spectrum.

14   They secured a lucrative contract to supply sporting equipment to numerous schools.

11.5.2   /sm/, /sn/, /ʃr/, /sf/

a)   Words

smack, small, smart, smash, smear, smell, smile, smirk, smoke, smooth, smother, smoulder, smudge, smug; snack, snail, snake, snap, snatch, sneak, sneer, sneeze, sniff, snip, snippet, snob, snoop, snooty, snooze, snore, snort, snout, snow, snuff, snug; shrew, shrewd, shriek, shrill, shrimp, shrine, shrink, shroud, shrub, shrug; sphere, sphincter, sphinx

b)   Phrases

a cloud of smoke, a sweet smile, drinks and snacks, crisp snow, a snooker player, flying shrapnel, a shrill shriek, a funeral shroud, a dwarf shrub

c)   Sentences

1   What was the sphinx's riddle?

2   A cloud of smoke obscured the bridge.

3   Drinks and snacks were included in the cost.

4   She shrugged her shoulders and looked resigned.

5   It was beyond the sphere of influence of his parents.

6   There's not a shred of evidence for these speculations.

7   The electrician relaxed and flashed him a grateful smile.

8   The nuclear programme was cloaked in a shroud of secrecy.

9   I picked up the crunching sound of his boots in the crisp snow.

11.6   Final clusters

As in the case of the initial clusters, the final clusters have been combined into larger groups. The exercise material, which includes words, phrases and sentences, has been presented in the following order: (1) clusters beginning with a stop, (2) clusters beginning with a fricative, (3) clusters beginning with a nasal, (4) clusters beginning with an approximant and (5) clusters containing dental fricatives.

11.7   First consonant = stop

11.7.1   /pt/, /pts/, /kt/, /kts/

a)   Words

abrupt, accept, adapt, adopt, bankrupt, concept, disrupt, erupt, except, intercept, interrupt, script; chopped, clapped, dripped, dropped, escaped, gripped, hoped, kept, leapt, slapped, slept, slipped, snapped, stepped, stopped, swapped, swept, trapped, tripped, typed, wept; accepts, adapts, adopts, concepts, disrupts, erupts, intercepts, interrupts, scripts; act, aspect, attract, collect, connect, contract (n.), correct, detect, direct, district, elect, exact, expect, fact, insect, object (n.), perfect (adj.), project (n.), protect, respect, select, strict, subject (n.); attacked, checked, joked, knocked, leaked, liked, locked, looked, marked, packed, panicked, parked, picked, soaked, talked, tricked, walked, worked; acts, aspects, attracts, collects, connects, contracts (n.), corrects, detects, directs, districts, elects, expects, facts, insects, objects (n.), projects (n.), protects, respects, selects, subjects (n.)

b) *Phrases*

adopt a child, went bankrupt, striped shorts, a film script, dropped a hint, a conflict of interests, the terms of a contract, when you least expect it, in point of fact, change the subject, talked nonsense, lost contact, in a strict sense, booked tickets, acts of violence, dropped the subject, resolve a conflict, a statement of fact

c) *Sentences*

1   The striped shirts are sold out.
2   I lost contact with my old friends.
3   She spoke with a perfect French accent.
4   The child slept wrapped in a soft blanket.
5   They joked and laughed as they looked at the screen.
6   There was no script for the play so they had to improvise.
7   I've booked tickets for six adults for tonight's performance.
8   The street kids were believed to have been involved in acts of violence.
9   Trevor had an excellent command of a broad range of critical concepts.
10 This had to be typed quickly, so please excuse any spelling and grammar mistakes.

11.7.2 /bd/, /bz/, /gd/, /gz/

a) *Words*

clubbed, described, dubbed, grabbed, robbed, rubbed, scrubbed, sobbed, stabbed, throbbed; clubs, crabs, cubes, describes, globes, grabs, herbs, jabs, jobs, knobs, mobs, probes, proverbs, pubs, robes, rubs, scrubs, shrubs, stabs, throbs, tribes, tubs, tubes, verbs, wardrobes, webs; bagged, begged, dragged, drugged, fatigued, flagged, hugged, jogged, pegged, plagued, plugged, shrugged, tugged; bags, begs, digs, dogs, drags, drugs, eggs, flags, fogs, frogs, hugs, jogs, jugs, legs, logs, mugs, pegs, pigs, plugs, rags, rugs, shrugs, snags, tugs, twigs, wigs

b) *Phrases*

robbed the bank, chopped the herbs, test tubes, sports clubs, grabbed hold of, pruned the shrubs, cats and dogs, collect twigs, soft-boiled eggs, dropped the bags off, soft drugs

c) *Sentences*

1   He stretched and crossed his legs.
2   Here's a list of the best pubs in Essex.
3   I had cornflakes and soft-boiled eggs for breakfast.
4   I first pruned the shrubs and then scrubbed the floor tiles.
5   The traffic that once clogged the streets now flows freely.
6   I don't understand the difference between proverbs and maxims.
7   Alex grabbed hold of the suspect's wrist, but he managed to escape.

11.7.3 /tʃt/, /dʒd/, /ps/, /pst/

a) *Words*

approached, attached, bleached, coached, crouched, fetched, itched, marched, matched, patched, reached, scorched, scratched, sketched, snatched, stretched, switched, touched, watched; alleged, charged, damaged, dodged, emerged, managed, merged, nudged, packaged, raged, ridged, staged, urged, verged, voyaged, wedged; collapse, corpse, eclipse, elapse, lapse, perhaps, traipse; caps, chips, claps, clips, cups, dips, drips, drops, escapes, gaps, grapes, grips, groups, heaps, hips, hoops, hopes, keeps, leaps, lips, maps, reports, ropes, scrapes, shapes, ships, shops, sleeps, slips, slopes, snaps, steps, stops, straps, stripes, taps, tips, traps, trips, troops, types, weeps, whips, wipes, wraps, zips; collapsed, corpsed, eclipsed, elapsed, lapsed, traipsed

b) Phrases

attached a document, coached a team, switched places, caged birds, lodged a complaint, charged to your account, the building collapsed, hopes and dreams, flights of steps, lapse into silence, armed troops, unfulfilled hopes

c) Sentences

1   I've attached the document for reference.
2   My aunt shrugged and lapsed into silence.
3   America has troops based all over the world.
4   They lodged a complaint against their parents.
5   She cleverly dodged all the difficult questions.
6   These items will be sent and charged to your account.
7   Thousands of buildings collapsed due to the earthquake.

11.7.4 /ts/, /dz/

a) Words

quartz, blitz, ersatz, glitz, hertz, klutz; admits, bats, beats, bets, bits, bites, boats, boots, cats, charts, chats, cheats, coats, creates, debts, doubts, eats, fits, flights, floats, forgets, gates, goats, hats, hates, heats, hits, hurts, huts, knits, knots, lights, meets, nets, nights, notes, pets, plates, plots, puts, rats, rates, regrets, roots, rots, seats, sets, sheets, shirts, shoots, shorts, shouts, shuts, sits, spits, sports, spots, suits, sweets, baskets, biscuits, blankets, buckets, budgets, carpets, carrots, exits, experts, efforts, habits, idiots, jackets, magnets, markets, minutes, packets, parrots, pockets, profits, rabbits, riots, secrets, visits; adze, backwards, forwards, towards; adds, awards, beads, beards, beds, birds, boards, brides, buds, cards, clouds, codes, cowards, fades, feeds, floods, grades, guides, heads, hides, hoods, includes, lids, loads, methods, moods, needs, nods, reads, rides, roads, seeds, sheds, sides, swords, weeds, words

b) Phrases

bend over backwards, dense clouds, slashed their throats, blocked roads, crossed swords, clothes baskets, sheets and blankets

c) Sentences

1   She wept buckets at the end of the film.
2   All kinds of thoughts raced through my mind.
3   Despite their best efforts they lost their homes.
4   We were forced to change the dates of our flights.
5   The roads were blocked due to the avalanche and landslides.

11.7.5 /ks/, /kst/, /ksts/

a) Words

annex, axe, box, climax, coax, complex, crux, fix, fox, helix, hoax, mix, ox, reflex, relax, six, tax, wax; blocks, books, brakes, bricks, checks, jokes, knocks, lakes, leaks, likes, locks, looks, makes, marks, oaks, panics, parks, picks, remarks, rocks, sacks, seeks, shakes, shocks, smokes, snakes, soaks, socks, speaks, sticks, strikes, takes, talks, ticks, topics, tracks, tricks, wakes, walks, weeks, works; next, text; axed, boxed, coaxed, fixed, indexed, mixed, taxed, waxed; contexts, texts

b)   Phrases

a sports complex, fixed interest rates, a draft text, mixed feelings, stopped in their tracks, a range of topics, greatest works

c)   Sentences

1   Alex left with mixed feelings.
2   He constantly takes my remarks out of context.
3   The player's contract's due to expire next spring.
4   Abstract words make these texts difficult to comprehend.

11.8 First consonant = fricative

11.8.1 /sp/, /sps/, /spt/, /sk/, /sks/, /skt/

a)   Words

clasp, crisp, cusp, gasp, grasp, hasp, lisp, rasp, wasp, wisp; clasps, crisps, cusps, gasps, grasps, hasps, lisps, rasps, wasps, wisps; clasped, gasped, grasped, lisped, rasped; ask, asterisk, bask, brisk, busk, cask, desk, disk, dusk, flask, grotesque, husk, kiosk, mask, mollusc, musk, picturesque, risk, task, tusk, whisk; asks, asterisks, basks, busks, casks, desks, disks, flasks, husks, kiosks, masks, molluscs, risks, tasks, tusks, whisks; asked, basked, busked, masked, risked, tasked, whisked

b)   Phrases

clasp hands, a wasps' nest, speak with a lisp, gasp in astonishment, his mask slipped, masked balls, the front desk, a desk lamp, a slipped disc, whisk the eggs, health risks, risk management, a blank mask

c)   Sentences

1   She asked me round for lunch.
2   Blend the ingredients with a whisk.
3   We had crisps and nuts with our drinks.
4   He was teased because he spoke with a lisp.
5   This student works as an assistant at the help desk.
6   I gasped in amazement when I realised how old he was.
7   Sandra seems to have an intuitive grasp of the concept in question.

11.8.2 /st/, /sts/, /zd/, /ʃt/

a)   Words

arrest, best, boast, chest, coast, contest (n.), cost, dust, fast, first, fist, forest, ghost, guest, host, last, list, lost, mist, most, must, nest, past, post, rest, taste, test, toast, trust, waste, wrist; addressed, based, chased, crossed, decreased, dressed, faced, forced, guessed, hissed, kissed, noticed, passed, placed, pressed, promised, raced; arrests, boasts, chests, coasts, contests, costs, fists, forests, ghosts, guests, hosts, lasts, lists, nests, posts, rests, tastes, tests, toasts, trusts, wastes, wrists; accused, advised, amazed, amused, apologised, browsed, bruised, buzzed, caused, dazed, diseased, gazed, paused, pleased, realised, recognised, refused, revised, seized, sneezed, squeezed, surprised, teased; astonished, blushed, brushed, crashed, dashed, finished, flashed, flushed, pushed, rushed, smashed, splashed, squashed, vanished, varnished, washed, wished, crushed

b) Phrases

an arrest warrant, thump your chest, count the costs, the earth's crust, a dense forest, ground frost, conduct an inquest, a conflict of interests, built to last, an ant's nest, build a nest, glimpse the past, the strength to resist, a staunch socialist, a chunk of text, crossed legs, a speck of dust, dashed his hopes, flashed through my mind, washed his hands, plant a forest, a wasps' nest, a link with the past

c) Sentences

1   We pushed him to accept the challenge.
2   There wasn't a speck of dust to be found.
3   My cheeks flushed when I was embarrassed.
4   It crossed my mind that the incident might have changed him.
5   My aunt recognised the symptoms in a split second and called an ambulance.

11.8.3   /ft/, /fts/, /vd/, /fs/, /vz/

a) Words

craft, daft, draft, drift, gift, left, lift, loft, raft, shaft, shift, soft, swift, theft; briefed, coughed, laughed, sniffed, stuffed, surfed; crafts, draughts, drifts, gifts, lifts, lofts, rafts, shifts, thefts; achieved, approved, arrived, behaved, believed, carved, curved, deserved, dived, improved, loved, moved, observed, proved, received, removed, reserved, saved, served, shaved, shoved, starved, waved; beliefs, chiefs, cliffs, coughs, laughs, sniffs, surfs; achieves, approves, arrives, behaves, believes, carves, caves, curves, deserves, detectives, dives, doves, drives, forgives, gives, gloves, graves, improves, leaves, lives (v.), loves, moves, nerves, observes, olives, proves, receives, removes, reserves, saves, serves, shaves, shoves, starves, waves, knives, loaves, scarves, wives

b) Phrases

arts and crafts, a draft agreement, prevent a draught, a gift box, lifts my spirits, loved him to bits, moved with the times, proved him innocent, saved their lives, damaged nerves, drives me wild, proves my point, forgives and forgets, perfect a craft, a first draft, exchange gifts

c) Sentences

1   This film gives me the creeps.
2   She moved in with her boyfriend.
3   He who laughs last laughs longest.
4   Sift the flour into the bread ingredients.
5   I felt they deserved a gift for their efforts.
6   There are too many chiefs and not enough Indians.
7   His enthusiasm lifts my spirits and takes my mind off life's problems.

11.9 First consonant = nasal

11.9.1 /md/, /mz/

a)   *Words*

aimed, alarmed, ashamed, assumed, bombed, calmed, claimed, climbed, combed, dimmed, doomed, drummed, farmed, foamed, formed, framed, harmed, named, resumed, schemed, screamed, seemed, shamed, steamed, warmed, welcomed, zoomed; aims, alarms, assumes, atoms, beams, bombs, claims, climbs, combs, crimes, crumbs, dims, dreams, drums, exams, farms, flames, forms, frames, games, gems, gums, harms, homes, items, names, palms, plums, poems, problems, programmes, resumes, rooms, schemes, screams, seems, storms, sums, swims, teams, themes, thumbs, times, victims, warms, welcomes

b)   *Phrases*

dimmed the lights, violent crimes, named and shamed, resumed his post, felt at home, solve problems, innocent victims, household items, pleased to welcome, alleged crimes, in ancient times, talks were resumed

c)   *Sentences*

1   We thumbed a lift to Belfast.
2   I dimmed the lights and closed the curtains.
3   Negotiations between the groups were resumed last month.
4   I felt profoundly ashamed that I'd brought disgrace on my parents.
5   He finished his exams three weeks ago but won't get the results till August.

11.9.2 /mp/, /mpt/, /mps/, /mf/, /mfs/

a)   *Words*

bump, camp, clamp, cramp, damp, dump, jump, lamp, limp, lump, plump, pump, ramp, shrimp, slump, stamp, stump, swamp, thump, wimp; attempt, contempt, exempt, pre-empt, prompt, tempt, unkempt; bumped, camped, clamped, cramped, dumped, jumped, limped, lumped, pumped, slumped, stamped, thumped; glimpse; bumps, camps, clamps, cramps, dumps, jumps, lamps, limps, lumps, pumps, ramps, shrimps, slumps, stamps, stumps, swamps, thumps, wimps; lymph, nymph, triumph; nymphs, triumphs

b)   *Phrases*

a waste dump, a desk lamp, a botched attempt, a moment of triumph, jump through hoops, a failed attempt, the merest glimpse, his latest triumph, hailed as a triumph, jump to conclusions

c)   *Sentences*

1   He walks with a limp after the accident.
2   We had grilled shrimp with fresh herbs.
3   I apologised for having jumped to false conclusions.
4   It was hailed as one of the greatest triumphs of science.
5   You're encouraged to put your own stamp on the project.
6   She pumped me for the names and contact details of the candidates.

11.9.3 /nz/, /nzd/, /nd/, /ndz/

a) **Words**

bronze, cleanse, lens, summons; balloons, bargains, beans, begins, bins, brains, chains, cleans, clowns, coins, crowns, designs, earns, fans, fines, fortunes, grins, groans, guns, humans, learns, lemons, lines, lions, loans, machines, moans, moons, opens, pains, pans, pens, phones, pins, plans, planes, scans, shines, spins, sprains, stains, towns, trains, tunes, turns, twins, vans, warns, wins, zones; bronzed, cleansed, summonsed; band, behind, bend, blind, defend, demand, depend, end, find, friend, grand, ground, hand, husband, kind, land, lend, mind, pond, remind, round, second (n.), send, sound, stand, wind (n.); chained, cleaned, crowned, designed, drowned, fanned, fined, gained, grinned, groaned, ironed, lined, loaned, opened, phoned, pinned, planned, scanned, stained, trained, tuned, turned, warned; bands, bends, blinds, defends, demands, depends, ends, finds, friends, hands, husbands, kinds, lands, lends, minds, ponds, reminds, seconds (n.), sends, sounds, stands, winds (n.)

b) **Phrases**

round the bend, a strange blend, distant lands, myths and legends, let's pretend, a round of golf, a gust of wind, husbands and wives, cleanse a wound, a contact lens, gold coins, pots and pans, twists and turns, bend over backwards, the end justifies the means, the end of the world, find fault, hand over fist, hold hands, of sound mind, second best, stand a chance, stand on your hands, take the wind out of your sails, a round of drinks

c) **Sentences**

1   Let's pretend it never happened.
2   He reminds me of my first boyfriend.
3   She seemed completely blind to his faults.
4   You can find some excellent second-hand phone bargains here.
5   The first round of interviews for the post will be conducted next month.
6   The new government banned all strikes, demonstrations and processions.
7   There's a glaring discrepancy between his predictions and his observations.

11.9.4 /nt/, /nts/, /ns/, /nst/

a) **Words**

amount, aunt, blunt, burnt, client, count, dent, faint, front, giant, hint, hunt, joint, lent, meant, mint, paint, point, print, rent, sent, spent, tent, vent, want, went; amounts, aunts, clients, counts, dents, faints, giants, hints, hunts, joints, mints, paints, points, prints, rents, tents, vents, wants; acquaintance, ambulance, appearance, audience, balance, bounce, chance, confidence, convince, dance, defence, difference, distance, entrance (n.), evidence, experience, fence, glance, mince, nonsense, once, performance, prince, science, sense, sentence, silence, since, tense; against; balanced, bounced, chanced, convinced, danced, experienced, fenced, glanced, minced, sensed, sentenced, silenced, tensed

b) **Phrases**

an equivalent amount, a fox hunt, roast a joint, specks of paint, a prolonged absence, on first acquaintance, a guest appearance, a twinge of conscience, a grand entrance, a profound influence, blind obedience, a frequent recurrence, a sequence of events, lapse into silence, an act of violence, against all odds, a second chance

c)   ***Sentences***

1   I wasn't convinced by his arguments.
2   Different clients have different needs.
3   He was frank and didn't mince his words.
4   She doesn't stand a chance against her opponents.
5   The tests were performed in strict compliance with the regulations.
6   He'd held a string of jobs, the most recent as an assistant to an accountant.
7   I just want the most important points, not the whole content of his writings.

11.9.5 /ntʃ/, /ntʃt/, /ndʒ/, /ndʒd/, /ŋz/, /ŋd/

a)   ***Words***

bench, branch, bunch, clench, crunch, drench, flinch, inch, launch, lunch, munch, pinch, punch, ranch, staunch, stench, trench, winch, wrench; branched, bunched, clenched, crunched, drenched, flinched, inched, launched, lunched, munched, pinched, punched, winched, wrenched; arrange, challenge, change, exchange, lounge, orange, range, revenge, sponge, strange; arranged, challenged, changed, exchanged, lounged, ranged, sponged; bangs, beginnings, belongs, belongings, blessings, boomerangs, brings, buildings, ceilings, clearings, clings, cravings, dumplings, dwellings, earnings, evenings, flings, gangs, gongs, hangs, herrings, kings, lungs, mornings, oblongs, pangs, puddings, railings, rings, sings, songs, springs, stings, strings, swings, things, tongues, weddings, wings; banged, belonged, longed, pinged, ringed, thronged, twanged, wronged

b)   ***Phrases***

accept a challenge, orange zest, an act of revenge, a clenched fist, the best of the bunch, when it comes to the crunch, change your mind, exchange words, pre-tax earnings, count your blessings, no strings attached, the kings and queens of England, swings and roundabouts

c)   ***Sentences***

1   My husband still clings to the past.
2   I longed for a moment of silence and rest.
3   He flinched when the verdict was announced.
4   I arranged the journals and books on the shelves.
5   She felt wronged by her cousin's constant accusations.
6   The girls exchanged confidences about their boyfriends.
7   Tourism in these countries evolved from modest beginnings.
8   The revelations of the goings-on behind the scenes shocked me.
9   By a strange coincidence he bumped into one of his old classmates.
10   The guests were a mixed bunch of Brits, Germans and Scandinavians.
11   They rummaged through my belongings and sprayed paint on my clothes.

11.9.6 /ŋk/, /ŋkt/, /ŋkts/, /ŋks/

a)   ***Words***

bank, blank, blink, chunk, drink, frank, ink, junk, link, monk, pink, rank, shrink, sink, skunk, stink, tank, thank, think, trunk, wink, zinc; defunct, distinct, extinct, instinct,

succinct; banked, blinked, inked, linked, ranked, thanked, winked; instincts; jinx, larynx, lynx, Manx, minx, pharynx, sphinx; banks, blanks, blinks, chunks, drinks, inks,
links, monks, ranks, shrinks, sinks, skunks, stinks, tanks, thanks, thinks, trunks, winks

b) *Phrases*

a bank account, my mind went blank, a direct link, sink to such depths, sink fast, thank
heavens, think outside the box, his first instinct

c) *Sentences*

1   My instincts told me to trust my friend.
2   His response was succinct and to the point.
3   When did the lynx become extinct in Scotland?
4   We observed a distinct improvement in his health.
5   He likes to think he's in control of his own destiny.
6   The elephant uses its trunk to grab objects and spray dust on itself.

11.10 First consonant = approximant

11.10.1 /lp/, /lps/, /lpt/, /lt/, /lts/, /ld/, /ldz/

a) *Words*

gulp, help, pulp, scalp, yelp; gulps, helps, pulps, scalps, yelps; sculpt; gulped, helped, pulped,
scalped, yelped; adult, assault, belt, bolt, built, cult, dealt, default, dolt, dwelt, exalt,
fault, felt, guilt, halt, jilt, jolt, kilt, knelt, lilt, malt, melt, moult, quilt, result, revolt, salt,
silt, smelt, spelt, spilt, spoilt, stilt, tilt, vault, volt, wilt; waltz; adults, assaults, belts, bolts,
cults, faults, halts, insults (n.), kilts, melts, moults, pelts, quilts, results, tilts, vaults, volts,
wilts; bald, bold, build, child, cold, field, fold, gold, hold, mild, mould, old, scald, scold,
shield, sold, told, wield, wild, world; appealed, boiled, called, chilled, cooled, crawled,
curled, drilled, filed, fooled, healed, pulled, rolled, ruled, sealed, skilled, smiled, thrilled;
builds, fields, folds, holds, moulds, scalds, scolds, shields, wields, worlds

b) *Phrases*

beyond help, plant bulbs, pulped books, nuts and bolts, a pinch of salt, a spoilt child,
dance a waltz, find fault with, a sense of guilt, adopt a child, the end of the world, a
bold statement, build bridges, cold hands, an old friend, rolled gold, wild animals,
a twinge of guilt

c) *Sentences*

1   Can you help me fold the sheets?
2   He gulped down the rest of the milk.
3   I noticed that his hands smelt of onions.
4   Don't be lulled into a false sense of security.
5   Help yourself to cereals and toast for breakfast.
6   I felt in my bones that it would result in violence.
7   She's cast in a different mould from her husband.
8   He knelt beside the patient and checked for a pulse.
9   Our efforts have improved the accuracy of the results.
10   It wouldn't be the end of the world, but it'd be a change.
11   The fluorescent bulb blinked, so I knew it had to be replaced.
12   Gabriel disagreed with the prevailing view held by scholars in the field.
13   They were equipped with shields and helmets to protect themselves against the
     hooligans.

11.10.2 /ltʃ/, /ltʃt/, /ldʒ/, /ldʒd/, /lk/, /lks/, /lkt/, /lm/, /lmz/

a) *Words*

belch, filch, mulch, zilch, squelch; belched, filched, mulched, squelched; bilge, bulge, divulge, indulge; bulged, divulged, indulged; bulk, elk, hulk, ilk, milk, silk, skulk, sulk, talc, whelk; elks, milks, skulks, sulks, whelks; bulked, milked, skulked, sulked; elm, film, helm, realm; elms, films, helms, realms

b) *Phrases*

divulge secrets, skimmed milk, the defence of the realm, a silent film, goat's milk, a film script

c) *Sentences*

1 Her skin was soft as silk.
2 Don's filched my pencils.
3 His pockets bulged with coins.
4 The bulk of the text is about the artist.
5 Breast milk remains the best for a child.
6 There has been a revived interest in silent films.
7 Should politics be kept outside the realms of science?
8 She loves the sound of the squelch of her boots on the damp ground.

11.10.3 /lf/, /lv/, /lvz/, /lvd/, /ls/, /lst/, /lz/

a) *Words*

elf, golf, gulf, self, shelf, wolf; absolve, delve, dissolve, evolve, involve, resolve, revolve, solve, twelve, valve; absolves, delves, dissolves, evolves, involves, resolves, revolves, solves, valves, elves, selves, wolves; absolved, dissolved, evolved, involved, resolved, solved; else, false, impulse, pulse, convulse, repulse; whilst; pulsed, convulsed, repulsed; aisles, appeals, bells, bills, boils, bulls, calls, canals, chills, cools, crawls, curls, details, dolls, drills, falls, feels, files, fools, girls, halls, heals/heels, hills, howls, kneels, meals, pulls, rolls, rules, schools, seals, sells, shells, skills, smells, smiles, spells, spills, steals, styles, tails, tells, thrills, tools, trails, walls, wells, wheels

b) *Phrases*

the Gulf states, self-obsessed, my first impulse, the sound of bells, bend the rules, against the rules, act like a fool, spilt the beans, self-confident, a faint pulse

c) *Sentences*

1 Did humans evolve from apes?
2 She was very involved with sports.
3 Carol's first impulse was to scream.
4 The blood pulsed through my veins.
5 The priest absolved him of all his sins.
6 We discussed the details of the contract.
7 Paul's shelves were crammed with books.
8 The wind carried the sound of distant bells.
9 He speaks with a pronounced Welsh accent.

11.11 Final clusters with dental fricatives

11.11.1 /θs/, /ðd/, /ðz/, /dθ/, /dθs/, /ŋθ/, /ŋθs/, /lθ/, /nθ/, /nθs/

a) Words

   maths, births, breaths, faiths, froths, cloths, deaths, growths, heaths, hearths, moths, myths; breathed, bathed, clothed, loathed, mouthed, unscathed, soothed, wreathed, writhed; bathes, breathes, loathes, mouths, seethes, soothes; breadth, hundredth, width; breadths, hundredths, widths; length, strength; lengths, strengths; filth, health, stealth, wealth; absinthe, hyacinth, labyrinth, month, plinth, millionth, billionth, ninth, tenth, thirteenth, fourteenth, fifteenth, sixteenth, seventeenth, eighteenth, nineteenth; hyacinths, labyrinths, months, plinths, billionths, eighteenths, fifteenths, fourteenths, millionths, nineteenths, ninths, thirteenths

b) Phrases

   a change of clothes, people of different faiths, the length and breadth, in the best of health, every ounce of strength, at arm's length, a test of strength, a sixth sense

c) Sentences

   1   She loathes stylish clothes.
   2   My husband isn't in the best of health.
   3   He emerged unscathed from the accident.
   4   He summoned all the strength he had left.
   5   The animals huddled together for warmth.
   6   Tracy swims twelve lengths in six minutes.
   7   The results have improved in recent months.
   8   Find the length and the width of the rectangle.
   9   The moths left holes in my clothes and blankets.
   10 Six twelfths and three sixths are equivalent fractions.
   11 Bruce was surprised by the depth of his feelings for her.
   12 A scientist claims to have found evidence of a sixth sense.
   13 He amassed a vast amount of wealth from his investments.
   14 Land mines have caused thousands of deaths to innocent civilians.

Chapter 12

Connected speech

The following features are of a different type from those treated so far. Phonemes are realised in particular ways and are combined in particular orders to form words. This is relatively straightforward for learners. When it comes to features of connected speech, however, it can't be said that these phenomena absolutely must occur in the contexts described, but only that they very commonly do; this raises the question of whether the learner should attempt to imitate these patterns of native speech.

Firstly, it's certainly advisable to learn about connected speech because it will help with listening comprehension. It's easier to understand speakers if you know when to expect sounds to change, appear or disappear. Secondly, connected speech phenomena are not unique to English, but at the same time they are not universal. This means that learners have connected speech habits which are almost certainly different from English habits and that applying those patterns to English will result in mispronunciations. Thus, one reason to learn about English patterns of connected speech is to help avoid this. Finally, depending on the learner's background, certain connected speech processes can make English pronunciation easier: why make such an effort to pronounce /skt/ in *asked* when you don't have to?

12.1 Citation forms vs. connected speech forms

The pronunciation of a word can vary depending on its phonetic environment. We have seen an example of this in the case of words which have strong and weak forms (see section 8.3), the strong form being used in stressed environments and the weak form in unstressed environments. The context of the surrounding sounds also has an important influence on a word's pronunciation. When we quote a word in isolation, we give what is known as the **citation form** of the word, and this is the pronunciation recorded in dictionaries. However, words are rarely uttered in isolation, but are rather preceded and followed by other words. As a result, adjacent sounds influence each other across word boundaries, which often causes a change in the phonemic structure of a word. A pronunciation of a word influenced by the sounds in surrounding morphemes, syllables or words is known as a **connected speech form**.

The three connected speech processes are:

- **Elision**: A phoneme present in the citation form is lost in the connected speech form.
- **Assimilation**: A phoneme in the citation form changes into another phoneme in the connected speech form.
- **Liaison**: A phoneme not present in the citation form appears in the connected speech form.

12.2 Elision

12.2.1 Consonant elision

The most common kind of elision involves /t/ and /d/. The alveolar plosives can be elided when they stand between two consonants and belong to the same syllable as the preceding consonant (see Table 12.1). For example, /t/ can be elided in *last lesson* /'lɑːs 'lesn̩/ and *facts* /fæks/, and /d/ in *brand new* /'bræn 'njuː/ and *hands* /hænz/, but not in *his twin* /hɪz 'twɪn/ or *this drink* /'ðɪs 'drɪŋk/. The following consonant may be in a suffix, the second element of a compound or a following word.

Word-final alveolar plosives are often realisations of the <-ed> inflection, but this doesn't block elision (see Table 12.2 for examples). Rather than being elided, /t/ usually undergoes glottal reinforcement or replacement.

An exception to this pattern of elision is that /t/ isn't elided in the clusters /lt/ and /nt/: *I felt sad* remains /aɪ 'felt 'sæd/, and *front door* remains /'frʌnt 'dɔː/. An exception to this exception is contractions with *not* (see section 8.15), which frequently lose their final /t/ before vowels as well as consonants (but not before a pause). This is particularly true of the disyllabic contractions: *I couldn't say* /aɪ 'kʊdn̩ 'seɪ/, *I shouldn't ask* /aɪ 'ʃʊdn̩ 'ɑːsk/, *I hadn't known* /aɪ 'hædn̩ 'nəʊn/, *It hasn't changed* /ɪt 'hæzn̩ 'ʧeɪndʒd/.

Table 12.1 Elision of alveolar plosives between two consonants

Sequence	Suffix		Compound		Phrase	
-ft + C	lifts	/lɪfs/	software	/'sɒfweə/	lift me	/'lɪf mi/
-st + C	firstly	/'fɜːsli/	coastguard	/'kəʊsgɑːd/	best friend	/'bes 'frend/
-kt + C	collects	/kə'leks/	fact-finding	/'fækfaɪndɪŋ/	react badly	/ri'æk 'bædli/
-pt + C	accepts	/ək'seps/	scriptwriter	/'skrɪpraɪtə/	kept quiet	/'kep 'kwaɪət/
-nd + C	hands	/hænz/	grandfather	/'grænfɑːðə/	stand still	/'stæn 'stɪl/
-ld + C	fields	/fiːlz/	childcare	/'ʧaɪlkeə/	hold tight	/'həʊl 'taɪt/

Table 12.2 Examples of elision of <-ed> endings

Sequence	Example	
-bd + C	We clubbed together.	/wi 'klʌb tə'geðə/
-gd + C	I shrugged my shoulders.	/aɪ 'ʃrʌg maɪ 'ʃəʊldəz/
-ʤd + C	He managed to do it.	/hi 'mænɪʤ tə 'duː ɪt/
-vd + C	I saved my breath.	/aɪ 'seɪv maɪ 'breθ/
-ðd + C	She mouthed the answer.	/ʃi 'maʊð ði 'ɑːnsə/
-zd + C	It amused me.	/ɪt ə'mjuːz mi/
-md + C	I calmed down.	/aɪ 'kɑːm 'daʊn/
-nd + C	He fanned the flames.	/hi 'fæn ðə 'fleɪmz/
-ŋd + C	It belonged to me.	/ɪt bɪ'lɒŋ tə mi/
-ld + C	I appealed to them.	/aɪ ə'piːl tə ðəm/
-pt + C	He stopped talking.	/hi 'stɒp 'tɔːkɪŋ/
-kt + C	He was tracked down.	/hi wəz 'træk 'daʊn/
-ʧt + C	I switched channels.	/aɪ 'swɪʧ 'ʧænl̩z/
-ft + C	I stuffed my face.	/aɪ 'stʌf maɪ 'feɪs/
-st + C	I was forced to do it.	/aɪ wəz 'fɔːs tə 'duː ɪt/
-ʃt + C	I brushed my teeth.	/aɪ 'brʌʃ maɪ 'tiːθ/

A less frequent kind of consonant elision is the elision of /k/ in final /sk/ clusters when a consonant follows: *masked* /mɑːst/, *risked* /rɪst/, *tasked* /tɑːst/. Although there are few words ending in /sk/, this kind of elision is common in the word *ask*: *I'll ask them* /aɪl 'ɑːs ðəm/, *They asked us* /ðeɪ 'ɑːst əs/, *We asked both of them* /wi 'ɑːs 'bəʊθ ə ðəm/.

12.2.2 Vowel elision

One kind of vowel elision has already been described under syllabic consonants (see section 8.2). Words such as *deafen* and *cycle* have the basic form /'defən/ and /'saɪkəl/, which usually results in the pronunciations /'defn̩/ and /'saɪkl̩/ with syllabic consonants. When a suffix beginning with a weak vowel follows, the syllabicity of the consonants can be lost: *deafening* and *cycling* becoming /'defnɪŋ/ and /'saɪklɪŋ/. Through this process a schwa is elided from these and other words which fulfil these conditions.

A similar process occurs when schwa is followed by /r/ and then a weak vowel; e.g. *history* /'hɪstəri/ becomes /'hɪstri/, *separate* (adj.) /'sepərət/ becomes /'seprət/, *category* /'kætəgəri/ becomes /'kætəgri/. If the following vowel is not weak but strong, the schwa is not elided: *hyphenate* = /'haɪfəneɪt/ or /'haɪfn̩eɪt/, not */'haɪfneɪt/; *idolise* = /'aɪdəlaɪz/ or /'aɪdl̩aɪz/, not */ 'aɪdlaɪz/; *separate* (v.) = /'sepəreɪt/, not */'sepreɪt/.

12.3 Assimilation

Assimilation in English is most often **anticipatory**, meaning that a sound is influenced by a sound which follows it. Less often, assimilation in English is **perseverative**, meaning that a sound is influenced by a sound which precedes it. In the case of anticipatory assimilation, the change happens because the articulators are getting reading to make the next sound while still articulating the present sound; i.e. they anticipate the following sound. When the assimilation is perseverative, the articulators are still in the position for the earlier sound when they are articulating the present sound; i.e. some aspect of their position perseveres into the following sound.

12.3.1 Place assimilation

English alveolar plosives /t d/ and the alveolar nasal /n/ take the place of articulation of a following plosive or nasal (for examples, see Tables 12.3 and 12.4). This means that:

- /t/, a voiceless alveolar plosive, becomes its bilabial equivalent, a voiceless bilabial plosive /p/, when the following sound is bilabial /p/, /b/ or /m/.
- /d/, a voiced alveolar plosive, becomes its bilabial equivalent, a voiced bilabial plosive /b/, when the following sound is bilabial /p/, /b/ or /m/.
- /n/, a voiced alveolar nasal, becomes its bilabial equivalent, a voiced bilabial nasal /m/, when the following sound is bilabial /p/, /b/ or /m/.
- /t/, a voiceless alveolar plosive, becomes its velar equivalent, a voiceless velar plosive /k/, when the following sound is velar /k/ or /g/.
- /d/, a voiced alveolar plosive, becomes its velar equivalent, a voiced velar plosive /g/, when the following sound is velar /k/ or /g/.
- /n/, a voiced alveolar nasal, becomes its velar equivalent, a voiced velar nasal /ŋ/, when the following sound is velar /k/ or /g/.

Table 12.3 Place assimilation: examples of alveolar consonants becoming bilabial

Assimilation	Bilabial					
	/p/		/b/		/m/	
/t/ → /p/	wet paint	/'wep 'peɪnt/	jet black	/'dʒep 'blæk/	white mice	/'waɪp 'maɪs/
/d/ → /b/	a bad person	/ə 'bæb 'pɜːsn̩/	a loud bang	/ə 'laʊb 'bæŋ/	red meat	/'reb 'miːt/
/n/ → /m/	brown paper	/'braʊm 'peɪpə/	a thin book	/ə 'θɪm 'bʊk/	lean meat	/'liːm 'miːt/

Table 12.4 Place assimilation: examples of alveolar consonants becoming velar

Assimilation	Velar			
	/k/		/g/	
/t/ → /k/	hot coffee	/'hɒk 'kɒfi/	quite good	/'kwaɪk 'gʊd/
/d/ → /g/	a red gate	/ə 'reg 'geɪt/	a bad group	/ə 'bæg 'gruːp/
/n/ → /ŋ/	green covers	/'griːŋ 'kʌvəz/	twin girls	/'twɪŋ 'gɜːlz/

Table 12.5 Place assimilation: examples of alveolar consonants becoming palato-alveolar

Assimilation	Orthography	Pronunciation
/s/ → /ʃ/	this shop	/'ðɪʃ 'ʃɒp/
	nice shoes	/'naɪʃ 'ʃuːz/
	a famous ship	/ə 'feɪməʃ 'ʃɪp/
	a close shave	/ə 'kləʊʃ 'ʃeɪv/
/z/ → /ʒ/	is she	/'ɪʒ ʃi/
	his shirt	/hɪʒ 'ʃɜːt/
	Lee's short	/'liːʒ 'ʃɔːt/
	because she	/bɪ'kɒʒ ʃi/

In the case of /t/, this is also the context where glottal replacement or glottal reinforcement (see sections 2.7.2 and 2.7.3) can take place. In this case, instead of assimilation taking place, [t] could be replaced by [ʔ], or assimilation could take place, with the resulting voiceless plosive being accompanied by glottal reinforcement.

The alveolar fricatives /s/ and /z/ also frequently undergo assimilation. When they are followed by palato-alveolar /ʃ/, their place of articulation changes to palato-alveolar (Table 12.5):

- /s/, a voiceless alveolar fricative, becomes its palato-alveolar equivalent, a voiceless palato-alveolar fricative /ʃ/, when the following sound is palato-alveolar /ʃ/.
- /z/, a voiced alveolar fricative, becomes its palato-alveolar equivalent, a voiced palato-alveolar fricative /ʒ/, when the following sound is palato-alveolar /ʃ/.

When /ən/ follows the velar plosives /k g/ or the bilabial plosives /p b/, the plosives can be released nasally (see section 2.8) and the tongue remains in position, resulting in a homorganic syllabic nasal, i.e. [m̩] after /p b/, or [ŋ̩] after /k g/; see Table 12.6. The more frequent a word is, the more likely this assimilation is to occur, but the variant with /ən/ is still more

Table 12.6 Place assimilation: homorganic syllabic nasals

Assimilation	Orthography	Pronunciation
/ən/ → /m̩/	happen	/'hæpm̩/
	ribbon	/'rɪbm̩/
/ən/ → /ŋ̩/	taken	/'teɪkŋ̩/
	pagan	/'peɪgŋ̩/

Table 12.7 Place assimilation: examples of coalescent assimilation

/t/ + /j/ → /tʃ/		/d/ + /j/ → /dʒ/	
I know what you said.	/aɪ 'nəʊ wɒtʃu 'sed/	Did you see it?	/dɪdʒu 'siː ɪt/
I've got you a present.	/aɪv 'gɒtʃu ə 'preznt/	Could you wait?	/kʊdʒu 'weɪt/
Can't you wait?	/'kɑːntʃu 'weɪt/	They made you do it?	/ðeɪ 'meɪdʒu 'duː ɪt/
Why don't you go?	/'waɪ 'dəʊntʃu 'gəʊ/	Would your brother try?	/wʊdʒɔː 'brʌðə 'traɪ/
He said that you did.	/hi 'sed ðətʃu 'dɪd/	He said you did.	/hi 'sedʒu 'dɪd/
I've got your key.	/aɪv 'gɒtʃɔː 'kiː/	I found your key.	/aɪ 'faʊndʒɔː 'kiː/
Couldn't you try?	/'kʊdn̩tʃu 'traɪ/	I've read your book.	/aɪv 'redʒɔː 'bʊk/

usual, and it's this form which learners are advised to use. This is an example of perseverative assimilation.

12.3.2 Coalescent assimilation

The assimilations we have looked at so far involve a phoneme changing into another phoneme under the influence of a following phoneme. In the case of coalescent assimilation, two phonemes influence each other and combine to form a third phoneme: /t/ and /d/ combine with /j/ to form /tʃ/ and /dʒ/. This process is most common and most complete when it involves *you* or *your* and is frequently heard in *could you, couldn't you, did you, didn't you*, etc; see Table 12.7.

12.3.3 Voicing assimilation

Unlike many other languages, English has very few examples of voicing assimilation. This is a phenomenon whereby a voiceless consonant becomes voiced under the influence of an adjacent voiced consonant, or a voiced consonant becomes voiceless under the influence of another voiceless consonant (perhaps more correctly termed 'devoicing assimilation'). English doesn't have the former, and learners should therefore take care not to say *jukebox, scapegoat, white-collar* as */'dʒuːgbɒks, 'skeɪbgəʊt, 'waɪd 'kɒlə/. Devoicing assimilation is also rare in English, the only common words and phrases being *have to* /hæf tu/, *has to* /hæs tu/, *had to* /hæt tu/, *used to* /juːs tu/, *supposed to* /sə'pəʊs tu/.

12.3.4 Manner assimilation

Manner assimilation involves the voiced dental fricative /ð/ becoming identical to a preceding /n/, /l/ or alveolar fricative. This is an example of perseverative assimilation. It is

Table 12.8 Manner assimilation: examples of dental consonants assimilating to the preceding consonant

Assimilation					
	Unstressed			Stressed	
/ð/ → /n/	It's on the table.	/ɪts ɒn nə 'teɪbl̩/		And then it rained.	/ən 'nen ɪt 'reɪnd/
/ð/ → /l/	Will they manage?	/wɪl leɪ 'mænɪdʒ/		Although it's sad	/ɔːl'loʊ ɪts 'sæd/
/ð/→ /s/	That's the idea.	/'ðæts si aɪ'dɪə/		What's this?	/'wɒts 'sɪs/
/ð/ → /z/	Was the baby healthy?	/wəz zə 'beɪbi 'helθi/		How's that?	/'haʊz 'zæt/

most common in unstressed positions, e.g. *on the, will they, that's the, was the* /ɒn nə, wɪl leɪ, ðæts si, wəz zə/, but is also heard in stressed syllables, e.g. *and then, although, what's this, how's that* /ən 'nen, ɔːl'loʊ, 'wɒts 'sɪs, 'haʊz 'zæt/ (see Table 12.8). Since many learners pronounce /ð/ as /d/, it can be a useful strategy to employ these manner assimilations. Remember to lengthen the assimilated sound as there's a clear difference between elision and assimilation of /ð/. If you don't lengthen the consonant, *on the table* will sound like *on a table*.

12.4 Liaison

When a certain set of vowels, let's call them the **liaison vowels**, is immediately followed by another vowel, an /r/ is inserted between them. This happens both within words when suffixes are added, and between words. For examples, see Table 12.9.

The liaison vowels are schwa, NURSE, PALM, THOUGHT, SQUARE, NEAR and CURE. See also section 5.4.

As the examples in the table demonstrate, there's a correspondence between /r/-liaison and the letter <r> in the orthographic form of the words. This reflects the fact that /r/ was formerly pronounced in all words with the <r> spelling (and still is in **rhotic** accents; see sections 2.14.7 and 5.4), but since the time at which English spelling was standardised, /r/ has been lost in non-prevocalic positions (i.e. at the ends of words before a pause and before consonants) in the GB accent. When an original /r/ was in word-final position, it remained if a suffix or word beginning with a vowel immediately followed. This pattern continues to the present day and explains why, when a vowel immediately follows, an /r/ appears at the end of the connected speech form of words which have a final liaison vowel but no final /r/ in their citation form.

Table 12.9 Liaison vowels

Liaison vowel	Intra-word		Inter-word	
schwa	sugary	/'ʃʊgə/ + /i/ = /'ʃʊgəri/	cover up	/'kʌvə/ + /ʌp/ = /'kʌvər 'ʌp/
NURSE	purring	/pɜː/ + /ɪŋ/ = /'pɜːrɪŋ/	stir it	/stɜː/ + /ɪt/ = /'stɜːr ɪt/
PALM	starring	/stɑː/ + /ɪŋ/ = /'stɑːrɪŋ/	far off	/fɑː/ + /ɒf/ = /'fɑːr 'ɒf/
THOUGHT	gory	/gɔː/ + /i/ = /'gɔːri/	pour out	/pɔː/ + /aʊt/ = /'pɔːr 'aʊt/
SQUARE	scary	/skeə/ + /i/ = /'skeəri/	repair it	/rɪ'peə/ + /ɪt/ = /rɪ'peər ɪt/
NEAR	nearer	/nɪə/ + /ə/ = /'nɪərə/	cheer up	/ʧɪə/ + /ʌp/ = /'ʧɪər 'ʌp/
CURE	curing	/kjʊə/ + /ɪŋ/ = /'kjʊərɪŋ/	cure us	/kjʊə/ + /əs/ = /'kjʊər əs/

/r/-liaison is so common in English speech that its use is often analogically extended to words with final liaison vowels which never historically contained a final /r/ and therefore are not spelt with /r/: *visa application* /ˈviːzər ˌæplɪˈkeɪʃn̩/, *Yamaha instruments* /ˈjæməhɑːr ˈɪnstrəmənts/, *saw it* /ˈsɔːr ɪt/, *idea of* /aɪˈdɪər əv/, *drawing* /ˈdrɔːrɪŋ/. This phenomenon has been called 'intrusive /r/'. Most learners will find that this doesn't come naturally to them because they are influenced by the spelling. Since this kind of /r/-liaison is variable, it isn't necessary to imitate it.

Suggested reading

In addition to reading the following works, those wishing to take their phonetic studies further can consult the IPA website at www.internationalphoneticassociation.org for information regarding its Certificate of Proficiency in the Phonetics of English. The Summer Course in English Phonetics (SCEP) at University College London regularly contains a strand preparing students for the exam.

Pronunciation dictionaries

Jones, Daniel, Roach, Peter, Esling, John and Setter, Jane (2011) *Cambridge English Pronouncing Dictionary*. Eighteenth edn. Cambridge: Cambridge University Press.

Wells, John C. (2008) *Longman Pronunciation Dictionary*. Third edn. Harlow: Pearson Education.

English phonetics

Collins, Beverley and Mees, Inger M. (2013) *Practical Phonetics and Phonology*. Third edn. Abingdon: Routledge.

Cruttenden, Alan (2014) *Gimson's Pronunciation of English*. Eighth edn. Abingdon: Routledge.

Roach, Peter (2009) *English Phonetics and Phonology: A Practical Course*. Fourth edn. Cambridge: Cambridge University Press.

Wells, John C. (1982) *Accents of English 1: Introduction*. Cambridge: Cambridge University Press.

Phonetic transcription

Lecumberri, M. Luisa García and Maidment, John A. (2000). *English Transcription Course*. London: Arnold.

Tench, Paul (2011) *Transcribing the Sound of English*. Cambridge: Cambridge University Press.

General phonetics

Ashby, Michael and Maidment, John (2005) *Introducing Phonetic Science*. Cambridge: Cambridge University Press.

Ashby, Patricia (2005) *Speech Sounds*. Second edn. London: Routledge.

Ashby, Patricia (2011) *Understanding Phonetics*. Abingdon: Routledge.

Catford, J. C. (2001) *A Practical Introduction to Phonetics*. Second edn. Oxford: Oxford University Press.

Knight, Rachael-Anne. (2012) *Phonetics: A Coursebook*. Cambridge: Cambridge University Press.

Ladefoged, Peter (2005) *Vowels and Consonants: An Introduction to the Sounds of Language*. Second edn. Oxford: Blackwell.

Ladefoged, Peter and Johnson, Keith (2010). *A Course in Phonetics*. Sixth edn (with CD-ROM). Boston: Thomson Wadsworth.

Roach, Peter (2001) *Phonetics*. Oxford: Oxford University Press.

Index

Page numbers in **bold** indicate tables. Page numbers in *italic* indicate figures.

Taylor & Francis eBooks

Helping you to choose the right eBooks for your Library

Add Routledge titles to your library's digital collection today. Taylor and Francis ebooks contains over 50,000 titles in the Humanities, Social Sciences, Behavioural Sciences, Built Environment and Law.

Choose from a range of subject packages or create your own!

Benefits for you

›› Free MARC records
›› COUNTER-compliant usage statistics
›› Flexible purchase and pricing options
›› All titles DRM-free.

Benefits for your user

›› Off-site, anytime access via Athens or referring URL
›› Print or copy pages or chapters
›› Full content search
›› Bookmark, highlight and annotate text
›› Access to thousands of pages of quality research at the click of a button.

REQUEST YOUR **FREE** INSTITUTIONAL TRIAL TODAY

Free Trials Available
We offer free trials to qualifying academic, corporate and government customers.

eCollections – Choose from over 30 subject eCollections, including:

Archaeology	Language Learning
Architecture	Law
Asian Studies	Literature
Business & Management	Media & Communication
Classical Studies	Middle East Studies
Construction	Music
Creative & Media Arts	Philosophy
Criminology & Criminal Justice	Planning
Economics	Politics
Education	Psychology & Mental Health
Energy	Religion
Engineering	Security
English Language & Linguistics	Social Work
Environment & Sustainability	Sociology
Geography	Sport
Health Studies	Theatre & Performance
History	Tourism, Hospitality & Events

For more information, pricing enquiries or to order a free trial, please contact your local sales team:
www.tandfebooks.com/page/sales

Routledge
Taylor & Francis Group

The home of
Routledge books

www.tandfebooks.com